Susan

Lady Caroline Lamb

Lady
Caroline
This Infernal
Woman
Lamb

SUSAN NORMINGTON

Susan Normington

HOUSE OF
STRATUS

This edition published in 2001 by House of Stratus, an imprint of
Stratus Holdings plc, 24c Old Burlington Street, London, W1X 1RL, UK.

www.houseofstratus.com

Typeset, printed and bound by House of Stratus.

A catalogue record for this book is available from the British Library.

ISBN 1-84232-162-5

For David and Richard

ACKNOWLEDGEMENTS

I should like to thank the owners of the following collections who have allowed me to consult, transcribe and publish papers in their archives and who received me with such kindness:

The Bessborough Papers: By courtesy of Lord Bessborough with acknowledgements to the West Sussex Record Office and the County Archivist.

The Chatsworth Collection: Manuscripts from both the fifth Duke's Group and the sixth Duke's Group by permission of the Trustees of the Chatsworth Settlement.

Castle Howard: Letters of Georgiana, sixth Countess of Carlisle, by permission of Mr Simon Howard.

Hertfordshire Record Office: Panshanger Papers by permission of the Head of Archives and Local Studies.

Hartley Library, University of Southampton: The Broadlands Archives by permission of the Broadlands Trustees.

Lovelace-Byron Archive, Bodleian Library, by courtesy of Lord Lytton.

I am most grateful to Mr Peter Day, at Chatsworth, Dr Christopher L Ridgeway, at Castle Howard, Dr Christopher Woolgar, at the University of Southampton, Kate Day of Hertfordshire Record Office and Mr Peter Wilkinson, Chief Archivist, West Sussex Record Office, for all their help and advice. I should also like to thank the Directors of Coutts & Co. and the bank's archivist, Tracy Earl, for showing me the papers connected with the letting and furnishing of Lady Caroline's house in Conduit Street. My thanks also go to Mr Paul Hopkins, County Archivist at Northampton County Record Office, who put me in touch with Dr Frances Harris, the author of *Holywell House: A Gothic Villa at St Albans*. I am most grateful to Lord Ralph Kerr who, as well as introducing me to Howard Usher's *William Lamb, Viscount Melbourne and The Owners of Melbourne Hall*, made it possible for me to consult the Lothian Papers at the British Library. I should also like to thank Dr C Wright for his advice on the Althorp Papers. My thanks are also due to Jonathan Gross who generously allowed me to read proofs from his life of Lady Melbourne, *Byron's 'Corbeau Blanc'*, and to John Murray who have allowed me to quote from *Byron's Letters and Journals*, edited by Leslie A Marchand, 12 volumes, 1975-82, *The Late Lord Byron*, Doris Langley Moore and various letters and journals.

During the writing of this book I have been lucky enough to visit places well known to Lady Caroline. According to local folklore she still visits them all. Her ghost plays practical jokes at Brocket Hall, sits by the fountain in the grounds of Melbourne Hall and sneaks in and out of Albany. Her presence has been felt at 50 Albemarle Street and she sometimes startles Scottish civil servants who have seen her, wearing an attractive green dress, on the upper landings at Dover House, formerly Melbourne House and now the Scottish Office.

I should like to thank Kate Thomas of CCA Europe Limited for showing me round Brocket Hall and sharing its legends; Miss Elizabeth Oliver for guiding me round Byron's rooms at Albany and Mr Eric Miller for showing me Dover House. I am also most grateful to the Cambridgeshire County Council's Libraries and Information Service and in particular to the librarians at the Huntingdon and Ramsey Libraries for their help and interest.

CONTENTS

LIST OF ILLUSTRATIONS

1. Lady Caroline Lamb, by Eliza H Trotter
(Courtesy of The National Portrait Gallery)

2. William Lamb, Viscount Melbourne, by Sir Thomas Lawrence
(Trinity College, Cambridge, UK / The Bridgeman Art Library)

3. Georgiana, Duchess of Devonshire and her daughter, Lady Georgiana
Cavendish, 1784, by Sir Joshua Reynolds
(Chatsworth House, Derbyshire, UK / The Bridgeman Art Library)

4. William Cavendish, 5th Duke of Devonshire, engraving by W J Hullarnd
(Mary Evans Picture Library)

5. Elizabeth, Duchess of Devonshire
(From *The Two Duchesses*, Vere Foster, Blackie and Son, 1898)

6. Henrietta Frances (Spencer), Countess of Bessborough, from a drawing
made for scenery of Richmond House theatre painted by J Downman,
engraved by F Batolozzi, 1797
(Mary Evans Picture Library)

7. Frederick Ponsonby, 3rd Earl of Bessborough, engraving by C Warren
published in 1791 after a drawing from life by W H Brown
(Mary Evans Picture Library)

8. Chatsworth House, Derbyshire
(© Travel Ink/David Guyler)

9. Sketch from Lady Caroline Lamb's commonplace book
(Hertfordshire Archives and Local Studies)

10. Sketch from Lady Caroline Lamb's commonplace book
(Hertfordshire Archives and Local Studies)

11. Georgiana, Countess Spencer
(From the collection at Althorp)

FOREWORD
by Sarah Miles

I very rarely look back at my life with regrets. This is not, I hasten to add, because my life has been so utterly pristine – far from it – it is because, unlike Lady Caroline Lamb, I attempt to learn from the plethora of mistakes I continue to make, whereas Lady Caroline simply barged on regardless, which is far more courageous, endearing even.

I do find myself having one regret now, however. Had Susan Normington's biography, Lady Caroline Lamb, been around before my husband, Robert Bolt, had made his film of the same name, I believe that not only would I have played the role differently, but that Robert's script might have gained a clearer insight – who knows?

Susan Normington's research finds Caroline's grandmother, Lady Spencer, a vividly colourful character, painted with a much more eccentric brush than I was aware of. The plain unpretentious table that she kept, the odd food she placed in front of Lady Caroline, her exotic habit of wearing a riding habit most of the time would have certainly rubbed off on Caroline, insidiously influencing her formative years, quietly moulding her character into the creature she became. Indeed it is Lady Spencer who must be held partly responsible for influencing Caroline's doomed destiny.

Caroline had a deeply inquisitive, inquiring mind. This should have been a blessing, but both her mother and grandmother saw her hunger for knowledge as a liability, and I'm sure this attitude was one of the main attributes shaping the pattern of the manic depression that was to follow. I firmly maintain that if Lady Spencer had been more forthcoming regarding her grandchild's thirst for religious and spiritual guidance, Caroline might have turned out differently. Imagine being locked up in a cupboard for asking questions about God. The poor child was obviously in need, yet all she got for her lust for knowledge was a dark cupboard.

Had Caroline's curiosity been embraced, she might have turned towards her own spirituality for self-awareness and self-knowledge, giving her the essential tools necessary to rebuff her madly volatile and often uncontrollable nature. It was as if Caroline was simply too intelligent for her sex, having to pay a heavy price for her brilliance. She was a woman born out of her time if ever there was one, and was forced to suffer hugely because of it.

I often wonder if Caroline could have fulfilled her destiny had she been given the opportunity to go to university. Here she and I are so alike – both born with talent, yet no education. I refused to toe the line and was expelled from three schools, the last when I was merely fourteen, with not a single exam under my belt. Likewise, Lady Caroline had no proper education to speak of, and with no scholarship under her belt, essential for fine prose and poetry – how could she ever become a writer of true merit? She didn't lack talent, just education and self-discipline.

The whole fiasco with Byron was, I believe, Caroline's frustration with her own talent and her inability to create her own 'Childe Harold' that could have taken society by storm. Since her own work lacked the discipline of education, she would damn well bask in the glory of Byron's reputation. It wasn't Byron she was besotted with; it was his poetry and the euphoric adulation that surrounded him. And therein lies the tragedy and with it the timelessness of Caroline's story – a story that is universal, a story that will outlive us all. For Caroline learned too late that it was her husband, the great Parliamentarian, William Lamb, whom she truly loved and respected above all others.

William could have been her teacher. He was steady as a rock, a faithful, besotted husband, indeed a witty, intelligent and nourishing influence. She had him right there beside her, and right there is where he would have remained for the rest if their days, but Caroline couldn't see him. She was blinded by the 'Byronic Legend', and when she adjusted her eyes from the blinding light, William had gone.

William had been advised to put his career before his devotion to Caroline, for she would surely have killed him along with his career if he didn't get away. Had he remained in England, would Caroline have been able to readjust, reassess, re-establish some kind of relationship that could have saved her life? Only after William had gone did Caroline realise the extent of her love, but by then it was all too late. Too late.

I know others will enjoy this book as much as I have. It has so much colour and texture. There is an undeniable truth running all the way through which makes it an irresistible read, even though I am one of the converted! Another thing it does, alas, is make me want to wake up old Robert Bolt from the dead and say 'Hey! Let's have another crack at making *Lady Caroline Lamb!*'

Sarah Miles

INTRODUCTION

Lady Caroline Lamb, like her ancestor, Sarah, Duchess of Marlborough was a strong-willed woman. Intelligent, well educated, practical in emergencies, she canvassed enthusiastically for her husband, William Lamb, Queen Victoria's first Prime Minister. His indifference provoked an affair with Sir Godfrey Webster, which was ended by his mother, Lady Holland. Still believing she was ignored, Caroline set out to attract the attention of Lord Byron. Instead of enjoying a gallant pretend affair, they fell in love so passionately that when he tried to end it she did not believe he was acting voluntarily. Convinced that William's parents, Lord and Lady Melbourne, had influenced him she parodied them, their family and friends in her novel *Glenarvon*. The success of the book inspired her to become a professional writer. With the support of the successful Irish author, Lady Morgan, she published two more novels despite the Melbournes doing everything they could to prevent her. Her choice of William Lamb for a husband had disappointed her family who had hoped she would marry her cousin, Lord Hartington. Caroline could not reconcile the difference between her sophisticated and tolerant family and the coarser, ambitious Melbournes. This eventually destroyed her marriage and ruined her.

As far as possible I have allowed the characters to speak for themselves through their letters and diaries, which accounts for the often eccentric language and grammatical quirks. It would be wise to bear in mind that Byron often wrote what his correspondents wanted to read rather than the complete truth; Lady Melbourne protected Caroline to avoid unpleasant repercussions falling on her family; Lady Cowper repeated damaging gossip to her brother William Lamb in an attempt to break up his marriage; Caroline dressed up her sins as virtues and Lady Morgan is sometimes unreliable. Nevertheless, I believe the balance of sympathy lies with Caroline who, because of the vindictive small-mindedness of the Melbournes was not allowed to develop her talents as a writer. Four years before she died Lord Hartington, by now 6th Duke of Devonshire, commented, 'She might have been saved had she not got into the hands of these blackguards'.

1

'Caro Ponsonby, wild as a hawk and impertinent as a squirrel'

On 2 June 1805, Lady Caroline Ponsonby went to Devonshire House to a small reception given in honour of her marriage to William Lamb, the second son of Lord Melbourne. Lady Elizabeth Foster wrote, 'She looks prettier than ever I saw her,' adding, 'sometimes she is very nervous, but in general she appears to be very happy.'[1]

Caroline's presents were spread across a table in one of the gold and white salons of the London home of her uncle and aunt, the Duke and Duchess of Devonshire. Apart from her wedding dress and veil, presents from the Duke and Duchess, most of the gifts were pieces of jewellery, including a pair of diamond and gold bracelets, a pearl necklace, several brooches, a cross made of pearls and one of burnt topaz, heavy gold amulets set with cameos and a large aquamarine. Lord and Lady Melbourne gave her a diamond wreath and a set of amethysts, in contrast to the modest hair bracelet from her friend, Caroline St Jules.

At half past seven the following evening, the family gathered in the drawing room of Caroline's home on the corner of Cavendish Square and they waited a few moments while Caroline composed herself. When she entered the room, clinging to her father's arm, the Duchess remarked, 'It was the prettiest thing I ever saw'. She wore a wedding dress with a high neck and long lace sleeves. Pieces of matching lace were let in to the 'transparent muslin' of the bodice and skirt, a large aquamarine secured her veil and around her neck shone her new pearl necklace. She was nervous and trembled when she saw William and the Reverend Preedy waiting but 'walked up steadily and never gave way or wanted support'. She repeated her vows firmly and in a clear voice. The Duchess thought William's tender encouragement was 'quite beautiful, and the difference of her light figure and his manly one very striking'.[2]

It had been a long day full of stress for Caroline. In the morning a friend of her mother had a fit of hysterics in the library and her cousin, Georgiana Morpeth, was on the point of giving birth. Outside, a crowd had gathered in the square waiting to see her leave and she could clearly hear murmurs and laughter, which added to her agitation.

Although she had loved William since she was twelve, a few days before the wedding she began to have doubts and regrets. She was fearful of her new life with its responsibilities and the thought of leaving her parents made her sad. She told her mother, Lady Bessborough, that she felt 'rather low and frighten'd'. Her mother comforted her, saying that if she appeared unwilling to go with William his feelings would be hurt.

Caroline's good resolutions crumbled when the carriage was called to take her on her honeymoon. She turned to William, begging him to let her stay. He gently explained that her home was with him now. She stared back at him, open-eyed in terror and clasped her father's arm saying, 'This is my home, these are my parents, share all I have – dwell with me where I have ever dwelt; but think not that I can quit them thus'. Lady Bessborough 'made a great struggle' to remain calm but Emily Lamb, William's sister, her cousin Harriet Cavendish, and Caroline St Jules all wept in sympathy. Still wrapped in her father's arms Caroline cried out several times 'I will not go, I will not,' hoping that if she screamed loudly enough William would relent. She was almost out of control when he stepped between the crying women and picked her up in his arms. She lay there, motionless like a doll as he carried her through the curious crowd in the square to the carriage. It was a little after nine o'clock when they left for the short journey to Brocket Hall, Lord and Lady Melbourne's country house in Hertfordshire.

Caroline came from a family noted for its eccentric, intelligent, strong-willed and emotional women. Her distant cousin, Sarah Ponsonby, ran off with Lady Eleanor Butler to become famous as one of the 'Ladies of Llangollen'. Her great-great-great grandmother, Sarah Jennings, the formidable Duchess of Marlborough, was the confidante of Queen Anne. Caroline inherited both her glorious copper-coloured hair and her stubbornness from the Duchess.

In order to understand Caroline it is necessary to appreciate the family and the values into which she was born and how her character was chiefly formed by her grandmother, the Dowager Countess Spencer, her mother, Lady Bessborough, and her aunt, the Duchess of Devonshire. These three women were Caroline's instructors and protectors and their personalities and experiences were important factors in her development. After her marriage to William Lamb, Lady Melbourne attempted to guide her but her advice was frequently ignored.

Caroline's grandmother, Margaret Georgiana Poyntz, was seventeen when she secretly married John, first Earl Spencer, at his twenty-first birthday party. Like Caroline, she was an unconventional, practical person. She disliked fuss and frills and often wore a riding habit to avoid dressing formally. She kept a plain and unpretentious table and made no concessions to eating fads. When Caroline remarked that her meal consisted of nothing but 'egg shells and turnip tops',[3] Lady Spencer replied, 'Take it or leave it.' She kept snakes and, at fifty-four, taught herself German. Her restless and enquiring mind ensured that she was never bored and any scheme to improve the lot of others was sure of her interest. When she was first married she loved to game, giving card parties at Althorp, the family home in Northamptonshire, where large amounts of money changed hands. Although she conquered her own passion for gambling, it became a curse for her two daughters.

Lord and Lady Spencer had three children: Georgiana, born on 9 June 1757, George John, born 1 September 1758, and Henrietta Frances, on 16 June 1761. Lady Spencer encouraged all her children to have open and enquiring minds. It was from her that Caroline inherited contempt for many of society's pointless conventions.

Georgiana was charming rather than strictly beautiful. She was tall with a clear complexion, good teeth, a laughing mouth and red-gold hair. Horace Walpole described her as 'a lovely girl, natural and full of grace'. When she was sixteen she was married to her cousin, William Cavendish, fifth Duke of Devonshire. The Duke was twenty-four, a withdrawn, quiet young man who preferred the company of dogs to people. Both his parents had died before he was sixteen, leaving him with one of the largest estates in the country – Devonshire House in London, a Palladian villa at Chiswick, Bolton Abbey and Londesborough Hall in Yorkshire, Chatsworth House and Hardwick Hall in Derbyshire and Lismore Castle in County Waterford. He was Lord High Treasurer of Ireland, Governor of County Cork, the titular head of the Whig party, the wealthiest man in England and a good catch.

A few weeks after the marriage contract had been signed, the Duke was invited to dinner at Lord Spencer's mansion in Wimbledon and afterwards to walk unchaperoned in the garden with Georgiana. After he left she could not remember what they had talked about, apart from the weather. She had a hazy recollection of his saying he was conscious of the great honour she was doing him, but her only clear memory was that when he broke two wine glasses at dinner, Lady Spencer had merely smiled. On 5 June 1774, four days before her seventeenth birthday, Georgiana Spencer and William Cavendish were married at the parish church in Wimbledon. Georgiana was half in love with her husband and completely in love with the freedom that marriage offered. The honeymoon was spent at Wimbledon to allow time for her to be presented at court before they left for Chatsworth.[4]

Her sister Henrietta, or Harriet (pronounced Harriot) as she was known in the family, was a tall, elegant woman noted for her dancing, self-confidence and wit. She did not have the same reputation for beauty as her sister but her quiet charm, intelligence and kind nature made her equally as popular. She had successfully warded off proposals of marriage from the Duke of Roxborough and Lord Trenton but in November 1780 she consented to marry Frederick, Viscount Duncannon, only son of William, second Earl of Bessborough and a cousin of the Duke of Devonshire.

Georgiana squandered a fortune at the card tables and exhausted her credit in six months. She was too afraid to tell her husband, so she confided in her mother who approached him on her behalf. The Duke silently honoured her debts. She struggled to find something useful to do and with her mother's encouragement she approached the Duke's cousin, the scientist Henry Cavendish. With his help she opened a small laboratory at Chatsworth where, under his supervision, she studied chemistry and geology. When the Duke discovered how she was passing her time he ordered her to stop, saying, 'Now that you have performed your duty in waiting upon Mr Cavendish, I would prefer for you not to visit him again'; he added, 'He is not a gentleman – he works.'[5]

The Duke's natural coldness made Georgiana nervous. Five years after her marriage, childless and unhappy, she wrote a two-volume novel, *The Sylph*. The hero, a man of fashion, is modelled on the Duke who sneers at his unsophisticated bride (Georgiana). Heartbroken, she confides in an older, worldly-wise woman, Lady Besford (Lady Melbourne) who pokes fun at the younger woman's belief that marriage is a source of happiness. She cynically advises her to enjoy her husband's title, rank and the liberty it gives her but to keep her distance from him and avoid disagreements. At first *The Sylph* was credited to Fanny Burney but it was not long before the identities of the characters were recognised by the Devonshire House set and the name of the author discovered. Georgiana said nothing, the family remained silent, she retained her good name and her relationship with her husband's family did not suffer.

In 1782, Lady Spencer asked Georgiana to befriend Lady Elizabeth Foster, the daughter of the Bishop of Derry. Elizabeth had married John Thomas Foster, the son of Dr John Foster of Dunleer, a Member of the Irish House of Commons and an old crony of her father's, in 1776. Within four years they were separated and their two sons, Frederick and Augustus, went to live with Dr Foster. This left Lady Elizabeth the choice of either living in genteel poverty with her sister, Lady Erne, in Bath, or relying on the charity of other relations.

Georgiana invited her to stay at Chatsworth and Lady Elizabeth's charming and amusing ways quickly made her presence indispensable to her hosts. The friendship blossomed. They were inseparable and gave each other nicknames. The Duke was 'Ca' or 'Canis' reflecting his love of dogs; Lady Elizabeth was Bess or 'Mrs Rackey', probably because her big dark eyes and pointed face reminded the other two of a racoon; and Georgiana answered to the unflattering nickname 'Mrs Rat'.

In December, after nine childless years of marriage, Georgiana thought she was pregnant. In her excitement she wrote almost hourly bulletins to her mother, full of terrified hope and plans. She was ecstatic when her hopes were confirmed and attributed the miracle to the happiness, laughter and steadying power that Lady Elizabeth had brought to her household. To outsiders the triple friendship was open to misunderstanding; uncharitable rumours rippled across London and Lady Spencer began to regret bringing Lady Elizabeth to Georgiana's attention.

On 12 July 1783 Georgiana's daughter was born, just six days after Harriet's second son, Frederick, and the delighted grandparents arranged for a double christening to be held at Wimbledon Park. The Duchess' little girl was named Georgiana Dorothy. Georgiana in honour of her mother and grandmother, Dorothy after the Duke's sister, the Duchess of Portland. The baby was known in the family as Little G.

Earl Spencer died suddenly in Bath on 31 October, leaving his energetic wife a widow at the early age of forty-six. She immediately handed her homes, Althorp, Wimbledon Park and Spencer House in London to her son, John and his wife Lavinia. By 3 November she had already moved into Holywell House on the outskirts of St Albans. The old, warm, red brick building, overlooking the river Ver and the Norman Abbey, a favourite residence of Sarah, Duchess of Marlborough, had hardly changed since her death. The main London road had been diverted round the house. It was so close that Lady Spencer could hear the coaches labouring up the hill and the chatter of passers-by. In widowhood she adopted an orderly, simple life, rising early to read and pray. She ate dinner at three and during the rest of the day visited the sick, comforted the bereaved and enthusiastically supported schools for the children of the poor. If there was any time left in the day she spent it in her flower garden.[6] She was the source of common sense to her daughters and to her granddaughter, Caroline.

As Duchess of Devonshire, Georgiana was the principal Whig hostess in London and when she threw open the doors of Devonshire House the *bon ton* flooded in. It was the custom in London to dine at four or five in the afternoon, attend an opera or play in the early evening, and then drop into Devonshire House for supper, conversation and cards. Night after night sedan chairs and carriages decanted revellers at Georgiana's door where they could be sure of meeting the best people, the wits, foreign literary lions and royalty. The gold and white salons on the ground floor were filled with the sound of conversation and debate until dawn and beyond. The Prince of Wales was a frequent visitor. He formed a deep friendship with Georgiana, calling her his 'sister' and for a short while he showed interest in Harriet, leading Lady Spencer to hope that he would ask for her hand. He did not but later agreed to be godfather to Harriet's grandson, and his namesake, Augustus Lamb. He passed his evenings playing whist and faro, enjoying gossip and cultivating the Whig orator, Charles James Fox. He had no firm political principles, but cultivated Fox to annoy his father, who loathed him. Other regular visitors included James Hare, a compulsive gambler, Charles Grey, Lord John Russell, the Duke of Leinster, Lord Robert Spencer and Richard Brinsley Sheridan, who was in love with Harriet and was gaining a reputation as a drunk. The Prince was no slouch with the bottle either and more often than not ended the night being pushed into a coach, driven home and put to bed by his valet.

Fox was a constant visitor. His father, the first Lord Holland, a dyed-in-the-wool Tory, engineered his election to Parliament while he was still under age and out of the country. His Stuart charm, vitality and passion blinded Georgiana to his slovenly appearance, cumbersome body, dark saturnine face, blue chin and bushy black eyebrows, his inheritance from Charles II and his mistress Louise de Kérualle, the Duchess of Portsmouth. Surprisingly, Fox had once prided himself on being a Macaroni, a leader of fashion, dressed in silk waistcoats and tottering round on red high-heeled shoes, sporting a large blue wig. Now he slouched about in a soiled blue frock coat and buff waistcoat, the colours of the American rebels, which he wore to irritate George III. He was a compulsive gambler, tossing away thousands of pounds, borrowing more and losing those. Destitute at thirty he borrowed stakes from the waiters at his club or the chairmen carrying him to and fro. He could drink and gamble for eighteen hours without fading, then brightly debate in the House of Commons.

Fox introduced Georgiana to politics and held her spellbound with his liberal theories. 'Would I were a man,' she wrote, 'to unite my talents, my hopes, my fortune with Charles', to make common cause, and fall or rule with him.'[7]

Lord and Lady Spencer had followed the Whig tradition of uniting and consolidating large estates by marriage. The Whigs regarded themselves as the representatives of the countryside. They were the political descendants of the victors of the 'Bloodless Revolution' of 1688 that replaced the Stuart monarchy with William of Orange. They believed that the power of parliament should be at least equal to that of the king and they had been eroding the powers of the crown ever since they gained office in 1714. The Hanoverian kings, George I and

George II, had paid for their right to reign by surrendering many of the powers that the Stuarts had enjoyed, to such a degree that George II complained he was merely 'a prisoner upon the throne'. When George III succeeded him in 1760, he declared that he was proud to be an Englishman and set himself the task of winning back the powers the Whigs had stolen and using to the full those prerogatives the crown still enjoyed.

By 1772 the loose association of noble landowners that formed the backbone of the Whig party began to fragment under the pressure of ideology and the loss of power, which had now passed to Lord North and the Tories or 'the king's friends'. Old Whiggery had no shame in accepting power, parliamentary seats, ambassadorships and sinecures as a reward for the part their families had played in 1688. The New Whigs, under the influence of Charles James Fox, held the view that these positions were trusts held for the good of the people. They opposed the king's policies in America and Whig ladies showed their opposition by dressing in the revolutionary colours.

After resuming office in December 1783, following the collapse of the North administration and the loss of the American war, the Whigs themselves fell from power and the king appointed twenty-four-year old William Pitt as his chief minister. Three months later Parliament was dissolved and an election was called. Three candidates came forward for the two seats of the Westminster constituency, Admiral Lord John Hood, a hero and popular Tory, Sir Cecil Wray, a Whig turncoat, and Fox, 'the Man of the People'.

This gave Georgiana the opportunity to show her support for Fox and she did not hesitate in asking the Duke to give his permission for her to canvass on Fox's behalf. Westminster was a unique constituency in which every male householder qualified for a vote. It was also one of the largest and most difficult to canvass. Corruption was rife and all the candidates bribed, fed and provided the electors with beer for the entire forty days of the campaign. Wray and Hood paraded through the streets protected by bully-boys dressed as sailors and armed with coshes, while Fox led his supporters, Irish chairmen, riffraff and troublemakers waving banners declaring 'Fox and Liberty'. When the two groups came in range they fought each other with drunken passion.

Undeterred, Georgiana rallied the support of other Whig ladies, including Mrs Crewe, Mrs Bouverie, her husband's sister (the Duchess of Portland) and Harriet. She designed a special blue and buff costume for herself and her sister, topped by a hat decorated with a fox's brush and a cockade with the word 'Fox' embroidered in gold. Each day from dawn to dusk the two sisters rode round the constituency in an open carriage, touting for votes. Almost as soon as Georgiana began canvassing the tide turned in Fox's favour. He felt guilty at exposing her to the dangers and indignities of the streets and half-heartedly asked her to stop.

'Nothing can wipe away the filth they've thrown,' she told him, 'let's *use* it – don't let us be defeated by them. You've admitted that my – our – driving about in carriages has done good. Well, I'm going to get out of my carriage. I'm going to *get* the votes. I can, I know it.'[8]

According to popular story, the sisters stopped at a butcher's shop and asked the owner for his vote. Still dressed in his shirtsleeves and bloody apron, he offered Georgiana his own and five more if she would kiss him. 'Why then,' she is reported to have said, 'take one.' Within hours placards appeared all over Westminster announcing, 'Several PAIR OF RUBY POUTING LIPS of the FIRST QUALITY, to be kissed by rum Dukes, queer Dukes, Butchers, Draymen, Dustmen and Chimney Sweepers. Please to enquire at Devon & Co. Crimson Pouting Warehouse Piccadilly.' 'It is very hard,' Georgiana wrote to Lady Spencer, 'they should single me out when all the women of my side do as much... My sister and Lady — were both kiss'd, so it's very hard I who was not should have the reputation of it.' Lady Spencer watched, with growing distaste, as her daughters' reputations were being tainted in the rough and tumble. She hated politics and believed elections were a waste of time and money.

The results were declared on 17 May 1784: Lord Hood 6,694 votes, Fox 6,233 and Sir Cecil Wray 5,998. A boisterous victory procession formed lead by a horseman waving a banner inscribed 'Sacred to Female Patriotism'. At the head of the drunken cavalcade was Fox who was carried in a chair decorated with laurel, myrtle and flowers. He was attended by thirty-two men in white who in turn were followed by the Dukes of Devonshire and Portland, Georgiana, Harriet and the Duchess of Portland, each in their own carriage. The procession made its way from Covent Garden to Devonshire House where the Prince of Wales was waiting on a specially constructed platform. According to Lord Pitt Lennox's account in *Fashion Now and Then*, 'the gates were thrown open, and discovered upon the balustrades the heir apparent surrounded by the first Whig families in the kingdom'. Later the mob staggered off to break the windows of the local residents.

A few weeks later, Lady Elizabeth joined the Duke and Georgiana at Chatsworth and under her spell of laughter and batting eyelids the Duke became almost skittish. They were so happy and delighted when Lady Elizabeth accepted Georgiana's invitation to remain with them permanently. Lady Spencer was alarmed and foresaw dangers in the passionate friendship, so when Lady Elizabeth developed a nagging cough she suggested to them that she should go to the south of France for the sake of her health. In December 1784 Georgiana discovered she was pregnant and once again attributed the wonder to the happy atmosphere generated by her friend. The gossips giggled and whispered, 'She was always simple, my dear, but now she is positively gullible.' On 29 August 1785, in the comfort of Devonshire House, Georgiana gave birth to a girl who she called Harriet Elizabeth (nicknamed Hary-o in the family). Just two weeks previously, in Vietri, a small fishing village on the Gulf of Salerno, Lady Elizabeth had given birth to Caroline Rosalie Adelaide, the Duke's bastard daughter.

On 11 November, Dr Denman sent word that the birth of Harriet's third baby was imminent. Lady Spencer raced from St Albans to Cavendish Square in an hour and twenty-five minutes, but she had to wait for another two days before Harriet 'was brought to bed of a lovely little girl – who seems very lively and in perfect health'.[9] The Duncannons were delighted with their daughter. Caroline told Lady Morgan, many years later, 'My mother wished ardently for a girl'. They already had two sons, John William, born 31 August 1781, and Frederick, born 6 July 1783.

Caroline was a small, delicate baby and Lady Spencer a demanding grandmother. When Caroline was barely a month old she wanted to know if she still squinted and if she had begun to put on weight. In January Caroline was inoculated and Lady Spencer swept her three granddaughters out of London to Holywell House to avoid an outbreak of smallpox. Despite all Lady Spencer's efforts Caroline did not gain weight and, at six months, she developed a cough.

Minor health matters were overshadowed by a rumour that Harriet, neglected by Duncannon, had run off with a lover. Lady Elizabeth wrote from Naples. 'Why won't you tell me if all I hear of dear Harriet and Harum (Duncannon) is true?' Lady Melbourne bustled in with advice and both she and Lady Elizabeth believed that the rumour would be scotched if Harriet appeared in society and brazened it out, but Harriet was too downcast to think of leaving Cavendish Square.

The Duncannons were reconciled and on 31 July 1787, William Francis Ponsonby was born. In October smallpox broke out in St Albans and Lady Spencer refused to see any of her grandchildren. 'I wish I was rich enough to offer to inoculate the whole town to get it over, that it might not be such a constant hindrance to my seeing some of you or your brats', she told Harriet. When Caroline developed a minor rash, Harriet jumped to the conclusion that it must be smallpox. 'How could you be such a goose?' Lady Spencer asked.[10]

By now Georgiana was in serious trouble with the Duke. Her gambling debts were enormous and the Duchess of Portland had begun a whispering campaign accusing her of being unfaithful. To prove her point she provided her brother with a list of Georgiana's supposed lovers, including the Prince of Wales, Fox and Count Fersen, an old flame of Lady Elizabeth's and friend of Queen Marie Antoinette. The one person she did not mention was the twenty-two-year old supporter of Fox, Charles Grey. Georgiana recognised his latent talent and political promise and together with Fox fostered his development. He was passionately in love with her and she was flattered by his admiration and agreeably startled by its violence. He frequently gave way to public outbursts and his possessive attitude towards her was so overwhelming that Lady Melbourne, who was careful never to give offence in public herself, took him to task. The Duke disliked this friendship and, annoyed at her enormous gambling debts, told Lady Spencer that he was seriously beginning to consider a separation or banishment.

Lady Elizabeth arrived back with her magic before the final decision was made and on 15 November the trio arrived at Hardwick Hall for a prolonged visit. It was there in the house of glittering windows, 'more glass than wall', that Lady Elizabeth led the Duke through his options. He could formally separate from Georgiana but this would mean that she would have to leave too, because it would not be decent to live under the same roof unmarried; or he could forgive Georgiana and continue to try for the heir he so desperately wanted. The Duke chose the second option, telling her, 'I of course shall never mention it to her, unless you desire me'. Lady Elizabeth could not resist the pleasure and explained the position to Georgiana, not forgetting to tell her about Caroline Rosalie Adelaide and the circumstances surrounding her birth. Georgiana was completely demoralised and, although no prude, she was shocked and hurt.[11]

Georgiana's addiction to gambling bewildered her banker, Thomas Coutts. 'I *will* venture and *endeavour* to give a faint idea of how much it shocks me to think what your Grace puts into hazard by indulging a passion for play. There is nothing your Grace can acquire; you have already titles, character, friends, fortune, power, beauty, *everything* superior to the rest of the world. Permit me also to add *conjugal happiness* to the list, and to say that all these, the first article only excepted to the list, you risk to gratify this destructive passion.'[12]

In July 1787 the Duke and Duchess, accompanied by Lady Elizabeth, took their children to Bath for two months. After several anxious weeks and a visit to a physician, Lady Elizabeth told the Duke she was pregnant. This time she did not bother to hide the cause of her delicate health from Georgiana.

She left for France where she was reunited with her daughter, who had taken as her surname St Jules, from the Comte St Jules of Aix en Provence, one of her mother's former admirers who agreed that she should use his name. The Duke's son, Augustus William James, was born on 26 May at Rouen and he was given the surname Clifford after the Duke's grandmother, Charlotte Boyle, who held the title Baroness Clifford.

Lady Spencer knew what had happened but never commented on the Duke's conduct. She simply refused to visit or dine with the Devonshires if there was any danger of meeting Lady Elizabeth. Her hostility was obvious and society drew its conclusions. The only way to stop the speculation was if she would agree to receive Lady Elizabeth. Eventually, to please Georgiana, Lady Spencer relented and invited all three to an uncomfortable evening at Holywell.

Georgiana hired twenty-three-year-old Miss Selina Trimmer, a devout Christian who shared Lady Spencer's child-rearing philosophy, to be the governess for five-year-old Little G and baby Harriet. Her mother, Mrs Sarah Trimmer, wrote moral stories for children, the most famous being the *Sacred History selected from the Scriptures, with Annotations and Reflections adapted to the Comprehension of Young Persons.* Little G and Hary-o were joined in the nursery by thirteen-year-old Charlotte William, a half sister, the result of a brief liaison between the Duke and a young milliner before his marriage. James Hare urged Lady Elizabeth to push her children into the Devonshires' nursery too and, with understandable misgivings, Georgiana agreed.

Caroline, or Caro as she was affectionately called in the family, lived in London with her parents in their mansion on the corner of Cavendish Square and Margaret Street. In the summer the family went to their splendid villa in Roehampton, where her father passed long hot afternoons playing cards with the Prince of Wales in an alcove in the garden.

In June 1789, Lady Elizabeth accompanied the Duke and Duchess to Spa. Georgiana hoped the healing waters would increase her chance of becoming pregnant and relieve the Duke's gout. They paused in Paris to visit Monsieur and Madame Nagel, who ran a small school where they left Charlotte William to complete her education. 'Luckily,' Georgiana ingenuously told her mother, 'there is only one other pensioner, Mlle de St Jules, a young Ly from the provinces, and as she is very young Madame Nagel will attend entirely to little Charlotte.' She neglected to mention the presence of little Augustus Clifford.

Georgiana was uneasy, frightened that the Duke would discover how much she owed. In fact she was so short of money that she was reduced to borrowing from her brother John and her servants in order to pay off the moneylenders. She owed money to twenty-five people, amounting, she said (she did not always tell the complete truth) to £61,917 (about £5 million today). She ignored James Hare when he urged her to tell the Duke, saying, 'There is no situation so desperate where there is not something to be done.' In Paris she cultivated a friendship with Susan, Fanny and Sophia Coutts, and advised their father on how to introduce his 'sweet girls' to society. In return Coutts was understanding and discreet about her debts. At the end of September, believing she was pregnant and knowing that the birth of a direct heir would release from the Dukedom entailed moneys from which she hoped the Duke would pay her debts, she told Coutts 'before I lie in (if I really am with child) I shall lay everything before him'.

The Duke was convinced that the baby would be a boy and refused to allow Georgiana to return home in case she miscarried on the way. Their friends were astounded at his decision and, even when they pointed out how dangerous it would be to stay in the Low Countries now that the seeds of revolution were spreading out from France across Europe, the Duke refused to reconsider. Instead he sent for his daughters and Miss Trimmer to join them in Brussels. Georgiana had correctly guessed the parentage of little Caroline St Jules but she still hoped to fool her mother by describing the child as a protégée of the Duchesse de Polignac, a friend of Lady Elizabeth. 'I have got you a charming little companion in Mademoiselle de St Jules,' she wrote to Little G, 'She is like Caro Ponsonby but she don't speak English.'

Lady Caroline stayed with her grandmother in March when her parents went to see Georgiana in Brussels. Lady Spencer sent regular reports on Caroline's progress to Harriet, telling her that she was healthy and '3 feet 3 inches high and could read well and could point out all the large cities on her map of England'. She added that Caroline was 'the most accommodating, good-humoured child' she had ever seen.[13]

The Belgian authorities suspected the Duke of sending seditious letters to England and despite his robust denials the family was expelled from the country. They made the dangerous journey to Paris with Georgiana in considerable discomfort and about to give birth at any moment. They were met on their arrival by a horrifying rumour – that it was Lady Elizabeth who was pregnant, not the Duchess. In an attempt to allay speculation Lady Spencer, who had hurried across from England, asked the Dowager Duchesse Deremberg and the Secretary at the British Embassy, Lord Robert Fitzgerald, to witness the birth. She also authorised her confidential maid, Ann Scafe, to keep a journal. Lady Elizabeth went to the opera and deliberately shared a box with a well-known rake, Lord St Helens, and showed the world her well-dressed slim figure.

When Lady Elizabeth returned to their rented house in Passy, she found the Duchess' bedroom crammed with people. 'At a little after one o'clock in the morning the twenty first of May 1790 her Grace was safely delivered of a fine boy – his title is Marquis of Hartington – the second title of the Duke of Devonshire.' Ann Scafe added the comment to her journal, 'There never was a more welcome child.'[14]

Lady Spencer's measures were not enough to silence the gossips and speculation on the relationship between the Duke, the Duchess and Lady Elizabeth continued. It was widely accepted that Lady Elizabeth had given birth to a boy who was taken from her and swapped for the Duchess' newly born daughter. (In 1816 Caroline revived interest in Lord Hartington's birth by centring the plot of her novel *Glenarvon* on changelings. Two years later the canard was embroidered to suggest that Hartington did not marry because he knew he was an impostor.) In August 1790 the Devonshire House nursery expanded to include Caroline St Jules and, before long, Augustus Clifford was slipped in almost unnoticed.

In February 1791 Harriet became seriously ill with what appears to have been tuberculosis complicated by a minor stroke. She was giddy, spat blood, her left arm and leg were numb and she suffered from what Georgiana described as 'spasms'. Dr Richard Warren was called in. He was a highly respected physician who had treated the Duke of Devonshire, the Duke of Portland, the Prince of Wales and the King. He prescribed the warm waters of Bath.

Now that Georgiana had performed her duty by providing the Duke with an heir, she allowed herself to fall in love with Charles Grey. They were indiscreet and, according to Lady Holland, Grey became 'fractious and exigent'. Lady Elizabeth and Lady Melbourne tried unsuccessfully to restrain Georgiana and it was only after Lady Spencer had taken her to task that she agreed to break off her affair and join her sister in Bath.

Her wanton behaviour and mounting debts had enraged the Duke to the point that he seriously considered starting separation procedures. He had correctly guessed that she was pregnant by Charles Grey, although since she had put on so much weight it was difficult to tell. He arrived unexpectedly in Bath and demanded to see Georgiana and Lady Spencer alone. Through the thin wall of her bedroom Harriet could hear raised voices and then the tap of Georgiana's footsteps as she ran to her room. Unable to stand the suspense she sent her sister a note. The answer confirmed her fears. The Duke wanted a separation. Harriet spoke to Dr Warren and persuaded him, using her cough and 'spasms' as an excuse, to order her to the south of France. She then asked him to suggest to the Duke that Georgiana should come with her as her nurse-companion. She believed that if they stayed away long enough the resulting scandal would force the Duke to relent. The Duke grudgingly allowed Georgiana to leave but he forbade her to see any of the children before she left.

Bad weather in the Channel delayed Lady Elizabeth, Caroline, Charlotte William and Caroline St Jules. Four days later Lady Elizabeth wrote reassuringly from Calais to the other travellers, Lady Spencer, Georgiana, and to Harriet and Duncannon, who had already arrived in Paris, 'Both Carolines were very sick & both were very patient. I must add both are now well and hungry'.[15]

At Lyons, on 19 December, they embarked on a flat-bottomed boat and sailed on the Rhône past Avignon to Tarascon where the group parted. Caroline, her parents and Lady Spencer went to Hyères. Georgiana, Lady Elizabeth, Caroline St Jules and Charlotte William went to Aix en Provence. While she waited for the birth of Grey's child, Georgiana was overcome by despondency. She made her will and wrote a letter to her son Hartington, to be given to him when he was eight. It began dramatically, 'My dear little boy. As soon as you are old enough to understand this letter it will be given to you; it contains the only present I can make you – my blessing, written in blood.' On 20 February 1792 she gave birth to a girl in the home of the Comte de St Jules where she and Lady Elizabeth had 'staid behind', as Duncannon told his father, Lord Bessborough, 'to see some relations of that little French girl you have seen at Devonshire House'. The baby, Eliza Courtney, was taken to England, adopted by her paternal grandparents and brought up at Hawick in Northumberland.

Harriet missed her sons, John and Frederick, and spent a great deal of time writing to them at school at Harrow. Her health was slowing improving and she was walking with the help of crutches. She told them that Caroline was happy, spoke French 'very tolerably' and was learning to play the harpsichord. In March the party regrouped in Nice where they met Lady Webster (later to become Lady Holland) whose husband, Sir Godfrey Webster, was a gambler and hard drinker who beat her during fits of depression. In May they were carried across Mont Cenis in chairs and although Harriet and Lady Elizabeth suffered from the cold, 'Lady Spencer was in her element gathering alpine flowers among the snow'. Georgiana took up mineralogy and told Little G, 'You wd laugh to see me climbing up hills with a hammer in my hands.'

Caroline St Jules was universally admired. She was 'a dear little girl' with 'great good sense' and 'sweetness of disposition' and 'a wonderful piety for such a little creature'. It is not surprising that in the face of such perfection Caroline Ponsonby rebelled. Lady Spencer complained to Miss Trimmer, who was living at Devonshire House with Hartington and his sisters. 'I am sadly fritted about poor little Caroline who has been for some days past so naughty and perverse that I sometimes think all the pains I have taken with her are thrown away. At other times she seems improved and when she will try to be so is a very amiable child'. However, she was 'invariable attentive at her prayers'. It was this and 'the recollection of what a little ill-tempered child her mother was at her age is all I have to keep me from desponding about her'.[16]

In June 1792 Lord Duncannon was recalled to England for six months. During his absence it became clear to Harriet that she could not control Caroline and she handed her over to her mother. Lady Spencer set her to work but Caroline refused to do arithmetic. This did not bother Lady Spencer, who told Miss Trimmer that, 'the fancy for them will come again as I have reason enough to be very sure she can do anything of that kind when she chooses to set about it'.

Although Little G was in England, Georgiana celebrated her ninth birthday by distributing clothes and flowers to nine poor children. In the evening she provided music and dancing. Georgiana told Little G, 'Caroline St Jules, with her usual goodness said that she liked the morning much the best' but Caroline Ponsonby was 'very naughty'. However, by the time she left to go to bed she had managed to make everyone laugh and they all had agreed that 'the little faults she makes are very entertaining'.

In August 1792 the two Carolines met the writer Edward Gibbon at his beautiful house in Lausanne, where they danced and sang for him. Caroline Ponsonby was a light-hearted, spirited little show-off and with her heart-shaped face and large eyes she looked like an elf. Gibbon was enchanted. Georgiana was dismayed and wrote, 'Caroline Ponsonby does what she will with him', and says 'anything that comes into her head, which is quite distressing'. Caroline was curious about everything and constantly asked 'Why?' When she received an answer she asked another question about the answer she had just been given. Her search for knowledge drove her family to distraction but Gibbon thought her amusing. He liked to play the fool with her by wearing his green jockey cap back to front. In one of their games with a puppy, Caroline told him that his big face frightened 'the little animal'. This embarrassed Georgiana, although she had to agree that Gibbon had 'the misfortune of being very ugly'.[17]

Caroline's grandfather, William, second Earl of Bessborough, died on 11 March 1793 aged 89 and for the second time in a year her father was forced to return to London alone. It was a dangerous journey. The French had declared war on Britain on 1 February and a civil war was ripping France apart. To avoid most of the difficulties he made his way through Verona, Innsbruck, Stuttgart, Wiesbaden and Bruges to Ostend. He passed close to the battlefield of Neerwinden, 'which was still very offensive from the carcasses of the horses &c, tho' most of the human bodies have been buried by the peasants'.

The French Revolution was coming to its bloody climax and family correspondence was dominated by fear for the safety of Marie Antoinette, a friend of Lady Spencer, who had entertained the Duke and Georgiana at Versailles three years before. They watched with mounting horror as French antagonism rose towards the Queen. Her situation, after the execution of her husband, Louis XVI, on 21 January 1793, was desperate. All attempts to rescue her failed and to the horror of her English friends, on 16 October, she was executed.

Despite their allegiance to the Whig party and their support for the American rebels, neither Georgiana nor Harriet had recognised the growing unrest in France for what it was. They believed the French were preparing to establish a constitutional government. They did not realise that what the world was seeing was the first act of vengeance by people who felt they had been oppressed for centuries. 'How much the greatest event that ever happened in the World! And how much the Best!' Fox had exclaimed with glee when the Bastille fell. But now the glory had gone. Harriet told John and Frederick, 'I believe the national character of the English, the generosity & real courage of their nature, would alone preserve them from ever acting as the French have done.'[18]

A month after Marie Antoinette had crossed the bloody scaffold in her best high-heeled satin shoes there was a mass exodus of *émigrés*. Georgiana generously invited the Duc de Grammont, his wife, the daughter of Madame de Polignac, his son the Duc de Guiche and daughter Corisande to Chatsworth where Corisande joined Little G and Hary-o in the schoolroom.

Georgiana and Harriet turned their sightseeing expeditions into educational experiences for the girls. They boiled eggs in the Hot Springs of Piscarella, examined samples of lava at Portici and watched ancient documents being restored at Herculaneum. Caroline St Jules was so fascinated by the baker's oven at Pompeii that they had difficulty in dragging her away. One of the highlights of their visit to Naples was lunch with the King and Queen at the Royal Farm where they were amazed by the mechanical dining table which allowed them to dine without servants. Georgiana described for Little G how 'the middle circle of the table contains the dinner & by pulling a bell brought up wine, water, bread &c.c'. The girls were allowed to walk up Mount Vesuvius but they were forbidden to go near the crater, which was active and occasionally threw up volleys of stones, some the size of a man's hand and still red-hot. John Daniel, Lord Bessborough's footman, had a lucky escape during one of these eruptions. The girls waited with Lady Elizabeth at a cottage half way up the volcano while Lady Spencer, Georgiana and Harriet walked to the edge of the crater. They returned with singed eyebrows and scorched protective handkerchiefs.[19]

In August 1793 the Duke forgave Georgiana and by 18 September she was reunited with her children at Dartford. As a peace offering, he gave her a new blue carriage with silver springs. Meanwhile, Lord Bessborough returned to Italy with his youngest child, six-year-old Willy, who was Caroline's favourite brother and the closest to her in age and temperament. They were lively, exuberant, curious and eccentric children. Willy's chatter and comments had amused his father and fellow travellers during the long journey. 'His great rage is at present to go into a nunnery to see the nuns', Lord Bessborough told Harriet. 'He says he understands after he is 7 they will not let him in.' Willy also had a few of Caroline's less attractive traits; 'Dear Willy is perfectly well but we have had some sad quarrels, a little in the stile of Caro's, when he grows tired.'

The children enjoyed the winter warmth of Naples, the blooming roses, carnations and the out-of-season green peas. They planted a garden and Caroline looked after her pet fox and passed many pleasant hours teaching tricks to Roma and Scappa, dogs which Lady Spencer and Harriet, now Lady Bessborough, had received as presents.

Members of the English colony in Naples included Lord Granville Leveson-Gower, Lord Holland, Charles Beauclerk, Lord Borington, Lord Morpeth, Lord Digby, Lord Berwick, Lady Plymouth, Lord and Lady Henry Fitzgerald and Lady Ann Hatton. Lady Webster joined them in February 1794 and promptly fell in love with Lord Holland. Lady Bessborough was amused and flattered to find that the young, spectacularly handsome Lord Granville, the youngest son of the Marquis of Stafford, was paying court to her. She pretended not to be affected but could not help being flattered, particularly as he was twelve years her junior. In the warm, relaxed expatriate life of Naples she allowed herself to be drawn towards him. Her submission is all the more curious as for her entire adult life she had been surrounded by admirers, from the Prince of Wales to Sheridan, none of whom she had any difficulty in keeping at arm's length.

The party broke up in the spring and they had barely reached Rome on the way home when Lady Bessborough began a series of letters to Lord Granville that ended only with her death in 1821.

Caroline's first recorded letter was written in Milan, in French, to her brother John; *'J'espère que tous mes amis se portent bien. Ce sera un grand plaisir pour moi de les revoir.'* As they got closer to home, Willy and Caroline became very excited and as they travelled through Germany Willy ran about shouting 'yaw, yaw, neon'.[20]

They arrived back at Cavendish Square in July 1795 after an absence of almost three years. Lady Spencer returned to Holywell a month later. She was welcomed by a peal of church bells and lighted candles in the cottage windows.

Lady Bessborough resumed her former routine of late nights, parties and gambling at Devonshire House. This left her susceptible to illness and when she caught a cold from Caroline in October, all her former ailments, weakness, shivering, coughing and the spitting of blood returned. Dr Warren recommended that she should go to the comparative warmth of the West Country and Lord Bessborough rented 'Stone House', a large furnished mansion not far from Teignmouth. Georgiana, Dr Drew and Lady Anne Hatton were invited and the winter days passed pleasantly. In the mornings they played chess or rode out in the countryside. In the evenings they played music or listened to Dr Drew read aloud while the ladies sketched and Lord Bessborough played cribbage. Lady Bessborough read Choderlos de Laclos' *Les Liaisons Dangéreuses* and noticed a similarity between the conniving anti-heroine Madame de Merteuil and Lady Melbourne. Lady Holland also remarked that Lady Melbourne's behaviour 'often puts me in mind of Madame de Merteuil'.

Since arriving in England, Caroline had become stubborn, perverse and argumentative and, on occasions, violent. Lady Spencer consulted Dr Warren, who recommended that she should be isolated her from her brothers and cousins. He believed that if she could no longer show off or turn the schoolroom into a battlefield she would become bored and behave properly. Miss Trimmer took Caroline to the Duke of Devonshire's villa at Chiswick. When Caroline was naughty, she was ignored, and when she was disobedient she was dosed with sal volatile or spoken to so sharply that she was reduced to tears. It did not take long before Miss Trimmer was able to write to tell Lady Spencer that Caroline had improved in every way. The two women agreed that it was impracticable to leave her at Chiswick indefinitely so, on 7 April 1796, Lady Bessborough met Miss Trimmer to discuss Caroline's future. After several hours of discussion they came to the conclusion that they would hire a reliable person to be a combination nurse and governess. This was not an easy task and it was not until June that Lady Bessborough found a girl, Mary, who met all her requirements. Caroline liked her, and tried to improve. Her good conduct was rewarded by being allowed to spend days with her brothers in Cavendish Square or with her cousins at Devonshire House. Just when everything seemed to be going well, Caroline fell from grace by quizzing Lady Spencer on religion, which was a subject she knew her grandmother disliked discussing. Her punishment was to sit in a 'cupboard' with Mary until it was time to go to bed with a dose of laudanum laced with lavender oil.[21]

Georgiana had suffered headaches for several months and needed peace and quiet, so it was agreed that the noisy young Ponsonbys and Cavendishes should go to Worthing for the summer where their high spirits and horseplay would not disturb her. Lady Spencer went ahead to look for suitable lodgings. At first she despaired of finding anywhere large enough or with sufficient privacy, for, 'if my poor little Caroline gets into one of her screaming passions there will be no concealing it.'[22] Eventually a house was hired which was big enough to hold all the servants, cooks, footmen, children, and Miss Trimmer and her sister Julia who were left in charge. Although Caroline still needed 'constant watching', Miss Trimmer told Lady Spencer, 'I cannot express the pleasure it gives me to see her so much better & when I see her pleased with being commended for being good & really strive to get the better of any little perverseness that comes upon her, it quite oversets me & I can sometimes scarcely refrain from shedding tears over her.'[23]

When Dr Warren examined Caroline in the autumn he was pleased with her progress and declared that she would be 'well quite soon'. She was an emotional child and could never hide her feelings. Once she became attached to a person or an object she could not let go. When Lady Spencer gave Lady Bessborough one of Roma's puppies, she asked 'I beg you will not let it be called Caroline's nor suffer her to have any dog or living favourite for I know by experience nothing agitates her so much – it arises from too much anxiety about what she loves but it should be avoided.'

Georgiana's headaches became more frequent and increased in intensity. There was also something seriously wrong with one of her eyes. She spent almost all her time in darkened rooms in excruciating pain. Dr Warren decided to operate. A tourniquet was applied to her neck forcing blood into her head, and leeches were put on the eyeball. This desperate measure did not cure the headaches and three expert surgeons, John Gunning, Gustavus Hume and Jonathan W Phipps, who specialised in treating cataracts, were asked to examine her. The eye and the surrounding area were now viciously inflamed, and the whole area had swollen to the size of a woman's clenched fist and stuck out from her face like a doorknob. She underwent a second operation on 3 August 1796 and at first she made a good recovery, her skin cool and her pulse regular, which led Lady Spencer to hope that the worst was over. It was not. In December the doctors were recalled and they applied 'causticks behind her ears and a blister on the back of her neck for four hours'. Lady Bessborough had never seen such suffering and her attempts to hold and soothe Georgiana brought back her 'spasms with great violence'.

In November Lady Elizabeth's estranged husband, John Foster, died and Georgiana invited her two sons, Augustus and Frederick, to consider Devonshire House as their home. This upset all the children. None of them liked Frederick's boring jokes or Augustus' pedantic ways and Miss Trimmer had difficulty in maintaining her professional attitude as she regarded Lady Elizabeth as an interloper and undoubtedly knew the secrets behind the births of Caroline St Jules and Augustus Clifford. Hary-o and Caroline in particular disliked Lady Elizabeth, and made fun of her mannerisms, whining voice and affected baby talk. Together with Little G, they made special efforts to hide their feelings in front of Caroline St Jules because they knew she was Lady Elizabeth's protégée but when they were alone they linked arms and paced up and down mimicking Lady Elizabeth. 'A thousand pards, dearest Georgiana, for not writing sooner, for 'oo know dearest love that I 'ave so 'ittle time for 'ose things 'at it is impossible for me to 'ite.'[24]

They were a mixed group. Hartington (usually called Hart in the family) was a quiet boy who loved to read. He was proud, passionate and slightly deaf. Little G was the easiest to get on with, gentle, serious, pliant and lazy. Hary-o was clear-sighted, strong-minded, inconsistent, either violently happy or plunged in despair and very greedy. Caroline St Jules was sensitive, self-effacing and pious. Corisande de Grammont was frivolous and flirtatious, which Miss Trimmer put down to her misfortune of being born French. Caroline was charming, clever, 'wild as a hawk and impertinent as a squirrel.'

In his guidebook to Chatsworth, which Hartington wrote in 1844, he reminisced affectionately about the fun they had in the smoky nursery. He described Miss Trimmer sitting primly at her desk, the children giggling behind a screen and how Caroline would take the lead in gently teasing her. This would produce a wave of giggles and little squeaks from Hartington, Little G and Hary-o.

In May 1797 Caroline and her mother spent some time in Holywell with Lady Spencer. In contrast to their usual practice they were up and dressed for prayers before breakfast at eight. Lady Bessborough gave Caroline her lessons and afterwards they visited Lady Spencer's girls' school. Dinner was at three, then they walked in the garden, read or embroidered until teatime. The evenings were devoted to music until nine when the bell rang for prayers and by ten o'clock 'not a mouse is stirring in the whole house'. This regular pattern of life was in stark contrast to the unsupervised rough and tumble Caroline enjoyed with her brothers at Cavendish Square. She told Little G, 'We played Pope Jone every night almost for money till nine or a little past. My brothers went yesterday to Harrow, before they went they hunted some rats & John threw me a dead one which blooded me'.[25] Lady Spencer disapproved of these easy-going ways and she particularly disapproved of Lady Bessborough's habit of sleeping for half the day. She asked her, 'How does Caroline go on for the many hours in the day she is with her brothers before you are stirring? I fear that dear child has too steady a determination not to be restrained, and too much unhappy invitation of temper and Spirits to bear contradiction.'[26] Later, Caroline told Lady Morgan that she and her cousins were neglected by their mothers and were so out of touch that they believed everyone ate off silver plates, that horses ate beef and did not know that bread was made of flour or butter from cream. She also said that she was ten before she could write, though there is clear evidence in the Althorp Papers that not only could she read and write but also that she wrote verse and composed and performed music.

Caroline was fluent in Italian and French but her formal education had been neglected. To remedy this, Lady Bessborough hired a German-speaking governess, Mademoiselle Muller. Caroline took an immediate disliked to her and flatly refused to work, saying, 'My faculties are suspended and my blood is congeal'd'. Mademoiselle Muller left. Lady Spencer was worried about Caroline's progress and feared that she would fall so far behind that she could never catch up, but Caroline forced the issue and the matter of a governess was avoided for three years until Lady Spencer pressed Lady Bessborough into employing Miss Rowden. She was a highly accomplished young woman, the daughter and sister of clergymen. Caroline disliked her and sulked. She said that she preferred 'washing a dog, or polishing a piece of Derbyshire spar, or breaking a horse to any accomplishment in the world'. She later told Lady Morgan that she felt she had been a trouble, not a pleasure to her parents all through her childhood and that she should have been a soldier instead of a 'forward, talking girl'. The parting was friendly and Miss Rowden celebrated her brief stay with a poem dedicated to Lady Bessborough, before returning to London to take up a post in a seminary for young ladies run by Monsieur St Quentin and his wife at 22 Hans Place.

In August 1798 the Bessboroughs spent their annual holiday at Margate. The children arrived in high spirits. Willy nearly fell over the banisters. He was saved by John who caught hold of his coat-tails while simultaneously restraining his mother from impulsively following Willy. A few days later Caroline narrowly escaped death. She was returning home with her parents in a curricle (a light two-wheeled carriage pulled by two horses) when Lord Bessborough lost his way in the darkness. Furious with himself and cross with Harriet and Caroline for being nervous, he handed the reins to Harriet before getting down to get his bearings and to soothe the whinnying, rearing horses. She held the reins in one hand and with the other helped Caroline climb down. It was then that she saw they were perched on the edge of a deep chalk pit; she did not dare move and then, to her horror, she realised that Caroline had vanished. An hour or so later she returned with a rescue party. She had run into Margate and gone to the playhouse, the only place she knew, and raised the alarm.

In May 1799, Caroline was confirmed with Caroline St Jules and Little G at Westminster Abbey. They wore plain white dresses with matching headbands and demure expressions; even Lady Spencer was impressed by their 'calm seriousness' when they took their First Communion.

Miss Trimmer deeply disapproved of Lady Melbourne and regretted her close friendship with Georgiana, which had begun soon after the young Duchess entered Devonshire House as a bride. Lady Melbourne's father was Sir Ralph Milbanke, the fifth baronet, and the family owned estates in north east England. Elizabeth Milbanke grew up at Halnaby Hall, near Durham, with her two brothers – John, who died in 1800, and Ralph, who later became the sixth baronet. In April 1769 Elizabeth had married Sir Peniston Lamb, who was elevated to the Irish peerage a year later as Lord Melbourne, Baron of Kilmore in the County of Cavan. The more established Whig families considered them to be *nouveaux riches* but Lady Melbourne set out to be the premier Whig hostess. She expensively and tastefully decorated the family mansion in Piccadilly (now part of Albany) as the backdrop to her political ambition. Although ten years older than the Prince of Wales she became his mistress and flattered him as they walked in the gardens behind Melbourne House (designed by another lover,

Lord Egremont). However, when she saw Georgiana's success as a hostess she decided to befriend and guide her rather than risk humiliation as a rival.

Lady Sarah Lennox described her 'commanding figure exceeding middle height, full of grace and dignity, an animated countenance, intelligent features, captivating manners and conversation; all these and many other attractions, enhanced by coquetry'. Men appreciated her blue eyes, pretty, unpowdered brown hair and mordant wit. Georgiana admired her intelligence and valued her advice but her deep affection blinded her to her friend's manipulations and flashy charm. Lady Bessborough was not so easily deceived.

Lady Melbourne's eldest son, Peniston (born 1770) was the only child Lord Melbourne could confidently call his own. In 1777 she gave birth to twins; the boy was stillborn, the girl died three days later. The probable father of these children and of William (born 1779) and his sister, Harriet Ann (born 1789) was the immensely rich Lord Egremont, the owner of Petworth. Emily (born 1787) looked like her mother but it was rumoured that her father was Francis, 8th Duke of Bedford. Frederick (born 1780) was assumed to be the son of Frederick, Duke of York, and George (born 1784) a by-blow of the Prince of Wales.

The Lamb brothers were large, noisy and liked to swear and play practical jokes. They thought it was enormously funny to embarrass people. At a house party at Brocket they sent Lord John Townsend to Corisande's bedroom convincing him it was his own. Hary-o was disgusted when William and Frederick arrived late at an assembly at Melbourne House 'very *drunk* and the former talked to me in a loud voice the whole time of the danger of a *young womans* believing in *weligion* and *pwactising mowality*'. She was equally revolted when William and Tom Sheridan turned up at Devonshire House for supper so drunk that 'they disputed till they almost fought'.[27] They had broken the unwritten rule that allowed a man to drink as much as he liked so long as he 'carried his wine like a gentleman'.

Little G and Caroline began to show an interest in the darkly handsome William Lamb and after sitting next to William at supper at Devonshire House Caroline told Emily that she had eaten well and 'being near your *gentlemanlike* brother of course neither found it dull or formal'. She later wrote, 'He thought of me but as a child, but he liked me much.' However, William's first interest was in Little G. This was not surprising, because as the second son of a peer he was expected to make his own way in the world. Although he had chosen a career in law it must have occurred to him how much more convenient and comfortable life would be as the Duke of Devonshire's son-in-law.

In August 1800 Lady Bessborough hit her head when she fell down the stairs at Roehampton. Five doctors were called in and they recommended that her head be completely shaved except for little tufts on either side. (This medical whim had caused Caroline to lose her long red-gold hair in June, when she complained of a sore throat.) Lady Bessborough returned to Cavendish Square and stayed out of sight throughout September and October. She had few visitors apart from Georgiana, who brought her baskets of fruit daily.

Lady Bessborough had conducted her six-year affair with Lord Granville in a circumspect and delicate way and it seemed as though her relationship with her husband had not suffered. Nor did it apparently change during that autumn when, still ostensibly recovering from her fall, she gave birth to Lord Granville's daughter, Harriet Emma Arundel Stewart (Stewart was Lord Granville's mother's maiden name). Caroline was with her grandmother at Holywell during her mother's indisposition.

In November, Lady Spencer celebrated Caroline's birthday with a poem.

Full fifteen years of lengthen'd childhood past
Have made thy anxious friends misjudge of Thee;
Oh show them all, my much lov'd child, at last
That from these follies thou art now set free.

Catch each advantage which thy Parents' Love
With liberal hands have on thy youth bestow'd;
With gentleness let friendship thee improve,
And humbly seek the assistance of thy God.[28]

Twenty-three Cavendishes, Bessboroughs, related Cavendishes and Ponsonbys sat down to Christmas dinner at Chatsworth and in one week they ate fifteen sheep and two oxen. The amount of food and drink consumed by those who could afford it was amazing. Pitt had kept himself going by swallowing glasses of port all day and beautiful women sipped themselves headlong into cirrhosis. To soothe their overworked digestion they took vast quantities of patent medicines – Godbold's Vegetable Balsam for constipation and asthma, Velno's Vegetable Syrup for everything else. They drank gallons of claret, tokay, hock, sherry, port and champagne and, even discounting the smaller bottles of the period, the aristocracy were as great boozers on wine as the lower classes were on gin.

Fashionable London, which covered an area roughly from Pall Mall to Park Lane and from the Haymarket as far north as Hanover and Grosvenor Squares, was deserted in winter. The aristocracy retreated to their country estates to hunt in the morning and eat and drink themselves into a stupor during the afternoon. Frequently, after a long day in the field and a heavy dinner, the gentlemen did not join the ladies for conversation and cards until after eleven or twelve o'clock. By that time they were 'very much elevated by wine'; but, according to William Lamb, 'it tended to increase the gaiety of society, it produced diversity'.

The most important guest at Chatsworth that Christmas was George, Viscount Morpeth, the twenty-six-year-old son of Frederick, fifth Earl of Carlisle. The Duke and Duchess of Devonshire were anxious to encourage a marriage between him and Little G, but Lord Morpeth was diffident and his lack of self-confidence worried Georgiana. It was a great relief to everyone when he pulled himself together and proposed. The couple were married on 21 March 1801 and the first of Little G's twelve children, George, was born the following April.

The cold winter brought back all Lady Bessborough's ailments and Caroline, in the way at Cavendish Square, was sent to stay with Lady Spencer. 'Poor little soul' she wrote, 'how difficult it is to know what to do with her – & yet at times how sweet a creature she is.'[29] When Caroline offered to give her dog to her grandmother, Lady Spencer refused. 'This would be too great a sacrifice', she told Lady Bessborough. 'She really has taught it a great many tricks and it is an intelligent little beast.' Caroline's behaviour improved so remarkably that Lady Spencer's maid, Jenny, noticed, saying, 'She will be the sweetest of them all at last.' Her only fault, according to Lady Spencer, was that she washed her face too enthusiastically, leaving it flushed and rough.[30]

In May, Caroline attended her first ball. It was held at Devonshire House in honour of Hartington's birthday. In her excitement Caroline managed to spoil her dress but Lady Spencer was not sympathetic, telling Lady Bessborough, 'I am not very sorry for dear Caroline's disaster, because she really is of an age to look in the glass and not let herself be made a figure of – tell her I long to see her that I may scold her.'[31] Caroline used this minor disaster as an excuse to ask for a maid of her own. Lady Spencer remarked tartly, 'the longer that wish dwells upon her mind ungratified the better'.[32]

Another joint family holiday was arranged, this time in Ramsgate. On 26 August Hary-o and Hartington arrived at their lodgings, a pair of semi-detached houses in Chatham Place, about half a mile from the sea. Duncannon and his brother William arrived on the evening of 9 September. Caroline and Lady Bessborough arrived later. They had been delayed at Sittingbourne when Caroline suddenly felt bilious. On hearing that the Melbournes were expected in the town, Hary-o told Little G, 'I dread their arrival, as if I was only to see them once a month, Miss Trimmer would keep up a constant reproof; she is perfectly kind and good-humoured, but you know how she hates Lady Melbourne. Just before we left town, she was angry with me for a week, because I happened to take Frederick's arm at Vauxhall'.[33] The days passed quickly with trips to Margate and Dover, swimming, expeditions to the Downs and formal breakfasts. In the evenings, when they were not at the theatre, they strolled along the pier or walked on the cliffs and laughed their way through suppers. 'Car Ponsonby behaves very well and does not give us as much of her company as I was afraid she would', Hary-o remarked rather cattily to Little G.

It was a summer of flirtations, but none surprised or alarmed Miss Trimmer so much as the one between Caroline and William Lamb – 'those creatures of earth and air.' (William was recovering from an affair with a 'Lady of no very strict virtue' who had discovered he could not afford to buy her luxuries and moved on to a richer man.) Corisande exaggerated her accent and coquetted furiously in front of Duncannon. Miss Trimmer did not approve of such precociousness but even gentle Caroline St Jules sidled up to rough George Lamb and gazed at him with her doe-like eyes. More serious than any of these was the stalking and attack on Duncannon by Lady Jersey, who regarded him as a potential husband for her daughter, Elizabeth.

Lady Bessborough disproved of the match. She disliked Lady Jersey and thought Duncannon was too young to be married. She told Granville; 'John admires her, and is of course flattered with the fuss they make with him, but I am sure he has not a thought further than liking to talk to a very pretty girl who marks a strong preference for him, and fear of Ly Jersey laughing at him and telling him he is in leading strings if he refuses any supper or party she asks him to… What I dread for John is all this going on till he is really seriously in love with the girl, who is very lovable, or till it is so much talk'd of, and he has made his attentions so particular that Ly J will have a right to complain if it goes no further.' Lady Bessborough took her son aside and pointed out 'the impropriety of his attentions if he meant nothing by them and the danger at his age of mistaking fantasies for real affection.' Duncannon decided to play safe and returned to London. Lady Bessborough was extremely annoyed when she heard that 'the Lambs chose to make the greatest joke of my disliking it, which they found out from Ly Ml and told him if they were him they would talk to and marry who they liked and when they liked and not be kept under tutelage by their mother'.[34]

A week or so later the Duchess, Lady Bessborough, Corisande and Caroline spent a few days at Brocket Hall. Corisande kept Hary-o supplied with gossip and the salient details were passed to Little G at Castle Howard. 'There was an extraordinary flirtation between William Lamb and Caro Ponsonby, and they seem, I hear, mutually captivated. When the rest were at games etc., William was in a corner, reading and explaining poetry to Car.' William was a born teacher and in his firm soft voice he discussed the works of Theocritus with Caroline. She had read some of William's articles and poetry, which were full of Foxite thoughts and idealistic ambitions. She admired his vision, fantasised about the author and half fell in love with her dream. Corisande was amused to watch William following Caroline all over the house and playing any game she wanted, including Hunt the Squirrel and Hunt the Slipper. In the mornings they sat 'reading tales of wonder together on the *tithertother*' and William told Caroline he was in love with her. He later said he would not have known what to do with himself had she refused him. Caroline remembered that day as the second happiest in her life. The first had been in July 1800 at a special breakfast at Chiswick to celebrate Little G's presentation at Court. Caroline had walked slowly through the garden with William, her hand resting lightly on his arm and then she had willed time to stop because she was 'as happy as I ever wished to be'. Caroline could never disguise her feelings and at the end of the visit to Brocket she got into the coach, burst into tears and 'roared' all the way to Roehampton. Corisande said, 'She is the oddest compound of sentiment and oddity, of 50 and 5, that I never was so amused in my life.'[35]

The Cavendishes, Ponsonbys and miscellaneous distant cousins gathered at Chatsworth in December 1801 to celebrate Christmas. It was bitterly cold and just the weather for snowball fights, skating and trying out the new sledges and the fashionable go-carts that the Duchess had provided. Lord Bessborough had a bad attack of gout but, not wishing to be left out of the fun, he wrapped up well and sat in a chair, which Duncannon pushed round on the ice. In his exuberance Duncannon misjudged a corner, the chair broke and Lord Bessborough shot across the frozen lake. He was laid up until February.[36]

In March 1802, the Treaty of Amiens ended the conflict between Britain and France, which had begun in February 1793. It opened the floodgates to aristocratic tourists, enabling them to resume their Grand Tours and cross France in relative safety. Lady Elizabeth was one of the first to arrive in Paris with Caroline St Jules and Frederick Foster. The Bessboroughs were eager to follow but Lady Spencer believed that Paris was an unsuitable place to take Caroline. 'I hear such accounts of the indecency of the French Theatres that I think you should enquire about them before you take young women especially to them.' Despite her warning, the family joined Lady Elizabeth in late December. Lady Bessborough described how they trembled with vicarious horror as they crossed 'that shocking Place de la Concorde, with ye remains of the Guillotine'. Like everyone else they were curious to see Napoleon Bonaparte and on 6 January they watched a military review from a balcony at the Louvre and had a 'perfect view of the Carrousel, which was filled with troops'. The First Consul wore a hat without lace and was dressed in a plain blue uniform. Sitting on Louis XVI's old grey horse he rode slowly along the line of soldiers followed by his generals in their brilliant uniforms and medals. Lady Bessborough was struck by the 'dead *morne* silence with which he was receiv'd by the populace, not one acclamation, but an evident appearance of discontent'.

Half of London society were in Paris and the Bessboroughs' days were filled with gossiping with old friends, walking along the boulevards, sipping tea and lounging in the Tuilleries, dinners, operas, receptions and shopping. Lord Bessborough bought bronzes for his collection while Caroline and her mother admired the delicacy of Angoulême china. They dined with Talleyrand and attended a party where Josephine Bonaparte and her soulful daughter Hortense were guests. Lady Bessborough ignored party allegiances and cultivated a friendship with the Duchess of Gordon, her sister's Tory rival, who invited both Lady Bessborough and Caroline to her ball. It was so enjoyable that Caroline refused to leave until after four in the morning. *'Je n'y tiens pas, c'est une vie de chien que nous menons'*, Lady Bessborough told Granville, 'out all morning to see Sights, and up all night with ye Girls at balls without end'. She woke one morning with a headache and a touch of queasiness, a state not unknown to modern tourists, 'I believe owing to the water, as Caro and all the servants are the same'.

Caroline sketched two pictures of herself, one on either side of the Channel. The English girl in a short, childish dress waves to her double in France who is in the height of fashion, with a long train and a feather in her hair. She wrote below:

Farewell to England & farewell to frocks
Now France I hail thee with a sweeping train
Subdued at length I'll bend my stubborn locks
And enter on a life of art and pain –

Farewell to childhood & perhaps to peace
Now life I sail upon thy glamorous stream
And oh may wisdom with each year encrease,
And prove my follies but an Infant's dream.

Another drawing in her commonplace book shows a Frenchman advancing on Caroline with open arms and a big smile saying, *'Mademoiselle, voulez-vous dancer?'* Caroline half turns her back, her arms firmly folded, her little nose well in the air, *'Non monsieur, je ne veux pas,'* she replies. No doubt she had William in mind when she wrote beneath the sketch:

French Man smile not thus on me
I hate your race; I hate your nation
In vain you bend your supple knee
I care not for your adulation
I love a man of English race
Who never learned to fawn or dance
He has an English heart & face
Oh there is no such man in France.[37]

On 20 February the Bessboroughs set off for home. Not long after leaving Paris, one of the carriage wheels broke. Lord Bessborough sent Lady Bessborough and Caroline ahead to wait for him while it was mended. They sat in the relay post, a filthy inn, for seven hours watched continuously by the scruffy owner and his friends. Lady Bessborough was afraid that they would be murdered for their money but Caroline remained calm, as she always did in face of danger. She complained that she was hungry but they had already given their picnic of eggs, cheese and brown bread to their hosts. Eventually Lord Bessborough rescued them and they limped into Abbeville at six o'clock to have the wheel professionally repaired. Six hours later they were on the road and almost immediately another wheel broke. This was repaired at Montreuil and after an uncomfortable day waiting they began their interrupted journey only to travel three miles before a third wheel broke. Bad luck followed them to Calais where they were delayed by gales in the channel.[38] When Caroline went to Holywell Lady Spencer could not resist a jab. 'Your dear girl is arrived very safe, my dear Harriet, but I cannot boast of her looks'.

All through the spring and summer of 1803, Georgiana provided evening balls and morning dances for the young people at Devonshire House. Hours were spent practising quadrilles to the French music Lady Elizabeth had brought back. Caroline was in her element, demonstrating the complicated steps she had learned in Paris from the actress, Madame Vestris. In April she and Hary-o were presented at Court.

In September, Georgiana became seriously ill with stomach pains and headaches. Lady Bessborough and Lady Spencer rushed to Devonshire House and the Prince of Wales made his physician, Sir Walter Farquhar, available should she need him. The Duchess was in exquisite pain for thirty-six hours and bleeding or lying in a bath of warm water could scarcely alleviate it. Farquhar ordered the Duke, who was feeling miserable with gout, to take her to Bath. The result of the Duchess' frequent and disabling illnesses showed on her face and body. Lady Holland uncharitably remarked, 'Her figure is corpulent, her complexion coarse, one eye gone, and her neck immense.'

Caroline stayed with her grandmother at Holywell in December 1803 before spending Christmas with her at Althorp, the home of her uncle, Earl Spencer, and his wife, the former Lavinia Bingham. As usual letters flew from Holywell and Althorp to Cavendish Square with reports on Caroline's health and behaviour. To treat her upset stomach, caused by over-eating, the Spencers' family doctor, Dr Kerr, prescribed a diet of 'plain meat of whatever sort she likes with Turnips, Carrots or Potatoes'. She was dosed with an emetic and cucumber root, which 'worked upwards and downwards'. She scratched her chilblains and wore Lady Spencer's shoes, which were too small and pinched her feet severely.[39]

In July 1804, Lady Bessborough's lover, Lord Granville, was appointed Ambassador to the Court of St Petersburg and offered to take seventeen-year-old Willy as his secretary. This was a painful double blow for Harriet as she had recently discovered that she was pregnant. Granville delayed his departure for as long as he could but he was forced to leave in October, almost a month before she gave birth to their second child, George Stewart.

William Lamb was called to the bar in the Michaelmas Term of 1804, and Caroline, tongue in cheek, suggested that she dress in black and follow him around as his clerk.

On 24 January 1805, William's elder brother, Peniston, died of consumption. 'The Melbourne's were in a shocking state,' Lady Bessborough told Granville, 'His lungs were completely decay'd, and Farquar says he thinks Emily in a very precarious state.' Peniston was the second of their children to die of the disease. Harriet had died of a similar complaint on 4 June 1803 when she was thirteen years old. The other children, particularly Emily and Frederick, never forgave their parents for ignoring the doctors' advice to send her to a warmer climate.

William was now Lord Melbourne's heir and expected to inherit his brother's annual allowance of £3,000 but Lord Melbourne refused to give him the same amount, despite his wife's pleas, thus underlining the fact that he did not believe William was his son. William abandoned his law practice – as the heir to the family title and estates it was considered more suitable for him to enter Parliament. Family feelers went out to find him a safe seat.

He spent the spring at Melbourne Hall, the family seat in Derbyshire and at the Bessborough villa in Roehampton, in close contact with Caroline. Hary-o was shocked when Caroline told her in her usual headstrong way that she had confessed her love to William before he had formally declared himself to her parents.[40] 'I fell in love when only twelve years old,' she told Lady Morgan, 'with a friend of Charles Fox – a friend of liberty whose poems I had read, whose self I had never seen, and when I did see him, at thirteen, could I change? No, I was more attached than ever... Afterwards he offered to marry me, and I refused him because of my temper, which was too violent; he however asked twice, and was not refused the second time, and the reason was I adored him.'[41]

William wrote to Caroline, 'I have lov'd you for four years, lov'd you deeply, dearly, faithfully – so faithfully that my love has withstood my firm determination to conquer it when honour forbade my declaring myself – has withstood all that absence, variety of objects, my own endeavours to seek and like other, or to occupy my mind with fix'd attention to my profession, could do to shake it.'[42]

Caroline's complex personality held no surprises for him. She was enchanting, intelligent, could sketch, compose poetry, speak and read French and Italian and totter along sufficiently well in Greek and Latin to enjoy classical plays at Harrow. She painted, sketched and played the organ. With her sharp little chin, perfect complexion, golden-red curls, wide, hazel eyes and darting ways she sometimes seemed more like a fairy than a human being. Her faults were hidden by her pretty ways. She still could not control her temper; she was over-possessive and she became unhappy if she was not the centre of attention. Her manner was direct and she did not waste time with pleasantries. Like her mother, she lived on her nerves and her emotions. Lady Bessborough once said, 'I can never love anything *a little*'. Nor could Caroline.[43]

Lady Bessborough was not pleased with William's courtship but she felt it would be wrong to stand in the way of Caroline's happiness, so she asked her to wait a little while longer until she knew William better. She told Granville, 'He has a thousand good qualities, is very clever, which is absolutely necessary for her; and, above all, she has preferr'd him from childhood, and now is so much in love with him that before his speaking I dreaded its affecting her health. But on the other hand, I dislike the connection extremely; I dislike his manners, and still more his principles and his creed, or rather no creed.'[44]

On 2 May Caroline stayed up until her mother returned from Devonshire House. Holding William's letter in her hand she flung her arms round her neck, saying that she loved William better than anyone else in the world, except her, but she would give him up if it would please her. Lady Bessborough was dismayed but she wrote to her brother, John (Lord Spencer) to ask him, as head of the family, to allow the marriage. The next day Caroline and Lady Bessborough lived in suspense until he gave the match his approval. Too nervous to tempt fate, Caroline had barred William from Cavendish House until Lord Spencer's decision was known, but now she agreed to meet him at Drury Lane Theatre. When Lady Bessborough and Caroline arrived, William was already waiting in the box. Lady Bessborough told Granville, 'I never saw anything so warm and animated as his manner towards her, and of course he soon succeeded in obtaining every promise he wished.' Afterwards he followed Lady Bessborough into the passage behind the box. She told Lord Granville, 'I was very nervous and on telling him I knew Lord B joined with me in leaving everything to Caro's decision, he answer'd: "and that decision is in my favour, thank heaven!"' Overcome with delight he threw his arms around her and kissed her. As soon as the play was over Caroline and Lady Bessborough rushed to Devonshire House to break the news. This triggered 'a most tragic scene with poor Hart, who on hearing what had pass'd went into violent hystericks, reproach'd Caro bitterly, saying he look'd upon her as his wife, that no plan he had ever form'd of future pleasure or happiness was separated from her, that she might think it hard to wait for him but that he would have waited any time for her and had always been in hopes his papa would let him marry her when he was 18 – in short, it ended with his being so ill we were oblig'd to sent for Farquhar'.[45]

William returned to Brocket and Caroline went to see her Lady Spencer. Although she had Lord Spencer's approval, nothing could be done without her grandmother's blessing. William wrote, 'I am much more anxious about it than I can express, and I listen for the postman's knock with cold hands, and indescribable anxiety. Your peace of mind is I know so connected with yr Dear grandmama's happiness.'[46]

'I do not know him at all,' Lady Spencer told her best friend, Mrs Caroline Howe, 'those who do speak highly indeed of his talents and understanding and assure me that tho' he was formerly rather a dashing cast of character – he is now everything that can be wished. She came by way of asking my consent & approbation but I soon perceived by her conversation & his letters such a mutual & vehement attachment which has subsisted in silence for some time that my sentiments could instantly be of no importance'. After Lady Spencer had met William she asked Mrs Howe, 'Have you seen him? He is very black but certainly handsome, that is he has a lively intelligent countenance with an air of sweetness when he speaks & smiles and a very good figure'. She told Harriet, 'I can only say how fervently I hope your dear girl may be happy. She must run some risques, & there seems in the present choice at least the advantage of mutual attachment. God grant they may be as happy as I wish them.'[47] Lady Bessborough told Granville, 'My Caro's Marriage is settled and declared, and their love for each other and his behaviour have quite reconciled me to it. Indeed, it is impossible to see the change in her and have a doubt. I believe all her ill health, all the little oddities of manner and sauvageries that us'd to vex me arose from the unhappiness that was constantly preying upon her.'[48]

Preparations for the wedding began, 'My whole day passes,' Lady Bessborough wrote, 'in seeing milliners and Mantua Makers.'[49] The Prince of Wales beamed with delight when he heard, saying, 'I am *so* happy, oh! But so very happy.' The Lamb family lawyer, Charles Cookney, was called in to negotiate the marriage settlement and it was agreed that Caroline should receive £400 pin money and William's allowance would be £1,500. This was later raised to £1,800 (about £85,000 today). They were also given possession of the three rooms on the first floor of Melbourne House at Whitehall. (In 1792 the Melbournes had exchanged houses with Frederick, Duke of York. The Duke moved to Piccadilly and the Melbournes to his cold mansion in Whitehall.)

Lady Melbourne was happy, for not only was William about to marry into one of the most influential Whig families in the country but Emily had recently been engaged to Peter Leopold de Grey, fifth Earl Cowper. Lady Elizabeth commented, 'These are certainly two as pretty marriages as possible. "The Melbournes", as the Queen good-naturedly said, "wanted this consolation after their trying misfortunes and they are very happy with it." '

William wrote in his autobiography; 'A passion which I had long cherished but had repressed, while prudence forbade the indulgence of it, now that it felt the obstacles removed out of its way, broke forth and became my master. I was married on the Third of June 1805 to the Lady Caroline Ponsonby, the only daughter of the Earl of Bessborough.'

2

'Being married is a state of great sufferance for a girl'

The stress of her wedding day had left Caroline agitated and nervous and for two days she remained at Brocket alone with William. He would not allow her to see anyone, not even her mother. On 8 June she accompanied Lady Bessborough and Lady Spencer on a tour of the wooded grounds. She seemed to be well and in good spirits but her 'nervous agitations' had increased. This disappointed Lady Spencer as she had hoped that William would be firm and encourage Caroline to control herself.[1]

Lady Bessborough told Lord Granville, 'We are out all the morning and in the evening William reads to us while she and I draw. He is delightful, and his manner to me every thing I could wish.' She told Caroline, 'William may pride himself on his good conduct, for to nothing one atom less kind & delightful than he is, could I have yielded you…as I told you so gravely the other day he really appears to me like my *natural* son.'[2]

William and Caroline were deeply in love. He explained, 'You don't marry out of reason you marry because you fall in love'. Caroline compared him to an angel. She told Little G, 'He is kinder more gentle, more soothing, more indulgent, talks nonsense better and coaxes me more than a woman could and with all that he is perfection.' However, it was difficult for Caroline, with her romantic dreams, to accept that gallant words inevitably led to the bedroom and although she probably guessed what was expected in the physical side of marriage, the robustness of the act shocked her. 'Really being married is a state of great sufferance for a girl in every way,' Lady Bessborough told Lord Granville, 'I do think it is very hard that men should always have *beau jeu* on all occasions, and that all pain, moral and physique should be reserved for us.'[3] Within a month of her wedding, Caroline composed a poem for Hart in which she compared herself to Titania, who left Oberon in fairyland and was 'doomed to become a mortal bride'.

To mortal scenes of deeper weight
My steps alas are doomed by fate
And all the ills that wait on life
Attend me since another's wife.
… What since befell her no one knows
But certain 'tis overwhelmed with woes
She deeply mourns her broken vows.[4]

Caroline was never to have a home of her own. She and William lived in other people's houses, in rented rooms or in mansions belonging to the Melbournes all their married life. Of all these unsatisfactory options her favourite residence was Brocket Hall. William's grandfather, Matthew Lamb, built the redbrick mansion on the site of a much older house in parklands, on the banks of the river Lee not far from Welwyn. The first Lord Melbourne, William's father, widened the course of the river to create the impression of a lake beside the house, a bridge and an artificial waterfall. Annual race meetings, popular with the Prince of Wales and his friends, were held on the course laid out in the grounds.

Lady Melbourne furnished and decorated the interior with the intention of creating an impressive, comfortable meeting place for members of the government who, she hoped, would extend their patronage towards her family. A portrait by Sir Joshua Reynolds of the Prince of Wales sheltering from a storm, hung in the drawing room, a present from the Prince in the year their son George was born. On the opposite wall Lady Melbourne placed a portrait of herself holding Peniston, Lord Melbourne's only child. The magnificent ceiling in the sixty-foot long ballroom was decorated with a series of panels representing morning, noon and night, surrounded by smaller pictures of frolicking babies illustrating the signs of the zodiac and the four seasons. These smiling infants were often copied and imitated by Caroline in her commonplace books.

The single gilded staircase lit by a delicate glass dome led to a landing, then divided to continue up to the principal bedrooms. Prominent, in the middle of the first floor landing, were the heavy wooden double doors of Lord Melbourne's room. His huge bed sat under an elaborately carved arch that had survived from the earlier house; and an interior door opened into Lady Melbourne's room, which was lit by large bay windows. A 'secret' door led on to the landing to allow her to flit across to the Prince of Wales' apartment.

It was not long before Caroline tired of the quiet country calm of Brocket and pined for the excitement of London. She compared herself to a soul just arrived in Paradise, very happy 'but still a little cut off from all it had been accustomed to love & live with.' As William's absences on business grew more frequent, she brooded over the brief romance that he had had with Little G. This, she told her cousin, became 'some little species of insanity, which they say people have on one particular subject'. She told Little G, 'He does not scruple to say he loved you very sincerely, yet his situation & both your ages then would have made it very disagreeable and his character was much less formed than it is now.' William tried to reassure her of his love, saying that even if he had loved Little G first, Caroline would be his last.[5]

Lady Spencer was curious to meet Lord and Lady Melbourne and invited them to spend an afternoon at Holywell with Caroline and William. They were so charming that she told Mrs Howe, 'Their behaviour to her and hers to them is cordial, kind & unaffected & as such behaviour always goes straight to my heart, I felt the same to them'.[6]

Lady Melbourne was contented with the match but she implied that it was Caroline who had benefited from it the most. She snubbed Lady Bessborough and told her that she hoped the 'daughter would turn our better than the mother, or William might have to repent of his choice.' Lady Bessborough did not believe her when she later tried to shrug off the remark as a joke and told her that she hoped and believed that Caroline would be a better wife. She added, tongue in cheek, 'especially with the help of your advice.' Georgiana attributed Lady Melbourne's sharpness to jealousy but William's obvious affection for his mother-in-law fuelled a rumour that they were lovers. Lady Bessborough was unconvinced. She believed Lady Melbourne was trying to keep her in her place.[7]

Caroline and William could not move into their new home in Whitehall because the rooms were needed for Emily's wedding reception on 21 July but Lady Bessborough made 'a very comfortable apartment' for them at Cavendish Square when they returned to London on 27 June.[8]

'I cannot fancy Lady Caroline married,' Augustus Foster wrote to Lady Elizabeth, 'I cannot be glad of it. How changed she must be – the delicate Ariel, the little Fairy Queen become a wife and soon perhaps a mother.'[9] When Hary-o saw her in London, she told Miss Trimmer that Caroline was 'amiable as possible and already most amazingly improved by being as gentle and posée as if she had been a matron in the country for 20 years instead of days. It is impossible to believe that she is a wife and it seems quite like a dream to have her here again in that capacity.' Lady Bessborough too found it difficult to adjust, saying that Caroline's behaviour was 'unlike a *wife*, more like a School Girl'.[10]

By August Caroline was back at Brocket. She was unwilling or too embarrassed to talk to her mother so she confided in Little G; 'For your life do not mention this circumstance to anybody for as I am not yet a week past my time – it may very likely be nothing.' By September she was sure she was pregnant and felt slightly frightened. 'I am with Child, G. Tell me fairly what you think & how *you* felt when you were so first. Had you ever little unaccountable pains, many fears that you were going to miscarry – were you nervous, apt to be frightened, very hungry, very dry, very sleepy & very languid? – Did a great deal of exercise give you a pain in your back? Were you restless? Pray tell me also, for I have nobody else to ask, though it seems an extraordinary question to ask, but is it bad for you to *sleep* with your husband at the time in the most significant sense of the word – I am anxious to know for I must let nothing be done that can hurt my darling boy who I love already more than anything.'[11] She told Little G that she did not see enough of William and although it was delightful at Brocket she was not content and felt 'like a horse in clover looking out for new pasture though I shall never find better.' However, when William was with her she glowed with pleasure and enthused to Little G, 'Today, for the first time, I went out to shoot with him. It was pretty to see the dogs & my beautiful husband with all his black hair over his brows & a great colour from the eagerness & animation he felt pacing over the stubble fields with his gun on his shoulder & me on his arm. Sometimes we rode & then he gently led my horse. I was delighted.'

Hary-o was in love with Duncannon, Caroline's carefree and flirtatious brother. She was unhappy when he was not with her and uneasy when he was. Her mother's well-meaning attempts to engineer occasions for them to be alone made her even more uncomfortable. He was a flirt, but when she confronted him he laughed, saying, 'What nonsense!' He would 'not be dictated to *by any woman living.*' In September he fell in love, proposed and was accepted by Lady Maria Fane, daughter of the tenth Earl of Westmorland. Caroline told him, 'I began to think you were vying with Don Juan in the list you meant to produce of broken hearts & plighted vows.' Eager to welcome Lady Maria she dashed off a note: 'I am quite impatient to know you & to love you, which I hear are one & the same thing.' Her spontaneous, affectionate message was passed from hand to hand. Lady Elizabeth commented to Augustus Foster, 'You may retract all your sorrow about Car Ponsonby's marriage, for she is the same wild, delicate, odd delightful person, unlike everything. Witness her dating to Lady Maria Fane her first letter of congratulation... *"Heaven knows what day"* '.[12]

Caroline looked pretty, plump and a little pale but was 'the happiest of human beings'. No-one could have guessed her condition from her appearance 'excepting indeed from her moving about and walking, which she does,' Hary-o said, 'with caution as if one quick step would be fatal.'[13]

For some time after their marriage, William and Caroline lived in a delicious mist of passion, fighting and making up. On 23 October they argued so loudly in Lady Holland's box at Covent Garden, during a performance of Nicholas Rowe's 'The Fair Penitent', that they almost drowned out the actors.[14] Four days later William stormed out of Whitehall yelling that he would not be home till very late. Caroline flounced round to Cavendish Square where she ripped off her wedding ring and sent it back to Melbourne House. She decorated herself with large quantities of her mother's jewellery, slapped on too much rouge and, with her mother and Hary-o, went to see Mrs Siddons perform in another of Rowe's plays, 'The Tragedy of Jane Shore'. She calmed down during the evening and by the time Hary-o dropped her off at Whitehall she was still half-indignant at William but also a little frightened at what she had done.[15] She had nothing to fear. William was prepared to indulge her in every way. She fascinated and enchanted him. They both had violent tempers and after their spirited disagreements Caroline would sometimes sulk or kiss him, stroking his head and whispering loving words in his ear. She laughed at one moment and stamped her foot the next, telling him, 'you must not contradict me in anything'. In the heat of the moment she often threatened to run back to Cavendish Square and when words failed she grabbed the first thing that came to hand, tea sets or fire irons, and hurled them at him. William idolised her but she knew he did not have the will or the knowledge to control her. Their spats were so famous that when Hary-o saw them at Chiswick, she remarked that 'They were very happy and, contrary to custom, at peace.' Caroline told Little G, 'We have had not so much as a sentence of disagreement since I saw you and if it is possible never will again. Indeed it requires the greatest ingenuity to be able to quarrel with such a man as William.'[16] During periods of armistice Caroline sat on William's lap, shared his chair, read the same book and they played at 'Spillikens, with their arms round one another's necks'. 'Caroline and Wm. Lamb flirt all day long *é felice adesso*', Lady Elizabeth told Augustus Foster.[17]

A meeting was held at Cavendish Square to prepare for the elaborate theatrical house party Lord and Lady Abercorn planned for Christmas. The chosen play was 'The Rivals'. George Lamb was cast as Squire Acres and William as Captain Absolute. It promised to be an enjoyable and spirited affair. 'I am so afraid of not being asked to the Priory that I do not know what to do,' Hary-o told her sister. Not only was she not invited but on 16 November Duncannon married the meek Lady Maria, 'who watches and listens to him as if he was an oracle.' Plain and disappointed, Hary-o told her sister, 'I gave up my *ci-devant* true love without a sigh.'

Despite Lord Abercorn's facetious edict saying his guests must not discuss politics or become ill, Caroline developed alarming symptoms and Lady Bessborough braved fog, rutted roads, highwaymen and Lord Abercorn's displeasure to nurse her. By the time she left on 2 November, Caroline was much better and 'I hope safe from what she apprehended'.[18] A month later Lady Bessborough returned, 'I went to the Priory, which is more like Bedlam than a house in the Country, fill'd with people all acting and spouting their different parts together.' Although Caroline seemed better, her accoucheur, Dr Richard

Croft, refused to allow her to be moved for six weeks. She fascinated Maria Duncannon who sat next to her for hours looking at the fragile elf-like face. Maria remarked she could not believe that something so delicate could produce anything so substantial as a child, but if she did, it would be a little thing with wings that would fly away as soon as it was born and no one would be able to catch it. On 8 December Caroline wrote cheerfully to Lady Spencer, 'I am quite recovered now from my indisposition but keep extremely quiet. I have got milk. The child has not moved yet.'[19]

In addition to 'The Rivals', George Lamb's comic opera 'Who's the Dupe?' was performed on 20 December. Lady Bessborough enjoyed it immensely, and called George the best actor she had seen by far. Hary-o thought that William was 'too much occupied with his beauty and expression of countenance and makes crooked smiles to the audience, when he ought to be attending to his companions. He is also rather tame as a lover and looks much alarmed as Caroline sits and watches him and would probably go into fits if an expression or look of well acted tenderness was to escape him.'[20]

Family letters for the last week of December are full of illness. One of the Duchess' eyes was painfully inflamed, Hary-o had a sore throat and Caroline St Jules could not speak. Lady Bessborough had a fever, 'They call it an influenza, whatever it is, I have got it, tho' not so bad as my poor Caro, who has been again blooded.' Caroline had a pain in her chest which, according to Hary-o 'she will fancy very alarming though everybody she consults (which is in other words, every soul she sees) assure her that it is nothing but a muscular pain in her back and that her fears are all fancies.'[21] William 'never leaves her a moment and seems to love her more than ever, but she is too exigent and with so good a husband might spare herself the trouble… She is so jealous of him. Her maid told mine that when he goes to the *piccola*, which is the only moment he is away from her, she sends her to watch him and find out where he is and if he comes straight back. This would be terrible with any other people, but I really believe it succeeds in this case, for they seem the happiest of human beings.'[22]

On 9 January 1806, despite the snuffles, coughs and colds, Lady Bessborough, Georgiana, Caroline and Maria sat in a little room high in the pediment of a building at Temple bar to watch Nelson's funeral procession. The news of his death had been received in November with great outpourings of public grief. Never at a loss to improve a dramatic moment, Lady Elizabeth swathed herself in heavy mourning with black cockades and the word 'Nelson' embroidered on all her trailing drapery. She indulged in extravagant sobs, sighs, grunting and groans, exclaiming that she wished she could have 'died in his defence'. A wish Hary-o devoutly shared.

Less than a month later, forty-six-year-old William Pitt died of drink. When Georgiana, well known for her Whig allegiance, applied to the Archbishop of Canterbury for seats at the funeral of the Tory Prime Minister, His Grace misunderstood her motives and replied sharply that 'Westminster Abbey was not a place of public amusement.'

William, eager to begin his parliamentary career, left Caroline at Brocket to claim the safe parliamentary seat of Leominster bought for him by his father for two thousand guineas. Caroline's labour began during the evening of 31 January. She was weak from the cold and bloodletting and during the night she was delivered of a premature, stillborn daughter. The news of her difficult labour was rushed to William who immediately started for home. Although the servants tried to prepare him for the worst he still hoped the baby would be alive when he arrived. 'Think how melancholy!' Lady Bessborough wrote, 'He met the little coffin going out of the house.' Both parents were devastated but William did not once mention to Caroline his own great disappointment as he comforted her.

Little G, the future mother of thirteen, broke the news to Hartington the following day. 'Caro Lamb is quite well & safe but was brought to bed last night of a dead child – It was a little girl – she is however quite well & will recover sooner than if she had gone on – She will have children enough.'[23]

In March Georgiana's frail health failed and, fearing she might die, she tried to make provision for her children. Hartington would inherit the dukedom and Little G was safely married but she feared that Hary-o, with her forthright manner, might become an old maid. She had intended to form a trust for Eliza, Charles Grey's child, but any money she acquired had slid across the gambling tables and the only way she could see to insure her future was to appeal to Hartington's good nature. The sixteen-year-old boy quietly listened to his mother's account of Eliza's birth, absorbing its significance. 'How could you, dearest Em, how could you?' he murmured (all the children addressed their mother as 'Em', as in 'M for Mother'). 'I was already a beauty, a toast and a Duchess and wholly neglected by my husband,' Georgiana replied timidly. Hartington was shocked but he recognised how much it must have cost his mother to confess and he loved her more for her courage. None of the Devonshire House children had ever questioned the presence of other children in the nursery. Lady Shelley wrote that, 'the Duchess's admirable daughters had never mixed in her evening coterie, and were brought up in that strict propriety which characterised the daughters of our Grandees in those days. Children were never admitted to hear the gossip of their elders, and knew nothing of the world until they married.'

Georgiana now was in continuous pain from kidney stones and blinding headaches. In addition to her physical miseries, creditors were pursuing her. She had constantly lied about the extent of her debts and even now she was too afraid to tell the Duke, so she turned to her mother and asked for a hundred pounds. Lady Spencer sent twenty, putting the balance into a draft, which she handed to Lady Bessborough saying 'you will easily understand the danger there is of my letting your dear sister know that I can do this, as it would then be constantly expected.' She attributed a great part of Georgiana's unhappiness to the 'old and hopeless story of money difficulties.'[24]

Georgiana developed shivering fits on 11 March, followed by headaches and bouts of biliousness. Her complexion became yellow with touches of orange as jaundice took hold but Doctor Farquhar insisted she was improving. Caroline tried to divert her attention from her pain with a poem:

Gentle sleep, thy blessing shed –
Soothe her weary soul to rest;
Angels, guard her suffering head,
Calm the troubles of her breast.

'Tis for others' woes she weeps,
By their sorrows quite opprest;
Angel, guard her while she sleeps,
She, who blesses, should be blest.[25]

On 21 March Georgiana's condition deteriorated and Lady Bessborough remained at Devonshire House all night. She rallied the next day only to relapse two days later. By 28 March it was clear she was dying. The Duke asked Miss Trimmer to stay, 'for I shall not be in any state of mind to attend to anybody, or receive or give any comfort whatever.' Georgiana died of an abscess of the liver in the early hours of 30 March 1806, a few weeks short of her forty-ninth birthday – her eyesight ruined and her 'liver decayed'. Lady Bessborough wrote, 'Anything so horrible, so killing as her three days agony no human being ever witness'd.' Devastated, prostrate with fatigue and grief she went to Roehampton and shut herself away for three weeks. Her only visitor, the Prince of Wales, remarked, 'The best-natured and the best-bred woman in England is gone.'[26]

Lady Elizabeth dreaded that Lady Spencer would oust her from Devonshire House before she had consolidated her position and mounted a charm offensive, but she miscalculated badly when she sent her a freshly cut lock of Georgiana's hair. Her intention was so transparent that Richard Sheridan hooted with laughter at her letter in which she exhorted him to 'try to drink less and speak the truth.' He exclaimed, 'By G-d! I speak more truth than *she* does.' He described to Thomas Creevey how she had '*cried* to him' the night before, 'because she felt it her severe duty to be Duchess of Devonshire.'

Far away at Castle Howard, Little G and her new baby were less affected by Georgiana's death than Hartington and Hary-o, who were still living under their father's protection. Hary-o was desperately unhappy. She had expected to take her mother's place as mistress of Devonshire House but Lady Elizabeth remained, undermining and usurping her position and, even more irritatingly, insisting on taking her into society as though she were her mother. She later described Lady Elizabeth's character as 'unparalleled, I do believe for want of principle and delicacy, and more perverted than deceitful for I really do believe she hardly herself knows the difference between right and wrong now.' Hartington and Hary-o were circumspect in their public dealings with Lady Elizabeth but Caroline made no attempt to disguise her feelings, amusing the family and embarrassing Lady Elizabeth by obliquely comparing her relationship with the Duke to that of Louis XIV and his mistress, later his wife, Madame de Maintenon.

Hartington turned to Lady Spencer for comfort and arrived at Holywell on 11 June tired, dusty and tearful but, with the resilience of youth he 'drank a gallon of tea, ate loads of roast lamb, pease & gooseberry fool, drank a quantity of beer & of water & finished all with a plentiful saline draught.' Ever cautious, Lady Spencer arranged for a 'bason extraordinary' to be put in his room; but it was not necessary.[27]

Caroline had suffered with bouts of queasiness since May. Lady Bessborough hoped she was not pregnant, fearing that another child so soon after her recent disappointment might permanently damage her health. Mrs Howe wrote, 'If Lady Car. Lamb should be breeding, I hope she will wear the laudanum plaister on her back which has done such wonders. I have the right receipt if it is wanted.'[28] Lady Cork and Lady Spencer agreed, with a proviso that she should drink a potion of laudanum and egg. Lady Spencer said, 'I really think it would be advisable to do something of this kind by way of prevention.'

In the hope that sea air and bathing would restore her health, Caroline went to Littlehampton with her mother. By 22 August the alarm was over. Lady Spencer was pleased to 'hear she is not with child, as I think when this unlucky complaint in her bowels is quite gone she will have a good chance of invigorating her constitution by tonic medicines and sea bathing.'[29]

Caroline's natural ebullience returned. She told Lady Holland about a recent practical trick when she dyed her hair, put on boys' shoes, buckles and clothes and 'jumped like a Harlequin, laughed heartily and had no mercy on anyone.' In quick succession she impersonated a Scotsman, a Yorkshire clergyman and a London wit before returning to her own character.[30] She asked Lady Holland if she could come to Holland House and within days she was invited together with her parents and William to attend a dinner in honour of the Prince of Wales. Lady Holland was banned from some aristocratic houses because she was both a divorcee and the mother of an illegitimate son, but invitations to her salon were highly prized by writers, poets and Whig politicians – men whose reputations were not easily damaged. Her dinners were run like theatrical productions and the guests were carefully chosen. The company consisted of eight or ten men with three or four women including a 'diner out' who had the responsibility of leading the conversation and making the evening interesting and successful. The most popular of these were Thomas Moore, Henry Luttrell, Samuel Rogers and the Reverend Sydney Smith. 'Dinners were not, as now, a jumble of pairs like the animals entering the arc. During my early life, the dazzling brilliancy of table talk shone brightly', Lady Shelley reminisced, 'then came a change; people wished to hear their own voices, and dinner-table wit sank away for ever!'

Fox was dying of dropsy (congestive heart failure). Lady Bessborough saw him in June and was horrified by his changed appearance. 'His face and hands are dreadfully drawn and emaciated, his complexion sallow beyond measure, his bosom sunk – and then, all at once, a body and Legs so enormous that it looks like the things with which they dress up Falstaff.' The Duke lent him his villa at Chiswick and there, on 7 August, Fox was tapped to relieve the pressure of the water in his lower body. 'Sixteen quarts of amber-coloured water was drawn off', but the relief was temporary. The next day, as he was admiring the Duke's picture collection 'a *gush* of water burst from the wound.' He never recovered and lingered until 13 September, then died without a struggle.

On 10 October Caroline, Hary-o, Lady Elizabeth and Lady Bessborough watched his funeral procession from a rented room in Pall Mall. The Duke, William and George Lamb followed the coffin to Westminster Abbey. William composed a poem on his hero, which Caroline copied into her commonplace book. Lady Bessborough remarked that 1806 had been 'a wretched year both public and private.'[31]

Lady Spencer observed in October that Caroline and William were 'on the best of terms possible & very happy in each other, & I think her in every respect much improved.' Caroline flung herself into William's favourite pursuits, to the amusement of the Lambs. She obtained Lord Melbourne's permission to copy a portrait of William by Cosway and was so anxious that it should be safe when she was not working on it that she ordered it to be hung high up on the wall. As she was preparing to begin copying she called for a footman to get it down. He came with a ladder and as he went to rest it on the wall his hand slipped and the top sliced clean through the canvass causing 'a Devil of a hole.' 'I have written to her', Lord Melbourne said, 'telling her not to be so over careful another time, so now we shall have some damned accident happen t'other way.' Lady Melbourne pursed her lips but George 'shook his sides with laughing.'[32] Lady Bessborough remembered that Hary-o had once said, 'It is not enough for a man and woman to like one another and marry, but they must also marry Father and Mother, Brothers and Sisters on both sides, *jusqu'au petit cousin.*' She commented to Lord Granville, 'I like William of all things, but I could dispense with some of his entours'.

William's rowdy family was a trial. It was difficult to ignore the brothers' revolting table manners, their snorts and guffaws and Emily's disconcerting habit of bursting into song at the dinner table. Caroline could not help comparing this to the amusing conversation and fastidious conduct that was the hallmark of Cavendish Square and Devonshire House. The Lambs made fun of her and jeered at William for his devotion to her. It was difficult for Caroline to pretend to be amused by their crass jokes or to endure their tittering. They scoffed at her simple Christian faith, laughed at her opinions, sneered at her talents and deliberately goaded her into temper tantrums and then treated her as though she were a spoiled child. Caroline based her description of family life at Monteith, in her novel *Glenarvon,* on the behaviour of the Lambs. She wrote, 'They are different to me, I can never assimilate myself to them. I was everything in my own family, and I am nothing here.'

Emily, in particular, resented Caroline. She was jealous and compared William's attention to Caroline to those of Lord Cowper, who, barely six months after the wedding, was 'very inattentive'. Hary-o wrote, 'although, she says he loves her excessively he is always from her... She seems tolerably contented, though I hear she is reduced to rejoice when he comes home drunk, as he talks more to her then than at any other time.'[33]

Hary-o was flattered and rather surprised when Emily became friendly, accompanying her to church, discussing morals, and inviting her to Brocket. Hary-o suspected this was a ruse to annoy Caroline, who had also recently invited her to Brocket. William once described his sister as 'pale like a rose.'[34] Lady Bessborough agreed saying, 'Emily is pretty, but she does not seem to me good natur'd – or sincere. She flatters Harriet violently to her face and takes every opportunity of cutting at her. Tho' I do not think H handsome, she is not ugly; as that is mere matter of opinion... Emily chuses to add to ugliness, her being the greatest gull that ever was, and what she calls dull and stupid; this most certainly is not true, and poor Harriet all the while thinks that Emily doats on her.'[35]

At the opening of the new Parliament on 19 December, William was chosen to move the Address in reply to the Speech from the Throne. Caroline was very proud of him and was determined to watch the event. She encouraged everyone to think she was at Holland House then dressed herself in her brother William's clothes and, with the help of Mr Ross, Lord Morpeth's secretary, she was smuggled into the House of Commons where she listened to William's speech. Lady Melbourne was extremely angry at the breach of propriety but let it be known that if William did not disapprove of Caroline's behaviour she would say nothing.[36]

From the beginning Caroline looked to William to lead and instruct her. He loved to teach and she wanted to learn to please him. She was already a fair linguist, classical scholar, poet and an accomplished artist. Her commonplace books are filled with amusing sketches and watercolours of her family, friends, servants and dogs. She had been protected from unpalatable and unpleasant aspects of life and her mother said that 'there never was a purer, more delicate mind existing than hers, and certainly as innocent from sins as any human being that ever breathed.' William began to introduce her to the works of historians, philosophers and metaphysicians. It was exciting and, like her heroine in *Glenarvon*, Calantha, Caroline 'threw off at once the shackles, the superstition, the restrictions, which, perhaps, overstrained notions of purity and piety imposed.' William's worldly, cynical outlook was at odds with the devout, God-fearing, charitable views held by Lady Spencer and Caroline was confused. 'I know not what to believe, or what to doubt.' She told him, 'Hide me in your bosom – let us live far from the world for you are all that is left me now. I look no more for the protection of heaven, or the guidance of parents; – you are my only hope – do you preserve and bless me; for I have left everything for you.' She wanted to please him so much that when he criticised her writing she hired a teacher to help her improve it.[37]

Her apartment at Melbourne House became the rendezvous for Whig politicians and their wives. The ladies came for supper and gossiped until their husbands returned from the House of Commons. Lord and Lady Melbourne could monitor all Caroline's guests from their apartment on the ground floor and even at the end of the day there was no privacy since both couples retired up a small spiral staircase to sleep in adjoining bedrooms on the third floor.

In January William was busy with parliamentary business and left Caroline alone in the huge empty rooms. She begged him to stay, saying she felt unwell, but he ignored her and dismissed her tantrums and regular 'nervous attacks'. Lady Spencer told Lady Bessborough, 'I think the physicians (not yours) should tell her that much might be done by her trying to resist them. This will be of the greatest use in hysterical complaints but I do not know whether it will have any effect in fainting and giddyness.'[38] On 14 January Caroline and Lady Caroline Lennox watched George Lamb flirting outrageously with Caroline St Jules. 'I could not help remarking the difference between a husband and a lover!'[39]

Caroline remarked dryly. By the end of the month it was clear that she was expecting another child. 'But her uncertain health prevents one's knowing what is her state or almost what to hope', Lady Elizabeth told Augustus Foster.[40] It was a difficult pregnancy, full of mysterious pains, weakness and restlessness. Caroline missed the comfort of Cavendish Square and the love and attention of her parents. She longed for privacy and a home of her own. Before their marriage, Lady Spencer had dismissed William's comparative poverty, saying that 'perhaps it is so much the better. I always think it is an advantage to learn the value of money by experience.' Now she said, 'I cannot help wishing they had some little place they could call their own (I am sure they would enjoy it much).'[41] Caroline went to Holywell in April and under her grandmother's regular routine, good plain food, walks in the garden and sympathetic conversation, her spirits were lifted. She confessed that she dreaded returning to Whitehall. 'God knows,' Lady Spencer told her daughter, 'I should be glad to have her, yet, as she had settled with her husband to return on Wednesday, I have advised her keeping steadily to her engagement and if she feels she is less well in London he will the more readily let her come here again. I am so fearful of a husband finding he can live comfortably without his wife that I dare not advise her staying.'[42]

This was the first summer that Caroline had missed her annual seaside holiday with her parents. Lord Bessborough wrote from Hastings, 'We miss you sadly, and all the places remind us of the pleasant company we had last year'. Caroline St Jules stayed with them for three weeks and all the while she was carrying on a clandestine correspondence with George Lamb. Hary-o was amazed that such a meek and mild girl could love the overweight, uncouth, red-haired, red-faced young man. Lord Minto described him as a stunted version of his father, the Prince of Wales. George's influence on Caroline St Jules was so marked that Caroline remarked to Little G, 'I think she is more experienced that she used to be – or than I was before I married. Oh those Lambs they do enlighten one's mind.'

Caroline was not the only one expecting a child that summer. Maria Duncannon was waiting for the first of her fourteen children and Corisande de Grammont was in her third month. She had married the diminutive Viscount Ossulston, noted for his roving eye, in July the previous year. The young women talked endlessly about their babies until Hary-o felt quite worn out by the discussions and comparisons and hoped it would all soon come to a happy conclusion.[43]

Corisande's daughter was born in early August; Maria Duncannon's daughter, 'a fine fat little thing,' was born next and urgent preparations were going on at Melbourne House for Lady Bessborough to be with Caroline during her confinement. Her labour began on 28 August and it lasted until one o'clock the following afternoon when she gave birth to a very large boy. An hour later William wrote to Lady Holland and Little G: 'Caroline is just (that is about an hour ago) brought to bed of a very strapping boy considering the size of its mother. – She is very quiet & well tho' with a little remains of pain from the severity of the labour which lasted however only about an hour.'[44] Three weeks later Caroline wanted to go to Roehampton with her parents but Lady Spencer would not hear of her leaving the house until she had been churched. 'Pray remind her of it if it has been forgotten,' she told Lady Bessborough sharply.

William's increasing affection for the baby pleased Caroline, 'but, of course,' she explained, 'he is less so than I am in outward demonstration'.

His little eyes like William's shine –
How great is then my joy,
For while I call this darling mine,
I see 'tis William's boy.

In fact he looked so much like William that when he smiled it looked as though he was about to rub his hands and swear. Through the love they felt for their child, William and Caroline rediscovered their love for each other and this inspired her to write:

If e'er in thought or word I rove
From the first and only love,
If e'er my inmost heart should frame
A wish thy presence could not name,
May I unworthy of thy care,
No more thy faith unaltered prove,
Or rest securely on thy love.
But now, beyond description, blest
My mind employed, my heart at rest,
I tranquil seek thy guardian breast;
And there removed from vain alarms
Find shelter in a husband's arms
Such love I feel is pure and chaste,
By no unhallowed thought disgraced
But like clear streams its course runs even
Admired by man – approved by Heaven,
May blessings down thy youthful head,
May earth its choicest gifts afford;

May Heaven its fairest bounties shed
To bless my husband and my Lord.[45]

A splendid christening was planned and although Emily's sixteen-month-old son had already been baptised at St George's Hanover Square, he was included in the ceremony. Both children were named after their godfather, the Prince of Wales, George Augustus Frederick. Caroline's son was known as Augustus and his cousin, Frederick. Four days before the christening Augustus developed cowpox which 'pitted him sadly & made him look thin & pale,' but, Caroline insisted 'he really is a beautiful baby.'[46]

Sheridan had been in love with Lady Bessborough for many years and was determined to attend the christening though he was not welcome. In January 1805, Caroline had received a series of letters 'fill'd with every gross disgusting indecency that the most depriv'd imagination could suggest' and he was the chief suspect. He was also under suspicion for sending 'indecent prints' to Hary-o and Caroline St Jules. Although there was no conclusive proof, Lady Bessborough firmly believed that the writing on the 'infamous letter' was his. When he asked her if he could come to the christening she told him that it was Lady Melbourne's right to invite the guests; after receiving the same answer from Caroline he approached Lady Melbourne, who refused, adding that the party was for close friends and relatives.

In the October evening Melbourne House looked like a Greek temple, with its pretty decorations and the flickering torchlight illuminating the pillars at the entrance. At five o'clock the huge wooden doors were thrown open with a great clatter and standing on the step next to the Prince of Wales was Sheridan. He announced that the Prince had chosen him to be his attendant for that evening and trotted behind him as they climbed the grand circular staircase to Caroline's apartment.[47]

The Prince did not leave until two in the morning, 'so you may suppose,' Lady Bessborough told Granville, 'the time hung heavy'. The guests valiantly played word games and Sheridan, who had placed himself opposite Caroline, watched her with his piercing eyes. This disconcerted her and she suddenly got up from the table, leaving Lady Bessborough to take her turn in the game.

Parlour games were popular. The evidence of an amusing evening playing a form of Truth or Consequences at Brocket is preserved on small slips of paper folded in three with space for three epigrams. The list of the subjects included Miss Trimmer, Lady Shelley, the Prince of Wales and Lady Cork. A round was dedicated to William and began, 'He who is answerable for all the impropriety that may be written this evening as he was the author of all last night.' This was followed by, 'One may not write against him; and what can be said in his favour?'

Then, 'William Lamb, God damn, God damn, William Lamb,' and 'A lamb –! He's a wolf in sheep's clothing, God damn, I hope that's not obscure. William Lamb, God Damn.' William had the last word with, 'I'll teach you who I *am*.'[48]

George was a gossip and he liked to jeer at Caroline. He told Hary-o that she was 'absurd with the child; rides out upon the high road, the Horse or Ass (I do not know which it is) led by pages in full dress, the baby on her lap and her maid and nurses following on foot, and then wonders why the Turnpike men laugh at her.'[49] He took special pleasure in describing rows between William and Caroline and how Caroline had thrown cups and saucers at William, but Lady Elizabeth overheard and said that in her opinion they both had tempers and were equally to blame.

Emily's nose had been out of joint ever since Augustus had been born and she persuaded George to say he was the most frightful creature he had ever beheld. Hary-o thought this was very unpleasant and took George to task. He was uneasy, blushed, and told her to keep her voice down because he was afraid that Lady Elizabeth or Lord Melbourne might hear.[50] It was clear to Hary-o that the Lambs harboured a great deal of spite against Caroline. Lord Egremont, William's father, referred to her as 'that nasty, infamous mad woman' whom William had married against his will. Caroline St Jules, who sided with George, said, 'Her passions ought to be treated like all other nervous disorders which require scolding, or at least a firm decided manner but both her [Lady Bessborough] and William indulge her till she is naughty.' Lady Bessborough mistrusted Lady Melbourne and referred to her as 'The Thorn' while Lord Egrement referred to her as 'the old Baggage, the mother of the Monster'.

It was fashionable for ladies to keep little armies of pages and some of the little boys came and went as the ladies passed them around between them. Three of Caroline's favourites were Thomas Bentley, Tom Hughes and Francis Corray, who pleased her so much that she wrote:

From Little Hampton town I came,
And Francis Corray is my name,
My face is fair my eyes are blue,
My heart is sound – my thoughts are true,
& never sure in any age
Was seen so good a little page

To Lady Carolina Lamb
A faithful follower I am
I feed her dogs & fetch her gloves
& watch her whensoever she moves

I learn my lesson, sing & play
& keep each merry Holyday
For never sure in any age
Was seen a happier little page.

My coat was of dirty blue
Is now with silver fine & new
My breeches & my waistcoat white
Are all men's envy & delight
My hands I clean, my hair I comb
& ever am so fine at home
I do not think in any age
There ever was so smart a Page.

Your servant Madam, This way Sir
Lie down you dog, get out you cur
My only business seems to be
To spend a life of liberty
Or dec't in lace & silver trim
To follow up my Lady's whim,
Yet sure so many at her age
Ne'er Lady had for little Page.[51]

Caroline took a great interest in the page's uniforms down to the smallest detail. She instructed her tailor, Mr Baker, to ensure that the waistcoats 'must each have three rows of buttons down the front', and 'six rows of round silver buttons for the coat & red waistcoat & three more rows for the drab one & 3 rows for the belt which is in all 12 rows at 1s. per dozen.'[52]

Caroline and William spent the autumn quietly at Brocket and on 21 November welcomed Lord Bessborough and Lady Bessborough, but their visit was spoilt by the arrival of Sheridan. He was a longstanding member of the Devonshire House Set, a crony of the Prince of Wales and well known to the Lambs. Lady Melbourne had expected to see him at Brocket the week before while she was entertaining the Prince of Wales but Sheridan neither turned up nor replied. When Caroline sternly told him he had mistaken the date and that his rudeness had irritated Lady Melbourne, he merely looked sheepishly at her and asked if he could stay the night. Lady Bessborough begged her not to let him stay any longer. She was frightened and embarrassed. She and Sheridan had been friends in the past, some say more than friends, and in 1790 their behaviour had so outraged Lord Bessborough, then still Lord Duncannon, that he began a suit in Doctor's Commons for a separation. He was persuaded to withdraw it only after the Duke of Devonshire intervened. From then on Lady Bessborough tried to avoid Sheridan, telling her servants to say that she was not at home if he called. This had only made the situation worse. He did not go away but sat, completely drunk, outside her front door for hours.

That evening Sheridan trotted behind Lady Bessborough and asked her to forgive him and shake hands. The next day 'when his carriage drove to the door, he shiver'd and cough'd, complain'd of a cold, of a head ache, said he had never met with so good a bed; every one was silent. He lik'd being at Brocket of all things; not a word. At last he ask'd whether it would be inconvenient to them to allow him to stay.' Caroline could not think of a reason to refuse. He drove Lady Bessborough to distraction by following her everywhere, in and out of rooms, up and down stairs until he cornered her in the nursery. He threw himself on his knees before her. She refused to take him seriously and he jumped up with a vicious look on his face and 'vow'd vengeance'. As he handed her into her carriage the next day he squeezed her hand with such force that her rings cut into her fingers and brought tears to her eyes.[53]

Caroline's London assemblies were noted for the wit of the conversation and the vivacity of the hostess. Miss Berry, the bluestocking writer, described the aftermath of one evening: 'we came away at half-past twelve, and walked beyond the Admiralty to the carriage. Many of the company were not away till near three, and the Prince of Wales and a very few persons supped below stairs in Lady Melbourne's apartment, and were not gone till past six – Sheridan of the number, who was completely drunk.'[54]

There was a certain amount of rivalry among the young mothers. Hary-o thought Augustus was 'the finest child,' Corisande's 'the prettiest' and Maria Duncannon's 'the fattest'. On 3 May, after dining at Lady Melbourne's, Caroline took Miss Berry to the nursery 'to see her little boy asleep, who a very few hours after was seized with fits and his life despaired of.' Miss Berry wrote in her journal, 'He is too big for his age – only eight months.'[55] Although Augustus was the largest and healthiest child Hary-o had ever seen, she did not like the look of helplessness in his face. Caroline was also worried, and tried to explain his fits as teething symptoms.[56]

The summer of 1808 was the hottest ever recorded in England. From 11 to 19 July the thermometer only once dropped below 80 degrees fahrenheit and on the famous 'Hot Wednesday' it reached 99 degrees. Caroline, William and Augustus spent the days lazily at Holywell. William read aloud, Caroline made white satin shoes for herself and Lady Spencer busily made nets to protect her fruit from the birds. Augustus was being weaned and seemed to be doing well. He could sit upright and tried to speak but ignored all attempts to encourage him to walk.

In August Caroline was pregnant, 'fat and pretty but not in spirits'. Once again she confided in Little G: 'Our little boy is really grown as blooming & stout as your little Georgiana which is saying something. He has more colour in his lips than when quite a baby and is mottled all over. He is no thinner but quite lively & well so that everybody that sees him now for the first time says what a fine stout healthy boy he is – When I have said thus much I have said all, for though a year & a month old tomorrow he can neither walk alone or speak a word – but laughs like a Lamb and grows very like me in beam & fat. I continue perfectly well. We have been very comfortable indeed & my own William is returned. The only thing that makes me uneasy is that I have nothing at all wrong with me – never am sick, eat ravenously & would not know I was in any way differing from Wm. But that my clothes grow rather tight for me.'[57]

At ten o'clock in the evening of 30 January, two years after the stillbirth of her first child, Caroline's labour began and she was 'brought to bed at one of a nice little girl who, however, only lived the night thro' and died on Lady Bessborough's lap. 'Caro bears it with the greatest resignation, but it [is] a cruel disappointment.' Lady Spencer told Caroline not to grieve but to take comfort 'in knowing that she has done all she possibly could to preserve this poor little infant, & all that now remains is to submit with entire resignation to God's will.' This second calamity was more than Caroline and William could bear and it was not until early March that their doctor could reassure Lady Spencer that Caroline was recovering and that he was no longer uneasy about William.[58]

They put on brave faces and congratulated Caroline St Jules and George Lamb on their engagement. The couple were married on 17 May at Devonshire House and spent their honeymoon at Brocket. The bride's putative father, Comte St Jules, was nowhere to be seen, but her natural father, the Duke of Devonshire, gave her a marriage portion of £30,000 (about one and a quarter million pounds today). The Prince of Wales, the reputed father of the bridegroom, congratulated Lady Elizabeth and praised the Duke for his generosity.

Lady Spencer foresaw the possibility of friction between the two Carolines and rattled off instructions. 'Above all things I hope she & dear Caroline will agree & live cordially together without the little jealousies which in their situations are so much to be dreaded. Much will depend upon their not having tittle-tattle gossiping servants; & you will do well to warn Caroline,' she told Lady Bessborough, 'indeed both of them, from the beginning against ever suffering her maid, or any about her to talk of either George Lamb, or Caroline or of their servants "*ni en bien ni en mal*".'[59] From this time on, to avoid confusion, Caroline was referred to in the family as Caro-William and her new sister-in-law as Caro-George.

The baby's death, her ill health and stress had driven Caroline and William apart. Their rows were more bitter and the reconciliations fewer. By the time Emily held a house party to celebrate George's marriage, they were not on speaking terms. Caroline went alone to Panshanger Park, the Cowper's country house near Hatfield. She wrote to William, 'Condemn me not to silence, and assist my imperfect memory and occasionally call me friend – girl – darling…and all such names as show great love. I will on the other hand, be silent of a morning, entertaining after dinner; docile, fearless as a heroine in the last vol. of her troubles, strong as a mountain tiger. You should say to me, *raisonnez mieux et repliquez moins*.' She ended, 'I think lately my dearest William, we have been very troublesome to each other which I take by wholesale to my own account and mean to correct and leave you in retail a few little sins which I know you will correct… I only want my Angel boy & man to be perfectly happy… Dearest Mannie'.[60]

In July they went on holiday to the Isle of Wight. They were reconciled and Caroline was once again William's willing pupil. He succumbed to her charm and laughed off Emily's increasing criticisms. They spent their days reading, playing cards and sightseeing. Caroline would have been perfectly happy if she had not been worried about her brother, Frederick, who was serving in Spain, a Major in the 23rd Light Dragoons. The Duke of Gloucester, who was also staying on the island, sent her accounts of the recent military actions, which only added to her suspense. Frederick bravely led his men in a charge, which took five French squares at the battle of Talavera, but he treated the whole affair with typical sangfroid. 'You are a shabby set,' he told Maria Duncannon, 'not a single line from anybody but my mother and but six letters from her since I have been in the country.'

'We found the Lambs at Cowes,' Hary-o reported to Hartington, 'Caroline much more extraordinary and entertaining than ever leading the sort of life of people in a Harlequin Farce, perpetually shifting of scene, dress and company, lodging in an apothecary's, dining at the Duke of Gloucester's, enfant de famille at Mrs Knox's an Irish lady who gives assemblies in London, one minute on a Pillion, the next in a boat, but the wand to effect these changes always in Columbine's hand – Lady [Lavinia] Spencer exclaiming – "William Lamb is an angel, nothing like the school of adversity!" '[61]

William's business commitments forced him to return to London and Caroline wrote to him on the day he left, 'I wish you goodbye, and God bless and preserve you, and keep you from all harm both in body and mind. I have been playing all day with that pretty little Augustus of yours. He is the dearest child I ever saw, and shows where you are gone by pointing to the sea...your own faithful Wiffin.'[62]

Neither Caroline nor Hartington had guessed how close Lady Elizabeth was to the completion of her ambition, but Lady Bessborough, Lady Spencer and Lady Morpeth had harboured fears and suspicions for several months. 'With a cross heart, a bad pen, red ink & no time, I write these few lines to you my kind little cousin,' Caroline wrote light-heartedly to Hartington on 29 September; 'I have read the Rights of Woman, am become a convert, think dissipation great folly, & shall remain the whole year discreetly & quietly in the country. Caroline George is the delight of Brocket Hall. Give her three kisses for me & mind I never will give you another while you live – you are a bad good for nothing boy.'[63] On 11 October the news that Lady Elizabeth was to marry the Duke of Devonshire reached Caroline but the actual date of the wedding was unknown, leaving the family uncertain as to whether or not it had taken place. Out of respect to Georgiana and Lady Spencer, Lady Elizabeth offered not to use the title Duchess of Devonshire. 'She says the Duke advis'd this, I own I should rejoice at it, tho' we have no right to expect it,' Lady Bessborough told Granville. In the end it proved to be an empty gesture.

Caroline wrote in a rage to Hartington who was entertaining Caro-George at Chatsworth. 'The last letter I wrote to you my good Gd. Mama chose to read and observed that there were rather strong expressions in it. It was all about what now I find is declared & however little right I may have to censure that old Witch's conduct I shall never hear her called by the dear name she has assumed without regret & disgust... Pray tell me, how Caroline broke it to you & what that emblem of innocence thinks now of Lady E Foster – Is it possible she can still be like the Pharisees who had eyes and saw not & ears & heard not & has she all along cunningly & slyly been aware of the whole intrigue? I detest such petty artifices as she employs. If she will be wicked let her be so in the face of day, but when I think of the scene of deceit, plot, iniquity & wiles that serpent has made use of I shudder at the thought... I am cross as Patch at the triumph of hypocrisy & petty intrigues I see everywhere carried on. I am sure the Melbournes knew of this long ago & I am sure also, my good Cous, that you told old Bess you would not disapprove of it. O she is a deep one. She has flummeried up a certain young Marquis from his cradle. She knew well that the storm where it blew hardest would be over soonest & the former influence remain stronger than ever. This mistress of your papa's knows how to throw her chains about you – she had a word here & a word there & few can set aloof above her...the cool contempt & indifference I felt, from the time I knew that hypocrite's character, never left me & never shall, though civility for my uncle's & humanity's sake will I hope always keep me from being disrespectful... You once loved me as I always shall you, write not or not write, & when I see you I know you will take all steps to kiss me & appease me; but we shall see if I cannot once in my turn be cold too.'[64]

Hartington replied immediately. 'The thing in your letter that shocks, provokes and makes my blood boil, is this incredible marriage, and your letter is the first that has told me of it. My g[rand]-mother's representations I thought were exaggerated by her fears, and hardly till I see it can I believe that woman could have the assurance to take that name so sacred to us, and henceforward to be so polluted. Indeed, my own Car, you wrong me very much in thinking that I could have talked to her on such a subject, and I don't see how I am ever to speak to her again with patience. And is it not extraordinary that Caroline, who has been with me for a week, talking incessantly all day long, should not have said a word about it? But if it is so, she may have been told not, & I shall have a letter in form to announce it. When, I should like to know have you seen me fawn upon that crocodile, as you have the cruelty to say I do in your wicked letter? Do, dearest Car, write to me directly, tell me that you did not mean any of the bitter things you said, and above all that you do not believe I care more for you present than absent... And write directly, for [until] I hear again from [you] I shall not have peace by day or rest by night. And now forgive me, and beg my pardon, dearest of wild young women. I will write to you every day in the year for the future if you wish it. God bless you dearest.'[65]

The family held a war council to decide what public position to adopt should the Duke marry Lady Elizabeth. Lady Bessborough told Granville, 'If my mother trusted to her self alone she would do as I do, grieve over what renews so painfully former recollections but no more; but I know my brother's opinion sway'ed by Ly [Lavinia] Spencer, and Ld Morpeth too, seems to intimate that he wishes that on such an event all connections should cease between Devonshire House and us, and Harriet quit her father. This I highly disapprove of.' Lady Bessborough felt caught in the middle, 'Yes, I shall stand alone against my whole family and *her* children as favouring an event, which God knows, pains me more than any... I really love Bess, and think she has many more good and generous qualities than are allowed her, but I think she has the worst judgement of anybody I ever met with; and I begin also to think she has more *calcul* and more power of concentration than I ever before believ'd.'

The Duke wrote to Lady Spencer formally telling her of his intention to marry Lady Elizabeth. Two days later on 19 October 1809, at Chiswick, he married his mistress of twenty-seven years. Lady Spencer's parson, the Reverend James Preedy, conducted the ceremony. 'Poor Preedy, is an object of real compassion,' she wrote. 'He should not have gone to Chiswick but he was persuaded as we all have been that the marriage was over; & when he was in the house I do not well see how he could have avoided doing what he did... He is quite wretched.'[66]

Caroline accepted an invitation from Hartington to stay at Chatsworth and she nostalgically told her mother, 'I went over every spot of the house, looked & spoke to all the people who knew me, & seemed as glad to see me as I was to see them. Dear Beautiful Chatsworth & dear Hartington... You cannot think now delightful he was, & how affectionately he spoke of you & all this odious business.' She broke her journey home at Holywell and was alarmed to see how the Duke's remarriage had left her grandmother looking so 'terrible and pale'. Once back at Brocket she rushed to see Augustus who was fast asleep in the nursery. 'I only kissed his rosy cheek and longed to wake him. It is near a fortnight since I have seen him,' she enthused to her mother.[67]

Within days of returning from Chatsworth, Caroline asked to see Hartington. 'I will meet you at *la dear Douarière's* [their nickname for Lady Spencer] if not at B. Hall, if not here. Write, write, write, write, write, write, write, write, write, write. I will add nothing but 'write' till I have an answer & will send you a double letter unfranked twice a day by the General Post. Bad boy!'[68] 'Dearest Cousin,' he replied, 'I beg your pardon for not writing, but very certainly my talent and pleasure do not lie that way; the latter consists only in the receiving part of the business. I hope to see you in a week or ten days at St Albans or in town and till then entreat that you will write me many long letters.'

The repercussions of the Duke's remarriage continued. Lady Lavinia Spencer criticised it in 'terms of coarseness and violence that would astonish Billingsgate,' Hary-o told her brother, 'I am quite ignorant of Caroline's [Caro-George's] opinions and feelings and had rather continue to be so. The other Caroline [Caro-William] is like a volcano on the subject.'[69] Hary-o was constantly under Lady Elizabeth's eye and she furiously described her as perverted and unable to distinguish between right and wrong. 'Circumstances have altered her conduct and situation at different times but she has invariably been what even when I was a child I understood and despised.' The family agreed it was essential that they find her a husband. Coincidentally, Granville's passion for Lady Bessborough had faded and he had decided that the time had come to marry and produce heirs. He took her into his confidence and she set out to smooth the way towards a *marriage de convenance* with her niece.

Charlotte, Duchess of Beaufort, Granville's sister, invited the pair to Badminton to enable him to evaluate Hary-o and gauge her suitability for the position of his wife. 'I had a conversation today of some length,' he told Lady Bessborough, 'in which she was agreeable, and shewed that good Sense which I always knew she possessed'. Hary-o was confused and flattered by his attentions and wrote to Miss Trimmer saying, 'I never felt so much in need of the friendship and advice of those I love and esteem.' She was inevitably jealous of her aunt but she allowed herself to fall in love with Granville. He proposed on 14 November and she accepted. They were married on Sunday, Christmas Eve, at Chiswick in the presence of the Duchess of Beaufort, Lady Harrowby, Hartington, Caro-George and her husband. The new Duchess of Devonshire exclaimed 'May she be as happy as I wish her and believe she will be.' Two days after the wedding Granville told Lady Bessborough, 'Every hour I passed with Harriet convinced me more and more of the justice and liberality of her way of thinking and of her claim upon me for unlimited confidence. She is indeed a perfect angel.' (It is not clear when she realised the true parentage of nine-year-old Harriet or five-year-old George Stewart but she generously gave them a home. In 1824 Harriet married Lord Godophin and George became his father's secretary.)

'Nothing but a long expressive letter from you can remove the affront I labour under at being excluded from my own cousin's wedding. Mrs Scafe is shocked at it. Pray send one a favour & cake, if not I shall positively turn green with jealousy & yellow with melancholy,' Caroline wrote cheerfully to Hartington. 'Send me an account of the ceremony – no soul writes me a word of what happened – who was affected? – How Ld G behaved, if Harrio was unhappy – how she was dressed – what she wore – let me know all these things & mind you come and see us at Christmas – Was Mama at the ceremony?' The string of orders and instructions ended, 'God bless you little Cousin Hartington.'[70]

In the New Year William left Caroline at Brocket with Augustus, who had been ill for a month. She felt abandoned and although William wrote to her regularly from London, his letters were full of parliamentary gossip but without the loving asides she was used to from Hartington. One began, 'Dearest love,' (since you do not like the other beginning) I am quite well & strong after sitting up until four o'clock this morning', and it was not until several paragraphs later, between reports of debates, that he enquired after Augustus.[71]

The relief Caroline felt when Augustus recovered was overwhelming. She wrote to Hartington at Holywell:

Friend of my heart accept this letter
The child thank God is rather better
But spight doctors drugs & pill
Has been most wonderfully ill.
Tis true he did not wheeze or hoope
But yet we thought he had the croupe
His breathing was so short & thick
We were obliged to make him sick
But Lucas says the cough & heat

Today have sounded a retreat
To that I may in safety say
The inflammations giving way
I'm writing to you lovely spark
With nurse & Selly [Miss Trimmer] in the dark
So that I neither care nor ken
Which way I turn my crazy pen.
But when some light assists my hand,
I'll draw the picture you command,
Paint Flora in a flowing robe
With either breast just like a glove,
Her skin like snow on frozen river,
Her hair the colour of your liver,
Her wide jaw bone and figure tall!
Leave it to me, I'll paint it all,
But as I am much pressed for time
Accept the sense & leave the rhime.

...I have scarcely been out of the boy's room since you left me & am so full of nursery jokes I hardly know how to write sense... Pray drive over & see a disconsolate widow bereft of all she holds most dear.'[72]

Augustus was placed with Miss Trimmer until a suitable governess could be found. At the end of March Caroline employed Miss Thomasina Webster who immediately fell in love with Augustus, calling him her own 'little pet Lamb'. She encouraged him to call her 'Moome', which, she explained, was a Gaelic word describing someone who loves and takes on the duties of a mother to children other than her own. Through her kindness and understanding Augustus did not have so many temper tantrums, which lessened the number of fits. Lady Spencer approved of Miss Webster but still had concerns about Augustus. She told Lady Bessborough, 'There is no judging as to character & principles what he is, but he seems at last to wish to do well – tho' as I have already said, there is a familiarity in his manner that will disgust many – as it did me.'[73]

William spent more and more of his time away from home and Caroline became resentful. 'That first ardour – that romantic passion, which we both experienced, was far too violent to last – contrary to general opinion on this subject,' she told Lady Melbourne. 'It has lasted far longer on his side than on mine & with its enthusiasm has ceased also its inconveniences. My temper is calm, we never quarrel, never shake the house with storms of passion as we did for the first three years. I can command myself now & he rejoices in the change yet he looks not for the cause – gratitude, affection even love remains in my heart

57

but those feelings which carry with them such a charm and existed so many years unabated have lately been on the decline.'[74]

It was not unusual for the wives of aristocrats to be neglected and most found ways of amusing themselves with good works or discreet love affairs so, by his own lights, William did not think that Caroline was particularly hard done by. He passed his time in his library or club and in the evening he frequently dined out at the great Whig mansions, where the food was nourishing but boringly predictable. The most frequent dishes on the menu were mulligatawny or turtle soup, salmon or turbot surrounded by smelts, saddle of mutton, roast beef, chicken, game, tongue and dishes of badly cooked French delicacies accompanied by mounds of boiled potatoes, pickles and stuffing. All the vegetables, which were unfashionable anyway, were cold and the desserts were take-away puddings and pies from Grange or Owen, pastry cooks in Bond Street. The diners drank port, sherry, hock, claret and burgundy from the time the soup was placed on the table until they fell under it.

Caroline was determined to regain William's attention, jolt him out of his rut and revive the enjoyable turmoil of their early years. Knowing that he would disapprove she went out of her way to cultivate older, more worldly women. She came home late with colourful tales of riotous parties and amorous advances but William remained unperturbed. He smiled at her in his lazy way and commented that she was far too cold and inhibited sexually to be attractive to other men.

Caroline described the situation in *Glenarvon*: 'They were dearer to each other perhaps, than any two who had been so long united in marriage. They loved each other with more passion, more enthusiasm than is often retained, but they were, from a thousand circumstances, utterly estranged at this time; and that apparently by mutual consent... When provoked Lord Avondale [William] was too severe; and when he saw her miserable and oppressed, it gave him more suffering than if he had himself been subdued... During the first years of their marriage, these tumultuous scenes but strengthened the attachment they felt for each other; but when Lord Avondale's profession absorbed his mind, he dreaded a recurrence of those quarrels and reconciliation's which had once so entirely engrossed his thoughts... Absent, pre-occupied, he saw not, he heard not, the misuse she made of her entire liberty. Some trifle, perhaps at times, reached his ear; a scene of discord ensued; much bitterness on both sides followed; and the conviction they no longer loved each other, added considerably to the violence of recrimination.' (Volume II, Chapter XIV)

In a fit of frustration Caroline told Lady Melbourne, 'William's love for me is such that he is almost blind to my faults.'[75] In desperation and bravado she set out to find the happiness she had lost.

3

'Mad – bad – and dangerous to know'

Sir Godfrey Vassal Webster hardly knew his mother, Lady Holland. He was the eldest son of her first marriage to Sir Godfrey Webster of Battle Abbey and had lived with his father's family since his parents' divorce in 1796. Sir Godfrey, overwhelmed by gambling debts, shot himself on 4 June 1800 leaving his children, Godfrey, Harriet and Henry, in the care of his brother-in-law and executor Thomas Chaplin. Lady Holland's only contact with her children was through Lord Egremont, who often invited them to stay with him at his country mansion, Petworth House in West Sussex.

After an undistinguished career at school, Sir Godfrey joined the 18th Light Dragoons and served in Spain. He returned in the autumn of 1809 and soon afterwards met Caroline. He was handsome, uncomplicated, jolly and dashing in his glamorous uniform; and his bravery in battle appealed to her romantic streak. He had led thirty men against one hundred French in a skirmish, killing twenty and taking five prisoners.

He was flattered that a beauty with such powerful connections should seek out his company and he cautiously played the game of romance with Caroline. He never overstepped the mark, but his admiration and loving words gave Caroline pleasure. She revelled in secret assignations and kisses 'snatched up with a great deal of fear'. Her craving for excitement led her to hide behind a set of doors at the Assembly Rooms in Argyle Street, within inches of discovery, and make him place a bracelet, made from his own hair, on her wrist.

Caroline's furtive behaviour made Lady Bessborough suspicious, especially when she caught her reading one of Sir Godfrey's letters, which she tried to hide behind her back. 'The consequence of all this,' Caroline told Lady Holland, who was more annoyed than shocked, 'is that we have mutually promised to give up all correspondence, all appointed meetings.'[1] She loosely interpreted that promise as meaning that she could still see him 'in public by accident' and as a 'common acquaintance'. She told Lady Holland, 'I am not lost enough to break

59

everybody's heart & my own by abandoning my husband & child.' However, she refused to return his presents, gold chains, crosses and a puppy.

As part of her campaign to be noticed, Caroline had the bodices of her dresses cut so that almost all of her breasts were revealed, she flirted and indulged in what Lady Holland called 'titillating displays'. She thought Caroline's behaviour exceptionally stupid and briskly told her to mend her manners, but she was not in the mood to oblige. When Lady Melbourne scolded her she went on to the attack, saying she was neglected and blaming William for her breaches of good taste. She wrote that William 'called me prudish said I was straight-laced – amused himself with instructing me in things I need never have heard or known – & the disgust that I at first felt at the world's wickedness I till then had never even heard of – in a very short time gave way to a general laxity of principles which little by little unperceived by you all has been undermining the few virtues I ever possessed.'[2]

In a fit of bravado, Caroline wore Sir Godfrey's bracelet in public and made a great fuss of the puppy. The next day she received a letter from Lady Melbourne; 'I only write you a few lines for the purpose of preventing yr coming to me loaded with falsehood & flattery under the impression that it will have any effect. Yr Behaviour last night was so disgraceful in its appearance & so disgusting from its motives, that it is quite impossible it should ever be effaced from my mind. When anyone braves the opinion of the World, sooner or later they will feel the consequences of it & altho at first people may have excused your forming friendships with all those who are censured for their conduct from yr youth & inexperience, yet when they see you continue to single them out & to overlook all the decencies imposed by Society – they will look upon you as belonging to the same class. Had you been sincere in yr promises of amendment or wished to make any return to Wm for his kindness – you would have discarded and driven from your presence any persons or things that could remind you of the unworthy object for whose sake you had run such risks & exposed yourself so much, but on the contrary you seem to delight in everything that recalls him to you & to nourish and foster those disgraceful feelings which have caused so much unhappiness to those who ought to be dearest to you. A Married Woman should consider that by such levity she not only compromises her own honour & character but also that of her Husband – but you seek only to please yourself – you think you can blind yr Husband and cajole yr Friends.'[3]

Sir Godfrey made plans to leave England; Caroline was defiant and demanded to see him one more time before he left. She told Lady Melbourne, 'Sir G Webster says he will rather die than leave England without speaking to me alone and I would rather quarrel with my whole family, lose my reputation and have my heart broke than not do it'. She proposed a bargain: 'If I may see him tomorrow and if you will not tell my mother, the Duchess or Frederick what passed tonight I will be as gentle and docile as a lamb. I will try and conquer feelings, which are now too strong for my reason to command, I will put myself in your & my Mother's hands & be guided by you but if I am driven to despair I will deceive you all. I speak not as a menace & I care not for what may be thought or said... If I may see him quietly and without witnesses here in the drawing room, if I may so far be trusted without injurious suspicion it is well. If not prevent me – and remember you have done so.'4

Caroline's letters to Lady Holland became long and rambling as she tried at first to justify her behaviour and later to blame William for corrupting her morals. When Lady Holland remained unconvinced, Caroline condemned her for neglecting Sir Godfrey when he was a boy. Caroline played the same psychological games that had been so successful when she was a child. She threw tantrums, then apologised, and then asked for help to improve her behaviour, usually from her accuser. If this did not work, she turned her sins into a joke and tried to laugh herself out of trouble and when the storm subsided she continued her life as though nothing had happened. She had the ability to convince herself that she was genuinely sorry and even wept.

Caroline came to her senses with a jolt when the puppy snapped at Augustus. 'Great God,' she wrote to Lady Melbourne, 'if this dog should go mad and bite William's child, what would become of me – I went into the garden and took a long walk. The dog suddenly dropped before me in a fit, foaming at the mouth – it turned my heart sick. I trembled all over. I took it home & prayed I might be forgiven... A sudden terror came into my head as I looked on my blooming Augustus that I might be punished for my conduct by the loss of what I neglected – your kindness, my mother's, my husband's – my own husband's – all occurred to me – I tore the bracelet off my arm and put it up with my chains in a box by itself – I have written to desire someone will fetch the dog – on my knees I have written to William to tell him, not any falsehood, not as you say, any stories to conceal my guilt but the whole disgraceful truth. I have told him I have deceived him. I have trusted solely to his mercy & generosity – yet as I have not said any of you know anything about it do not mention it to him unless he does to you but write to me my dearest Lady Melbourne, write & tell me you forgive me for I am indeed very miserable, very repentant... Pray do not name the person to William or say anything about it.' She added, 'From what danger I have been saved – Good God I tremble when I think of it – I was indeed on the brink of perdition & about to encounter misery, infamy and ruin with perfect levity... Dear William may he never know what a little ungrateful serpent he has nourished in his bosom. God bless him & all of you & me too if I am not past hope – I have written to tell Sir Godfrey I will see him once more and after that

61

I am at your orders.' She added in a conspiratorial postscript, 'Of course you must not restore it [the puppy] till a proper lie is invented to cover the sin. To be reduced to this is indeed humiliating?'[5]

On 3 May she told Lady Holland, 'I have not written before because I am sick of false promises. You many depend upon it now however that I will do everything you say if you wish. I am humble enough now believe me & shall write no more flippant letters God knows – your son has this moment left the room – we are good friends there is no pique now – but I thought you would like to know I have done with the whole thing… I have had a lesson I shall not easily forget, believe me – I will do nothing by halves tho' I have no doubt I am more innocent than I appear, yet this is the last you ever shall hear about me on the subject.'[6] She claimed that she would have risked everything for Sir Godfrey and it was his 'forbearance' and 'his real friendship' for her that preserved her from 'despair & infamy'. She added, 'As to William, he is & pray God he may ever remain, ignorant of what would break his heart.' Lord Holland wrote at the top of the paper, 'A monstrous silly passage – the common cant of every woman in similar circumstances.'[7]

Lady Holland had cause to doubt Caroline's sincerity when Sir Godfrey suddenly walked into her box at Drury Lane where she was watching a performance with Caroline. 'All I can say with truth is that I did not know he would come to your Box & believe me so far – for why should I add untruths to my other faults?' Caroline asked. She added, 'As to what you say about my liking to excite interest & anxiety in those I love, it was unkind. I neither wish it nor imagine this to be the means. Conduct like mine may create contempt & ridicule, – & may, if pursued, deeply wound & afflict the hearts of those I love, but I should hope few would feel interest or waste their sensibilities on so bad a subject. I shall make no promises but perhaps you will one day see that my adoration for William & my gratitude & interest for him are not all hypocrisy & words.'[8]

When Lady Holland refused to speak to Caroline until she stopped seeing Sir Godfrey, Caroline wrote, 'No human power shall ever dissolve the friendship or allow the sentiments I feel for him some call your son.' She continued in a fit of rage, 'I will sooner give up wealth, comfort, peace of mind & every other good & follow that man than I will hear him continually made an object of scorn & abuse & denied the common privilege of meeting & speaking to me when I please.' Caroline was remorseful after the tantrum passed; 'My dearest Lady Holland, I entreat you to forgive the very improper letter I wrote last night, that I am miserable for it you may believe by my writing this.'[9] Lady Holland remained silent. Caroline tried again, 'I feel ungrateful, uncomfortable, unhappy & all the Uns imaginable at not having seen you for so long.' She tried to coax the older woman to attend a pageant at the Assembly Rooms in Argyle Street. 'You shall be dressed like the Persian Ambassador & I will accompany you in whatever shape you please... As I am Queen of Argyle St. I could get you a Box. Pray come – Hate refusals.'[10]

Lady Holland's refusal to accept her extravagant claims of innocence drew another letter from Caroline. 'You have just cut me across the heart, right into it, believe me. I can only say that I am grieved at what has happened & that without loss of time I will do all in my power to repair it. How wrong I have been William never will know. I do not think were I to tell him he would believe it – but I have not deceived him. I hope you do not think I could – no young man ever yet behaved so well to any woman as your son has done, so respectfully & so well in everything. I did not deserve it & cannot but feel the difference of his conduct & many others who are termed *gentlemen*.'[11] Caroline had succeeded in her intention to convince everyone that she was having a full-blooded adulterous affair with Sir Godfrey. She told Lady Holland, 'I took you in at the time as I did all my friends and half London. I did it to excite interest & succeeded – that I acted my part well, shewed my cleverness & now might like a good little woman amuse myself with something – those were your very words. I have had no wish to excite any emotion in anyone – I have just followed the caprice of the moment as I generally do – made a great fool & vexed those who cared about me.'

Once the rumour mill began turning it was difficult to stop. Caroline was accused not only having an affair with Sir Godfrey but also with his half-brother, the fickle, romantically inclined Henry Holland. Horrified, she promised not to return to London, write or see Henry until she knew how to conduct herself, 'which', she told Lady Holland, 'may probably never be, for tho' old enough I am not wiser than when I was but twelve... It is the misfortune of those who have once strayed from the truth that they never afterwards are believed.'

Sir Godfrey left the country. In 1814 he married Charlotte Adamson, the handsome daughter of a claret merchant, by whom he had four sons. He left his wife to bring them up alone and lived under an assumed name for many years before his death in 1836.

Caroline was weak and in shock, as she usually was after violent emotional storms, but she was happy and forgiven. She left little Augustus with Lady Holland while she spent a few days with Lady Spencer, in the peace of Holywell, before she returned to Holland House. 'It has been very pleasant indeed here & Lady Holland has been most extremely kind to me,' she wrote to Duncannon. 'I am much better in health but have hardly been out at all in the gay world.' She discounted the King's seventy-second birthday party at St James's Palace and an outing to Astley's Royal Amphitheatre to see 'the popular Grand Equestrian and Pedestrian spectacle, called THE BLOOD-RED KNIGHT' with its 'grand attack on the Usurpers' Castle, and his defeat by warriors on real horses, some of which are seen immersed in water.'

In answer to a scolding letter from Georgiana Morpeth, Caroline replied, 'You ask me whether I felt sure of my future & conduct – alas I have acted so ill that I have lost much of that vain confidence I used to boast of but if feeling once more little short of adoration for Wm & perfect, perfect happiness, can prevent my making myself odious & wretched then I think I may say I am sure I will act very differently in future. You cannot think how painful it is to me to recur to that subject. How I once liked to talk of it is the only thing that surprises me, but indeed, William's behaviour to me since has been such that I must have been bad indeed not to have been touched by it.'[12]

'How has dear Caroline's great imprudence been received at Whitehall?' Lady Spencer asked Lady Bessborough. 'Dear child, she knows not the pain she gives to you & me, & too probably the misery she is preparing for herself; and all this not from vice but vanity, inordinate vanity... Dear Caroline's perverseness makes me wretched whenever I think of it. You may shew her this letter if you like it, for I cannot write to her.'[13]

In July a large party from Devonshire House went to see the *Queen Charlotte* launched at Greenwich. Harriet dined with the Sheridans, 'who all sung and got royally drunk' while they waited for the ceremony to begin and were almost drowned when their skiff was caught in the wash of the newly launched vessel. It was a rare opportunity for Caroline to raise her eyebrows at her cousin; 'Harriet is far from well. I hope it is not in consequence of this intemperance,' she wrote primly to Lady Holland.[14]

The storms of the spring were forgotten and Caroline and William were at peace with each other and with his family. They spent a few days at Panshanger and accompanied Emily and Lord Cowper to the annual Hertford Ball, 'where everybody looks & nobody speaks to you.'[15] Caroline discovered a large swelling on her head, which she thought was one of the first symptoms of dropsy. Hary-o refused to take her seriously but Caroline was so concerned that she returned to London to be treated for what she described as 'puffs on my brain (which are dispersing by section and spirituous applications)'.[16] The following month Caroline joined her parents on their annual holiday at Brighton, William went shooting and Augustus went to stay with his grandparents at Melbourne House.

Caroline wrote brightly to Lady Melbourne, 'We have an excellent House [Belle Vue] and are living a very gay irregular life – which with Balling, riding on the downs, walking & talking requires all the health & spirits I possess... This place delights me – I make acquaintance with everybody, love & like everyone without taste or distinction & am in such spirits I can scarcely keep upon ground.' The Prince of Wales invited them to the Pavilion but it was so hot that the visit was postponed. Caroline asked to have news of Augustus and told Lady Melbourne, 'The little time I have had has been fully taken up in writing to William.'[17] He responded by calling her his 'dearest love' and encouraged her renewed interest in Greek by sending her his own translation of Theocritus' epitaph on the death of his baby son. It was the same work that they had read together on the tithertother at Brocket so many years ago.[18]

In the autumn Caroline accompanied William and Lord Palmerston on a shoot and was delighted when William proved to be the better shot. Palmerston attributed his failure to the high wind and William's good fortune to a lull in the wind, 'which, was a knack he had through life, which stood him in good stead in politics as in sporting.' They were welcomed home by 'the most beautiful little boy you ever saw,' who, 'trots after Wm in a pink sash and petticoats'.[19]

Caroline worried about Hartington. He had been deaf from childhood and was prone to catch cold but recently he had developed a persistent cough accompanied by bouts of sneezing. 'Now my heart of hearts, I conjure you on my knees, I entreat you if you are not quite the thing to come immediately to town,' she wrote. 'I am safe but not overwell; however I neither had my neck broke or got into the newspapers, tho' I behaved a little wild, riding over the Downs and about the sands, with all the officers at my heels, in a way not very decent for one of my cloth. I am like the song of Rosa, in love with everybody & am always abused for it… What a world it is dear sweet coz, what a flimsy patched work face it has, all profession, little affection, no truth. That you love me I feel sure, dearly, and deeply though you now & then see my faults, but indeed it is but bad speculation to gaze on the black of every object. Mine are unfortunately all on the surface. I am pitted all over but it is but skin deep. Many a fair outside covers a blacker heart. Dear little man, take care of yourself, & when we meet in a better & happier world we will be unco virtuous.'[20]

She tried to amuse him with family gossip, nonsense and doggerel. 'Your letter, Sweet Coz, made me stretch my lips to my ears. We vulgarly call this laughing, & so, if you wish to cause me merriment straight ways send me more nonsense; there is comfort in writing it to one who will take it down as a cockatoo swallows a spoonful of castor oil, which I know is your case for in many respects you resemble that sagacious bird.'

My love to Mrs Lamb the Duchess & the Duke,
Now profit by my kind reply but more by my rebuke,
& if you wish to hear from me pray write a pretty letter,
& I will try and answer it like any honest debtor,
So God preserve thee cousin dear & mend thee with his Grace –
& keep within thy heart of hearts for me no little place.[21]

Caroline developed a friendship with Lady Oxford, formerly Jane Elizabeth Scott, whom she had met at Holland House. She had married Edward Harley, fifth Earl of Oxford, when she was twenty-two. She liked to think of herself as an intellectual, held romantic views on the French Revolution and even sympathised with the bloodthirsty Jacobins in a woolly-witted way. She referred to herself as Aspasia (the Greek adventurer, famous for her learning, wit and beauty) and advocated freedom, liberty and free love. Lord Oxford had given her her head and this resulted in five daughters and two sons by various fathers, including Lord Oxford himself. The attractive tribe was known collectively as the Harleian Miscellany (a pun on the famous collection of manuscripts, published in 1744, in Lord Oxford's library). Caroline was very impressed by her worldliness and quoted her freely. She asked Lady Holland, 'Did you hear that Lady Oxford told Dr Bailey this year when she was in the act of dying that she would not be buried with the Harleys having found it too great an annoyance to live with them?' Lady Oxford's posing and undergraduate humour did not amuse William and he was dismayed at the speed with which Caroline picked up and parroted her half-thought-out views.[22] Lady Holland warned Caroline of the dangers of being associated with Lady Oxford. Caroline, in an attempt to regain Lady Holland's approval, replied: 'You cannot think how good & amiable and *docile* I mean to be, & as to Aspasia I shall see her but seldom. I abjure all my follies & flightiness from this hour exactly (fi past 5) Monday... I mean henceforward to be a pattern wife.' She added, 'I have too tender a conscience to be wicked & cannot rest at night if I have in the least deviated from my duty.'[23]

Miss Sydney Owenson, the celebrated author of the 1806 best seller *The Wild Irish Girl*, had recently arrived in London and was swiftly taken up by Whig ladies, becoming the talking point at society gatherings where she sang her own songs, accompanying herself on the harp. She had an unprepossessing appearance with one shoulder higher than the other and a squint. Her curly black hair was cut short and she usually wore a white muslin dress, with a flower tucked into the bosom, under a red Celtic cloak. She was highly intelligent and could count among her friends the political writer and novelist William Godwin (the widower of Mary Wollstonecraft), and Richard Phillips, her first publisher, who had been imprisoned for publishing a cheap edition of Tom Paine's *The Rights of Man*. Caroline invited Miss Owenson to Melbourne House and offered to collect her from her lodgings in her carriage but promptly lost her address. Despite this unpromising beginning they became firm friends, frequently meeting at the Dowager Countess of Cork's receptions at her pretty mansion in New Burlington Street. Lady Cork, as Mary Monckton, had turned her mother's house into a literary centre where Dr Johnson, Sheridan, Edmund Burke and Sir Joshua Reynolds were sure of enjoying an entertaining evening. She continued the tradition after her marriage to Edmund, seventh Earl of Cork, and invitations to her salon were highly prized. Miss Owenson was enchanted by Caroline and flattered to be included in her circle. At a crowded party at Devonshire House she sat on the second flight of stairs between Caroline and the novelist 'Monk' Lewis, while Lady Oxford perched a few steps higher and watched the passing parade. 'At two in the morning,' Miss Owenson wrote later in *The Book of the Boudoir*, 'Lady C— L— proposed that we should go and sup snugly at M— House and return to waltz when her Grace's rooms should thin; – and so we did.'[24]

Caroline enjoyed the Waltz – the fashionable new dance that was considered lewd in some circles. In the past the only contact between dancing partners was a light touch of the hand but now young men could, with perfect propriety, place their arms completely around young women who were unprotected by petticoats and stays and wore only scanty, loosely fitting dresses. Corisande Ossulston sanctimoniously warned Caroline of the dangers of such behaviour. Caroline responded by describing her assailant as a hypocrite; one of those women who 'liked to simper of an improper book, ride and *flirt*...then go home to their Lords pleased, like the Pharisees of old, that they are not like this sinner whom passion & feeling alone impelled reluctantly to ruin & infamy...

I likewise waltz & think no wrong
For O sees harm but I see none
For if you do not waltz too long
& turn the same with every one
How can there be the least of evil
E'n if the mad turned out the devil
Then I will waltz let who say no
For who cares much for little O.'[25]

Lady Spencer wrote anxiously to Lady Bessborough, 'How is dear Caroline? I have written her a few rather serious lines in answer to a letter I had from her which rather vexed me, telling me she had jumped over a couch at some assembly. Dear Child she does not know how much she lowers her character by such improprieties. Thank God they are only childish, but that is unfit for her situation.'[26]

Sydney Owenson also saw the danger in her friend's behaviour, but could do little to stop her. Meanwhile Miss Owenson had caught the eye of Lady Abercorn, who was so impressed that she offered her the position of her companion, and before long she was indispensable. She had succeeded in making her way from being the daughter of a travelling storyteller to the toast of the Whigs. Lord and Lady Abercorn were so anxious to keep her in their household that they looked for suitors on her behalf. Charles Morgan, Lord Abercorn's surgeon, appeared to be the most likely candidate and to make him more attractive Lord Abercorn arranged for him to be knighted. They were married on 20 January 1812 in the Abercorn's Irish mansion, Barons's Court, Tyrone. Thackeray's daughter said that her father had modelled Becky Sharp, another young woman who lived on her wits, on Lady Morgan.

Good resolutions seldom lasted long with Caroline. On her sixth wedding anniversary she refused to leave a dancing party with William, even after he had reminded her of the significance of the date. She pointedly did not follow him home until after five in the morning. Later she wrote, 'As I drove home my heart reproached me & tho' tired to death I could not sleep… My husband is angry with me – I do not wonder.'

In July the Duke of Devonshire's health failed. He had hardly ever been ill, apart from the occasional attack of gout; but now at sixty-two he was having difficulty breathing and Sir Walter Farquhar was called in. Within days the Duke's condition worsened, hastened by purging, clystering and bloodletting. By the end of the month he could sleep only if he was propped up on pillows to ease the 'spasms on the chest'. On 28 July he ate a hearty meal and took a turn on the terrace at Devonshire House, but the improvement did not last more than a few hours; by the following evening he could not breathe at all unless standing up. Mr Walker, the apothecary, had just tied the tourniquet to the Duke's arm before opening the vein when his Grace's head lolled back and he silently died in the Duchess' arms. Some said he was another of Sir Walter Farquhar's victims. On 5 August, twenty-one carriages, tributes from friends and members of the Royal Family followed the hearse from Devonshire House to the outskirts of London where metalled road ended. There they turned back, leaving the Duke to continue his slow journey north to be reunited with his 'Beautiful Duchess', in the family vault in the Church of All Saints at Derby.

Lady Bessborough rushed to Chiswick to comfort the Duchess, who bore her loss with great courage, composure and surprising cheerfulness. She continued to take her place in the drawing room even though 'George Lamb's and dear Hart's riotous Spirits would almost oppress one at a gayer time.' The Duchess did not mind the horseplay. She even seemed to encourage it and went out of her way to amuse Hartington. He misunderstood her well-meaning efforts and doubted her grief was genuine. When he saw her pale and wan face, the best he could say was, 'I see she wears no rouge.'

In her desire to promote her children's future the Duchess lost all discretion and told Lady Bessborough, 'for the first time entirely and *circumstantially*,' how Caro-George and Augustus Clifford came to be born. George Lamb had already discussed the circumstances of his wife's birth with Lord and Lady Holland and he told Lady Bessborough that Caro-George knew now who her father was but that she had known for a long time that the Duchess was her mother.[27]

The Duchess managed to offend all her step-children in her scramble to assume the rank and privileges she believed were her due. She suggested that Clifford, as the Duke's son, was entitled to use the Cavendish arms and crest. She took possession of the Cavendish family jewels and said she would keep them until Hartington married. She alienated the entire family by announcing that she would stay at Chiswick for a year and strongly hinted that she would like it as her dower house. Even Lady Bessborough, who was quite fond of her, thought she was behaving foolishly. Sir Samuel Romilly, the family lawyer, instructed her to hand back the jewels and Lady Bessborough was chosen to tell her that she could not live at Chiswick.

Hartington, bolstered by the antagonism of Caroline, his sisters, Uncle and Aunt Spencer and his grandmother, gave the Duchess one week to leave. She had gone by November. Instead of feeling pleased he was subdued; 'I now know why my Duke felt melancholy,' Caroline told him, 'he has the heart of an Angel & he knew he had been too hasty, too suspicious… You felt that you had ferrited the maim'd fox out of its last hold – the safe corner to which it still clung from the dangers & taunts of a rigidly just world. You had been told it would encroach & you dropped a hasty exclamation & it made you sick to think you had done so – am sure of it & I feel the same – We both act precipitately.'[28] Hartington replied, 'Thought I at St Albans it will be better not to talk much to that flightsome young woman, and now lo! She accuses me of cruelty to the oppressed. Know then, dear cousin, that I was on my knees almost to persuade the fox to remain in her den on less wonderful expense than what had gone on, but she wouldn't – and I do assure you that twasn't that what made me melancholy, nay much am I rejoiced in the spirit at so amicable a riddance, being moreover certain that through life I shall cherish, assist & support the poor body in her old age & crepitude.'[29]

Lady Melbourne had cultivated Daniel Giles, 'a pleasant bachelor of fifty, very popular in County Society', and Member of Parliament for St Albans. She had dazzled and flattered him by introducing him to her powerful Whig friends. During a stroll in St James's Park she had delicately suggested that when the time was ripe he might consider passing his safe seat to George or Frederick, so that 'William might secure the seat for a future occasion.' Mr Giles seemed happy with the prospect until he discovered that he had become the butt of jokes and a figure of fun to William's aristocratic friends. After hearing himself described disparagingly as 'the Hertfordshire Brewer' he told Lady Melbourne that he had no intention of being 'a mere tenant for another' or a 'warming pan' for William.[30]

William did not appear disappointed and passed the autumn hunting and shooting at Brocket while Caroline rode about the countryside, visiting the neighbours with Augustus who she called her 'bosom friend'. She boasted that he spoke French fluently and was William's delight; 'We are united like 3 flames or 3 oaks or what you will.'[31] The bitterness of the past appeared to have been forgiven and forgotten. This happy state was confirmed by Caro-George in November; 'I am just come from Brocket Hall. They are all going on very jollily there,' but she could not resist a passing jab by adding, 'Caroline is a little less mad than usual.'[32]

In July 1811 Lord Carlisle's former ward, George Gordon, sixth Lord Byron, returned to London after a two-year tour of the near east and installed himself at Reddish's Hotel in Albemarle Street. The two men were distantly related through Isabella Byron, the earl's mother, who was also Byron's great-aunt.

Byron's father, Captain John Byron, was a charming rake who ran off with a divorced heiress, Amelia, Marchioness of Carmarthen. Their brief, passionate union produced three children of whom only one, Augusta Mary, survived. As soon as the exhausted Amelia died, taking her annual income of £4,000 with her, John Byron turned to the marriage market at Bath. Barely a year later, on 13 May 1785, he married his second 'golden dolly', Miss Catherine Gordon of Gight. It took him less than two years to squander her money, sell her estate to Lord Haddo and flee to France. On 22 January 1788 his son, George Gordon Byron, was born, his right foot twisted out of its natural position. For the first few months Mrs Byron looked after both children until Augusta was claimed by her maternal grandmother, Lady Holderness, and brought up at Eckington, north of Chesterfield. When Lady Holderness died in 1801, Augusta was farmed out on a rota basis to various branches of her family, including the Duke of Leeds, the Earl of Carlisle and General William Harcourt.

George Gordon Byron succeeded to the title by default. In 1796 the heir, William Byron, was killed in Corsica at the battle of Calvi. Two years later Byron's great-uncle, the fifth Lord, sometimes known as the 'Wicked Lord', died in the neglected family home, Newstead Abbey, and Byron was brought from Scotland to be educated like a gentleman. John Hanson, the Gordon family lawyer, persuaded Lord Carlisle to become his guardian and they placed him at a small boarding school in Lordship Lane, Dulwich. His mother was notoriously difficult to deal with, uncouth and loud but sensible and good hearted. She was devoted to her son and frequently visited the school and withdrew him for weekends against the advice of Dr Glennie, the headmaster. After a particularly noisy argument, Dr Glennie appealed to Lord Carlisle who responded, 'I can have nothing more to do with Mrs Byron – you must now manage her as you can.' However he continued to oversee Byron's education from afar and secured his place at Harrow by obtaining an annuity of three hundred pounds from George III.

To celebrate his coming-of-age in 1809, Byron provided a roast ox and gallons of beer for his tenants at Newstead Abbey in Nottinghamshire. At the time he owed over £10,000 and his mother heartily disapproved of the expense, which led him to declare that he had only two courses of action – to blow his brains out or find a 'golden dolly'. Mrs Byron had no doubts: 'He must marry a woman of *fortune*'. The enormous debt forced him to consider selling Newstead Abbey. However, the building was little more than a romantic ruin. The wind whistled through the cloisters, deserted cells and the broken west wall of the façade. The surrounding hills were barren with scarcely a tree to be seen for miles except for lonely clumps of Scotch firs. The fifth Lord Byron had done his best to ravage the estate so that there would be nothing of worth left for his son, who had married against his wishes, to inherit. Byron moved in to the Abbey when he became of age and furnished a few rooms at great expense. He invited his friends to stay, hired them monks' robes, fake tonsures, ropes of beads and crosses from a theatrical costumier. At dusk they put on their costumes and swished about the Abbey indulging in horseplay with maids and scaring each other by jumping in and out of old stone coffins. Robert Rushton, Byron's page, was almost shot by one of the terrified guests. After dinner Byron passed round the skull of a former monk, set in silver and filled to the brim with burgundy, for each guest to sip from. These juvenile jokes and pranks were later transformed by Byron's enemies to wholesale orgies, but his housekeeper, Nanny Smith, said 'They played some mad pranks; but nothing but what young gentlemen may do, and no harm done.'

Byron met Augusta again when he was fourteen and she eighteen at General Harcourt's house in Portman Square. They were immediately attracted and enchanted by each other. Augusta sent letters to him at Harrow and helped him to defy his mother and undermine her influence during his adolescent rebellion. Mrs Byron was well aware of what was happening but she was unable to break their alliance. In 1807 she proudly sent a copy of Byron's first published work, *Hours of Idleness*, to Lord Carlisle who immediately replied acknowledging the book.

Augusta's favourite friends at Castle Howard were Lady Charlotte Leveson Gower and Lady Gertrude Howard. Their twittering and giggling irritated Hary-o who thought Augusta insipid. She told Little G that to be with her for any length of time was enough to make one die of boredom. She was amused by Augusta's passion for her handsome, hard-drinking, hard-riding cousin Colonel

George Leigh of the 10th Dragoons and had little sympathy when he ignored her. Augusta was timid and shy with strangers but could be lively when she felt at ease and never tired of talking about her clever brother. She looked like the Carlisles; tall, slim, with large eyes set in a long oval face; her lips were full, her teeth were good, her freckled skin was clear but she had a slightly receding chin. She wore her long dark brown hair in curls, which tumbled from her small head over her fashionably sloping shoulders. She had a good ear for music and a pretty voice, made more interesting by the family inability to pronounce R's, a trait which Byron and later his daughter Allegra inherited. In 1807 Augusta married George Leigh and settled down at a stud farm owned by the Prince of Wales at Six Mile Bottom near Newmarket. Within three months Leigh had resumed his bachelor life. Hary-o described him as *'le moins marié que possible* and every body excepting his wife meets him at every place in England save Six Mile Bottom.'

As soon as he came of age, Byron wanted to take his place in the House of Lords and asked Lord Carlisle for advice. He replied explaining the technicalities of taking a seat but did not offer to sponsor him. Quick to take offence, Byron felt insulted and responded by describing him in his new satire, *English Bards and Scotch Reviewers*, as a 'hymnster, *petit-maître*, pamphleteer! so dull in youth, so drivelling in age.' He made the situation worse by adding in the second edition the lines 'No Muse will cheer with renovating smile, the paralytic puling of CARLISLE.' When he learned that the earl suffered from a nervous disorder he was overcome with remorse. 'I thank heaven I did not know it – and would not, could not if I had. I must naturally be the last person to be pointed on defects or maladies.' On 13 March he attended the House of Lords and took the oath with very bad grace. On 19 June he told his mother, 'The world is all before me, and I leave England without regret, and without a wish to revisit anything it contains except yourself and your present residence.' He gaily sailed away to the Mediterranean on 2 July 1809.

In November 1811 the Duchess of Devonshire wrote, 'Lord Byron is come back…very much improved and regretting his satirical poem'.[33] He bought up all the unsold copies of the satire, 'which,' the Duchess remarked, 'is a great sacrifice to have made and ought to conciliate everybody… The misery is that his severest lines were on Lord Carlisle, and therefore Lord Morpeth has not yet and can't bear to meet him.'

The Irish poet Thomas Moore was offended by several references in *English Bards and Scotch Reviewers* and wrote to Byron, challenging him to a duel. By the time the letter was delivered, two years later, Moore had married, mellowed and changed his mind. Samuel Rogers, the banker, poet and man of letters, was curious to meet the new poet and he invited him to dinner at his elegant house in St James's Place, overlooking Green Park. The menu included soup, fish and mutton. Byron refused every course and ended up with a plate of potatoes, which he mashed up with vinegar. A few days later Rogers bumped into John Cam Hobhouse, a friend of Byron's since his days at Cambridge and asked, 'How long will Lord Byron persevere in his present diet?' Hobhouse replied, 'Just as long as you continue to notice it'. Rogers discovered later that after Byron left his house he had gone to a club in St James's Street where he ate a hearty meal.[34]

Within days of arriving in London Byron met a distant relative, Robert Dallas, a former lawyer who made a living from translating books on the French Revolution. He showed him a narrative poem, *Childe Harold's Pilgrimage*, which he had written on his travels. Dallas was convinced it would sell and took it to the publisher John Murray, who passed it to his literary advisor, William Gifford, who gave it his approval.

Lord Holland had also been a victim of *English Bards and Scotch Reviewers*. Byron had attacked him in the mistaken belief that he had sponsored a vicious review of *Hours of Idleness*, which had appeared in the Whig journal *The Edinburgh Review*. Fortunately, Rogers mediated on his behalf and he was forgiven. Byron regularly attended the House of Lords and prepared his maiden speech with the help and advice of Lord Holland. On 27 February 1812 he spoke, taking as his subject the Nottingham Frame-breaking Bill and the rioting 'Luddites'. He urged conciliation and forgiveness. (In fact the disturbances ended when the bill he had opposed was enacted and frame-braking became a capital felony.) He glowed with pleasure as peers scrambled to be introduced and said that the speech had given him the best advertisement he could want for *Childe Harold's Pilgrimage*.[35] That evening he dined at Holland House for the first time and on 10 March *Childe Harold* was published.

Caroline was an avid reader and liked to be in the vanguard of literary fashion, so when Rogers offered her a proof copy she galloped through it and immediately wrote a fan letter. '*Childe Harold*, I have read your Book & I cannot refrain from telling you that I think it – & that all those whom I live with & whose opinions are far more worth having – think it is beautiful – you deserve to be and you shall be happy – do not throw away such Talents as you possess in gloom & regrets for the past & above all live here in your own country which will be proud of you – & which requires your exertions – pray take no trouble to find out who now writes to you – it is one very little worth your notice & with whom you are unacquainted but who from the first has admired your great and promising Genius & who is now so delighted with what you have written that it would be difficult for me to refrain from telling you what I think – as this is the first letter I ever wrote without my name & I could not well put it – if you take the trouble you may very easily find out who it is – but I shall think less of Childe

Harold if he tries – though the greatest wish I have is one day to see him & be acquainted with him.'[36]

Byron decided not to reply but when he discovered that the writer was 'a fine young woman distinguished for eccentric notions' he changed his mind and, according to Dallas, 'he became so enraptured, so intoxicated that his time, his thoughts, were almost entirely devoted to answering.' Since there were few ladies with those qualifications it is more than probable that Byron guessed the identity of the writer.

Caroline already knew a little about Byron from her gossiping cousin at Castle Howard and from her brother William, who had been a fellow member of the Cambridge University Whig Club. *Childe Harold* had spawned extravagant rumours about Byron. He was a man who had been 'educated nobody knows how, having passed his time in a foreign country, nobody knows where, from which he was driven it seems by his crimes.' No one believed him when Byron denied basing Childe Harold's adventures on his own exploits; instead they fell over themselves to be introduced. He told Thomas Medwin, a cousin of Shelley, 'I received everywhere a marked attention, was courted in all societies, made much of by Lady Jersey, had the entrée at Devonshire House, was in favour with Brummell (and that alone was enough to make a man of fashion at that time); in fact, I was a lion – a ball-room bard – a *hot pressed* darling!'

Caroline summoned Rogers to Melbourne House and demanded to meet Byron. Rogers teased her, saying, 'He has a club foot and he bites his nails.' She declared, 'If he is as ugly as Aesop I must see him!'[37]

The first opportunity occurred a few days later at Lady Westmorland's, but Caroline hung back, after watching groups of young ladies 'all throwing their heads at him', simpering and smirking. She would not compete for his attention, declined Lady Westmorland's offer of an introduction, and walked away. From the centre of the ring of coo-ing ladies Byron noticed Caroline leave. He felt piqued.

Byron was just twenty-three, nearly five feet ten inches tall with blue-grey eyes, a handsome nose, pale complexion and white, even teeth. His small head was covered with clusters of dark-brown glossy curls, except over his temples where he had shaved off a few locks to give himself an intellectual high forehead. His voice was low with just a faint memory of his youthful Scottish brogue. He wore newly fashionable long loose trousers, which disguised his twisted ankle and foot. He wore open-necked shirts with soft, flowing collars rather than the starched cravats favoured by his new friend Beau Brummell.[38] His good looks and famous 'underlook' (achieved by lowering his head and raising his beautiful eyes) sent shivers up the spines of respectable matrons and young girls alike. Fifty-year-old Lavinia Spencer demanded to be introduced and afterwards said,

'If I ever read countenances correctly I read either madness or wickedness in Ld Byron. He is not ill-looking but such eyes!'[39]

Byron's good looks were pale beside the tall, dark William Lamb, 'the most handsomest man alive' whom Caroline *'had married for love* and love the most romantic and ardent.' However she was not totally immune to his allure and that night she wrote in her journal that he was, 'Mad – bad – and dangerous to know.'[40]

1. This portrait of Caroline was exhibited in 1812, the year Byron came to fame and first saw Caroline. When, after their introduction by Lady Holland at Holland House, he asked to see her alone she agreed and from March until September they were inseparable.

2. **William Lamb:** Caroline's family was disappointed when she chose to marry William Lamb, later Lord Melbourne and young Queen Victoria's first Prime Minister. Lady Bessborough, Caroline's mother, had hoped she would marry her cousin, Lord Hartington, the eldest son of the Duke and Duchess of Devonshire.

3. **Georgina, Duchess of Devonshire with her daughter:** After nine childless years of marriage, Georgiana credited her pregnancy to the happiness her friend Lady Elizabeth Foster had brought to the household. The baby, named after her mother, was called 'Little G' in the family.

4. Georgiana Spencer married William, 5th Duke of Devonshire, when she was sixteen and he twenty-four. He was reputed to be the dullest and richest man in the kingdom, preferring the company of his dogs to that of people.

5. Lady Elizabeth Foster was separated from her brutish first husband and living in genteel poverty when she was befriended by Georgiana and taken to live at Chatsworth House. She seduced the Duke of Devonshire bearing him two children – Caroline Rosalie Adelaide de St. Jules in 1786 and Augustus Clifford in 1788. After Georgiana's death in 1806 and, against the wishes of his family, she married the Duke in 1809.

6. Caroline's mother, Harriet Spencer (Lady Bessborough) was not considered to be as lovely as her sister Georgiana, called 'the beautiful Duchess', but she was an elegant woman noted for her dancing, self-confidence and wit. She had many admirers, including the Prince of Wales and Richard Brinsley Sheridan.

7. **Federick Ponsonby, 3rd Earl of Bessborough:** Harriet Spencer was reluctant to marry but eventually accepted a proposal from the Duke of Devonshire's first cousin, Frederick Ponsonby, Lord Duncannon, later 3rd Earl of Bessborough. It was a happy marriage even though Harriet had two children by Lord Granville Leveson Gower – Harriette Emma Arundel Stewart, in 1800 and George Stewart in 1804. After the passion of their affair cooled they remained friends until Lady Bessborough's death in 1821.

8. Chatsworth House, in Derbyshire, the seat of the dukes of Devonshire where William, 5th Duke, his wife Georgiana and Lady Elizabeth Foster often stayed. It has been in the family for 450 years and is today the home of the 11th Duke and Duchess.

9. This sketch, taken from one of Caroline's commonplace books, shows her cousin Hary-o dancing while Caroline and William watch. Hary-o later married her aunt's former lover, Lord Granville Leveson Gower.

10. Caroline's sketch shows herself and William with her brother-in-law George Lamb and his wife Caroline St. Jules. To avoid confusion the two Carolines were known as Caro-William and Caro-George.

11. Georgiana, Countess Spencer was Caroline's grandmother. She disliked fuss and frills, kept snakes and at fifty-four taught herself German. She encouraged all her children to have open and enquiring minds but was constantly worried that Caroline's unconventional behaviour would harm her reputation.

4

'This dream, this delirium of two months must pass away'

The Duchess returned to London in January 1812 and settled at 13 Piccadilly Terrace, opposite Green Park and not far from Hyde Park Corner. There, in a 'drawing room of appalling solemnity', she received her friends and acquaintances. Devonshire House remained closed throughout the spring in contrast to Melbourne House, 'the centre of all gaiety,' where 'all the *bon ton* assembled' and practised waltzes and quadrilles in Caroline's enormous drawing room. Every day forty or fifty people, all young, gay and noisy, gathered to dance from twelve in the morning till near dinnertime. Caroline told Lady Morgan, 'I was the happiest and gayest of human beings. I do believe without exception.' William rarely attended these gatherings because, as he said later, 'I despised music when I was young beyond everything and everybody who liked it'.

A few days after Caroline had ignored him at Lady Westmorland's she was at Holland House talking to Lord and Lady Holland when Byron arrived. Lady Holland began to introduce them but he cut in saying, 'That offer was made to you before; may I ask why you rejected it?' Caroline did not answer the question but instead invited him to visit her at Melbourne House. 'I had just come in filthy and hot from riding,' she wrote the following day, 'when they told me that not only was faithful old Mr Rogers in the drawing room but he had brought with him another and different poet. Should I go up to my room and tidy myself before confronting him as I was? No, my curiosity was too great and I rushed in to be introduced to this portent'. In her account to Lady Morgan of the same occasion, she said she was resting on a sofa after her ride, talking to Rogers and Moore when Byron was announced. 'I flew out of the room to wash myself. When I returned Rogers said, "Lord Byron, you are a happy man. Lady Caroline has been sitting here in all her dirt with us, but when you were announced, she flew to beautify herself."' Byron asked for permission to call on Caroline that evening when she was alone. She agreed, and 'from that moment for more than nine months, he almost lived at Melbourne House.'[1] It is impossible to say which is the more accurate account but when Queen Victoria asked William where Caroline first met Byron, he told her it at was at Melbourne House.[2]

William had already met him at Lady Holland's on 8 March, and on 24 March all three attended a dinner at Holland House. Caroline invited Byron to a morning party at Melbourne House the following day. He accepted.

With the gift of hindsight Byron wrote, 'It was a fatal day; and I remember that in going upstairs I stumbled, and remarked to Moore, who accompanied me, that it was a bad omen. I ought to have taken the warning. On entering the room I observed a young lady, more simply dressed than the rest of the assembly sitting alone upon a sofa. I took her for a humble companion, and asked if I was right in my conjecture. "She is a great heiress," said he in a whisper that became lower as he proceeded; "You had better marry her and repair the old place Newstead." '

The young girl was Lady Melbourne's niece, Anne Isabella Milbanke, usually called by her friends and family Annabella. She was the daughter of Sir Ralph and Lady Milbanke of Seaham in County Durham and widely believed to be an heiress. In fact her father had lost a great deal of money fighting election campaigns to remain the Member of Parliament for Durham. This was her third season in London and she had not, as yet, found a husband. She impressed Byron who described her as 'piquant, and what we term pretty… Her features were small and feminine, though not regular. She had the fairest skin imaginable. Her figure was perfect for her height, and there was simplicity, a retired modesty about her, which was very characteristic, and formed a happy contrast to the cold artificial formality, and studied stiffness, which is called fashion.'

Annabella liked to observe, dissect and analyse people and describe them in word pictures which she called 'Characters'. Lady Melbourne made her uneasy, if not a little afraid, with her good looks, quick tongue and common sense. She refused to be introduced to Lady Holland whose reputation was tainted by divorce but she was desperate to be noticed by Byron. She thought William self sufficient with deplorable manners and Caroline silly, but not artificial. Later, her view hardened and she dismissed her kindness, envied her position and sneered at her conversation.

'Gueth how many pairth of thtockingth I have on?' Caroline lisped to her partner, William Harness, as she whirled round with him on the dance floor. Harness, a friend of Byron, was struck dumb at the intimacy of the question. 'Thixth,' she said, lifting her skirts to reveal her pretty little feet and ankles.[3] It was just the kind of behaviour Annabella deplored. She primly remarked, 'She does not do justice to her own understanding. She conceals its power under the childish manner, which she either indulges or affects.' Her disapproval did not prevent her from continuing to accept Caroline's hospitality.

Annabella had an impressive list of suitors but she was having difficulty finding a husband whose virtues matched her own. The earliest and the most persistent of her admirers was Caro-George's half-brother, Augustus Foster, who had entered the Diplomatic Service in 1804 and served in Washington and Stockholm before being appointed Minister to the United States of America by the Prince Regent in February 1811.

When Byron entered a room he used to go to the nearest chair or stand close to a wall or near a table in the hope that the flowing white cloth would disguise his lame leg. Young women dressed in fluttering white gauze dresses coo-ing and calling his name always surrounded him. 'I went to a *morning* party at Lady Caroline Lamb's where my curiosity was much gratified by seeing Lord Byron, the object of universal attention,' Annabella wrote to her mother. 'Lady C has of course seized on him, notwithstanding the reluctance he manifests to be shackled by her...all the women were absurdly courting him and trying to *deserve* the lash of his Satire. I thought *inoffensiveness* was the most secure conduct, as I am not desirous of a place in his lays.'[4]

Three days after they met Byron gave Caroline a hothouse rose and carnation. He bowed deeply and gazed up at her through his magnificent eyelashes, giving her the benefit of his 'underlook' as he handed the flowers to her saying, with a wry smile, 'Your Ladyship, I am told, likes all that is new and rare for a moment.' On Good Friday Caroline wrote in her very best handwriting on small sheets of paper decorated with sky-blue borders and delicately embossed at the top corners with scallop shells, 'The rose Lord Byron gave to Lady Caroline Lamb died despite of every effort to save it: probably from regret at its fallen fortunes. Hume at least who is no great believer in most things, says that many more died of broken hearts than is supposed. When Lady Caroline Lamb returns from Brocket Hall, she will despatch "The Cabinet Maker" to Lord Byron, with the flower she most of all wishes to resemble, as however deficient its beauty and even use, it has a noble and aspiring mind, and having once beheld in its full lustre the bright and unclouded sun, that for one moment condescended to shine upon it, never while it exists could it think any lower object worthy of its worship and admiration. Yet the sunflower was punished for its temerity, but its fate is more to be envied than that of many less proud flowers. It is still permitted to gaze, though at the humblest distance, on him who is superior to every other, and though in this cold and foggy atmosphere it meets no doubt with many disappointments, and though it never could, never will, have reason to boast of any peculiar mark of condescension or attention from the bright star to whom it pays constant homage, yet to behold it sometimes, to see it gazed at, to hear it admired, will repay all. She hopes therefore when brought by the little page it will be graciously received, without any more taunts and cuts about Love of what is new.'[5]

Caroline was not the type of woman that Byron usually admired (big, brown, buxom with dark 'antelope eyes'). She was small, thin with reddish hair and a gamin charm, which she sometimes emphasised by wearing one of her page's uniforms. Hary-o once said that she was 'the strangest person that ever lived, really half-crazy. She was not good looking but very clever and could be very amusing.' Caroline's innocence, affection, enthusiasm and bright intelligent eyes enchanted Byron and she was spellbound by his fantastic stories. He described his childhood in Aberdeen, his days at school and at Cambridge, how he travelled across Spain to Malta, his meeting with Ali Pasha (the fat, bearded despotic ruler of most of what is now modern Greece), how he was shipwrecked and hid in the mountains in fear of bandits. He described the remains of Actium near the bay where Anthony lost the world, the ruins of Nicopolis (a memorial built by Augustus to celebrate his victory), his stay in a Capuchin convent in Athens and how a widow with three beautiful daughters tried to sell him one. His reminiscences astounded her. He had swum the Hellespont, fallen dangerously ill and was nursed back to life by his servant. He had rescued a girl, sewn in a sack, from drowning and had fallen in and out of love with Mrs Constance Spencer Smith, an adventuress, in Malta and been a member of Lady Hester Stanhope's salon in Athens. All his stories were exciting and each had a grain of truth heavily padded with poetic licence. Deeply impressed, Caroline began to defer to his opinions as she had to William's.

His apparent indifference to his sudden success intrigued Caroline and his attention, affection and interest flattered her. She soothed his wounded feelings by her kindness and he enjoyed being fêted by the daughter of an earl. His previous experience with women had been confined to prostitutes, schoolgirls, maids and landladies' daughters. His self-esteem was sore from Lord Carlisle's snub and he felt vulnerable and slightly ridiculous when he discovered that his page, Robert Rushton, had slept with Susan Vaughan, his mistress and a maid at Newstead. Byron blamed Susan and dismissed her together with his former mistress and maidservant, Lucy.

Caroline showed him the thing she treasured most, Augustus, and Byron would sit for hours cradling the heavy child on his lap while they talked softly in the nursery high in the roof of Melbourne House. 'We went about everywhere together,' Caroline told Thomas Medwin, 'and were at last invited always as if we had been married – It was a strange scene – but it was not vanity misled me. I grew to love him better than virtue, religion – all prospects here.' She could not hide her delight in their friendship. Byron was more cautious remarking that 'friendship is a dangerous word for young ladies; it is Love full-fledged, and waiting for a fine day to fly.' In *Glenarvon* she describes a tender moment when he stood 'a breath' away from her and in his 'low vibrant voice' asked her for the rose she had tucked into the bodice of her dress. 'Must I?' she asked. 'You must,' he replied, smiling. 'With some hesitation, she obeyed, yet she looked round in hopes no vigilant eye might observe her. She took it from her bosom, and gave it tremblingly into his hands. A large pier glass reflected the scene to the whole company.'

Byron objected to the waltz; it may have been because his damaged foot prevented him from dancing or that he was jealous of Caroline's partners or just the paradoxical desire of the rake to take a high moral stance, but the light-hearted dancing parties ceased and he made Caroline promise never to waltz again in his presence. She wrote in her Commonplace book,

What! The girl I adore by another embraced?
What! The balm of her breath shall another man taste?
What! Press'd in the whirl by another bold knee?
What! Panting, reclined on another man than me?
Sir, she's yours – you have brushed from the grape its soft blue
From the rosebud you've shed its tremulous dew –
What you've touched you may take, pretty waltzer adieu.[6]

Whether Byron was at Lady Glenbervie's, Lady Cowper's or at Melbourne House, he was dogged by the serious Miss Milbanke who feigned disinterest and told her mother, 'I shall not refuse the acquaintance if it comes my way,' adding scathingly, 'his manners are in a superior degree such as one should attribute to nature's Gentlemen.' She longed to be noticed and he was sufficiently curious to make delicate enquires but went no further when both Caroline and Caro-George assured him that she was to be engaged to the Hon. George Eden. In telling the lie, Caro-George was protecting her brother's interests and Caroline was protecting her own interest in the social lion of the season. Annabella dismissed Augustus Foster's suit, saying that she felt it her duty to concentrate on finding a wealthy man. The Duchess said, 'I hope you don't make yourself unhappy about her; she is really an icicle.'[7]

Pretending to bow to superior male knowledge, Annabella sent Byron a selection of her poems for his comments. He returned them with a note to Caroline, 'I have no desire to be better acquainted with Miss Milbanke, she is too good for a fallen spirit to know or wish to know, & I should like her more if she were less perfect.'[8] He asked pretty Bessy Rawdon (niece of the Earl of Moira), 'Have you seen Miss Milbanke lately? I wish when next you see her you would be so kind as to give her a hint not to send me any more of her foolish little rhymes.'

Bessy, when she was an old lady, described him as being Satan incarnate with talent, beauty, genius, wickedness, hypocrisy and vice, but when he read his poetry the beauty of the words and his voice made his listeners forget his 'cloven foot... All the women adored him – I adored him and partly on that account, and partly because his manners were affected, the men hated him.' Hary-o was unimpressed and told Hartington, 'I have made acquaintance with him. He is agreeable, but I felt no wish for any further intimacy'.[9] The Duchess of Devonshire thought he had 'a pale, sickly but handsome countenance, a bad figure and amusing conversation, in short, he is really the only topic almost of every conversation – the men jealous of him, the women of each other. I have my accounts from Caroline (George), Caroline-William and Lady Bessborough – all agree in their accounts.'[10] Some women went to extraordinary lengths to meet him. Rogers was amused to receive an invitation inviting him to dinner with the postscript, 'Pray could you not contrive to bring Lord Byron with you?'[11] Byron had invitations from Lady Heathcote, Lady Jersey, Lord Grey, Lady Oxford and other leaders of London society. He was also taken up by members of the literary establishment – Miss Berry, Samuel Rogers and the poets Thomas Moore and Thomas Campbell. He attended a ball at the Argyle Rooms and he was welcomed at Holland House, Melbourne House and even Spencer House. Carriages delivering invitations to his rooms jammed the traffic in St James's. On 10 May the Duchess wrote to Augustus, 'He continues to be the greatest attraction at all parties and suppers. The ladies, I hear, spoil him and the gentlemen are jealous of him. He is going back to Naxos, and then the husbands may sleep in peace. I should not be surprised if Caroline William were to go with him, she is so wild and imprudent.'[12]

Caroline defied convention by travelling with him, unchaperoned, to Holland House. During one of these journeys, in his swaying carriage, Byron took her hand and pressed it to his heart so she could feel it beat and asked her to kiss him on the mouth. She hesitated at first but then 'it was more than I could prevent from that moment – you drew me to you like a magnet & I could not indeed I could not have kept away... Never while life beats in this heart shall I forget you or that moment when first you said you lov'd me – when my heart did not meet yours but flew before it – and both, intended to remain innocent of greater wrong.'[13]

It was too passionate, too sudden and Caroline drove it along too fast. At first he was amused and flattered and he compared her overwhelming love to an erupting volcano which poured lava through her veins. 'My poor Caro,' he wrote, 'you know I have always thought you the cleverest most agreeable, absurd, amiable, perplexing, dangerous, fascinating little being that lives now or ought to have lived 2000 years ago.'[14] The Duchess told Augustus, 'Your little friend, Caro-

William, as usual is doing all sorts of imprudent things for him. He admires her very much.'[15]

Sometimes, after visiting Caroline on the first floor, Byron would descend the stairs, cross the hallway, knock on Lady Melbourne's door and spend some time with her. He enjoyed her conversation, approved of her youthful, witty, pragmatic outlook on life and respected her opinions. 'She is doubtless in talent a superior – a *supreme* woman – & her heart I know to be of the kindest – in the best sense of the word – Her defects I never could perceive – as her society makes me forget them & everything else for the time. I do love that woman (*filial*) or (*fraternally*) better than any being on earth'. After her death he wrote, 'Her mind and heart were as fresh as if only sixteen summers had flown over.'

His affection and respect for her mother-in-law irritated Caroline. She told Byron, 'If I feel jealous of her I will remember her age & respect her – & if she speaks horribly I will recollect my faults & not answer – she has every fine quality & much good – but if I have too much of it, I think she is too wholly without sentiment & romance – she also wants that softness which my mother & *yourself* have, that *vielle court* manner which is to me prettier and more conciliatory than any other... But I love Lady M & think she has the *law* on her side and thereafter I will be very submissive & kind – for your sake also – for she is only too dear to you.'[16]

Byron, Caroline and William all had violent tempers. Byron inherited his from his mother, who used to throw cups, saucers and even fire irons at his charming, feckless father. When he was a small child Byron ripped his frock from top to bottom in a rage, then stood in sullen silence waiting for retribution. On another occasion he bit a large piece of china out of a saucer. He told Lady Blessington, the writer and socialite, that his rages 'were so disproportionate to the cause as to surprise me when they were over, and this still continues. I cannot coolly view anything that excites my feeling, and once the lurking devil in me is roused, I lose all command of myself.'[17] The animal magnetism that had drawn Caroline and Byron towards each other was not enough to keep the peace, as they both jostled for the limelight. Lady Morgan observed that the only subject which really interested and animated Caroline was herself and Byron's favourite topic was himself so they did not have to be together long before 'he would grow moody and she fretful'. When Lord Holland passed the couple at a reception he waved an antique censer towards Caroline, saying jokingly, 'You see, I bear you incense.' She replied, 'Offer it to Lord Byron, he is accustomed to it.'

Byron became pathologically envious of every man Caroline had ever shown any interest in and tried to force her say that she loved him better than William and that she hated Sir Godfrey Webster. She told Lady Melbourne that when she refused 'he went into such a furious passion & swore at me, & said, "Tell me if it is so," – & I said, "It is no use telling you what is false – It is true – but Sir Godfrey never made love to me – from the first he liked another – he never even shook hands with me but as an acquaintance." "But did you like him," he said & I answered "Yes!" and then he did abuse me & scorn me & mock me so and called me such horrid names…' Overcome with emotion, she threw herself on the floor where she was found by Lady Melbourne. White with fury and frustration, Byron left saying, 'By God you shall pay for this for I will wring that little obstinate heart.' Caroline vowed to Lady Melbourne 'never to go away with him – never come to say I preferred him to William.'[18]

Still shaking with rage Byron joined two school friends, 'Long' Baillie and Madocks, at a public hanging. He wrote to Thomas Moore that 'after sitting up all night I saw Bellingham launched into eternity, and at three the same day I saw Lady C—L— launched into the country.' John Bellingham, a shipbroker, had lost a great deal of money seven years earlier and had been unjustly imprisoned in Russia. He believed that Lord Granville, then Ambassador Extraordinary in St Petersburg, should have helped him. On 11 May he had armed himself and left his home St Neots, laid in wait for Lord Granville in the lobby of the House of Commons and had then shot Spencer Perceval, the Chancellor of the Exchequer, by mistake.[19]

When he was calmer, Byron wrote to Caroline, 'Moore is in great distress about us & indeed people talk as if there were no other pair of absurdities in London. It is hard to bear all this without cause, but worse to give cause for it. Our folly has had the effect of a fault. I conformed & could conform, if you would lend your aid, but I can't bear to see you look unhappy, & am always on the watch to observe if you are trying to make me so. We must make an effort, this dream, this delirium of two months must pass away, we in fact do not know one another, a month's absence would make us rational, you do not think so, I know it. We have both had 1000 previous fancies of the same kind & shall get the better of this & be ashamed of it… It is better that I should leave town than you, & will make a tour or go to Cambridge or Edinburgh. Now don't abuse me, or think me altered, it is because I am not, cannot alter, that I shall do this, and cease to make fools talk, friends grieve, and the wise pity.'[20]

Lady Bessborough was known for her soft heart and she often took in orphans and either kept them herself or found them homes. One such child was a hermaphrodite. 'She was consulted as to its name,' Caroline told Byron, 'It is not yet christened – it is of both sexes and a remarkably fine interesting child about six months old perfect in every respect. Shall it pass for a male or female – which be the safest? If you can throw any light upon the subject do but for your life do not name it to anyone – because in the first place it will seem as if I wrote to you which you know I *never* do & in the next it will appear a mighty strange sort of topic of discussion from me to you – so be discreet. Yesterday I received a letter from Lady M saying these words 'Caroline is there no end to your strange adventures will nothing cure you – I hear but do not believe that you have a female page – if so do not hope to make me laugh. You always think you can make people laugh at your follies but these are *crimes*.'[21]

Caroline did not want to be sensible. Samuel Rogers wrote, 'She absolutely besieged him.' In an early letter to Byron which Caroline showed Rogers she had 'assured him that if he was in want of money, all her jewels were at his service. They frequently had quarrels, and more than once on coming home I have found Lady Caroline walking in the garden and waiting for me to beg that I would reconcile them... But such was the insanity of her passion for Byron that sometimes when not invited to a party where he was to be she would wait for him in the street, till it was over! One night after a great party at Devonshire House to which Lady Caroline had not been invited, I saw her, yes, saw her, talking to Byron with half of her body thrust into the carriage into which he had just entered... In spite of all this absurdity, my firm belief is that there was nothing criminal between them.'[22]

William ignored Caroline's antics; the course of her new passion seemed to be very similar to her earlier one with Sir Godfrey Webster. He was tired of Byron's posturing and laughed at the extravagant claims Caroline made on his behalf. He knew she was not capable of complete abandon and that she still loved him. He understood her petulant and demanding nature and was willing to wait until the violent attachment had burnt itself out. He was well aware that a considerable part of Caroline's charm in Byron's eyes was her high position in society and that he 'liked being spoken of as a favoured intimate at Melbourne House.' He also knew, Byron had told Lady Melbourne, that he wanted the affair over so that he could marry an heiress, restore Newstead and take a more active part in the House of Lords.[23]

William's relaxed attitude infuriated Caroline. She told Lady Morgan that 'his indolence rendered him insensible to everything.' William once remarked, 'My mother always told me I was very selfish, man and boy, and I believe she was right, I always find some excuse for not doing what I am anxious to avoid'.[24]

Reports of Caroline's indiscretions reached Holywell. 'How is dear Caroline?' Lady Spencer asked Lady Bessborough. 'She fidgets me sadly as I daresay she does you, but I hope her good sense & excellent heart will in time find out that eccentricity is not a favourite qualification. Many have neither taste or sense enough to understand it, & most of those who have, despise it or dislike it.'[25] Although there had been a great deal of talk, Caroline had not yet done anything to have her barred from polite society. She told Georgiana Morpeth, 'William is quite delightful & I am as happy as the word can express. Lord and Lady

Melbourne are really kinder & more attentive to me than anything you can imagine.'[26] On 2 June the Duchess wrote, 'Caroline W Lamb is quietly, thank heaven! at Brocket with William and all of them.'[27]

On 4 June Caroline insisted on leaving Lady Spencer and returning to London. 'I could urge but a little against it as she assured me that Ld & Ldy Melbourne & her husband wished it,' Lady Spencer told Lady Bessborough, 'in short there is no arguing when such matters of fact are asserted. She was very amiable & Augustus extremely good, but he has a little effort now & then in drawing his breath, which I do not like. Pray observe it. One is afraid of saying anything to her (dear child) lest she would be doctoring or dieting him.'[28]

On 10 June Lady Spencer wanted to know how long Caroline intended to stay in town. She added, 'I hope she keeps out of scrapes. Where is William, it is long since I have heard of him.' She asked Lady Bessborough on 19 June, 'How is dear Caroline going on – she has so accustomed herself to represent things her own way that I never can depend upon what she says of the opinions of those with whom she lives.'[29]

Byron's progress through the fashionable drawing rooms continued. He met the Prince Regent and Sir Walter Scott, joined house parties held at Middleton, the Earl of Jersey's country house, and at Bowood, the Marquis of Lansdowne's country seat. At Middleton he refused to come down to dinner and ate biscuits and drank soda water in his room until someone remarked it was 'effeminate', then he dined with the others and drank until he 'sweated the claret'. He talked about his rise in society too much for good taste. 'He is a singular man,' Miss Berry commented, 'but I very much fear that his head begins to be turned by all the adoration of the world, especially the women.'[30] In a bitter moment Caroline told William that Byron was 'very ignorant before she and her friends had taken him up, and had always lived in the worst society; that he had read nothing but a few classical books'.[31]

Byron did his best to keep away from Caroline, although they were frequently invited to the same events. One evening he sat next to Mrs Amelia Opie, the popular writer, who was completely bowled over by his attention. She described his voice to Benjamin Haydon, the painter, as 'the most exquisite of any mortal's she had ever heard; it was so sweet that when he spoke it startled her as if the Devil was speaking.' She said, 'It gave one the idea, as if it was such a voice as had deceived Eve.' They sat watching a man fiddling with what appeared to be a glass flute. As he prepared to begin Byron asked, 'What is that fellow going to do?' Mrs Opie explained he intended to play it. Byron replied with a smile, 'Does he mean to let us *see* the notes as well as *hear* them?'[32] Caroline, who had been trying to catch his eye by playing the fool, sat on the edge of the sofa between them then wriggled backwards until she had edged and elbowed Mrs Opie out. On another occasion, a reception at Spencer House, Caroline saw Byron lean over another woman and in her agitation she bit clean through the rim of her wineglass.

Caroline suspected Byron's interest was flagging. She called his servant, William Fletcher, to Melbourne House and told him, 'I want you to take the little foreign page I shall send – in to see Lord Byron. Do not tell him beforehand but when he comes with flowers – shew him in.'[33] No doubt the 'little foreign page' was she. Caroline had begun to stalk Byron. He complained to Lady Melbourne that she watched him and had invaded his rooms 'terrier like' heavily disguised as 'a carman'. On 4 June Byron retreated to Newstead with his cousin, George Byron and John Cam Hobhouse. On 10 June a letter arrived delivered by a page whom Hobhouse suspected of being Caroline in disguise. By the end of June the affair had reached its crisis. The grand romance that Caroline demanded had become one-sided, killed by unreasonable demands, daily love letters, private assignations and public displays of jealousy. She had fallen in love with Byron in his character of Childe Harold the tragic hero and catch of the season, but her love was now turning into an obsession. All he wanted was peace, 'for I hate *scenes* and am of an indolent disposition.' He decided he had two options, either to extricate himself from Caroline's coils or elope with her.

Byron blamed the situation partly on Lady Bessborough for piquing his vanity by telling him that she was sure Caroline did not love him but was merely leading him on. Now all Lady Bessborough wanted was for the affair to end and she appealed to Hobhouse for help. He agreed, telling her that Caroline was the mischief-maker but that he would persuade Byron to leave London if she could keep Caroline under control. They were embarrassed when Caroline walked in on them during one of their plotting meetings and casually remarked that they looked guilty. Hobhouse exclaimed, 'Here's a pass for the world to come to!'[34]

'I wrote her a serious letter a few days ago,' Lady Spencer told Lady Bessborough, 'but probably she will not tell you of it. She is a dear child but trifles sadly with her own happiness.'[35] The family distrusted Caroline and called a conference at which it was agreed that as she was unwilling to break off the association she must accompany her parents on a prolonged holiday at the family estate in Ireland. Lady Melbourne did not disguise her relief. Caroline was making William look ridiculous and she was afraid that Byron did not have the courage to finish the affair.

'Have you heard from Caroline – I have not,' Lady Bessborough wrote anxiously to Lady Melbourne. 'I find she is writing to him... It is dreadful but I hope he is determined enough to make it useless. I have not told Caroline he is in town. Do you know how long he stops?'[36] In fact Byron had obligingly arranged to visit Harrow with Hobhouse on 28 July. That morning Caroline told Lady Melbourne, 'I have consented to go to Ireland – What more? – I think this unkindness but, after all, I deserve it'.[37] She was determined to see Byron as she knew it was her last chance to goad him into an elopement and just before noon, a person dressed as a cabman was seen hammering at the side door of Dollman's Hat Shop in St James's where Byron had his lodgings. The disguise had not even deceived the servants. It was clearly Caroline, wearing a page's uniform, under the shapeless coat. Scenting a scandal a small crowd gathered outside and when Hobhouse arrived he found Byron running distractedly between his bedroom, where Caroline was having hysterics, and the sitting room where Mr Dollman was urging him to throw her out. 'This ensured,' Hobhouse wrote in his journal, 'that nothing could possibly have happened – besides which both parties were too much agitated to admit a doubt of their conduct at that time'.

After a while Hobhouse coaxed Caroline to change into a dress, bonnet and shoes that he had borrowed from one of the maids and both men tried to persuade her to go home. She refused. Byron said, 'Then we must go off together, there is no alternative'. Hobhouse replied sharply, 'Indeed there is, you shall not go off this time.' 'There will be blood spilt,' Caroline threatened as she struggled with Byron to reach a court sword, which was lying along the back of a sofa. 'There will be if you do not go away,' Hobhouse replied. 'It shall be mine, then,' she exclaimed, but she was unable to escape from Byron's grip.

A servant called to Hobhouse to come down and calm Mr Dollman. Before leaving the room he took the precaution of ordering Fletcher to stay with the pair 'to prevent the possibility of anything criminal happening or anything which might be construed into a possibility of the thing to be dreaded taking place.' Caroline was quieter when he returned and agreed to leave but only if she could see Byron once more. By now the men were so anxious to be rid of her they would have agreed to almost anything. They knew that if a scandal was to be avoided, they must smuggle her out of Byron's rooms and back to Melbourne House without being recognised. Caroline had brought her own clothes in a small basket and Hobhouse suggested that she change into them at his lodgings across the park in Westminster. She would only agree if Byron stayed with her while she changed. Hobhouse was shocked and told her, 'Such a conduct would not be consistent with what I owe to both of you, to your mother and to myself.' She continued to argue until she was overruled by Byron.

Hobhouse put them in a cab, raced across St James's Park to open up his rooms and then waited until the cab appeared. He stopped it, ordered Byron out, got in himself and completed the journey with Caroline. He left her in his chambers, told her to lock the door and joined Byron in the street. They walked to Bailley's Coffee House and waited.

Caroline was dressed and argumentative when Hobhouse came back alone. She refused to return either to Melbourne House or Cavendish Square but after some persuasion agreed to go to a friend. A message arrived from Byron asking to see her and Caroline made Hobhouse promise not to interfere and suggested Highgate or Barnet as possible meeting places. Hobhouse knew that 'all apparent opposition would only make her as extravagant as before, & cause a scene, I consented to speak to him on the subject. God knows that from the very beginning I have done my best to keep my friend out of the scrape – My first wish was that he should give this lady, who by the common consent of all London has made a dead set at him, no power over him by consenting to any serious folly. My next desire was to prevent a public disclosure and an elopement. This latter event would, as B assured me and assures me, have certainly taken place but for the part I played in the transactions of yesterday.'

When the cab reached 5 Grosvenor Gate, the home of her friend Mrs Conyers, Caroline was agitated and tearful. She asked Hobhouse to arrange for her carriage, which she had left at Moore's Livery Stables, to pick her up and return her to Whitehall and to call on her the following day.[38]

Lady Spencer wrote to her daughter, 'Your letters, my dearest Harriet, convey a state of anxiety about dear Caroline without detail enough to say what occasions it. The one of this morning says you have had a delightful letter from Caroline & *hope all will be well.* Her uncertainty & instability of mind is indeed most melancholy but she loves her husband & as yet, he loves her. Is there any possibility of making her see what she risques in breaking such a bond?'[39] The uncertainty of the situation took its toll on Lady Bessborough's delicate health and when, at Holland House, she heard a rumour that Caroline had eloped, she collapsed.

On 6 August Caroline wrote to Lady Melbourne as though she had not a care in the world: 'We thank you very much for your entertaining letter – & Lrd M for his venison which was excellent – I think you will find our bills much less high this time but it is impossible to manage quite as well as we wish as many think they have the right to come… Dearest Lady Melbourne I shall never forget your kindness to me – love you most truly whatever you may think – Wm is very kind to me – I have made up my mind to go to Ireland – but this is gloomy weather for a journey.'[40]

Lady Bessborough was recuperating at Roehampton when Lady Melbourne told her that Caroline had invited Byron to Brocket. 'Your note put me quite in despair. From Caroline's letter and my mother's account of her I should have thought all was going smoothly. She writes cheerful letters full of plans for

Ireland & consulting me about her dress there – a long letter is full of nothing but her fondness for William and the anxiety that he would catch cold by being out in the damp.'[41]

Byron remained in London and Caroline's emotions fluctuated from wanting to become a nun to running off with him. Five times in one day she told her mother that she would leave London and live at Brocket but did nothing. 'It is useless to endeavour to judge of what changes every minute Caroline has,' Lady Bessborough told Lady Melbourne. She had toyed with the idea of telling Caroline that Byron 'flirts with *anyone*,' but thought better of it in case it fuelled another scandal.[42] Caroline haunted the places Byron frequented. John Murray knew that on at least one occasion she had slipped through his front door, crossed the black and white tiled hall and hidden in the little glass-domed waiting room. When she heard Byron's distinctive limping, dragging step, she ran out and waylayed him at the foot of the stairs. She told her mother that she had met him 'by accident' in the street. Byron was infuriated. She wrote to him, 'I am without excuse – I trust myself to your compassion. If you tell anyone that I attempted to see you I am lost – irretrievably lost. If not, be assured I will neither write nor send nor see you. I really leave London immediately at my own request. I merely called in hopes of seeing you one instant just to ask you to forgive my having broken all my promises. Be happy, but as I depend solely on your generosity, do not embitter the feelings of all my friends by telling them what a lost, worthless being they have lavished all their kindness upon. Oh, Lord Byron, think how inexcusable it must appear to others when it does so to you and pray excuse what I have done – yours more alarmed more wretched than you can think, Caroline.'[43]

Lady Bessborough did not dare tell Caroline what Hobhouse had told her, that Byron 'did not wish to see her & wished she was gone to Ireland. That when she was present she had such a power over him he could only do what she pleased, that he never was so much in love with anyone but she teased him to death & made him wretched and that a few weeks absence would cure him – but that *if she got at him again* she would force him to go away with her, and that he should blow his brains out a week after. Mr H said he knew Ld Byron had advised her not to come & preferred either to meet her at Brocket or on the road, that she had written a furious letter in answer – but can William really let her come? When I speak to him he only tells it her & she does not mind and talks him over & afterwards exalts over me telling me I was in hopes of keeping him away from her but she knows him better than I do. What can be done, my dearest Ly M? As I had not heard from her I wrote today as if I thought the Irish plan quite settled & added that I would go down to Brocket some day soon to consult with her & William. I dread getting a letter or message to tell me she is coming to *see me.*

Dear Lady M is there some way to stop her – if we could but get him out of town. Cannot you see him? If you see Lord Byron you had better not seem to know anything from me for Mr H was very anxious he should not know I had seen him.'[44] Byron was willing to refuse to see Caroline if he could rely on Lady Bessborough to deal with the stormy consequences. He told Lady Melbourne, 'It was with the greatest reluctance & something of *disgust* that I ever consented, with which I beg she may be acquainted.'[45]

Caroline inundated her mother-in-law with letters full of threats, recriminations, penitence, demands and vows that she would be good. 'We will not talk of consequences, I have weighed them – If reduced to despair I can bear up against anything & tho' you think so, I am not ungrateful. Perhaps for Wm's sake, for all of you, it were best to be rid of me – yet do as you chuse – I do sincerely promise you that I will go to Brocket & try for two months to live as I ought – If I cannot make myself a comfort to Wm & all of you – I will then leave you all – this country forever – but if possible I wish to remain – Oh do not drive me to act in a manner I must repent, do not – yet you all will – for I will see Lord Byron these two days, that I am resolved and, if refused, I have told you I will keep my intention – for your goodness to me – whatever becomes of me I shall be grateful, most grateful & as to Wm all I can say is, I am no longer fit to appear before him, to live under his protection – and this reconciles me in part to what you will call atrocious conduct – As to Lord Byron, he is innocent of every crime but love for one who did not deserve it and has behaved throughout in a manner does him honour.'[46]

To avoid Caroline, Byron refused invitations to the theatre, parties and dinners, asking Lady Melbourne to make his excuses. Caroline wrote daily, sometimes hourly and when it became clear she would not leave without seeing him he wearily agreed. 'I find two epistles – in the last the old story of the interview, to which if she still harps upon it I have no objection.'

Lady Melbourne could not understand why Byron remained in London until he told her that he was going to auction Newstead Abbey. 'The moment I can arrange this & I will not wait in hopes for further or better proposals, I shall leave town.' He added, 'You can have the goodness to state the real fact to Ly B & C. I do assure you I have Ldy B's comfort more at heart than my own convenience.'[47] When Caroline heard of the sale she asked him 'Why not have kept it & taken Biondetta [his pet name for her] there & have lived & died happy. Yet you give us both up. No ties can bind, but Newstead A bears your unkindness in sullen silence. I will kneel & be torn from your feet before I will give you up.'[48] On 9 August, following an Italian custom, she sent Byron a sprig of her pubic hair wrapped in a piece of paper marked *'ricordati di Biondetta'*.[49]

'What is to be done? If William will not stop her who can?' Lady Bessborough asked Lady Melbourne, desperately. 'Caroline must do, as she likes – as if it were easy to mother her – They drive me distraught… I will try to persuade her to go to Brocket tonight. I want you to write to WL. I have written – It does no good because he always tells it to her and she always undoes what I have done. If you beg him not to tell her he will be more afraid of making a quarrel between you and her than he is between us. Tell him how much harm it does *him* in the world as well as her to leave him. Also tell him, pray, she believes he is afraid of her and does not care what she does. Surely this would have effect and I would trust to your kindness not to press too hard anybody.'[50]

Lady Bessborough was afraid that the Melbournes were running out of patience and might ask for a separation so, at a little before eleven o'clock on Wednesday, August 12, she arrived at Whitehall. She intended to persuade Caroline to go to Roehampton with her and to stay there until William could join them on Friday. She hoped they could all leave for Ireland shortly afterwards. She met Caroline coming down the stairs in a bad mood and before she could say a word Lord Melbourne appeared. He was a short, fat, disagreeable man, who thoroughly disapproved of Caroline and immediately reproached her for the trouble she was causing.[51] Her answer was so rude and disrespectful that Lady Bessborough was frightened and ran off to find Lady Melbourne. By the time she returned Caroline was gone, leaving Lord Melbourne 'pale as death' screaming at a porter to stop her. At first the two women hoped she would come back after the first explosion of anger had died down, but as the hours passed it was clear this would not happen. Lord Melbourne told them that when Caroline boasted to him that Byron wanted to elope with her he had told her that he did not believe it and in any case she could go and be damned.

Lady Bessborough drove up and down Parliament Street in the hope of seeing Caroline, then hurried to Byron's rooms where she found him at home alone and as disconcerted as she was. In the late afternoon he sent a note, 'I trust that Ly C has by this time reappeared or that her mother is better acquainted than I am. God knows where she is. If this be the case I hope you will favour me with one line… As I am one of the principal performers in this unfortunate drama I should be glad to know what my part requires next? Seriously, I am extremely uneasy on account of Ly C and others.' At six o'clock he wrote, 'Not a word *of* or *from* her. What is the cause of all this. I mean the *immediate* circumstances, which has led to it. – I thought everything was nice & quiet in the morning till the apparition of Ly B. If I hear from her Ldy B shall be informed… I am apprehensive for her personal safety, for her state of mind – here I sit alone, – however I might *appear* to you, in the most painful suspense.'[52]

After fruitlessly driving round London for most of the day, Lady Bessborough dined with the Duke at Devonshire House. He had seen Caroline that morning and she hoped he might have some clue as to where she had gone. Soon after Lady Bessborough arrived, the driver of the coach Caroline had hired came with a bundle of letters. They confirmed Lord Melbourne's version of the events – that he had threatened to 'tell Wm everything &, in the most insulting manner, assured me Lord Byron would not take me if I wished in that he despised me. As to that I am as sure of Byron as I am of anything on earth – but I will not for worlds involve him in my ruin.' Caroline ended with the usual jumble of threats and urged Lady Melbourne to 'comfort my mother and take care of my boy.' Her letter to Byron was an extravagant farewell.

Byron followed the coachman and threatened, browbeat and bribed him to drive him to Caroline. She had taken refuge in the home of a surgeon who had taken her in, believing she had been abandoned. Byron, pretending to be her brother, forced her into the coach and returned her to Cavendish Square where Caroline was persuaded, under protest, to return to Melbourne House. Lady Bessborough was relieved and wrote to Lord Granville, 'William most kindly promise'd to receive and forgive her. The Melbournes too, were very good, and she seems much touch'd by their reception. But how long will it last? Oh, G,' she cried to Granville, 'what will come of it? I dread to think, and am afraid I never shall get her to go with me to Ireland. I dread, to it being known, for it was noon day, and she ran all up Pall Mall, conceal'd herself in a chemist's shop till she thought pursuit was over, sold a ring by which she got money to pay the hackney coach, ordered the man to drive thro' the first turnpike off the stones; he took her to Kensington (think of the bad look to the laquais employed at Holland House). There she borrowed 20 Guineas on a fine opal ring you have seen her wear, and her plan was going to Portsmouth and embarking in the first Vessel that sail'd from there, where-ever it might happen to be bound for. What an escape! She had taken a place in a stage, G. Dear G, all this will end ill; if it does not to her, it will be to me. I do feel very unwell, and have for the last hour spit up so much blood that I think some little vessel must have broken. Why is it not a large one? I do no good to any one, and am grown rather a burthen than pleasure to all those I love most.'[53]

The following morning Lady Bessborough said that if she could have persuaded Caroline to leave for Ireland she would have left the next day, 14 August, the day they had originally planned to go. However Caroline had a trump card. She announced that she was pregnant. William loved children, and was delighted and in his joy he almost allowed himself to believe that the journey to Ireland would make her miscarry. 'I know not what to do!' Lady Bessborough exclaimed, 'I never saw so distressing a creature, and yet when she thought me in danger almost distracted with grief and remorse, swearing one moment that she will destroy herself if I am ill the next that if Lrd Byr offers to stir out of London she will instantly fly – if not *with* him from everyone else.'[54]

That Friday morning Caroline called at Cavendish Square twice. Lady Bessborough told Lady Melbourne, 'I cannot tell you how very unwell or how very unhappy I feel… Caroline does not know or, I am afraid does not care how much she makes me suffer – I love her too much and unfortunately she knows it. What makes me think she has a sort of perverse pleasure in playing on my feelings is what passed today.' During her first visit Caroline had promised her mother that she would leave London and go to Brocket. She returned in the afternoon and 'took the final opportunity of telling me she was intending to go to Lord By's, that she came to prepare me for it as she had always promised & as before that she had told you & would write to Wm… I wish to make light of it to her & not appear to mind if not she sees the effect on me – I cannot have it – She really frightened me because I thought her in earnest – I did not like to tell her how unwell I felt but after some talking she ended as she did to you – by promises of doing all we wish. I begin to think as Wm does that *neither* intend going but both delight in the fear & interest they create… He is fair neither to us nor her. If he is not wishing it why does he stay?'[55]

A few hours later, the servants found Lady Bessborough collapsed on the floor of her carriage suffering from what Caroline called a broken blood vessel but was probably a slight stroke. Mrs Peterson, her confidential maid for almost thirty years, wrote immediately to Lady Melbourne. 'Thank God she by degrees got better – but indeed if she is to undergo many more such very miserable days as the few last have been it will quite kill her. I have written to Lady Caroline but fear she is lost to all feeling even for such a mother'.[56]

Mrs Peterson had known Caroline since she was a baby and was not afraid to tell her what she thought. 'Cruel & unnatural as you have behaved you surely do not wish to be the Death of your Mother. I am sorry to say you last night nearly succeeded in doing so. She had fallen in a Fit at the bottom of her Carriage & with the utmost difficulty her footmen got her out. Oh, Lady Caroline could you have seen her at that moment you surely would have been convinced how wickedly you are going on. She was perfectly senseless & her poor mouth Drawn on one side & cold as Marble we was all distracted even her footmen cryed out *shame* on you for alas you have exposed yourself to all London you are the talk of every Groom and Footman about Town. A few months ago it was Sir Godfrey & now another has turned your Head & made you forget what a Husband you have what an angel Child besides making you torture all your kind relations & friends in the most cruel manner. Your poor Father too was heart broken at seeing the wretched state you had reduced your Mother to we got Mr Walker quick as possible & thank God she is better – Lord Bessbro' would not let me send for you he said the sight of you would make her worse. You have for many months taken every means in your Power to make your Mother miserable & you have perfectly succeeded but do not quite kill her – you will one day or another fatally *feel* the wickedness of your present conduct. Oh Lady Caroline Pray to God for the strength of mind & resolution to behave as you ought for this is Dreadful.' She added, 'I feel by sending you this I offend you for ever but I cannot help it.'[57]

Despite everything, Caroline continued her campaign to see Byron. She wrote carefully to her parents including the same reasons in both letters but skilfully tailored to suit the personality and inclination of the recipients.

'My own dearest, kindest Mama – be assured of one thing – that I will go with you whatever happens. I have seen Crofts [the accoucheur] who objects, but that is nothing. Your will, your happiness, is everything; but I have only one request, I would not urge it if it could hurt you. Just delay for 5 days your journey from Roehampton. You do not know the agitations I have gone through nor what I have suffer'd. I will not speak of thinking I had lost you. Had it been so, I should not have recovered; as it is, my senses are really not straight again. I want a few days to compose me, to get right. Let me go with you to Roehampton, but let us remain there a little while before we set out. I ask this only because I know and feel that we all want a little repose and that afterwards a journey is very well. And now to shew you that I have no design in this, I do promise you, upon my honour and soul, that at all events, whether you grant it or not, I will not see Lord Byron. I know Mrs Peterson and others may think it is an excuse of mine saying I am with child, but at such a time would I, could I have the heart to do it? I know also, that I have deserved to be suspected; but let me go at all events, only just give me time to recover. I never was so unwell as last night; you know I said nothing of it, but if I were not so, I wish for a few days quiet. Will you, who are so good, so kind, so generous, you who, though I nearly killed you, I love better than anything on earth, for whose sake I will have given up what is too dear to me – will you, my M, ask for this delay, which however, if you have set your mind otherwise I will not urge. As to letting you go without me, could I? Would you consent? Ah, let us not part now! Trust in me at least at this moment; all deceptions are over now; you see my whole heart if you please. Do with me as you will, and only if you think such request reasonable grant it.'[58]

In the letter to her father she acknowledged that she was the cause of her mother's illness and asked for forgiveness. She offered to go to Roehampton where he could keep his eye on her and added, 'Wm is very anxious indeed that I should make this short delay for ten days for a particular reason, and I am certain my nerves are so shaken, and I have been ill these 3 days that to hurry off will make me quite so. I should never have thought of considering myself if Crofts and Sir H H [Henry Halford, the Prince Regent's physician] had not positively said that it was madness to take Mama on a journey of that sort, far from medical help, at such a time. They said delay it a month; I only ask ten days; and that my motive may not be suspected. Lock me up if you chuse during that time, but do not refuse this to your own child your only daughter, who with all her faults loves you so dearly.'[59]

She pleaded with Lady Melbourne to use her influence with Dr Farquhar to delay their departure. 'Living altogether comfortably & quietly, either at Roehampton or any where she pleases, is really far better for her than taking a long journey – seasickness & every other inconvenience. I know she has set her mind on it – but you can, you must persuade her not. We are all most anxious and I far the most as I feel I am the cause.'[60] On 15 August Lady Bessborough was slightly better. She had slept well and Sir Walter Farquhar prescribed cupping. Hary-o believed that Caroline deliberately kept 'every thing belonging to her in a state of agitation and anxiety from the extreme and alarming oddity of her character and conduct' and she hoped she would acknowledge her part in her mother's illness.

Byron was confused, railing against Caroline and her emotional tyranny but jumping to her defence when she was criticised. 'No one,' he told Lady Melbourne, 'has the right to interfere with *her* but yourself and Mr L[amb] & if she is to be persecuted for my faults – to be reproached with the consequence of misplaced affection but too well returned – by any but *you and yours* (who have acted so differently with a kindness which I did not believe to exist in human nature) I cannot and will not bear it, without at least taking my own just share of the consequence... Dear Ly M comfort & be kind to her, you *have been*, she owns it with the greatest gratitude. In everything of this kind the *man* is – & must be most to blame – & I am sure not less so in this instance than in every other. Act with me as you think proper – I seek not excuse – nor evasion – I have given you my *word* and it shall be observed – & I am sure Ly C will be the last to make me break it.'[61]

The situation was fast becoming farcical. Even the Prince Regent, no slouch himself when it came to scandals, was surprised. 'Now could you imagine, Dear Ly M,' Lady Bessborough wrote, 'that I had spoken to the P of Ld Byn – He began about my going to Ireland & then he told me the whole story of Caroline saying Ld Mel had been with him very much out of humour complaining that she drove him mad & *we* were almost as bad, that Ld Byn had bewitch'd the whole family, Mothers & daughter & all & that nothing would satisfy us but making a fool of him as well as of ourselves, & insisting on his asking Ld Byn to his house. The P said all this so rapidly & so loudly, interrupting himself now & then to exclaim,

"I never heard of such a thing in my life – taking the Mothers for confidants! What would you have thought of my going to talk to Ly Spencer in former times!" – that in spite of the subject & the circle I was near to laughing. But do not scold Ld Mel, for he was so very good-natured & so civil that I was quite delighted with him. I could not get away from Ld Byn when once he began talking to me – he was part of the time very pleasant & talking of other things – but he did tell me some things so terrifying & so extraordinary!!'[62]

Byron enjoyed his popularity, friendship with powerful politicians and access to grand surroundings and set out to make himself interesting and attractive by wrapping his past in a veil of mystery. He talked recklessly, calling his feckless father a doomed man and enlarged on the grim tales surrounding the fifth Lord Byron – that he was a murderer and a devil worshipper. The strange sights and ceremonies he had seen on his travels were exaggerated but far more dangerous to himself were the broad hints he made that he had taken part in forbidden, esoteric, erotic adventures. He posed and brooded and implied he was weighed down with guilt, having committed a hideous crime too terrible to be named. According to Hobhouse his greatest failing was 'a love of talking of himself to any sycophant that would listen to him'.[63] Augusta more than once jokingly remarked, 'Byron is never so happy as when he can make you believe some atrocity against him.' It was an affectation well known to his Cambridge friends who ignored it and accepted that 'his extraordinary love of a bad reputation, of exhibiting himself in the most unfavourable aspect, amounted almost to insanity.'

On 14 August Newstead Abbey was auctioned at Garroway's Coffee House. Not even Hobhouse's manful efforts to bid up the price twelve times could bring it up to its reserve of 120,000 Guineas. It was not surprising that few people were interested in buying Newstead. It was almost a ruin. The niches in the entrance hall had lost their statues. The family portraits had been sold and the entire building looked as though it was crumbling away. When John Murray saw it he commented that it would cost at least £100,000 to make it habitable. However, a few days later Byron accepted an offer of £140,000 from Mr Thomas Claughton of Haydock Lodge near Warrington and made arrangements to leave town. Before he went he agreed to one last meeting with Caroline. She triumphantly announced to Lady Melbourne, 'I have obtained my mother's leave.'

Byron hated emotional scenes. He had witnessed his parents' noisy emotional storms and his childhood and youth had been clouded by his mother's passionate tantrums. All his life he went out of his way to avoid confrontations. The infidelity of the two maids at Newstead, Lucy and Susan Vaughan, had left him with a distrust of women. When an affair was over he found it difficult to make a clean break. He dithered with Caroline and much later found it impossible to tell his last mistress, Teresa Guiccioli, that she must return to her husband, asking her brother to do it instead. His cold treatment of Claire Clairmont, mother of his daughter Allegra, changed her love for him into unremitting hatred.

They met. Caroline thought he looked sorry for her. He cried and she 'adored him' but felt as 'passionless as the dead'. He allowed Caroline to leave for Ireland believing he would follow her. He wrote, 'My Dearest Caroline, If tears which you saw & know I am not apt to shed, agitation which you must have perceived through the *whole* of this most nervous affair, did not commence until the moment of leaving you approached, if all I have said & done, & am still but too ready to say and do, have not sufficiently proved what my real feelings are, and must ever be towards you, my love, I have no other proof to offer. God knows I wish you happy, & when I quit you, or rather you from a sense of duty to your husband and mother quit me, you shall acknowledge the truth of what I again promise & vow, that no other in word or deed shall ever hold the place in my affections, which is, & shall be, most sacred to you, till I am nothing. I never knew till that *moment* the *madness* of – my dearest and most beloved friend; I cannot express myself; this is no time for words, but I shall have a pride, a melancholy pleasure, in suffering what you yourself can scarcely conceive, for you do not know me. I am about to go out with a heavy heart, because my appearing this evening will stop any absurd story which the spite of the day might give rise to. You think *now* that I am *cold & stern, & wilful?* Will even *others* think so? will your *mother* ever? That mother to whom we must indeed sacrifice much *more*, much more on my part than she shall ever know or *can* imagine. –"Promise not to love you" ah Caroline it is past promising. But I shall attribute all concessions to the proper motive, & never cease to feel all that you have already witnessed, & more than can ever be known but to my own heart, and perhaps to yours. May God protect forgive and bless you, ever & ever more than ever, your most attached BYRON. PS – These taunts which have driven you to this, my dearest Caroline, were it not for your mother & the kindness of all your connections, is there anything on earth or heaven would have made me so happy as to have made you mine long ago? & not less *now* than *then*, but more than ever at *this time*. You know I would with pleasure give up all here & all beyond the grave for you, and in refraining from this, must my motives be misunderstood? I care not who knows this. What use is made of it. It is to *you* & to *you* only that they are, *yourself*. I was and am *yours*, freely and most entirely, to obey, to honour, love and fly with you when, where, & how you yourself *might* and *may* determine.'[64]

Caroline left for Ireland, quietly encouraged by Byron's promises that they would meet soon. There was no more mention of a pregnancy. Far from her influence, Byron took the pragmatic decision to end the tormented affair and find a 'golden dolly'. 'You will not regret to hear that I wish this to end,' he told Lady Melbourne. 'It certainly shall not be renewed on my part. – It is not that I love another, but loving at all is quite out of my way; I am tired of being a fool.' He added coarsely, 'It is true from early habit, one must make love mechanically as one swims, I was once very fond of both, but now as I never swim unless I tumble into water, I don't make love till almost obliged.'[65] Hobhouse rejoiced, 'I congratulate you most sincerely on your release from one who certainly was not the Lamb of God which taketh away the sins of the world.'[66]

Byron hoped Caroline would stay in Ireland until his plans were complete but 'in the mean time I must write the greatest absurdities to keep her "gay" & the more so because ye last epistle informed that "8 guineas, a mail & a packet *could* bring her to London."' Caroline sensed he was slipping away from her but she could not understand what had changed him. He told Lady Melbourne, 'I shall not write any more to Ireland, if I can avoid it, in fact I have said & unsaid & resaid till I am exhausted. I would marry before they return, this would settle it at once.' He also told her, 'Do you suppose that at my *time of life,* were I so very far gone, that I should not be in *Ireland* or at least have followed into Wales, as it was hinted was *expected* – now they have crossed the channel I feel anything but regret.'[67] He was not telling the complete truth. According to Caroline, 'he wrote, every day, long kind entertaining letters. It is these,' she told Medwin that 'he asked Murray to look out and extract from when he published the Journal.'

Byron suspected that Lady Bessborough blamed him for Caroline's misery but he told Lady Melbourne, 'I am sure Ly B will be a little provoked, if *I* am the *first* to change.' He continued, 'She will doubtless expect her daughter to be adored (like an Irish Lease) for a term of 99 years. I say it again, that happy as she must & will be to have it broken off *anyhow* she will *hate* me if *I* don't break my heart.'[68] Nevertheless he did feel some remorse. Lady Melbourne would have none of it. 'What! Pass your time in endeavouring to put her into good humour & to satisfy her, & disguise from her that you are unhappy. Fine Dreams indeed – the first is much beyond yr Power & finding how ill you succeed, must inevitably prevent you from persisting in the last... If a little trifling expression of coldness at present would prevent this *finale,* how much more kind, to give a little present pain, & avoid her total ruin... She always told me you continually sd – that she had exposed herself so much before she was acquainted with you, that her character could not suffer, as it was already gone – I abused you at the time for giving it this turn tho' what you sd was perfectly true, & in my opinion exculpates you entirely... As a friend, I say flirt as much as you please but do not get into a serious scrape before you are safe from the *present one.*'[69]

As Lady Melbourne folded her letter for the post, two arrived from Caroline. 'Both letters,' she told Byron, 'are written the same day, one full of spirits, gaieté, dinners, parties &c, &c, the other *false* written to deceive one, talking of her unhappiness & affecting to be perfectly quiet & resigned… She is trying to act upon my feelings, & to make me tell her something about you. *This I shall not do.* She says you are angry, begs me to tell her why – entreats me to speak openly & she will not betray me, perhaps I have shown you her last letter – if so she will forgive me – & so on. I am now inclined to think that if you could get her into a quiet state by any means, it would be the best chance. You might agree to see her quietly when she returns, provided she made none of the scenes she is so fond of; it might *possibly* go off in that way, but it never can while she is in this constant state of irritation… The result of all this seems to me the best thing you can do is to marry, & that in fact you can get out of the scrape by no other means.'[70]

'Your are right in all you say about my love,' Caroline told Lady Melbourne. 'I know it is too violent but there is this to be said, the only two men who ever loved me insisted on it – would not be content with less and did all, all in their power to make me love them so by more than returning it. Those two are most different in character but after them no others can please. It is dangerous to be attached to one of this sort; they both acknowledge it because all after must appear a blank. Wm as you say, feels for me even more than affection & I do the same for him. – It is impossible not – but that most of the passion, though it lasted with us for above three years, must, as you too have remarked, cease to exist or change its object, – with him a new pursuit engrossing all his time & powers. Grant the fact that my attachment to Lord Byron grew in time to be a thing, as you say, that is madness & excess – You must easily believe that his conduct so unexpected, so sudden nearly killed me. Wm forgetting all jealousies really feels for me, you may ask him whether I have not tried to think of others and to forget myself, but I wish to speak reasonably to you if I can – my dearest Lady Melbourne, your kindness throughout has been generous & you will, I am sure, know I am grieved. Your letters have been received by me with scenes of passion and tears. Last night the storm in my room was, as William remarked, little exceeded by the storm of thunder & lightning without – the consequence is a calm on both sides this morning & if it will not tire you, I will now explain myself. You say I shall be sorry to hear Lord Byron is in spirits – believe me I wish him all happiness, health & spirits – I do forgive him from my very soul for making me the plaything & victim of his varying passions – never fancy I wish to cause grief to anyone – As I said when leaving Augustus, half the pain of parting is gone when we feel that it is not shared – but though I do think few women and no *men* [underlined three times] ever took blame to themselves as I always do without throwing it on the other side.'[71]

Lady Melbourne passed the letter to Byron with a note. 'I have no beliefs in the part about Wm unless it is that she can manage him more easily than she can any other person, and she thinks it as well to give it the appearance of fondness, if she determines to remain.'

Before Caroline left for Ireland she had found a loose page from a letter on the floor of her apartment. She picked it up, saw it was from Byron to Lady Melbourne but read it anyway. She was distressed by the way he spoke of her and quoted passages from it in a letter she sent Byron. 'Who was careless?' he asked Lady Melbourne. 'If you left it in ye way on purpose – it had a blessed effect – it is but another *winding* to our only *Labyrinth* – She quotes from it passages which I recollect – how could you Lady M – how could you "wear a pocket with a hole?" '[72] Lady Melbourne replied sharply, 'You are too suspicious… I cannot bear her having got that letter whether she opened it or found it, 'tis all one. It will be long before I forgive it. If it was either on my table or in my drawer she has added falsehood to her other iniquities, for in that case she could not think it was for her. I have not been in right good humour since I heard it.'

When Caroline heard these excuses she wrote to Lady Melbourne in a fury. Her writing straggled uncontrollably across pages covered with inkblots. 'Once more I assure you upon my honour I have never opened or intentionally read any letter of yours. I found a part of one on the floor – It was in a hand I was used to receive myself – I made no secret of it – I have committed no wrong… Once again, Lady Melbourne, I most solemnly swear to you by all that *you* may hold sacred, if it were not for my mother and the kindness I have received from you all, this day forth you should never see me again. Oh that I had not been weak enough to return when Lord Byron brought me back, that I had never returned but come it late, it will come at last, & such an exit I will make from this scene of deceit and unkindness that it shall expiate even my atrocious conduct, the canting sorrow of which you accuse me. Lord Byron has now sealed my destruction and it shall follow, mark these words & when it comes, remember it was not the mere impotence of frantic grief, but the firm resolution of a heart bitterly and deeply injured. I never more will write to you & thanks for the letters I have received. I shall not reproach you for them – I deserve unkindness from *you*. I never have, I hope I never have, accused Lord Byron. He or you best know why he behaves so ill to the woman he so lately professed to love. He is changed perhaps that is a reason, no we are not master of our affections, his love for another is no cause but I neither expected nor can bear insult, hate, suspicion & contempt. I will not bear it. He may love who he pleases. I shall never reproach him but he should not treat me with cruelty and contempt.' Still smarting she added a postscript. 'I found on the floor in my room in London a part of an open letter addressed to no one, & as I thought to me. I could not know it was to you. I left it exactly where I found it… I have been foolish enough to make myself very miserable. I am called atrocious, dishonourable and much more by you, selfish,

101

ungenerous, ay – frivolous by your friend – He says he knows *how* I behave. I shall write no more to anyone at all who writes unkindly to me, but as a last favour, I do request of you, if you can prevail upon yourself to do so, not to abuse me, or repeat what I say. You are quite right in resolving to have no more secret letters – but I do give you my assurance my Mama has never shewn anything you wrote or spoken to me about those things. She asked me yesterday what I had written to you and I said only quantities of nonsense. She asked me if there was anything that had occurred and I said not. If I have appeared impertinent consider what harsh terms you – and he both write… I have errors but I am not mean or cowardly – selfish is a word I dislike… Do not call me *canting*. I am not that… Let me not be thought a lovesick deserted lady that is all I request… I am free & independent of Lord Byron – I do not wish to move his compassion – I would give much *never* to be named to him more.'[73]

The family had received a warm welcome from their Irish tenants and settled into the comfort of Bessborough House, built by the first Earl of Bessborough in 1774 and designed by Francis Bindon. The large central block of blue limestone had wings at either end. Two curving stairways led up to the front door. The great hall was notable for its four Ionic columns of Kilkenny marble, each one carved from a single stone. The house was surrounded by five acres of wooded parkland close to the river Sir, which was noted for its unusually large salmon and trout.

Caroline passed her time by compiling a book of her poems to give to Mrs Howe. When it was fine she liked to walk to the post office at nearby Fiddown. She passed the church where her grandmother, Lady Caroline Cavendish, daughter of the fourth Duke of Devonshire, was buried. In *Glenarvon* she used the picturesque church, once famous as an Abbey and home of St Maidoc, as the meeting place of Calantha [Caroline] and Glenarvon [Byron].

At the end of September, Hart invited the family to come and admire the improvements he was making to Lismore Castle. To amuse the travellers Caroline speculated aloud on what it would look like and when the romantic ruins came in sight through the mist she let her imagination run riot. She described 'shivering ghosts and knights in armour' wandering through the deserted parkland and up to the portcullis. They let out a huge shout of laughter when they got closer and saw the castle. It was standing in the centre of a dirty village without even 'an acre of ground belonging to it.' Instead of being shown into Caroline's fine 'Gothic Hall' they entered 'two small dapper Parlours neatly furnish'd in the newest Inn fashion, much like a Citizen's Villa at Highgate'. Caroline at once struck a dramatic pose and declared her heart was broken.

Despite the new paintwork and furniture the rooms were uncomfortable and damp. A few days later, when everyone was present, Caroline flung open the door and announced loudly, 'Pray walk in, Sir, I have no doubt you are the rightful possessor, and my Cousin only an interloper usurping your usual habitation.' No one moved. They stared at the open door until, 'with great solemnity and many pauses, in hopp'd a *frog* closely followed by Caroline carrying a candle in each hand, "to treat the master of the Castle with proper respect".' Hart was only half amused.[74]

The stay at Lismore lifted her spirits. 'We are indeed very comfortable and gay – plenty of society, great variety of scenery & such good humoured kindness on us by all sorts of people it would be ungrateful and stupid not to be pleased.' She assured Lady Melbourne, tongue in cheek, 'I can assure you I am *very well behaved*. I make no difficulties anywhere or about anything'.[75] She promised not to have any fancies, hire more pages or accept any horses or dogs. She asked Lady Melbourne to give Augustus a kiss and tell him that she loved him dearly.[76]

William's seat of Portarlington, Lord Bessborough's pocket borough and bought for £5,000, was not secure and Lady Melbourne encouraged him to stand for the parliamentary seat of Hertfordshire, which Peniston had held from 1802 until his death in 1805. In 1812 the Whigs were a divided party. They considered themselves to be radicals fighting for freedom but as major landowners, and as Irish peers who did not qualify to sit in the House of Lords, or the younger sons of English peers, many of them were unwilling to resign their privileges to the rising number of successful manufacturers and wealthy tradesmen. The industrial revolution had created a new class who demanded a share in governing the country. They wanted to change the balance of power within the House of Commons and rid it of its traditional aristocratic monopoly. As the pressure for reform became greater, division increased within the Whig circles. Some saw the writing on the wall and threw in their lot with the reformers. The Duke of Norfolk was heard to toast 'Our Sovereign, the People'. The Whigs narrowly held on to power, calling on the loyalties of friendship, blood and placemen. The Prince of Wales now Prince Regent tried to encourage the formation of a coalition but the Whigs objected to any plum places being given to Tories. When a petition to form a coalition government was rejected by the House of Lords on 19 March, the Prince Regent finally turned his back on his old Whig allies and appointed a High Tory, Lord Liverpool, as Prime Minister. The decision was confirmed and in August an election was declared.

William disliked constituency work, neglected the voters and was a poor orator. He 'frightened' Caroline 'to death' when he spoke. He invariably lost the thread of the argument and staggered, bumbling to a ragged finish. 'I can walk in the shrubbery here at Brocket Hall and reason and enlarge upon almost any topic,' he wrote in his journal, 'but in the House of Commons, whether it be from apprehension, or heat, or long waiting, or the tediousness of much of what I hear, a torpor of all my faculties almost always comes upon me, and I feel as if I had neither ideas nor opinions, even upon the subjects which interest me most.'

Lord Cranbourne, a Tory and son of the Marquis of Salisbury, had spent the summer canvassing and working in the constituency and Lady Spencer thought he would win the election. 'It is anxiety for Wllm Lamb & not indifference about him that makes me speak so,'[77] she told Lady Bessborough. Caroline knew her grandmother was right but she was more concerned about the impact that the expenses of an election would have on their income. The cost of running in a general election often cost as much as £50,000 and they had barely enough money to cover their own needs, despite living rent-free at Melbourne House and Brocket Hall. Over the years William had developed a sophisticated but ultimately unsuccessful way of keeping creditors at bay, by regularly paying off small amounts from each bill in the hope that this would temporarily satisfy them. It was a ruse that could not last long and he was often embarrassed. Among his debts was a bill for a pair of trousers which remained unpaid for so long that his tailor, Francis Place, who later became a Radical politician, threatened to take him to court.

Sir Matthew Lamb had left £500,000 in property and £500,000 in cash but what had not been gambled away had been spent on Lady Melbourne's lavish parties. Lord Melbourne had been forced to let the family seat in Derbyshire, Melbourne Hall, to Sir William Rumbold and was now contemplating selling Melbourne House.

At the end of September William told his mother that he would not stand for election. 'I have no money. I am embarrassed to a certain degree by circumstances, which I am willing to explain. My income is insufficient. I am deprived of many things which I wish to have & in many things which I might be facilitated. I receive no assistance. Under these circumstances I have long since determined not to diminish my own income one halfpenny – in justice to myself I cannot do it. I cannot expect my Father to bear the whole burthen, & even if he were willing to take it upon himself, I do not know whether I could justify to myself the suffering a further debt to be accumulated upon my account, which must in the end lead to serious embarrassment & to the further dismemberment of the property. This is the state of the case.'[78]

Lady Melbourne showed the letter to Lady Holland with the comment, 'nonsense. – But I do not see at ye same time, how I can act in contradiction to sentiments so decidedly express'd'. In the event, Lord Cranbourne was defeated and Thomas Brand and Sir John Sebright were returned to Parliament as the members for Hertfordshire.

On 9 October Lady Bessborough discovered that Caroline had 'sent an express to England with orders to find Lord Byron where ever he may be.' She told Lady Melbourne, 'The doer does not know I know, but besides the folly of the thing I am concerned from the noise it has made at Waterford, for of course we are rather prominent people.' She continued, 'With all this she seems to quite doat upon William and the usual speech made me everywhere, is what charming spirits Ly C has, and how fond she seems of her husband. It is quite delightful to see them. When they say this to me, I want to bellow.'[79] Lady Bessborough could not understand William's attitude but it appears that he was more annoyed at Byron's treatment of Caroline, because it upset her, than afraid she would elope with him.

'*AT THIS moment*,' Byron wrote to Lady Melbourne, 'another *express* from Ireland!!! More Scenes! – ...I must now write to her – I wrote Ly Bessborough a letter, which she was fool enough to shew her.' Caroline was so miserable that William contemplated taking her to Sicily to stay with his brother, Frederick, now minister plenipotentiary *ad interim* at the Court of Naples and the Two Sicilies. Caroline wrote to Lady Melbourne, 'Nobody loves me now or ought – I wish to be dead – and they who wish it are not long in having their prayers heard... William is out of spirits about Parliament but he is right, without involving himself or Lord Melbourne in debt he could not have come in otherwise – it is a great disappointment.'[80] Byron would not be drawn on his thoughts about Sicily. He told Lady Melbourne, 'You & Mr Lamb are the best judges, to me it must be a matter of perfect indifference; & though I am written to professedly to be consulted on the subject what possible answer could I give that would not be impertinent? – It would be the *best* place for *her* & the worst for him (in all points of view) on earth, unless he was in some official capacity.'[81]

Caroline spent hours preparing an elegant, blue morocco-bound commonplace book for Byron. The first few pages are carefully lined and the handwriting is copperplate. 'This comes from one who suffers. When you open this book – you will be as far from me in distance as you are now in heart, yet I believe time which softens all resentment, will make you forgive many of my faults & you will perhaps remember that I was affectionate & true to you, that however separated I have been yours & though men can forget women do not, neither do they ever resent and what you bound to you once will be still yours while it exists however you may think to cut the chain *no* one knew how to unloose... I think of you as of one dead to me... You do not know what I have felt at parting with you... It shall be the study of my life to correct my faults, to remember any wishes and advice you may have been kind enough to give me – & to behave in future so as to make you look back upon the attachment you once professed for me with less pain – God bless you Lord Byron, be happy & take care of yourself.'[82]

On the following pages she told the story of a spaniel, Biondetta, a metaphor for herself, which she had given to Byron. 'It had all the fierceness of a tyger, or mountain cat when angry – but would nestle like a dove in his bosom when caressed. It was so small that he frequently carried it about and it was so happy when thus favoured that it grew presumptuous & would bite and bark at everyone who approached. One day he drew it from his bosom and gave it back to its former owner – kissing it and promising with tears to soon return – but Biondetta's faults were remembered & all her truth and kindness forgotten from that hour. Lord Byron never returned more. The dog sat and watched for him & would not feed or sleep till it heard that a new favourite filled its place & then growing furious it broke its chains and tried to bite & tear to pieces its rival. Lord Byron heard of its violence, so forgetting what strong feelings he had left raging in its head, discarded it forever, repudiated it, spurned it from him & spoke of his little spaniel with disgust & anger. Biondetta never recovered from this, from that hour it sickened & still watching for one kind word or message from its master, it died. The collar round its neck was Lord Byron's gift. It was returned to him after its death.'

The writing on the next page is uneven. 'It was one of the Blenheim Breed in right line – proud of its – blood – its conceit was what ruined it with its master he courted & favour'd it till it grew vain & when it sat in his bosom it looked as it would have defied the world then he humbled it too much & suffered others to taunt it & though it was duly fed and properly taken care of it absolutely pined itself sick – as everyone witnessed for its moaning and sighs became tedious and she was silenced by sharp words & scoffs. He refused to see it when dying, had he come it would have licked his hand and gazed once more upon his face as if to thank him – but Lord Byron had a low opinion of this race – and what affection he could feel he had bestowed on a prettier & finer animal. He even derided Biondetta & said it was a whelp of a vixen – but whatever it was – none ever lov'd him so before or since.'

In a frenzied joint letter to Byron and Lady Melbourne, Caroline accused their friends of turning him against her. 'They have all tried to blacken me – & will again & they are too many & too skilful not to succeed – besides I put myself in their power – in the power of everyone for when they tell me you said such and such things of me I fire up & say ten thousand worse of you & Lady Melbourne & of everybody to which *alone* of all accusations I plead guilty & for which I shall forever more grieve. But I can only say that as you have had the generosity to forgive me without one reproach & Lady Melbourne was the means by which I gained this good, I will rather be cut into pieces than ever speak unkindly or with disrespect of either of you again. At one time I was even jealous of her – I confess it. I thought she was gaining your confidence & esteem & I was loving *both*... Now all feelings of jealousy are past because, indeed, they cannot exist situated as we are. I even think we might be friends as you would have other attachments there could be no fear – but still as Lady Melbourne has not confidence enough in me to allow of this and as I make no doubt you will act as kindly by me as you may and ought, I will never more seek it till it is thought proper... There is another thing I wish to say while writing to both of you – & it is this, if I stay away or refuse to waltz or to shake hands with people I am accused by Lady Melbourne of doing it out of a romantic wish of pleasing you – Now be assured I do not flatter myself that you care in the least about it. Perhaps even you would be glad to hear I was dancing & amusing myself because you are, I am sure, good natured enough to be sorry if any one is unhappy whom you in the least care for. – But I do promise yourself & Lady Melbourne my motive for all this is quite different from what you may either of you think... I cannot think of a woman who has once acted as I have can be too reserved in future – People of course will laugh – and deride me & call it an affectation of prudery to atone for an excess of contrary conduct but if this affectation continues no one will, in the end blame it & no one will have the power to reproach me for what is past. The least thing now will be misconstrued, every unguarded word or look of mine will be looked upon with severity – I see the sharp censure already to start into words on every cold, formal face I meet. Let not Lady Melbourne think it is from a wrong motive or to cherish vain imagination & regrets that I follow the line of conduct I have resolved upon. She says love is all imagination, nothing else – & what is this saying – It may explain the seat of the evil but it cannot remove it – Everything in life is more or less imagination, but love need not lead to wrong – It does too often. It has with me – but may it not also guide to right and to duty & may I not be impelled to act better than I should naturally & to conquer a very turbulent & faulty character by those same feelings? Believe me I shall.'[83]

After she returned to Bessborough, Caroline wrote to Lady Melbourne again. 'My mind, my nerves my whole condition is so irritated that Wm says that he does not know what to do with me... I struggle to conceal my feelings from my mother, I am not stubborn, I am not selfish, but I cannot, will not bear this state much longer. Remember that I warn you, I do not menace – I am respectful, I wish to be so... Strangers even think me miserable. They suppose it is leaving my child – my mind is irritated – I will go away – depend on it.'[84] Sad and enraged at Byron's silence, Caroline begged Lady Melbourne to break her own friendship with him and not to write 'harshly to me who is near mad'. She ended the confused letter, 'Wm promises me I shall see him once more. It is only once more

I wish, only for one moment.' It seemed that the situation had not changed since they left London.

Byron had selected his 'golden dolly'. To Lady Melbourne's astonishment the heiress he had in mind was her priggish niece, Annabella Milbanke. When she asked him if he was sure, he replied, 'Miss M I admire because she is a clever woman, an amiable woman & of high blood, for I have still a few Norman & Scotch inherited prejudices on the last score, were I to marry. As to *love*, that is done in a week, (provided the Lady has a reasonable share) besides marriage goes on better with esteem & confidence than romance, and she is quite pretty enough to be loved by her husband, without being so glaringly beautiful as to attract too many rivals.'[85]

Lady Melbourne approached her brother, Sir Ralph Milbanke, and a tentative offer of marriage was made to Annabella. She refused. She had seen Caroline's antics and the interest Byron had shown in pretty Bessy Rawdon, Miss Margaret Mercer Elphinstone and a score of other ladies. He was not too cast down and remarked, 'My *heart* never had an opportunity of being much interested in the business, further than that I should have very much liked to be *Your relation*.' He asked Lady Melbourne, 'What shall I do – shall I *advertise*?'[86]

He spent August in Cheltenham with the Melbournes where he was fêted by the Jerseys, Cowpers, Hollands, Rawdons and the Oxfords. At Lord Holland's request, he composed an address to be read at the reopening of the Drury Lane Theatre, which had been burned down in 1809. He had an enjoyable affair with a sensual but gluttonous 'Italian songstress' whose noisy enjoyment of 'chicken wings, sweetbreads, custards, peaches & *Port* wine' rather repelled him as he affected to believe the only food women should be seen eating was lobster and salad. From Cheltenham he went to Middleton with the Jerseys. In October he stayed with the Oxfords at Eywood, their country house in Herefordshire where he enjoyed Lady Oxford's ripe favours under the nose of her complaisant husband, whom they nicknamed 'Potiphar'. For a while it appeared there would be an addition to the attractive collection of children but to Byron's relief it was a false alarm.

On hearing that Byron had proposed to Annabella, Caroline sent him a bitter recriminating letter. He told Lady Melbourne, 'She has hurt and disgusted me by her latter conduct beyond expression; & even if I did not love another, I would never speak to her again while I existed, & this you have my full consent to state to those whom it may concern... C threatens to revenge herself upon *herself*, by all kinds of perverseness. This is her concern... If Ly C wishes any interview pray explain for me that I WILL NOT meet her, if she has either pride or feeling this will be sufficient.'[87]

Caroline wrote to Lady Oxford, 'My dearest Aspasia, I only think Byron is angry with me. Will you write to him? Will you tell him I have done one thing to displease him & that I am miserable? Tell him I wrote him a cross letter I know but that I have a thousand times ask'd his pardon – He is tired of me, I see it by his letter. I will write no more, never tease him, never intrude upon him only do you obtain his forgiveness.'[88]

They left Bessborough and arrived in Dublin on 1 November. William dreaded his mother's reaction to his refusal to stand for Hertfordshire and played for time, delaying their departure. Caroline passed the days in writing letters, rehashing her troubles at enormous length. 'My opinion is,' she told Lady Melbourne, 'that whatever he may say to all of you, he would have been glad if I had left all for him – certainly he shewed no backwardness to this & when I told him of his saying he would take me if I threw myself upon him it would make him smile. So long as I knew him attached to me I would keep to every wish of his though separated from him & live only to make up to Wm for the past. I gave him leave to marry to do what he pleased and only said I hoped he would still remember me with affection not the less for having resisted involving him & my whole family in misery.' She described how Byron had gone down on his knees, and said that 'he would give nothing for a heart that could feel for any other living object but himself' and urged her, should anything happen to William, to agree that she would belong to him. They wrote pledges vowing to love no one but each other but when Caroline added to hers the words 'except William', Byron tore up the papers and said 'I will not have exceptions. If you ever dream of another I will make your heart ache & burn.'[89]

Lady Bessborough wearily wrote to Lady Melbourne, 'All I wish is to keep everything quiet and seeing him for her cannot be worse than writing to him the whole day.'[90] She was scarcely able to disguise her astonishment at William's continued indifference to the situation. Two letters arrived for Caroline, one from Lady Spencer full of advice and another with a coronet on the seal and Lady Oxford's initials beneath it. The writing was Byron's. After four pages of praise 'about some other person' it ended, '& as to yourself Lady Caroline, correct your vanity which is become ridiculous – exert your caprices on others, enjoy the excellent flow of spirits which makes you so delightful in the eyes of others and leave me in tranquillity.' Caroline assumed Lady Oxford was the instigator and commented, 'What will not a woman do to get rid of a rival? She knew that he still loved me.' Caroline tried to carry out her threat to commit suicide and would have succeeded in cutting her wrists if Lady Bessborough had not caught hold of the handle of the knife and defied her to draw the blade through her hand.[91] Referring to the letter, Caroline told Lady Morgan: 'It destroyed me. I lost my brain, I was bled, leached; kept for a week in the filthy Dolphin Inn.'

George Lamb warned Byron, 'I have just received a letter from Caro, which makes me fear she will take some violent or imprudent step. I thought I had been most *prudent and cautious* as the only thing I said to her, was that *if* as she told me you were altered to her, I hoped she had too much pride and good feeling to force herself upon you. This she says has thrown her into fits. She says that you never hinted at such a thing, and that she must hear from your own lips that you have changed before she will believe it – Do tell me if you have heard from her, and what I shall say to her, for they are all coming here, and I feel as if it was impossible *not* to do harm in some way. Whatever one says to her – I only wish never to hear anything more on the subject – I can't tell you how I dread their coming… Forgive me for troubling you, but I was afraid if you received a violent letter from her you would think I had repeated some things you said to me, which I never did.'[92]

The travellers arrived at Tixal Hall, the house the Granville's rented in Staffordshire, in time to join a cheerful house party consisting of the dandy Brummell and two of his close friends – the dark, beautifully-complexioned Lady Harriet Villiers and her husband, Richard Bagot, who was soon to be appointed Bishop of Oxford. Also in attendance were George Lamb and Caroline's half-sister, Harriet Stewart. A less welcome guest was Scappa, Lady Bessborough's souvenir from Naples. She liked to carry the old, smelly dog around in her arms, which disgusted Hary-o who was not a dog lover.

While the visitors unpacked, Hary-o wrote to her sister, 'My Aunt looks stout and well, but poor Caroline most terribly the contrary. She is worn to the bone, as pale as death, and her eyes starting out of her head. She seems, indeed, in a sad way alternately in tearing spirits and then in tears. I hate her character, her feelings and herself when I am away from her, but she interests me when I am with her; and to see her poor careworn face is dismal, in spite of reason and speculation upon her extraordinary conduct, she appears to me in a state very little short of insanity, and my Aunt describes it as at times having been decidedly so.' Caroline pulled herself together and was 'excessively entertaining at supper. Her spirits whilst they last, seem as ungovernable as her grief. My aunt is very gay and amiable, Poor Lord Bessborough *me pèse sure le coeur et l'esprit*. William Lamb laughs and eats like a trouper.'[93]

Despite all her protests and good intentions, Caroline rained letters on Byron and Lady Oxford, imploring him to see her and ordering him to return her presents. This was a crude attempt to embarrass him as she assumed he had already given them to Lady Oxford. When all failed she threatened to write and tell Lord Oxford about his wife's affair. Byron remarked, 'I am almost sure that *she* will write to Mr L[amb] if so – there will be a pretty scene.' Caroline was impervious to her mother's tears, Lady Melbourne's sharp tongue or her grandmother's strictures. On 27 November Lady Spencer wrote to Lady Bessborough, 'Dear Child, it is grievous to me how she trifles with her own & her husband's happiness.'[94] Caroline released her pent-up feelings by riding at breakneck speed round the grounds at Brocket and up and down the turnpike. 'You have told me how foreign women revenge,' she threatened Byron, 'I will show you how an English woman can.'

She ordered a large bonfire to be built with a straw effigy of Byron on top and invited children from Welwyn and the cottages near the gates of Brocket Hall to a ceremony. The girls wore white dresses made for the occasion and danced and skipped round the burning pyre. As the flames shot up into the cold winter sky, one of Caroline's favourite pages stood in the flickering shadows reciting the 'address', which she had composed. Sitting close to the fire was a basket containing copies of Byron's letters, presents and his portrait.

Is this Guy Fawkes you burn in effigy?
Why bring the traitor here? What is Guy Fawkes to me?
Guy Fawkes betrayed his country and his laws,
England revenged the wrong; his was a public cause.
But I have private cause to raise this flame
Burn also these, and be their fate the same,

('Put the basket in the fire under the figure,' Caroline told the page)

Rouge, feathers, flowers, and all those tawdry things
Besides those pictures, letters, chains and rings –
All made to lure the mind and please the eye
And fill the heart with pride and vanity –
Burn, fire burn, these glittering toys destroy,
While thus we hail the blaze with throats of joy –
Burn, fire, burn, while wondering boys exclaim,
And gold and trinket glitter in the flame –
Ah, look not thus on me, so grave, so sad,
Shake not your heads, nor say the lady's mad.
Judge not of others for there is but one
To whom the heart and feelings can be known.

Upon my youthful faults few censures cast,
Look to my future and forgive the past.

London, farewell, vain world, vain life adieu
Take the last tears I ere shall shed for you.
Young tho' I seem, I leave the world for ever,
Never to enter it again – no never – never.[95]

Caroline still tried to see Byron and under the pretext of owing him money she sent a banker's receipt to his bank. He told Lady Melbourne, 'I have returned it, & if the money is not removed from Hoare's & my name withdrawn, I shall most assuredly dispatch it with her compliments one half to the Magdalen asylum [a reformatory for prostitutes] & the other to St Luke's [a lunatic asylum] as a donation & return in kind for her bonfire.'[96]

5

'She is now like a barrel of gunpowder'

Caroline still refused to accept that her affair with Byron was over and in the New Year of 1813 tried to regain his attention by the only method she knew – behaving outrageously. She continued the guerrilla war of letters and threatened to have his family motto inscribed on all her servants' buttons with the addition of the word 'NE' before 'Crede Byron'. 'This is her own account,' Byron told Lady Melbourne, 'and may therefore be false.' It was falsely rumoured that he was sleeping with Lady Melbourne and Caroline. He wrote, 'Beseech her for her own sake to remain quiet. If this is disregarded it will be out of my *power* to prevent consequences *fatal* to her perhaps to others also, & which I most sincerely wish to avoid'. He suggested that Lady Melbourne 'remind her that the same man she is now trying by every serious & petty means to exasperate is the same who received the warmest thanks from herself & Ly B on the occasion of her *Kensington* excursion, one with whose conduct she has repeatedly professed herself perfectly satisfied & who did not give her up till he was assured that he was not abandoning a woman to her fate but restoring her to her family.'[1] Byron admired Lady Melbourne and was even jealous of her former lover, the Prince Regent. He later remarked, 'If she had been a few years younger, what a fool she would have made of me, had she thought it worth her while, and I should have lost a valuable and most agreeable *friend*.' Caroline feared that they were more than friends.

Byron had given Caroline three miniatures of himself. Shortly before she left for Ireland she sent them to the artist, George Sanders, for a few minor alterations. When they were not returned she suspected that Byron had reclaimed them. Unwilling to ask him directly she appealed to his old school friend, Lord Clare; 'You may perhaps prevail on him to give *you* one of the pictures he gave me... I do not want three but what would I give for one.' Lord Clare was silent. She approached Sanders, who told her that Byron had given one to John Murray for the frontispiece to a new edition of *Childe Harold*. Early in January Caroline made an appointment to see him in his new offices at 50

Albemarle Street. She handed him a letter which appeared to be from Byron authorising her to 'Take which picture you think most like but do not forget to return it the soonest you can.'[2] John Murray had never seen Caroline before and not having any reason to suspect such a charming messenger, he handed her the miniature. Caroline jubilantly wrote to Byron confessing what she had done. On 8 January Byron told Murray that he had been taken in by a forgery and asked that, in future, he would not give anything of his away without a covering letter bearing his seal as well as his signature.[3] In fact the text of the letter bore only a passing likeness to Byron's hand but Caroline had taken great care to produce an almost perfect signature. Later, Byron wrote at the bottom of the page, 'This letter was forged in my name by Caroline L for the purpose of obtaining a picture from the hands of Mr M January 1813.' Caroline was totally unrepentant and told Byron that she had now broken all but the sixth and ninth Commandments but would break those too if he did not allow her to keep the picture. Murray was amazed at the situation but Byron was confused and angry, saying 'I do not at all know how to deal with her, because she is unlike every one else.'

On 6 February, Miss Webster, Caroline's companion, marched into Murray's office and in Byron's presence announced, 'Mr Murray, Lady Caroline Lamb desires you will call tomorrow'. Murray, nonplussed, agreed. 'What was I to do?' Byron asked Lady Melbourne. 'If I said "*don't go*" to a person who knew nothing of *her* – & who dreamed only of an order for books &c he would have thought it very singular… The room being full I thought it best to say nothing.'[4] Murray met Caroline the following morning at Melbourne House. She charmed and flattered him until he agreed to accept a selection of her designs and pictures to show Byron as possible illustrations for his next work. Byron turned them down but he was disappointed as, he told Lady Melbourne, 'I regret this last blunder since she has been so quiet & silent since her arrival that I trusted our cares were over.'

To all outward appearances Caroline was leading a pleasant, calm, domestic life at Brocket Hall. She told Lady Holland, 'Wm is very well & we are very comfortable. Augustus looks radiant & is growing tender-hearted – He is Wm's delight and never from him – walks with him, reads to him and cuts as many jokes as George Lamb. He looks really beautiful in his new dress which is plain & not as I fancy you think, all gold and silver.'[5] When they left Holywell, after a family lunch, Lady Spencer wrote to Lady Bessborough, 'They all look pretty well, Caroline is certainly better & happier than she did some time ago, but Augustus is rather short breathed, but both his father & mother think him quite well.'[6] A few days before, on 9 February, William had begun his autobiography, which was to occupy his time until the end of March.[7]

Caroline continued to plead for an interview with Byron, not suspecting that he was planning to go abroad with the Oxfords in June. Lady Melbourne suggested to him that he should let her know so that they could avoid scenes if she found out by accident.[8] Byron reluctantly agreed to see her if Lady Melbourne was present. However, Caroline had recently asked to see Lady Oxford and Byron 'thought it as well to *lump* the interviews into one' on the grounds that Lady Oxford was less likely to be embarrassed than Lady Melbourne. 'You did not act with your usual judgement in preferring Ly O to me,' Lady Melbourne wrote ruefully, 'You might have depended upon my leaving the room if she had shewn a disposition to be quiet – & most assuredly in any case should not have been a listener.'

Caroline repeatedly asked for her letters, pictures, gold chains and rings to be returned. Byron told Lady Melbourne, 'The rings (among others a *Wedding* one, which she *bestowed* upon *herself* and insisted on my placing it on her finger) were all the manufacture of a Bond Street Artist… I give up pictures, letters &c to her tender mercies – let that satisfy her – the detestation – the utter abhorrence I feel at part of her conduct – I will neither shock you with nor trust myself to express. That feeling has become part of my nature – it has poisoned my future existence – I know not whom I may love but to the latest hour of my life I shall hate that woman.'[9]

Caroline agreed to return the miniature on condition that she could have a copy as well as a lock of Byron's hair. His reluctance led Lady Melbourne to write, 'Do send me some for the little bits I took by force will not satisfy her – and really when a Lady condescends to make such a fuss, for such a trifle – it is not for a Gentleman to *faire le difficile.*'[10] Instead of sending Caroline one of his own curls, Byron sent one of Lady Oxford's, telling Lady Melbourne, 'It was a lucky coincidence of colour & shape for my purpose – & may never happen again – & surely it is a very innocent revenge for some very scurvy behaviour.'

He took extravagant measures to avoid Caroline and in April forbade Murray to send her a preliminary copy of his new poem, *The Giaour.* Nevertheless Caroline managed to obtain one, probably from Samuel Rogers. She asked her mother to let her know Byron's movements, when he planned to leave the country and if he was going with Lady Oxford. She ended her letter with the words, 'Depend upon my prudence.'[11]

Caroline had cultivated John Murray, at first, in the hope that he would bring her closer to Byron, or at least be her advocate and conduit for letters and messages, but she soon valued him for his friendship and common sense. Despite their unusual meeting he became fond and a little sorry for her. He tried to warn her that forgery was not a prank but a crime. She was cheerfully unrepentant. 'So you give it as your opinion that I might be convicted? I know in that case who would have taken charge of me if the verdict had been transportation. But then it could not have been for more than two years at the most.'[12]

She still believed she could change Byron's mind and pleaded with Lady Melbourne to allow her to see him 'before he takes a long journey after which we may perhaps never meet more.' She explained that the reason she wanted to see him was to 'bid him adieu', part in peace and ask his forgiveness for her mistakes. At the same time she wanted him to acknowledge that they had been the result of his unkindness. 'I do not think I shall live till he returns,' she wrote dramatically.[13] 'I regret it & acquiesce with reluctance,' Byron told her. 'I have only one request to make – which is not to attempt to see Ly O, on her you have no claim – You will settle – as you please – the arrangement of this conference – I do not leave England till June – but the sooner it is over the better.'[14]

Despite his brave face, Byron was still susceptible to her charm and during the interview he was not as firm as he had intended. Caroline told Thomas Medwin, 'He asked me to forgive him; he looked sorry for me; he cried. I adored him still, but I felt as passionless as the dead may feel. Would I had died there! – I should have died pitied & loved by him, & with the sympathy of all. I even should have pardoned myself – so deeply had I suffered. But, unhappily, we continued occasionally to meet. Lord Byron liked others, I only him.' She copied into her commonplace book a letter she wrote to him soon after the meeting. 'One only word, you have raised me from despair to joy we look for in Heaven. Your seeing me has undone me forever – You are the same, you love me still. I am sure of it – your eyes, your looks, your manners, words say so. Oh God, can you give me up if I am so dear? Take me with you – Take me, my master, my friend. Who will fight for you, serve you, in sickness and health, live but for your wishes and die when that can please you – who so faithfully as the one you have made yours, bound to your heart of hearts? Yet when you read this you will be gone. You will think of me, perhaps, as one who gave you suffering – trouble. Byron, my days are passed in remembering what I once was to you. I wish you had never known me or that you had killed me before you went. God Bless and preserve my friend and master. Your Caro.'[15]

Lady Bessborough lived in fear that Caroline might elope and was tormented by the uncertainty. She was constantly restless, could not sleep at night and felt ill. She took to her bed, getting up once in a while to be cupped or to soak her feet in warm mustard water. Each time she closed her eyes she saw in her mind's eye Caroline and Byron running away and would awake in a wave of horror.[16]

It was impossible for Byron and Caroline to lead normal lives in London without running across each other at social events, lectures or receptions. One evening, Caroline left Lady Jersey's in tears because, she told William, Byron had offended her. William leapt to her defence and demanded to know what had happened. 'Now this is really laughable – if I *speak* to her *he* is insulted – If I *don't* speak to her – *she* is insulted,' Byron told Lady Westmorland. 'I am at this moment as ignorant of my offence as I then was of having offended. I saw her for one instant at a distance as she entered the room but she neither saw nor appeared to see me. I can say no more – & would not have said so much were I not desirous to vindicate myself to you (as her friend) from the imputation of affronts I did not offer & offences I do not understand.'[17]

Byron continued to reply to Caroline's letters. He justified this by saying that it was his method of keeping her calm and avoiding scenes until he could leave but he was left behind when the Oxfords sailed for Sicily on 27 June, the same day Augusta arrived in London. Byron and Augusta had much in common and the novelty of being together after having been parted for so long was enjoyable. They shared a sense of humour and Augusta could make Byron laugh. To take her mind off her debts and her children he took her to meet Madame de Staël at Lady Jersey's, to a masque at Almack's, with tickets provided by Emily Cowper, one of the leading patronesses of the club, and to a reception at Lady Glenbervie's where the sharp-eyed Miss Milbanke noticed them sitting on a sofa. Byron's delight in his sister's company excited the jealously of Caroline, Lady Melbourne and her niece.

Byron's finances improved considerably when Claughton, who had pledged £25,000 towards the purchase of Newstead, was forced, under threat of a lawsuit, to pay him £15,000. Claughton subsequently forfeited any rights to Newstead. (It remained unsold until 1818 when Thomas Wildman, a classmate of Byron at Harrow, bought it.) Byron generously gave £1,000 to Augusta to pay off some of her husband's gambling debts, lent his friend Francis Hodgson enough money to get married and then went on a monumental spending spree to equip himself for his postponed journey. His enthusiasm was infectious, and for a short while Augusta seriously considered going with him. She eventually refused as she was worried about leaving her feckless husband and would not go without taking one of her children, three-and-a-half-year-old Georgiana, eighteen-month old Augusta or two-month old George.

In an attempt to set himself free, Byron told Caroline that he was in love with Lady Oxford. The confirmation of all her fears so soon after their disagreement at Lady Jersey's added fuel to her smouldering resentment, which burst out at Lady Heathcote's waltzing party on 5 July. She was reminded, when she was asked to begin the dancing, of her promise to Byron never to waltz in front of him. She whispered to him, 'I conclude I may waltz now.' He replied, 'With every body in turn – you always did it better than any one. I shall have a pleasure in seeing you.' After a few minutes Caroline went into the small supper room and as he passed her with Lady Rancliffe on his arm, Byron said, 'I have been admiring your dexterity.' Seeing she was holding a dinner knife, he added, 'Do, my dear, but if you mean to act a Roman's part, mind which way you strike with your knife – be it at your own heart, not mine – you have struck there already.' Caroline murmured 'Byron' and ran off with the knife still in her hand. Mary, Lady Rancliffe, pretty little Bessy Rawdon's cousin, and Corisande Ossulston caught sight of it and began screaming. Caroline was seized and during the scuffle the knife cut her hand and blood dripped on to her dress. She fainted.[18]

'God knows what has happened,' Byron wrote to Lady Melbourne, 'but at 4 in the morning Ly Ossulston looking angry (& at that moment ugly) delivered to me a confused kind of message from you of some scene – This is all I know, except that with laudable logic she drew the usual feminine deduction that I "*must* have behaved very ill"... Ly W[estmorland] said "You must have done something, you know between people in your situation, a word or look goes a great way"... I am quite unaware of what I did to displease & useless regret is all I can feel on the subject. Can she be in her senses? – yet – I would rather think myself to blame – than she were so silly without cause.'[19]

'She is now like a Barrel of Gunpowder & takes fire with the most trifling spark,' Lady Melbourne wrote, 'She has been in a dreadful bad humour this last week, with her, when the fermentation begins there is no stopping it – till it boils forth, she must have gone to Ly H[eathcote's] determined to pique you by her waltzing & when she found that fail'd, in her passion she wish'd to expose you, not feeling how much worse it was for herself. Now she seems ashamed for the first time I ever saw the least mark of that feeling. It might have been kept secret but for Ly O[ussulston] & Ly H[eathcote] – the first from folly – the other from being entirely ignorant how to be goodnatur'd & from a wish to display her fine feelings... I knew they would talk & thought if it reach'd you it must make you uncomfortable & therefore desired Ly O[ssulston] to say to you there had been a Scene – but that she was calm'd & I would write to you next morning. At present I am trying to get her out of Town & hope I shall succeed. I was able to send for Fred, whom I know could hold her & I could not by myself & indeed I must do Ly Bl[arney] [Byron's nickname for Lady Bessborough, after the eccentric character in Goldsmith's *The Vicar of Wakefield*] the *justice* to say that her representations of her Violence in these paroxysms was not at all exaggerated. I could not have believed it possible for anyone to carry absurdity to such a pitch. I call it so, for I am convinced she knows perfectly what she is about all the time, but she has no idea of controlling her fury. She broke a glass & scratched herself, as you call it, with the broken pieces. Ly O & Ly H screamed instead of taking it from her, & I had just left off holding her for 2 minutes – she had a pair of scissors in her hand when I went up, with which she was wounding herself but not deeply – Pray if you answer her letters do not let her find out I have written you word of all this.'[20]

Society twittered with disapproval. 'I am perfectly horror struck, my dear Lady Holland, at the account I have received from town, of the scene at Ly Heathcote's,' the Duchess of Beaufort wrote. 'I have been told that poor Ly CL not only wounded herself in several places, but at last was carried out by several people actually in a straight waistcoat'.[21] Clergyman and essayist, Sydney Smith, was amused when he heard that 'Lady Caroline Lamb stabbed herself at Lady Ilchester's Ball [sic] for the love of Lord Byron, as it is supposed. What a charming thing to be a poet. I preached for many years in London and was rather popular, but never heard of a Lady doing herself the smallest mischief on my account.'[22] According to Frances, Lady Jerningham, a prolific letter writer and close friend of Mrs Fitzherbert, Caroline joined the ladies after supper in 'a bed chamber, took a glass of water and smashed it to pieces in her hand, by which means she was very much Cut, then in a moment produced a Knife and put it up to her throat. She was however stopped from doing serious Mischief, and they now say she is out of her Senses.'

All Caroline's past indiscretions were nothing compared with this. 'Do not speak of this horrid scene more than you can help,' she asked Lady Holland. 'I have long lost, and justly lost the opinion of others. My dishonour is complete. I neither seek to excuse myself nor have my errors shar'd. All I wish is to clear from gross misrepresentation the noblest, the most generous of human beings. William Lamb has ruined himself by excess of kindness for me. I feel it, and I trust to the generosity of the few friends I have left that they will, as far as they can, do me the only favour I shall ever ask at their hands. I am willing to do anything that is thought right, but I am resolved never more to appear in society, for which I am wholly unfit.'[23]

The newspapers published highly coloured versions of the event. Caroline asked John Murray, 'Whatever my faults and follies, is it necessary I should bear false calumnies? – And because part of a story is true am I to let my husband be dishonoured through my own imprudence? Do tell me if you read in the *Morning Herald* and some other papers the cruel account about a lady in High Life, & if you did, do you not think it ought to be contradicted?'[24] Lady Spencer wrote to Lady Bessborough, 'Dear child how cruelly does she trifle with her happiness, which has been & still, perhaps still, might be within her reach.'[25]

Caroline sent Byron a basket of gooseberries and grapes but made no more attempts to see him. Helped by William's extraordinary ability to ignore the unpleasant, the couple resumed their married life as though nothing had happened. In August the family visited Holywell and Lady Spencer thought they were 'very amiable and went to church'. Caroline described William to Murray as her 'best and only friend, whose goodness no words of mine can describe, to one who, however censured by the world for the mercy he has shown me is above every human being in nobleness of mind, integrity and kindness of heart.'

Byron retired to Suffolk with Augusta and her growing family. Frances, Lady Shelley, whose husband John was a member of George Leigh's hunting and gambling friends, described the Stud at Six Mile Bottom as a 'wretched small house, full of her ill-trained children, who were always running up and down stairs, going into "Uncle's" bedroom where he remained all the morning.' However, Byron was 'very patient with Mrs Leigh's children, who are not in the least in awe of him. He bore their distracting intrusions into his room with imperturbable good humour.'[26]

In October Caroline offered Murray copies of poems written by the Duchess of Devonshire, 'which,' she told him, 'you are not intended to see.'[27] He lent them to Byron who returned them with the comment, 'The Duchess' verses are beautiful, but I don't like *her* a bit better.' Murray was busy preparing to publish Madame de Staël's *De l'Allemagne* and, anxious to please him, Caroline suggested that William might help him in translating several passages. The offer was accepted. The original 1810 edition had been destroyed on the orders of Bonaparte's censors but Murray's edition was an immediate success and sold out within three weeks.[28]

Lady Jersey launched Madame de Staël into London society and within days she had met the Prince Regent, the Queen, the Duchess of York and the Duke of Gloucester. She fascinated Lord Melbourne, leading Lady Melbourne to complain that she was a show-off. At a reception at Lord Lansdowne's people knocked each other to the floor as they scrambled to climb on tables and chairs to get a glimpse of her. She was almost ten years older than Caroline, a plain, sturdily built woman with buckteeth in a wide mouth that almost never closed. She was formidable, enjoyed philosophical discussions, monopolised conversations and was truly happy only when the talk centred on her or on her writing. Caroline was piqued at William's interest and irritated when he praised her 'good eyes' and elegant arms. She dryly informed Murray that 'To air and water, not to mention soap, I think she has an antipathy.' Arguments between the two women were frequent and came to a head when Madame de Staël questioned Caroline about Byron. Caroline complained, to Murray, 'I do not see why strangers are to ask one these sort of questions and to gossip on all sides.'

The Duke of Devonshire had commissioned a portrait of Caroline from Thomas Phillips. She chose to wear a page's uniform, a velvet suit with sleeves lined with blue satin and a frothy lace ruff rising from a golden collar. She has a half smile on her haughty face and carries a charger covered in black and white grapes, which she is offering to someone beyond the picture. Phillips hung this next to his portrait of Byron and several people asked Caroline if she was offering him the grapes. She was embarrassed and angrily asked Murray to instruct Phillips to remove her picture from the exhibition.

In November, on the first anniversary of Caroline's return from Ireland, Lady Spencer found her at Brocket with Augustus. He seemed healthy enough but still suffering from the shortness of breath she had noticed in the spring.[29] William had gone to Panshanger to take Emily to the Hatfield Ball.

Byron abandoned his plans to go abroad and accepted an invitation from James Wedderburn Webster to join his house party at Aston Hall, near Rotherham. (Coincidentally it was in that house that his father had seduced Augusta's mother.) He amused himself by flirting with Webster's wife, Lady Frances, and giving Lady Melbourne a running commentary on his progress. He wanted to give Lady Frances a miniature he had commissioned from James Holmes and had given to Caroline. (Augusta thought it was the most lifelike of all the portraits and miniatures.) Caroline dutifully returned it, telling Murray, 'I cannot refuse, but if you knew how it did grieve me.' Byron rewarded her by telling Murray to send her an advance copy of the *Bride of Abydos*. She was overcome, 'such attention is deeply felt by one like me' she told Murray, using the opportunity to bombard him with questions. 'How is he who writes so well and is he going to remain with us – I hope so – is he sitting for the miniature which he promised me? Tell me that he is well... Pray write me word of all that is said & thought of the *Bride of Abydos*.' She enclosed a little picture of two young girls with a lamb. Copied beneath were lines from the *Essay on Man* by Pope:

The lamb thy riot dooms to bleed today
Had he thy reason would he skip and play?
Pleased to the last he crops the flowery food,
And licks the hand upraised to shed his blood.[30]

'If you think it pretty you would not please me more than showing it to the Giaour who used always to say those lines to me... He will not be displeased, trust me, or I would not ask you.'

Caroline spent much of her time drawing and sketching pictures, which she sent to Murray with requests for amusing books or to Byron in the hope that he would use them as illustrations. He moaned, 'C has been playing the devil about some engravings & fooleries.' In December Caroline told Lady Spencer that, 'Life has glided by. I walk, sleep, eat and read a little – and think a little – Wm is most kind to me and I think it is a sign that he has a very well functioned brain that he endures a life as solitary as that of a hermit. Augustus grows very sensible and good – He generally appears at our dinners. We get up at 8, breakfast at 9, lunch at 1, dine at six and go to bed at fi past 10. We read Herotes in Greek & Mad De Staël.'[31]

There was a large, noisy houseparty at Brocket during the holiday season and Caroline wilted among the Lambs. On Christmas Day she wrote, 'One line to you my dearest Grand Mama just to wish you every happiness upon it & to tell you that I think of you often and love you and honour you from my heart of hearts. Madame de Staël is here. She is a wonderful *Man*. She is very calm and good-natured but wants softness.' One morning Caroline knocked on her bedroom door and on entering she found her in bed dressed in a 'loose combing cloth upon a grey pelisse – the black locks covered with bran! & a chapeau plummet on the top of all.' Madame de Staël was unconcerned and happy to see her. Caroline told Murray, 'I like her a great deal better for receiving me so – She is after all a very good-hearted, good-natured woman.'[32]

News of the victory of the Battle of Nive reached London on 28 December and Caroline was anxious to hear if her 'gallant Ponsonby brother and Lord Wellington' were safe. She told Murray, 'We have the secretary at war [Lord Palmerston] here but he knows nothing.' Since the Battle of Leipzig in October there had been hope that the war with France would soon end. Napoleon's defeat had forced him to retreat towards France with the remnants of the Grande Armée. Throughout the winter of 1813-14 the Allies moved forward, scenting the kill. Napoleon fought back. They offered terms to avoid further slaughter. He pretended to agree, chicaned, played for time and lost. Meanwhile Wellington was fighting his way out of the Peninsula into France itself. In an attempt to protect Bayonne, the French, under Marshal Soult, attacked the combined armies of Spain, Portugal and Britain on the banks of the river Nive. The battle began at nine o'clock on 10 December 1813 and by the end of the afternoon the British and their allies had repulsed the enemy. The French suffered 2,000 casualties. Three German battalions deserted when their ruler changed sides. Caroline's fears for her brother and Lord Wellington were groundless. They were both safe and resting at St Jean de Luz.

Pleased with the sales of the *Bride of Abydos* (six thousand copies in four weeks) Byron began work on *The Corsair* on 17 December. It was in Murray's hands by the middle of January and on the street by 1 February 1814. Murray wrote, 'I sold on the day of publication, a thing perfectly unprecedented, 10,000 copies'.

1814 began like the last year. 'More letters one – two – three – from C who wants pictures – forgiveness – praise for forbearance – promise of future confidence – and God knows what beside… And as to pictures,' Byron told Lady Melbourne, 'I have no time to sit for a Sign Post. Just as I had got her quite out of my head – and she was quietly disposed with you and every one else – here she comes again.'[33]

Two days before Christmas the country was seized in the grip of severe misty frosts. The Thames froze from London Bridge to Blackfriars and people crossed the river on foot. Snow followed the frost. It fell day and night for six weeks making the roads impassable. Augustus rolled about in it laughing, made snowballs and made slides on the frozen lake. Lord and Lady Melbourne sat and fidgeted. They were expecting a visit from the Prince Regent. Each day the Prince promised to come and each day the trip was postponed. Eventually, Caroline told Murray, they were told that 'he had ordered his carriage and should be at Brocket at 4. All the servants were ordered out to meet him, carpets were put down in the court, everything was ready when another express arrived saying he was going to be blooded – and could not come till the next day. This is so ludicrous, Lord Melbourne has very wisely written to his other friends to say they may come and we think it appears certain his Royal Highness fears the passage.'[34] The Prince developed a diplomatic sore throat and the visit was abandoned. Caroline commented, 'I would not travel this weather. I hate to go slow. I run and gallop and drive as if for a wager, and otherwise I care not if I stay at home a year. I never have the windows shut, even in winter. Keep the feet warm, the head cool and the heart free, and you may defy the world the flesh and the devil – and Madame de Staël!'[35] On 24 January Caroline fell on the ice, hitting her head just above the temporal artery. The wound bled profusely and to staunch the blood Dr Lucas put leeches on it. She told Murray, 'It ought to shew you, that even in this world if we escape dying of a broken heart we may at all events finish with a broken head'.

Lord Melbourne was impatient to return to London. In an attempt to make a passage through the snow to the gates of Brocket he designed a primitive snowplough. It consisted of a triangular piece of wood that, at the broadest point, measured the width of a carriage, pulled by four horses. Augustus was allowed to go out with the men on the contraption and watch as it pushed the snow aside. He was delighted and clapped his hands declaring 'it was the most joyful moment of his existence.' Later, however, he was brought to Caroline to be scolded. She told Lady Spencer, 'The men accused him of sticking out his foot to trip up Master George – "How can you say so?" he said, "I was trying all I could to trip him *down!*"'[36]

Byron took Augusta to Newstead for the first time and settled in the few rooms that were habitable. They discussed his future and he wrote to Lady Melbourne. 'I wish I were married – I don't care much about beauty nor *subsequent* virtue – nor much about fortune… But I should like, let me see, loveliness, gentleness, cleanliness, something of comeliness & *my own* first born, was ever man more moderate?'[37]

Madame de Staël told Caroline that Byron had recently completed a new work and when Caroline questioned Lady Melbourne, she told Byron, anxious to put Caroline in the wrong, 'This I know was not true but merely to bring up your Name.' She was mistaken, 'I never said one word,' Caroline told Murray, 'for I act by his name as the Israelites did by that of their God, I name it not.' In an attempt to get into Lady Melbourne's good favour she promised to be good and asked for forgiveness. Lady Melbourne ridiculed her, telling Byron, 'She said she had written a detail of the reports that had been made to her which would be given to me if she died & that I should see how she had been work'd upon. The idea of *her* leaving a paper for *me* to see made me laugh.' No doubt she was thinking of the letter she had planted in Caroline's rooms in 1812. 'She is now cheerful enough to be very tiresome with her theories and her discussion which she is eternally beginning & always turn upon some supposed ill usage, which women receive from men, evidently alluding to you.'[38]

Marriage continued to occupy Byron's thoughts. 'I have no *heart* to spare – & expect none in return, but as Moore says "A pretty wife is something for the fastidious vanity of a roué to *retire* upon." – and mine might do as she pleased so that she had a fair temper – and a *quiet* way of conducting herself – leaving me the same liberty of conscience. What I want is a companion – a friend – rather than a sentimentalist.'[39]

In January Murray showed Caroline the illustrations for *The Corsair* which increased her desire to return to London. She threatened to drive herself to town in a phaeton, 'I dare say I shall not drive safe – but overturn myself and all I approach. Write to me for I am in a fever.'[40]

Byron struggled back to London through the thawing snow in February to find he was under siege from the Tory press for attacking the Prince Regent in the lines *Weep, Daughter of a Royal Line*, which had been published anonymously in March 1812 and which Murray had included in *The Corsair*.

Weep, daughter of a royal line,
A Sire's disgrace, a realm's decay;
Ah! happy if each tear of thine
Could wish a father's fault away!

Weep – for thy tears are Virtue's tears –
Auspicious to these suffering isles;
And be each drop in future years
Repaid they by thy people's smiles.

'I hear the Prince speaks very ill of him,' Caroline told Murray. 'It was absurd to put it in – How can he be surprised that those he trod on like reptiles so long should rise & bite when they can – For God's sake do not name me to him. Do not say I write to you. He tells everything to Lady Melbourne'.[41] She asked Murray to send her any articles for or against Byron and not to forget 'to write all you promised in the little book I left with you.' She continued resentfully, 'My letter shewn – my words misrepresented, my gifts offered and worn by such a woman as Lady Oxford!' (Lady Oxford had been seen in Rome with Byron's miniature peeping out from her sash.) Caroline complained, 'I am sick of the stupid newspapers – why throw dust on his sacred head? *You* called it forth. *You* published *Weep Daughter* and it was unwise was it not?'[42] Lady Melbourne thought Byron should sue the more colourful papers. Murray omitted the lines from the third edition but he was persuaded to replace them in the fourth. The success of *The Corsair* astounded Hobhouse. '13,000 copies sold in a month. The abuse showered upon Byron for the *Weep, Daughter of a Royal Line* helped it along.'

Lady Spencer was seventy-seven, frail and unable to write comfortably so she often dictated her letters to Miss Trimmer. In a spidery hand she wrote a last letter, 'Selina is out, my dear Harriet, so I am proud to be my own scribe & to say that I really think my cough is better. Was you at the Ball last night? The carriages passed my windows till after 5 today, & I was sorry not to be well enough to look out, as I should have seen some of their odd dresses.' Lady Bessborough and Caroline were grief stricken when she died on 18 March 1814. No longer would they be able to retreat to Holywell or ask the pious but worldly old lady for advice.

That spring Thomas Phillips exhibited three portraits of Byron. Caroline thought they were all bad likenesses, 'yet enough to make my heart break.'[43] She told Murray, 'I like him as he was even when I knew him first.' Hobhouse upheld this view. 'Went to see three pictures which are being painted of Byron by Phillips RA I see no resemblance in either one.'[44] For some time Caroline had been trying to persuade Murray to allow her to have a copy made of the miniature he was holding for Byron. She had found a suitable artist, Miss Eleanor Kendrick, who later became a miniature painter for William IV and had her work exhibited at the Royal Academy. 'I die for it', she told him. 'I have done with stabbing and burning – I have taken the veil.' She promised never to tell Byron and argued that 'however harsh, however false' he was behind her back, 'he is only too indulgent and kind' when she saw him and 'therefore do you not refuse what you know he would grant if I were to see him.' Murray reluctantly agreed; Miss Kendrick arrived at Albemarle Street at nine in the morning and three hours later the copy was finished.[45] The news reached Caroline just as she was about to leave for Brocket. She begged Murray to put it in his pocket and to bring it to Melbourne House immediately. 'To go into the country and not see, this is death – Do you fear my betraying any trust – Have I ever – do send it me.' On 15 April she wrote, 'Thank you a thousand times more than I will say.'

Byron no longer casually dropped into Whitehall to talk to Lady Melbourne. He dreaded to meet Caroline and to be subjected to emotional scenes. He continued to be a welcome guest in all the great Whig strongholds and a familiar figure at Holland House, where he shocked his fellow diners with his outrageous notions. A favourite topic was incest, a fashionable subject of conversation. As usual, he went too far. He implied that the original hero and heroine of the *Bride of Abydos* were brother and sister and not cousins, as they appeared in the final version. Since everything he said was scoured for personal experience, he had entered a dangerous area. He had made similar remarks during Augusta's stay in London the previous July and rumours and innuendoes reached out as far at Eton, leading Augusta's nephew to cross-question her. Caroline had suggested to Lady Melbourne in January that Byron was the father of Augusta's coming baby and said that he had shown her incriminating letters. She pointed to the rumour that Augusta and George Leigh were on the point of separating. Lady Melbourne challenged Byron. 'C is quite out,' he wrote, 'In the first place *she* [Augusta] was not under the same roof – but first with the H[arroby]s in B[erke]l[e]y Square and afterwards at her friends the V[illier]s nearer me.'[46] The rumour that Augusta and George were considering separation was 'utterly false & without even a shadow of foundation so you see her spies are ill paid or badly informed.'

The Third Earl of Chichester, Augusta's nephew, commented, 'Although Colonel Leigh abominated Lord Byron he absolutely and totally denied and disbelieved in Mrs Leigh's guilt.' The resulting child of the presumed act of incest looked like George Leigh and he treated her in exactly the same way as his other children. Therese Villiers, who had known Augusta since they were children, said, 'I think I am justified in saying very confidently that her mind was purity and innocence itself.' If there had been the faintest chance that the allegation had been true it is unlikely that the Prince Regent would have recommended Augusta to be a bedchamber-woman to his prim mother, Queen Charlotte, in March 1815.

Byron showed no signs of carrying a great secret on his soul when he attended the christening of his goddaughter and Augusta's fourth child, born on 15 April. The baby was named Elizabeth in honour of her godmother, the Duchess of Rutland, and Medora, either after a heroine in *The Corsair* (part of which was written at Six Mile Bottom) or after the Duke of Rutland's filly which had recently won the Oaks. The child was always called Libby in the family.[47]

Byron had little time for his shiftless brother-in-law, Colonel George Leigh, but he was conscious that physically he was no match for the tall colonel of the 10th (Prince of Wales' Own Royal) Hussars. His baggy white trousers, made of Russian Duck material, strapped firmly under his feet to hide his deformity, compared sadly with Leigh's gold braided jacket, red pelisse edged with white fur and scarlet shako with gold rosettes and cords. Leigh belonged to the horseracing, hard-drinking and gaming fraternity. He beggared himself and his family and had attempted to recoup his losses by cheating the Prince Regent by withholding money from the sale of his horses. This was a particularly shabby trick, considering that the Prince had provided him with a job, the running of his stud at Six Mile Bottom, and a house to go with it – an arrangement that had almost certainly been contrived by Lady Melbourne. Byron's present of £1,000 had lessened the grip of a few of his creditors but it had emphasised Leigh's inadequacy and aroused his envy. This was increased when Byron gave Augusta an additional £3,000 in May 1814 with the rider that she should encourage her husband to find a way of regulating his expenditure.

Augusta's attachment to Leigh puzzled and annoyed Byron: 'It is true she married a fool', he told Lady Melbourne, 'but she *would* have him – they agree & agree very well – & I never heard a complaint but many vindications of him'. In a reference to Lady Melbourne's help in arranging the match, he wrote, 'Poor soul – she likes her husband – I think her thanking you for your abetment of her abominable marriage (7 years after the event!!) is the only instance of similar gratitude upon record.'

Caroline visited John Murray so frequently at Albemarle Street that she claimed her black horse, Cameron (later renamed Glenarvon) could find his way there and back unaided. Murray discussed everything and anything that interested her enquiring mind, from ethics, poetry and Byron to politics, but what interested her most was writing. Lady Morgan had just written *O'Donnel*, a novel in three volumes, Murray was about to publish Sir Walter Scott's *Waverley* and Caroline began her first book. After one of their talks on a damp day in April, Caroline went home in the rain. She told Murray that it was 'remarkably warm and pleasant besides no drizzly rain that falls on me can wash away my sins, as the lady says to the friar. I was reflecting all the way home upon a new cause of misery which I have conjured up. I think I shall live to see the day – when some beautiful and innocent Lady Byron shall drive to your door & I picture to myself the delight with which you will receive her – how every remark of hers will be admired by you – and how bright she will appear to you compared to me – who is faded and fallen. I really believe that when that day comes – I shall buy a pistol at Mantons & stand before the Giaour & his legal wife & shoot myself… If you knew how good I was once, how sorry you would be for me now… Oh, that Lady Biron – How I feel secure that you will prefer her ten hundred times to me – Everyone will.'[48]

Caroline admitted to Lady Melbourne that she dreaded the thought of Byron marrying, to which she replied: 'It is my opinion that if you persisted in your present behaviour – that you will drive him to marry.' 'This,' she told Byron, 'made her look very grave.' Lady Melbourne told Caroline to treat Byron as she would anyone else or avoid him without appearing to do so. 'Or,' Byron commented, 'if we jostle – at any rate *not* to *bite*.'[49]

Caroline could not stop herself writing to him and many of the letters were tear-stained, written in such a passion that the pen-nib cut the paper and the writing was uneven, straggly, smeared and blotted. 'When I enter a room I know where you are by a row of beaming eyes all turned askance after you,' she wrote in a typical letter. 'I literally saw nothing but your ear for a whole hour one night – It is perfectly unlike any ear in nature.' (Byron's ears were small with unusually narrow sloping lobes, a characteristic he passed on to his daughter Ada.) 'I have often been nearer to it than the other night – too near even while I exist, to forget moments of perfect happiness – your wife will be happy – I am certain of it – though others doubt it – because you are a man any woman might live with forever & unless she tire you – you could not tire her… There is nothing in heaven or earth or under the earth like *you*… Why did God make a Being like you, if he did not give us the strength not to admire and love it? Are you a man? I doubt it. How many angry looks from Lady M – how many frowns will be my fate – and perhaps from you – The mouth will be turned with its corners to the ground – However, I cannot be worse off as someone said when they were in the pillory.'[50]

Byron agreed to return her letters and pictures saying, 'At the same signal it might be as well for her to restore *my* letters – as everybody has read them by this time – and they cannot longer be of use to herself and her five hundred sympathising friends'. In an attempt to please him and be near to him, Caroline tried to make friends with Augusta. 'Tell your sister to try not to dislike me. Let her not pass me by as Lady Gertrude Sloane does – & Lady Rancliffe… Make her forgive me if you can for I love that Augusta with my heart because she is yours and is dear to you.'[51] She had no inkling that Lady Melbourne was encouraging him to renew his suit with Annabella Milbanke, whom he described as 'the most prudish & correct person I know.' Caroline reverted to the old fear that he was in love with Lady Melbourne. 'Think of my situation,' she scolded, 'how Extraordinary! My mother-in-law actually in the place I held – her ring instead of mine – her letters instead of mine – her heart – but do you believe either she or any other feel for you what I felt. Ugly and thin & mad, despised as I am, you never, never love or will be lov'd by another – of that I am certain because, except for your own self, no one can love as well & devotedly & entirely as I could – & did – and this one day you will know.' After an evening spent listening to Byron read a selection of his works Caroline, in an incoherent letter, accused him of being capable of asking her to make his new favourite's bed. 'You are just a man to exact it & with my violence you would have made me do it – I have done all but that already – Have I not?' What really hurt her was that he 'thought of other *women while with me* of that I am sure'.[52]

At the end of March Byron took over Viscount Althorp's lease at A2 Albany. He was delighted with the space and freedom of the rooms and took a vicarious pleasure in living in Lady Melbourne's former home. 'Whilst I lived in that House,' she told him, 'no Misfortune reach'd me.' Caroline began to make furtive visits when she thought Byron was out. She put on her Carman's coat and mixed with the crowds flocking along Piccadilly, then slipped into the courtyard, passed the door of Byron's fencing instructor, Henry Angelo, and vanished down the steps on the left of the front door, not stopping until she was safely hidden in the whitewashed subterranean corridor which ran the length of the building. Carefully avoiding Mrs Mule, Byron's old, kind and unprepossessing servant whom he had brought from his former lodgings, she would announce herself at the servants' entrance, talk her way past Fletcher or Rushton and enter his chambers. The living room, formerly Lady Melbourne's library, at the back of the main building, was large and pleasant and lit by a bow window. A long table stood in front of the fireplace, usually covered in books. A miniature of Lady Oxford hung near a comfortable sofa and a large screen covered with prints of famous boxers on one side and actors on the other added a touch of colour. Byron's sabres and silver urns shone in the sunlight and the room was never silent, filled with the cawing and screeching of Byron's pet macaw and parrot.

On one of her clandestine visits Caroline found a copy of Beckford's *Vathek*. She could not resist writing on the flyleaf 'Remember me'. Byron was enraged by her brazen invasion of his home and her constant disregard of his wishes and wrote beneath her words;

Remember thee, remember thee!
Till Lethe quench life's burning stream,
Remorse and shame shall cling to thee,

And haunt thee like a feverish dream!
Remember thee! Ay, doubt it not;
Thy husband too shall think of thee;

By neither shalt thou be forgot,
Thou false to him, thou fiend to me.

'She comes at all times,' he complained to Lady Melbourne, 'at any time – & the moment the door is open in she walks – I can't throw her out of the window…but I will not receive her. The Bessboroughs may take her if they please – or any steps they please – I have no hesitation in saying that I have made up my mind as to the alternative – and would sooner – much sooner be with the dead in purgatory – than with her… She may hunt me down – it is in the power of any mad or bad woman to do so by any man – but *snare* she shall not – torment me she may – how am *I* to bar myself from her! I am already almost a prisoner – she has no shame – no feeling – not one estimable or redeemable quality. These are strong words – but I know what I am writing… I would lose an hundred souls rather than be bound to C[aroline] – if there is one human being whom I do utterly *detest & abhor* – it is she – & all things considered I feel to myself justified in so doing – She has been an adder in my path ever since my return to this country – She has often belied – & sometimes betrayed me – she has crossed me everywhere – she has watched – & worried & *guessed* – and been a curse to me & mine.'[53]

Caroline saw the situation differently. She was still his love, his Biondetta who would stand by him through thick and thin when everyone had deserted him.

If to love all that love thee should e'er be thy lot
By the World that now courts the condemned or forgot
When thy own fickle heart has all others estranged
Then remember Biondetta who never has changed.

Who had followed thy steps though in sickness and sadness
More firm in misfortune than those who upbraid her
Who followed thy steps – though to death and to madness
Then mourn o'er the grave where thy falsehood has laid her.

I know thou wilt say that this fool shall recover
But the blow never fails from the hand of a lover
Full home it was struck and it fell on a breast
By remorse and unkindness already depressed.

A smile even in death may illumine each feature
When hope fondly cherished – forever is past
And the heart that is noble and high in its nature
Though bowed and scorn'd will be firm to the last.[54]

On another occasion, when Byron discovered her hidden in his rooms, he desperately decided to shock her out of love. He let her believe that he had taken part in homosexual acts during the two years he was abroad in 1809 to 1811 and showed her papers which, she said later, implicated Augusta in incest. She told Medwin that when they parted Byron had pressed his lips on hers and said, 'Poor Caro, if every one hates me, you, I see, will never change. No, not with ill usage!' She replied, 'Yes, I *am* changed, & shall come near you no more'.

On 2 April Napoleon had been dethroned and shuffled off to Elba, leaving the settlement of Europe in the hands of a Congress in which he had no say. The Bourbons were restored in France and Louis XVIII, or as Byron preferred, 'Louis the Gouty,' enjoyed a triumphal welcome in England, which reached its peak when the Prince Regent invested him with the Order of the Garter. The summer of balls and masquerades began when Frederick William, Emperor of Russia, and Alexander, King of Prussia, arrived for a state visit on 6 June.

The visit of the Allied Sovereigns coincided with the anniversary of a century of Hanoverian rule and, as part of the celebrations, St James's Park was tidied up. It had been used as a camp for the militia during the Gordon Riots in 1780 and had become 'a long dirty field, intersected by a wide dirty ditch, thinly planted with rotten lime trees and surrounded by a wooden railing.' A 'Chinese' bridge was built over the canal, which supported a seven-storey wooden pagoda lit by gaslights and fireworks. The builders hoped that the 'girandoles of rockets, roman candles and *pots de brin*' would make the pagoda look like a column of fire on the opening night. Instead the top three storeys burst into flames and several of the workers drowned or burned to death. London was brilliant with lights. Every window in the houses surrounding the park glowed with candles and lamps were hung in the trees. The Mall and Birdcage Walk were illuminated with Chinese lanterns and an entrance fee of a half-guinea allowed the crowds to stroll about the park and lose their money in gaming tents and refreshment booths. Another firework display was held at the Temple of Concord, not far from Constitution Hall, which covered one-third of Green Park.

Caroline shook off her gloom and obtained an order of admittance to Carlton House for Murray to see the Emperors. 'What is the meaning of right and wrong?' she asked him, 'all is but appearance. Who that looks innocent can be thought guilty? What is Guilt? There is no such thing as conscience... If I cannot sleep in my bed – why should I lie down? There are balls and assemblies, operas and plays, and who dances more gaily than I am? Who dare say I am not good or happy?… Come and see the balloon on Friday. Thursday I sup out. Tomorrow there is a great ball, Saturday a supper. All the week is full of amusement. Be happy – let us all be merry. What is life given us for but to enjoy it? God bless you sir – and if there is a God pray that He may bless me – even me also.'[55] Full of her old ebullience and charm she wanted to reward him for keeping her secrets: 'I wish I knew what you would like – would you or your friends like a Marlborough spaniel – they are very rare – only the D of York, my cousin of Marlborough & I have the breed – I by descent – she by favour. Do you wish for baskets of violets – have you any want of cards to see Devonshire House – or the Elgin Marbles – only command me for upon earth I know of nothing more disagreeable than to labour under *continual* extenuated obligations.'[56]

On 16 June Lady Cork gave a reception in honour of the Prussian field marshal, Gebhard Leberecht von Blücher, who had defeated Napoleon at Laon and come to the aid of Wellington at Waterloo. Mrs Opie arrived late and found fourteen guests rattling round Lady Cork's pretty rooms 'where eternal twilights fall upon fountains of rose-water which never dry, and on beds of flowers which never fade, – where singing birds are always silent, and butterflies are for once at rest.'[57] Blücher had been delayed at the opera. He was present when the great debate began on whether or not the Prince Regent had bowed to his estranged wife. Each new arrival at Lady Cork's was asked 'Well what do *you* say? Did the prince bow to the pit or the princess?' Everyone had a different opinion. Mrs Opie turned to Caroline and said, 'How difficult it is to ascertain the truth!' 'Aye, indeed,' she replied, 'it teaches us to receive all reports doubtingly.' Just after midnight, when people began to drift home, Caroline suggested to Lady Cork and Lydia White, a wealthy Irish Bluestocking, that they should play charades in an attempt to keep the remaining guests. The trio left the room and returned armed with the poker and tongs from the fireplace. Mrs Opie explained, 'the word was *orage* – they dug for *or* and they acted a passion for *rage* and then they acted a storm for the whole word, *orage*.' Caroline disappeared but by now everyone had given up all hope of seeing Blücher. Then they heard the sound of cheering which grew closer and they leapt up, 'There's Blücher at last!' The door opened. A servant announced, 'General Blücher,' and in strutted Caroline in a cocked hat and a greatcoat. Amid the laughter Lord Hardwick arrived. He was taken aback when Caroline clasped her hands, lifted her pretty hazel eyes, fluttered her lashes and asked him for money. 'What for?' the startled man asked. She laughed as she replied 'for that *pretty hurra*. They did it so well!' She ran downstairs with the money in her hand to share it among the servants.[58]

The Duke of Devonshire's magnificent reception for the allied sovereigns on 19 June brought back memories of similar events held in his mother's heyday.

London was awash with foreign dignitaries and Byron preened himself in the company of Prince Radziwill, Prince Metternich, General Blücher and General Köller, who had just returned from Elba. Byron was elected to Watier's, the famous gambling club, and on 1 July attended its masked ball held at Burlington House in honour of the Duke of Wellington. He wore a monk's habit, and Hobhouse borrowed his Albanian costume made famous by his portrait by Thomas Phillips. Byron had paid the enormous sum of fifty guineas for it and eventually gave it to Margaret Mercer-Elphinstone for another masquerade. William wore a 'magnificent Italian dress' but the courtesan Harriette Wilson remarked that he 'looked so stupid, I could not help fancying that Lady Caroline had insisted on his showing himself thus beautiful, to gratify her vanity; for, to do William Lamb justice, his character is in truth a manly one, and I will venture to say that this sad tawdry dress was never one of his own choosing.'[59]

Caroline set out to irritate Byron and as soon as she arrived she attached herself to Hobhouse's arm and 'played the most extraordinary tricks.' She marched up and down so often in front of Byron that he thought she was about to make a scene. However, 'as she was masked & dominoed and it was in daylight there could be little harm & there was at least a probability of more quiet. Not all I could say could prevent her from displaying her green *pantaloons* every now & then – though I scolded her like her grandfather upon these very uncalled for and unnecessary gesticulations.' Which was just what she wanted him to do.[60]

Caroline was one of the first to be presented to Louis XVIII 'but almost all the other ladies had to wade through a passage & a room. I could not have squeezed myself through – worse than the mob at the door.' Crowds surged through the streets to see the King pass and Caroline was disappointed that Murray had not invited her to watch the procession from one of his windows. 'I, however,' she told him 'got into the thickest of the crowed, women fainting & men swearing & nearly reached your doors when the dread of appearing like Miss Benger [an unprepossessing bluestocking friend] exerting her energies before the beautiful *Corsair*, if he were there, made me retreat as fast as the immense crowd would let me. I write to make you one petition – Let me be there to see the King go away. I care not if it is at the roof of the house.'[61]

At the end of July Byron took Augusta and her children to Hastings. They spent three happy weeks swimming, eating turbot, walking on the cliffs and endlessly discussing his marriage. Augusta steered him away from his childhood sweetheart, Mary Chaworth, who had left her brutish husband and recently written to Byron. There still remained the slight danger that Caroline might persuade him to elope and Lady Melbourne hoped he would marry Annabella Milbanke. Byron briefly considered Lady Catherine Annesley and her youngest sister, Lady Juliana. Thomas Moore and Augusta liked Lady Adelaide Forbes and Byron ran an eye over shy Lady Charlotte Leveson-Gower, Lord Carlisle's niece. Augusta put out delicate feelers but, knowing the antagonism felt by the Carlisles towards her brother, she did not hold out great hope. She felt Annabella was not the best choice but she agreed to consider her in the event that Lady Charlotte refused him.

Annabella had not seen or heard from Byron for some time and, fearful he had escaped, wrote to him. She explained, as delicately as she could, why she had encouraged him to believe that she was engaged to Lord Auckland. 'The reasons which led me to believe the character of one person suited to my own have disappeared with opportunities for fuller investigation...nothing could induce me to marry him.' Byron replied, tongue in cheek, 'I did – do – and always shall love you... You would probably like me if you could; and as you cannot I am not quite coxcomb enough to be surprised at a very natural occurrence.' Annabella's reply was so verbose and ungracious that he assumed the courtship had collapsed. He replied briskly, 'Very well – now we can talk of something else.' Terrified that she had lost her chance, she clumsily flattered him by asking his opinion on a selection of modern history books and inviting him to stay at Seaham.

She need not have worried, Byron was at Six Mile Bottom with Augusta, where he ate a whole collar of brawn and made himself ill. He returned to London to receive good news. Murray had sold 6,000 copies of his new work, *Lara*, in four days. On 21 August he took Augusta and the children to Newstead on an extended holiday, reading, swimming, boating and relaxing on the lake.

The Duchess of Devonshire left her house at 13 Piccadilly, where she had lived 'in almost regal splendour', for Paris on 6 August where she joined half of London Society, including the Duke of Wellington, who had been appointed Ambassador, and Lady Oxford whose 'charming *soirées*' were famous. On 8 August William Ponsonby (though sometimes still called Willy in the family to distinguish him from William Lamb) married Lady Barbara Ashley Cooper. It was to be a happy and financially secure marriage. The bride was the daughter of Lord Shaftesbury and a considerable heiress.

Lady Bessborough too, decided to leave England and planned a prolonged tour of the Continent, ultimately arriving in Italy by way of Paris, Orleans, Nice and Marseilles. She wanted to take Caroline to remove her from Byron's influence and told her to be ready to leave in October. Caroline told Murray, 'I wish to leave my trunks with you & my cockatoo & two Blenheim puppies, 3 pages, Rushton, Seymour & Eden Green. If you do not write instantly counter orders they will be at your door.' Meanwhile she remained at Brocket and bombarded Murray with invitations, orders, presents and letters. 'I can send you fruit or fish or garlands,' she told him and added, 'God Bless Lara and send him every Joy. I hope his birds do not bite and scream quite as much as mine. Yours very sincerely, Cosimo di Medici.'[62] Byron was never far from her mind, 'God Bless the "Childe",' she told Murray, 'That I did love him is too certain, that I have not, cannot, shall not change is the fault of my nature for God be witness I tried hard for it this year.' When she did not receive an instant reply to an invitation, she wrote impatiently, 'Are you coming? If you have the least good nature forward *Waverley* to me by the Leeds coach. I cannot get it and I must read it this instant... Let me know how you are.' She signed herself, 'Yrs, Medora – oh never!'[63] She jokingly replied to one of his letters, 'You cannot express how much it will please you to hear from me in Switzerland – Is this a courteous way of entreating my silence till then?'

Augusta persevered in her attempt to entice Lady Charlotte Leveson-Gower to consider marriage to Byron and was disappointed but not surprised when, under pressure from her family, Lady Charlotte accepted a proposal of marriage from Henry Howard, the future Earl of Surrey, a man she scarcely knew.

'You see,' Byron said to Augusta, 'that after all, Miss Milbanke is to be the person; – I will write to her.' Augusta was unconvinced but when she read his letter she said, 'Well, really this is a very pretty letter; it is a pity it should not go. I never read a prettier one.' Byron exclaimed recklessly, 'Then it *shall* go.' He convinced himself that 'a wife would be the salvation of me' and having thrown the die, he became agitated and often sat on the steps outside the Abbey waiting for the post. He felt sure he would be rejected and daydreamed about the trip he would take with Hobhouse. They would go to Italy; he had always wanted to see Venice and the Alps.

Annabella immediately accepted his offer and, to make sure there should be no mistake or misunderstanding, sent her acceptance in duplicate – a copy to Newstead, the original to Albany.

Augusta and Byron were dining with a friend when the letter arrived. Just moments earlier, the gardener had found Byron's mother's wedding ring, lost in a flowerbed beneath her bedroom window many years before. Holding the unopened letter in his hand, Byron declared dramatically, 'If it contains a consent, I will be married with this very ring.' He silently read it, went white faced, looked glumly at Augusta and said, 'It never rains but it pours.'

6

'Everything she says, does or imagines must be public'

Shortly after returning to London from Newstead on 23 September, Byron wrote to Lady Melbourne. 'I thought – at least heard that C was gone to France – See her I will not – if I can help it – and if I did nothing could come of it now – though the consequences might be as unpleasant.' He did not know if she had learned of his engagement but suspected the servants might have told her. He dreaded seeing her as her recent half-hostile, half-mocking attitude made him uncomfortable.[1]

He told Lady Melbourne that he had never doubted that Annabella would accept his proposal, 'After all it is a match of *your* making.' In fact he was taken aback. He told Moore, 'I certainly did not dream that she was attached to me, which it seems she has been for some time'. More importantly he had relied on slipshod information. 'Her expectations, I am told are great: *what* I have not asked.' Nevertheless he was determined to make the marriage work and to make sure he could afford to give Annabella a good settlement, he decided to sell both Newstead and his estate in Rochdale.

The engagement was a triumph for Annabella, or as she described it 'an event that affords me the best prospect of happiness. The attachment had been progressive for two years and I now own it with feelings of happiness that promise to be durable as they are deep.' It was a brave attempt to persuade herself and others into believing that Byron had played the pale and anxious suitor for two years, while in fact she was one in a gallery of potential brides.

Byron invited Murray to Albany. His first words were, 'Can you keep a Secret?'

'Certainly,' replied Murray, 'positively, my wife's out of town!'

'Then I am going to be MARRIED!'

'The devil! I shall have no poem this winter then?'

'No.'

'Who is the lady, who is to do me this injury?'

'Miss Milbanke – do you know her?'

'No, my lord.'

Murray told his wife Annie that Byron then began to curse 'poor Lady C— as the fiend who had interrupted all his projects and who would do so now if possible. I think he hinted that she had managed to interrupt this connection two years ago. He thought she was abroad, and, to his torment and astonishment, he finds her not only in England, but also in London.'[2]

The Milbankes broke the news of the engagement to their relations in a series of letters and Annabella could not resist bragging to her friends, saying she wanted 'her happiness made known.'[3] Byron instructed Lady Melbourne to tell Caroline. 'It cannot be helped – She must do her worst – if so disposed.'[4] Caroline immediately asked Murray to call at Melbourne House. 'I am in town for 10 hours can you come and see me this evening – at nine or ten – if not when can I see you? – I am all alone in London.'[5] Her dream had come to an end.

Hobhouse noted the news in his diary on 30 September without comment. The following day he congratulated his friend and agreed to stand as groomsman at the wedding. In a charming letter Augusta told Annabella how much she was looking forward to calling her 'sister'. Lord Wentworth, Annabella's uncle, gave his permission and the lawyers were summoned. Sir Ralph and Lady Milbanke hid their disappointment at her choice. Formal announcements were placed in the *Morning Post* and the *Morning Chronicle*. When a notice contradicting the announcement was published in the *Morning Chronicle*, Byron suspected Caroline; 'no one else has the motive or malignity to be so *petty*'. However, on reflection he remembered Claughton's animosity towards him over the sale of Newstead and he apologised to Caroline.[6]

Hary-o received the news with astonishment. 'Lady Bessborough,' she told Lady Morpeth, 'writes us word that Miss Milbanke's marriage is declared and all the Melbourne family full of it. How wonderful of that sensible, cautious prig of a girl to venture upon such a heap of poems, crimes and rivals'. She quoted part of a letter Annabella had written to Lady Melbourne, 'in which she praises him with rapture and says she can never sufficiently wonder or rejoice at being the happy object of his choice, and only hopes to deserve it by her constant exertions &c.' She added that Lady Melbourne was highly emotional, though Caroline is 'calm and reasonable'.[7]

Caroline could not resist writing Byron one last letter. 'I must write farewell, not as you say to your favourites or they to you – not as any woman ever spoke that word for they never mean it to be what I will make it – but as nuns and those who die.' Teardrops puckered the writing paper. 'Thanks too for your patience and forgiveness in many trying scenes – & even receive thanks for your cruelty as it has humbled a very proud and vain character whom none but you ever dared to contend with before. From a child I have made everyone bend to me – The least contradiction the least control made me desperate – a word from those I loved & honoured was more than I could bear – and I felt so sure of never failing in what was honourable and in time that I could not bring myself even to pray to God for his support – could you but guess with such a character as mine, so like an untamed tygress – what I have suffered within these three years, you would perhaps judge me less harshly… It is not in my nature – either to feel remorse or shame – you have judged me severely not justly – my principles were most firm till my ill conduct shook them & sooner than feel wrong – I preferred to think right a mere nominal distinction – in short I loved you as no woman ever could love because I am not like them – but more like a Beast who sees no crime in loving and following its master – You became such to me – Master of my soul more than of anything else.' In her distress she smudged the wet ink with her finger, leaving a blot where the B of 'Beast' should be.[8]

Sir Ralph and Lady Milbanke became irritated and impatient when the marriage settlement had not been agreed, nor Newstead sold, by the middle of October. Byron's enthusiasm was flagging and George Leigh told Augusta that a bookmaker in Newmarket was taking bets on whether or not the marriage would take place. Since the announcement in the press, Byron had been honouring wagers he made in Brighton in 1808 when he took a guinea from each of his gambling cronies at odds of 150:1 against him marrying. Leigh advised him not to rush into marriage but Byron suspected his motive was to try to protect Augusta's inheritance rather than to prevent an unsuitable match.[9]

Byron's family lawyer, John Hanson, was unwilling to leave London to draw up the marriage contract. He was embroiled in a crisis. When his daughter, Mary Ann, had married the feeble-minded Earl of Portsmouth, in March 1814, Byron had been a groomsman. Now Portsmouth's brother and heir, Newton Fellowes, wanted the marriage annulled on the grounds of lunacy but Byron stood by Hanson and swore an affidavit saying the groom had appeared to be 'perfectly calm and rational' on his wedding day. Byron was now becoming increasingly uneasy as the days passed and Hanson dithered and procrastinated. His patience finally snapped when Hanson pleaded illness as an excuse for more delay, giving the Milbankes an excuse to break the engagement, which would leave him vulnerable to Caroline's attempts to compromise him into eloping.

He left London alone for Seaham on 29 October and spent the first night and the whole of the following day with the Leighs at Six Mile Bottom. It was late evening before he left and made his way to the coaching inn on the Great North Road, The Haycock at Wansford. The following evening he slept at Newark. Throughout the journey he was haunted by thoughts of Mary Ann Chaworth, 'the starlight of his boyhood'. She had been his first love when he was a plump, vulnerable, slightly pompous boy of fifteen and she a sophisticated young woman of seventeen, already pledged to dashing Jack Muster, reputed to be a by-blow of the Prince Regent. Their one-sided, six-week summer romance ended when Byron heard that Mary had supposedly said to her maid, 'Do you think I could care anything for that lame boy!'[10] The marriage had turned out badly and for some months Mary had been trying to get a separation from Jack. Augusta did not want him embroiled with another married woman and had advised him to ignore Mary's letters. When her overtures came to nothing she had a nervous breakdown. Lady Melbourne was well informed of the situation as Sophie Muster, Jack's mother, showed her copies of Mary's letters. Byron later told Medwin, 'Had I married Miss Chaworth perhaps the tenor of my whole life would have been different.'

He arrived at Seaham on 1 November and the extraordinary length of time he had taken to travel from London did not pass without comment. Lady Milbanke was particularly annoyed at what she saw as a slight to her clever daughter. Neither of the Milbankes had wanted Byron as a son-in-law but Sir Ralph told Mrs Clermont (Annabella's former governess and confidante) that she had 'persecuted' them to allow her to marry him.

When Annabella returned home after the 1812 season she had written an assessment of Caroline. 'She tries to disarm the condemnation of her friends by unreserved confession of her errors... Confidence in her integrity is also diminished by perceiving a delicate attempt at self-justification, through apparent candour of self-reproach. She has a peculiar grace in telling her story, which engages our interest, and tempts our judgement to take her part. She piques herself, and not without reason, on the *charm* of her evasive ingenuity; her apprehension is exceedingly quick, and she *manages* every feeling as she sees it rise in the minds of those whom she would persuade.'[11] She now asked Byron for his views and he told her that Caroline's 'whole disposition is a moral phenomenon (if she be not *mad*). It is not feminine – she has no real affection – or if any, it is to the very man she has most injured, WL – but everything seems perverted in her – She is unlike every body – & not even like herself for a week together.'[12]

Byron was taken aback when Annabella asked if he had any doubts about their engagement. He sank back into the sofa speechless for a few moments, then he murmured indistinctly, 'You don't know what you've done.' Annabella believed this meant he was struck with despair at the thought of losing her. It did not occur to her that he saw the door of freedom swing open but could not think how to honourably take the first step. He was not convinced she was truly in love with him and told Lady Melbourne, 'Her disposition is the very reverse of our imaginings. She is overrun with fine feelings, scruples about herself and her disposition (I suppose, in fact she means mine) and to crown it all is taken ill once every three days with I know not what... In short it is impossible to foresee where this will end *now* any more than two years ago; if this is a break, it shall be her doing not mine.' Lady Melbourne suggested he take a more physical approach. This produced a remarkable effect. Annabella was alarmed at the strong emotions and desires she felt when he touched her and was frightened and embarrassed. He had offended her modesty and she tried to avoid being left alone with him. '*Entre nous,*' he told Lady Melbourne, 'it is really amusing. She is like a child in that respect – and quite *caressable* into kindness and good humour'.[13] The sexual tension grew unbearable and Annabella ordered him to leave. He agreed that living so close together and not being married was uncomfortable.

Negotiations with Claughton for the sale of Newstead finally collapsed in the first week in December. 'Things must come round in the end,' Byron encouraged Annabella, 'for even if N[ewstead] and R[ochdale] are both sold at a loss they will at least leave us clear, and your settlement secured into the bargain. Well – "to marry or not" that's the question – or will you wait? Perhaps the clouds may disperse in a month or two. Do as you please.' This was hardly the letter of an impatient lover but Annabella ignored the hint and, as Byron later told Medwin, 'She married me from vanity and the hope of reforming and fixing me. She was a spoiled child.' Certainly she had received enough clues to deduce that Byron did not love her as most young men love their brides. Hobhouse later remarked, 'Miss Milbanke may have been deceived in the expectations she formed in uniting herself with Lord Byron, but she was not deceived by Lord Byron, she was deceived by herself. A little less passion and a little more reflection would have convinced her of the propriety of accepting Lord Byron's proposal of delay.'[14]

On 3 December the *Morning Herald* published lines of doggerel.

By Miss M-LB-K

Pray! Let a jealous rivalle strive in vaine
To drawe him, sated, back to lawlesse joyes.
For firmlie are our youthful heartes betrothed,
And our congenial soules fast bound in one!
Now since a spark of his poetic fire
Hath caught my glowing soule, I will become
Love's proxie for his Ninth prolifick Muse,
And yield him every ninth revolving Moone
A sweet Childe Harold to delight his Sire!

Lady Melbourne thought that the first two lines 'must mean C – They might have been better applied, & heavier loaded. The next 2 have no fault except not being matter of fact which I wish they were. The last remain to be proved.' She was anxious to see him married as soon as possible because she knew he was weak where Caroline was concerned, despite his blustering denials. Caroline, like everyone else, could not understand the delay and when she asked for a reason Lady Melbourne placed the entire blame on Hanson, adding, 'I hope she won't think of inquiring about it from him.'[16]

'I think her good resolutions seem to be ebbing,' Lady Melbourne wrote on 15 December. 'Last night she injured herself upon A[nnabella]'s name being mentioned, luckily no strangers were by. This morning she enquired if you were in Town. I said I did not know, which is fact, for I should not be surprised if you were gone to x [Augusta] – How can she allow you to put An[n]a[bella] into such an unpleasant situation. She ought to feel for her.'[16] Augusta and Byron frequently used crosses and noughts to refer to various people, events or actions. They favoured + while Lady Melbourne preferred x and on one occasion xxx. 'You say I put in too many of these hieroglyphics,' she told Byron, 'but as your *one* puzzles me I think it proper return to puzzle you three times as much.'

On his way back to London Byron spent a few dismal days at Six Mile Bottom. He was depressed and had decided to break the engagement but Augusta urged him to be careful and think again. He applied to the Doctor's Commons for a wedding licence and surprised Hanson by saying, as the official handed it to him, 'Pray, sir, what is the proportion of those who come here first to make marriages, and then afterwards to unmake them?'[17] He returned to the Leighs where he passed a gloomy Christmas, overshadowed by the wedding and by George's constant sniffles, complaints and demands for medicine.

At three o'clock on Boxing Day he met Hobhouse and began the journey north to Seaham. 'Never was a lover less in haste,' Hobhouse wrote in his journal as they crawled up the Great North Road in the grey, cold afternoon to Wansford.[18] The next day they left the warmth and comfort of The Haycock and made their way through the snow and bitter cold to Newark. Byron told Hobhouse that 'he was not in love with his intended bride; but at the same time he said he felt for her that regard which he believed was the surest guarantee of continued affection and matrimonial felicity.' He stressed that he did not want to marry until he had settled his precarious finances and 'was not precipitate or eager in hastening the match – and certainly, gave his wife's family and the lady herself every opportunity of delaying, if not breaking off the connection.'[19]

They were married on 2 January 1815 by the bride's uncle, the Reverend Thomas Noel, in the first-floor drawing room of Seaham Hall. At the words 'With all my worldly goods I thee endow,' Byron half smiled at Hobhouse. The couple left for their honeymoon at Halnaby Hall in Yorkshire and Hobhouse returned to London feeling 'as though I had buried a friend.'

Caroline asked Annabella what she would like as a wedding present and offered to be friends. '*We* are well disposed *towards* her,' Byron wrote to Lady Melbourne, 'and can't see why there should not be peace with her as well as with America'. He warned his co-conspirator, 'Recollect – *we* are to keep our secrets & correspondence as heretofore – mind that.'

Hanson had offered Byron his house at Farleigh in Hampshire but the legal disputes surrounding his daughter's marriage to Lord Portsmouth made it an unsuitable arrangement. Byron was disappointed, as he had hoped to be able to live cheaply in the country until Newstead was sold. Sir Ralph and Lady Milbanke suggested they settle at Halnaby Hall but Annabella ignored their kindness and authorised Lady Melbourne to find her a suitable house in London. Byron asked Hobhouse to see if it would be possible to rent the Duchess of Devonshire's house at 13 Piccadilly for a year. It fell to Lady Melbourne to make the final arrangements. The rent for a year was £700 (about £39,000 today). This was equal to the whole of Annabella's income, leaving them nothing to pay for the staff or for the upkeep of two carriages. The rent remained unpaid for two years.

Byron, revelling in his new status as Lady Melbourne's nephew by marriage, asked, 'Pray is there any foundation for a rumour which has reached me – that *les agneaux* are about to separate? If it is so, I hope that this time it is only on account of incompatibility of temper; and that no more serious scenes have occurred; in short, I don't know what to wish, but no harm to anybody, unless for the good of our family, which she is always embroiling. Pray tell me as much as your new code of confidence will permit, or what is still better, that this report (which came in a letter) is as the person says it may be a "wicked scandal."[20] Lady Melbourne replied, 'It may or may not be "wicked scandal", but as far as I am inform'd, it is not true. They are in the country to all appearance like two turtle doves – there may now & then be a little sharpness introduced but who knows that some part of the cooing of these same birds may not be scolding. Really she seems inclined to behave better than she has done – & is now only troublesome in private & a great bore in Society. This I know you never would believe – but I hope some day to see you undergo a dinner, when she wishes to shew off.'[21]

Byron was anxious to return to London alone to attempt to put his affairs in some kind of order. He still had not repaid the loan he had taken out to cover his Mediterranean expedition of 1809. Annabella refused to stay at Seaham, particularly when she discovered that he intended to break his journey at Six Mile Bottom. Augusta did not want visitors. Her house was too small, her children too noisy and she was short of money. She suggested they might be more comfortable if they rented a house in the neighbourhood but when they could not find one she rearranged her inadequate home with good grace. Annabella knew it was her presence that was causing Augusta's problems but she still insisted on accompanying Byron. A more sensitive woman might have postponed her visit. As it turned out, the fortnight at Six Mile Bottom became a nightmare. Byron resented both her presence and her assumption that she was always right. He told Henry Drury, his former schoolmaster and friend, 'She is a woman of Learning, which I have great hopes she means to keep to herself – I never touch upon it for fear of quotation.'

Miserable and insecure, he began to drink large amounts of brandy. Each evening, his inhibitions dulled by alcohol, he teased the women. He was coarse and offensive, drawing unfavourable comparisons and forcing them to play adolescent kissing games. He speculated aloud on whether or not they wore the new-fangled 'drawers', a word so shocking that Annabella could only write it in a private kind of shorthand when she later prepared her notes for her lawyers. He took pleasure in being boorish and deliberately went out of his way to humiliate her in front of Augusta. He took a special delight in taunting her by saying how he would have broken the engagement if Augusta had not stopped him. He laughed at her shocked face and jeered at her foolishness in believing he had been dying for love. He teased her by mischievously pointing at little Libby, Augusta's daughter, saying, 'You know that is my child'. He argued viciously with Augusta over her support for Lord Carlisle and his uncouth treatment of his guardian. She was relieved to see them leave on 28 March, telling one of Byron's friends from Cambridge, the Reverend Francis Hodgson, 'I am sorry to say his nerves and spirits are far from what I wish them. I think the uncomfortable state of his affairs is the cause, at least, I can discern no other. He has every outward blessing this world can bestow.'[22]

'Six Mile Bottom, Est possible!' Caroline exclaimed to Murray when she heard that Byron was staying with Augusta. She was not happy or well, complaining of faintness and blurred vision. She had not had a letter from her mother, who was now living in Marseilles, for a month and she worried her family was in danger of being caught up in a civil war.[23] She had written a new novel, illustrated it herself and had already shown it to Thomas and Edward Hookham, Publishers, of 15 Old Bond Street, friends of Percy Bysshe Shelley. She wrote to Murray, 'My head is set upon the publication of my novel & the vignettes with it – *They are pretty*. The novel is still very unequal. I am going to rename it. Answer me fairly as a man and not in jest. Is it your wish to undertake it? Hookham will not do the vignettes as *well* as I like. He fears the expense & wishes them to be done in an inferior style. There are 4. What do you say to it? I will speak to you seriously – My fear is that if I entrust it to you – You will not like it. Let me know without delay your real wishes & as such I will follow them, but do not say yes & then give them into other hands. This would be acting like B[yron]'.

Almost as soon as Byron and Annabella moved into 13 Piccadilly the traditional congratulatory visits began. Lady Melbourne insisted that Caroline accompany her. 'It was a cruel request,' she told Thomas Medwin, 'but Lord Byron himself made it. Mrs Leigh, myself, Lady Melbourne, Lady Noel [Annabella's mother had changed her name from Milbanke on the death of her brother, second Viscount Thomas Noel Wentworth] & Lady Byron were in the room. I never looked up. Annabella was very cold to me. Lord Byron came in & seemed agitated. His hand was cold, but he seemed kind. This was the last time upon this earth I ever met him.'

On 16 April Augusta asked her friend, Lady Shelley, to accompany her on a visit to Piccadilly to congratulate Byron and Annabella. She was apprehensive and only agreed because 'Mrs Leigh was so insistent, and reminded me of my brief acquaintance with her brother at Newmarket, that I consented to accompany her in paying my respects to the newly married couple. We mounted the stairs, and were about to be ushered into the drawing room when the door suddenly opened, and Lord Byron stood before us. I was, for the moment, taken aback at his sudden appearance; but I contrived to utter a few words, by way of congratulation. Lord Byron did not seem to think that the matter was adapted to good wishes; and looked as though he resented my intrusion into the house. At least I thought so, as he received my congratulations so coldly, and the expression on his face was almost demonical. Lady Byron received us courteously, but I felt, at once, that she is not the sort of woman with whom I could ever be intimate… I was not sorry when the visit was over. I felt like a person who has inadvertently dipped her finger into boiling water.'[24]

John Murray's son described Byron, shortly after his marriage, as 'a short man with a handsome countenance, remarkable for the fine blue veins which ran over his pale marble temples. He wore many rings on his fingers and a brooch in his shirtfront, which was embroidered. When he called, he used to be dressed in a black dress-coat (as we should now call it) with grey and sometimes nankeen trousers; his shirt was open at the neck. Lord Byron's deformity in his foot was very evident, especially as he walked downstairs he carried a stick. …Sometimes, though not often, Lord Byron read passages from his poems to my father. His voice and manner were very impressive. His voice, in the deeper tones, bore some resemblance to that of Mrs Siddons [the most famous tragic actress of the day].'[25]

Caroline once said that his voice made her 'heart bleed and men who never feel cry.'

The news that Bonaparte had escaped from Elba on the brig *Inconstant* and landed at Fréjus on 1 March reached 50 Albemarle Street through John Murray's European literary contacts. Hobhouse immediately wanted to leave for Paris but Murray warned him that Bonaparte was heading that way and the roads were full of English people making their way home. Augustus Foster wrote to his mother, who was staying in Marseilles with the Bessboroughs, that London was thunderstruck by the news and he was confounded. Nervous that her parents were in danger, Caroline asked Murray to send her any news he got from France. She added in her inconsequential way, 'Send me a book or two – and pray destroy my letters – my novel is much prettier than anything you ever read.'[26]

Twenty days after setting foot on French soil, Bonaparte reached Paris. He travelled along the mountain road to avoid the lower valley of the Rhône, where he had been frightened to tears by the fury of the inhabitants on his way to Elba. He descended from Grenoble to Lyons and from there, thanks to the protection of the Bonapartist factions and the incompetence and unpopularity of the Bourbons, continued to the Tuileries.

The Bessboroughs had been living under the protection of Marshall André Masséna, who described by Miss Berry as having 'thick black hair; a vulgar-looking, intelligent countenance, and rather a short figure,' but more importantly he was a turncoat. He deserted Bonaparte for the Bourbons and now turned his coat again. During his Bourbon phase he had talked freely with Lady Bessborough and she was now frightened that 'he would sooner put me in a dungeon by way of a gag than risk letting me go free and *talk*.' The family packed and moved swiftly to Nice and then Genoa.

They decided it was too dangerous to stay and started for home, despite the dangers the journey presented to the newly pregnant Barbara Ponsonby and Lord Bessborough's painful gout. They were in Milan in May and by June had reached Schaffausen where they heard that Frederick Ponsonby had been severely wounded at Waterloo. Leaving Barbara and Lord Bessborough to follow more slowly, Lady Bessborough and William Ponsonby left immediately for Brussels. On their way they braved Cossacks, Prussians and Austrian soldiers and heard 'the cannonading of the siege of Hüingen'.

The news of Wellington's victory reached London on 19 June and Caroline's first thought was for the safety of her brother Frederick. Major-General Denis Pack, who had been with him in the Peninsula campaign, told her that 'Ponsonby is quite idolised by the whole army – he is one of our most gallant officers.' Caroline wanted to leave for Brussels at once but William insisted she obtain Duncannon's permission. As soon as he gave it she placed Augustus with Miss

Webster and told Murray, 'I enclose you my drawings & Miss Webster will send you my MSS. It is in a dreadful state. I had only time to correct the 3rd Vol., which you read. All the rest is merely copied. I scarce think you can make it out. I am just setting out for Brussels & shall be obliged to you to write to me constantly there… I hope my journey may not be in vain.'[27]

When they reached Ghent on 1 July, William was told that Frederick was dead – but news arrived the following morning that he was seriously wounded but still alive. Caroline wrote to Duncannon, 'Only think what William suffer'd… He never told me. He behaved so well, so kindly, he suffered me even to reproach him for not proceeding to Brussels. But I can write no more as I scarce know what I say, & we are just setting off. Only this, he is really out of danger, quite out, dearest, dearest brother.' (28) Five days later Caroline wrote, 'I have just seen Frederick & thank God he is said to be out of danger. I arrived here half an hour ago. Nothing you ever heard of is like the crowd, but we have procured excellent apartments in this best hotel not far from my brother… How happy I feel at having come. Poor Fred wants the greatest care & attention. He seems very weak… The same surgeon attends him who attends the Prince of Orange. I am to see him tomorrow at 12. I scarce can write. I feel so very nervous but happy. Only his breath seems very affected, but the surgeon says he is doing well. He must not speak yet. He asked after you all & my mother & particularly wished me to have brought Augustus. Pray tell him as I have only time to write to you. For the post direct yr letters to me at l'Hotel de Flandre, Place Royale.' Frederick's most serious wound was in his chest, where a lance had pierced his lungs and he had been trampled by French cavalry.[29]

The post was erratic and it was impossible to find the English papers that Frederick craved. William told Duncannon on 12 July, 'Ld & Lady Holland are expected today. We hope they will bring some news of Ld & Lady Bessborough. We have heard nothing of them… Caroline is very low at receiving no letters & never hearing about Augustus.'[30] Caroline insisted that she had written to Duncannon every day and to Lady Melbourne. 'I believe none of my letters have reached you… Frederick is mending daily. I had a very good report to give you a few days since, but yesterday he had a regular fit of ague, & now be assured it was ague & not, as you will hear, a shivering fit, for I sent to the English physician who saw him this morning with Gunning the surgeon, & who said so. I am in hopes in a fortnight or 3 weeks to bring him home. I detest being here. I get no letters & am so uneasy about my mother that I do little but cry. The sights, too, render one miserable.'[31] An eyewitness described the funeral pyres, which burned on the field of battle for more than a week: 'it is only human fat that feeds the fire now. Thighs, arms & legs are piled on the fire. There were about fifty labourers round them, handkerchiefs covering their noses, stirring the fire and bits of bone with long forks'.[32]

'When you do not hear,' Caroline told Duncannon, 'remember that it is the horrid post. For example I conclude some of you have written to me & I feel certain Miss Webster has, now I have not received one single letter since I left Dover, where your kind note reached me. This of course makes me low & being away from England but everyone is low at Brussels. We expect the plague or fever. There is already one in the French Hospital… We are quite dull & uncomfortable – no books, no society, no letters & all the news comes back through England.'

She was overjoyed to receive a letter from Lady Melbourne. 'I cannot describe to you how totally cut off from news of every sort we are… The great amusement at Bruxelles, indeed the only one except visiting the sick, is to make large parties & go to the field of Battle – & pick up a skull or grape shot or an old shoe or a letter, & bring it home. Wm has been, I shall not go – unless when Fred gets better & goes with me. There is a great affectation here of making lint & bandages – but where is there not some? & at least it is an innocent amusement. It is rather a love making moment, the half-wounded Officers reclining with pretty ladies visiting them – is dangerous. I also observe a great coxcombability in the dress of the sick – which prognosticates a speedy recovery. It is rather heart-breaking to be here, however & one goes blubbering about – seeing such fine people without their legs & arms, some in agony, & some getting better. The Prince of Orange enquired much after all his acquaintance: he suffers a great deal, but bears it well. The next door to us had a Col. Millar, very patient, but dreadfully wounded. Lady Conyngham is here – Lady C Grenville – Lady D Hamilton, Lady F Somerset, Lady F Webster affected & Lady Mountnorris [her mother] who stuck her parasol yesterday into a skull at Waterloo. Perhaps a certain rivalship makes me see her less favourably, but indeed Lady F Webster is too ridiculous.' (Caroline was also flirting with the Duke of Wellington.) 'Mr Bradshaw, an amiable Dandy close by me, says it makes him ill for 2 hours after he has seen her. I conclude that you have heard that the D[uke] of Wellington fell desperately in love with her & 2 others, which was the cause of his not being at the Battle in time. The Dss of Richmond's fatal Ball has been much censured. There never was such a Ball – so fine & so sad. All the young men who appeared there shot dead a few hours after.'[33]

No one could spare a kind word to say about Caroline and she was routinely belittled. For two weeks she had overseen Frederick's nursing and kept the family informed of his progress under quite horrific conditions. She was resourceful and brave, her flighty side temporarily submerged by her innate common sense. No account was taken of the ghastly sights and smells she had endured and once the ladies arrived in Brussels the claws came out. Hary-o repeated stories to Lady

Morpeth, 'Caroline Wm said to the surgeon, "Pray, Sir, had not I better read to Colonel Ponsonby all day long?" He answered, "No, but if I might venture to recommend, it would be to hold your tongue."' In another letter she wrote, 'F Ponsonby is still feeble and wounded all over and was in dread of Caroline's sisterly persecutions, but she was soon prevailed upon to prefer parading about the town at all hours.' Fanny Burney, now Madame D'Arblay, added her voice to the sour condemnation. She described Caroline crossing the Place Royale 'dressed, or rather *not* dressed, so as to excite universal attention, and authorise every boldness in staring, from the general to the lowest soldier among the military groups constantly parading La Place, for she had one shoulder, half her back and all her throat and neck displayed, as if at the call of some statuary for modelling a heathen goddess. A slight scarf hung over the shoulder and the rest of the attire was of accordant lightness.'[34] The former Miss Burney no longer turned any heads at the age of sixty-three.

On 16 July Lady Bessborough arrived and was dismayed to see how weak and helpless Frederick seemed, 'but W Lamb & the people who saw him ten days ago say the amendment is miraculous.'

'I'm glad upon the whole that Caroline went,' Duncannon told his mother, 'as I think she may have been a comfort to Fredk altho' for some days I prevented her journey. I was nervous of the dreadful state in which Fred was at first & I really was afraid to let her go till we heard better accounts of him.'[35] William told Duncannon, after Lord Bessborough, Lady Barbara and the Hollands arrived that 'Both your father & mother look very well, though she is rather fatigued with the length & anxiety of her journey. Caroline has this morning received a letter from Maria [Duncannon] of 17th. She swears the accusations [of not writing] are unjust, as she has written continually. I hope she has, for I have trusted rather to her writing to you.'[36]

Caroline replied to Maria, 'Wm & I have a very pretty house in the Place Royale about/of a mile from my mother's, which is the best in Brussels. It is the fashion here to have tea parties from 8 till 11. I had a very large one last night, but do not often, as I remain much at my mother's. Fred may be pronounced well, the sort of rapid strides he has made for this last week is quite beyond our hopes, & our only anxiety is to keep him back.' As for returning home, 'Everyone wishes ardently to return. If Wm has a mind we shall go by Paris & meet them at Calais, but we both dread the Emperor's armies and crowd.'[37]

She need not have feared, for after fleeing the battlefield Bonaparte had abdicated and returned to Malmaison, the home of his beautiful, loyal, deserted, dead wife, Empress Josephine. He was alarmed at the news that the allied armies were approaching and enemy patrols had been seen edging their way towards St-Germain-en-Laye, which cut off his escape route to the west. Platov, the Cossack leader, was offering his daughter in marriage to any of his men who captured Bonaparte and Blücher announced he would shoot him out of hand. After receiving permission to take a ship from Rochefort, at his own risk, from the Minister of Marine, Bonaparte summoned his three official bastards to Malmaison. He said farewell to Charles Macon, his son by Elenore Denuelle, to Alexandre, his son by Maria Walewska and to the high-spirited Emilie, daughter of Françoise Pellaprat, the only one of his mistresses who personified his idea of what a woman should be. 'In France,' he said, 'women are too highly regarded. They are in fact nothing more than machines for producing children. One sex must be subordinate to the other.'

He had already smuggled three million francs to the banker Lafitte to be forwarded to America but he was not sure this would be enough and spoke to Josephine's daughter, Hortense, his stepdaughter and sister-in-law, who offered him a diamond necklace worth two thousand francs which she sewed into a sash. He had a flash of hope and changed into uniform and sent a message to the provisional government asking to resume command of the army in order to defend Paris. The request was emphatically refused and he changed back into civilian clothes, ordered carriages to be brought to the front door and slipped out by the back door. He crossed the park, walked through a door in the wall and climbed into an unmarked yellow barouche, which drove off as fast as the four horses could be whipped. He reached Rochefort on 3 July where he found British warships waiting. On 15 July he surrendered to Captain Maitland of *HMS Bellerophon*.

Hary-o was in high spirits. On 11 May she had presented Granville with his legitimate son and heir, Granville George, or the 'Little Governor'. She was overjoyed in July when Granville was created Viscount Granville of Stone. Her happiness was increased when Hart invited them to go with him to Paris to join in the victory celebrations and the restoration of Louis XVIII. They arrived at Calais on 26 July and reached Paris three days later. She was dismayed when she heard Caroline might come to Paris, saying smartly, 'I trust she will not – till I have left it.'[38]

Between Paris and Brussels Caroline was taken ill and stopped for advice from apothecaries at most of the towns they passed through. On reaching Paris she declared she was dying and sent for a doctor but by a strange accident the note was delivered, not to a doctor but to her new idol, the Duke of Wellington. Hary-o was not surprised, as she was sure that Caroline had set her cap at the Duke.

Paris was teeming with activity. Talma, the celebrated tragedian, Mademoiselle Georges and Mademoiselle Mars were playing at the Théâtre Français. In the evenings the English visitors could see the lights from the British camp shining in the Champs Elysées and listen to the haunting sounds of bugles and bands.

They mixed with Parisians sitting under the trees and watched the passing parade of French beauties dressed in loose robes, which hung like sacks from the throat to the ankles, with long sleeves gathered at the wrist and a shawl thrown over their shoulders. The ladies could hardly hide their smirks when they saw their English cousins in long waisted dresses and little shell bonnets.[39]

The main topic of conversation was the Duke of Wellington's ball on 1 August, to be held in the mansion formerly occupied by Marshal Junot, built by Grimod de La Reynière, an immensely rich, gluttonous farmer-general, who had choked to death on a lump of Strasbourg pie. From its raised terrace on the corner of the Avenue Gabriel it was possible to see the Champs Elysées and the former Place Louis XV, later Place de la Révolution, where, less than forty years earlier, 2,790 people were guillotined. The bloody square was renamed the Place de la Concorde.

The guests included a roll call of military commanders and diplomats, Castlereagh, Metternich, Nesselrod, Humboldt, as well as every British officer of distinction. They cut a handsome dash, the British scarlet mingling with the rich foreign uniforms, though the English thought the Austrians in their white uniforms looked like musicians. Diamonds blazed, stars, crosses and ribbons were seen on every chest. 'The King entered with his splendid cortège, and after being solemnly received by the illustrious host of the night, and shortly conversing with him, passed on among the gay crowd, and joined a circle, the centre of which was Lady Castlereagh, and one of its components the veteran Blücher. The Prince of Orange followed, pale from his recent wound, and with his arm in a sling. He spoke some time with the Duke of Wellington, and then joined the circle of Lady Castlereagh.'[40] Hary-o was put out when Prince Talleyrand, the Machiavellian French Prime Minister, 'waddled' past her without saying a word: 'I only had the satisfaction of seeing his dirty, cunning face and long coat for a moment. After him came Joseph Fouché, a little spare, shallow, shrewd-looking man, who seems to unite all parties in one common feeling – horror of his character.'[41]

Under the clear and starry sky jugglers walked in the brilliantly lit gardens and amused the guests. A feast had been laid out in the formal dining room and in several smaller rooms with individual round tables. At the table next to James Simpson, a young lawyer, were 'two very beautiful Englishwomen of high fashion. Lady W[edderburn] W[ebster] and Lady C[aroline[L[amb] keeping a chair vacant between them. In a few minutes the Duke of Wellington himself looked into the room when the ladies called to him that they had kept a place for him.' They were joined by Walter Scott 'and the four formed a very merry supper party. I could not help hearing their conversation, for it was rather loud, but there were no state secrets in it. Lady C[aroline] L[amb] startled us by an occasional scream.'[42]

The victorious Duke was under siege by three pretty and flirtatious ladies, Caroline, Lady Frances Wedderburn Webster, with whom Byron had dallied in 1813, and Lady Frances Shelley. According to Hary-o's rather jaundiced eyes, Lady Frances had a 'sort of hoisted-up look in her figure, tight sattin shoes, a fine thick plait of hair, blood shot eyes, parched lips and fine teeth.' She told Lady Morpeth, 'Lady Shelley pursues her pursuit with the most unremitting diligence and really makes herself very ridiculous as the Duke pays her no attention and she follows and watches him quite laughably. There is no harm in her, I am sure beyond inordinate vanity. There is I find, a very different case – Lady Frances Webster, that beautiful daughter of Lord Mountnorris, Lord Byron's "Genevra".' Lady Frances Webster's flirtation with the Duke proved lucrative for her philandering husband. In February 1816 he was awarded £2,000 damages against Baldwin and Moody, proprietors of the *St James's Chronicle*, who alleged she had been the Duke's mistress.

Hary-o complained, 'Nothing is agissante but Caroline Wm in a purple riding habit, tormenting everybody, but I am convinced ready primed for an attack upon the Duke of Wellington and I have no doubt but she will to a certain degree succeed as no dose of flattery is too strong for him to swallow or her to administer. Poor Wm hides in one small room whilst she assembles lovers and tradespeople in another; he looks worn to the bone.'[43] Caroline was too attractive, popular with men and happy for Hary-o to stomach. Once more the rumourmongers began their work. It was said that Caroline broke two busts of the Duke of Wellington because she thought they did not do him justice. They warned him that Caroline was dangerous and would not 'leave Paris till she had stabbed herself for him'.

James Wedderburn Webster liked to play the field and asked Byron for his advice before he moved in on Caroline. '*Keep clear of her,*' he replied. 'She is a villainous intriguant – in every sense of the word – mad & malignant – capable of all & every mischief – above all – guard your *connections* from her society – with all her apparent absurdity there is an indefatigable & active spirit of meanness & destruction about her – which delights & often succeeds in inflicting misery.'[44] A week later he regretted his words. 'I wrote rather hurriedly & probably said more than I intended or than she deserved – but I fear the main points are correct – she is such a mixture of good & bad – of talent and absurdity – in short – an exaggerated woman – that – that in fact I have no right to abuse her – and did love her very well – till she took abundant pains to cure me of it – & there's an end. I will give you one piece of advice, which may be of use,' Byron wrote to Webster, 'She is most *dangerous* when *humblest* – like a Centipede she *crawls & stings.* – As for "him" [William Lamb] – we have not spoken these three years – so that I can hardly answer your question – but he is a handsome man as you see – and a clever man as you may see – of his temper I know nothing – I never heard of any prominent faults that he possesses – and indeed she has enough for both – in short his good qualities are his own – and his misfortune is having her – if the woman was quiet & like the rest of the amatory world it would not so much signify – but no – everything she says – does – or imagines – must be public – which is inconvenient in the end however piquant at the beginning.'[45] In spite of his bitter words Byron had written to Caroline while she was in Paris, wishing her as much happiness with her regiments as he was having with 'Bell'. Caroline reciprocated by sending him a souvenir, a 'Legion of Honour' cross – picked up from the field of battle at Waterloo.

William came out of hiding long enough to take Caroline to dine with the Hollands, the actor-manager of Covent Garden, Charles Kemble, and his playwright wife, Maria Teresa. During the conversation he idly said that they would be leaving Paris the next day, but when someone else remarked that they had heard that Byron was thinking of coming to Paris, 'Lady Caroline immediately announced her intention of prolonging her stay.' The Kembles returned to their hotel a few moments before Caroline and William and watched as he carefully lifted her from the carriage and carried her over the wet cobbles. Their eldest daughter Fanny described the scene her parents witnessed: 'My mother's sitting room faced that of Lady Caroline's, and before lights were brought into it, she and my father had the full benefit of a curious scene in the room of their opposite neighbours, who seemed quite unmindful that, their apartment being lighted, and the curtains not drawn, they were, as regards the opposite wing of the building, a spectacle for gods and men. Mr Lamb on entering the room, sat down on the sofa, and his wife perched herself on the end of it, with her arm round his neck, which engaging attitude she presently exchanged for a still more persuasive air, by kneeling at his feet, but upon his getting up, the lively lady did also, and in a moment began flying round the room, seizing and flinging on the floor, cups, saucers, plates – the whole cabaret, vases, candlesticks etc, her poor husband pursuing and attempting to restrain his mad moiety, in the midst of which extraordinary scene the curtains were abruptly closed.'[46] The Kembles assumed that it was William's stated intention to leave Paris that had led to Caroline's furious display. They were not to know that crockery throwing was an established feature of arguments in the Lamb household.

Far from planning to leave for Paris, Byron was at Six Mile Bottom helping George Leigh sort out the terms of his father's will. It was a dismal visit, the children were ill, he tripped over a mousetrap, picked a fight with Augusta and left after five days having accomplished nothing but upsetting everyone. Annabella was pregnant and plans were made for her to return to Seaham for the birth, but Byron's financial problems were so serious that they did not dare leave the house in case the bailiffs broke in to seize the furniture. The marriage was turning sour and Byron secretly blamed Annabella for his recent expenses. 'Lord Byron tells me', Hobhouse wrote in his journal, 'he and she have begun a little snubbing on money matters. Marry not, says he.'[47] In September they kept up appearances and dined twice at Holland House where they were seen by Caro-George, who commented that, 'She is to lie in in November. He appears very happy, and is much improved by his marriage.'[48]

'Caroline William writes me word,' Hary-o told Lady Morpeth, 'that she detest Paris, which she says is gay without interest, noisy beyond bearing, that she is magnificently but uncomfortably lodged, alone or in a crowd; and that every countenance bears the stamp of suppressed ill-humour if native, pique if Austrian or Russian, open insolence or vulgar wonder if English, with the only exception of Hart, who sees everything *couleur de rose* and enjoys himself extremely.'[49]

By September the brilliant receptions were over and Caroline's thoughts returned to Augustus and domestic affairs. She asked Lady Melbourne to dismiss 'mademoiselle'. 'Pray tell her, I will settle with her on my return but not having further occasion entreat her to return to her parents. I will recommend her if I can. Pray let her be gone before I arrive.'[50]

On 13 October Annabella asked her mother, 'I suppose you see in the papers that *ma chère cousine* is returned, having imported, I believe, several improvements in iniquity?'[51] Caroline had brought back a silk scarf from Lyons for Annabella but it was slightly torn. She had worn it to avoid paying duty or having it impounded by 'the sharks'. She had also brought back a present for Byron, a book which had belonged to Napoleon, stamped with the Imperial Eagle. Annabella dryly commented to her father, 'With this French scarf & Lady Holland's necklace, of which I think I told you, my livery will be quite complete.' She brushed aside all Caroline's acts of kindness and overtures of friendship and disliked the thought that she might be happy. After seeing Caroline at the theatre she remarked to her mother, 'Lady CL is there every night, making herself conspicuously ridiculous with William.'[52]

The Honourable Douglas Kinnaird, a friend of Hobhouse, persuaded Byron to stand for election to the sub-committee that managed Drury Lane Theatre and both he and George Lamb were elected as new managers. He enjoyed the dinners and later used them as an excuse to stay out late and get drunk. He had a loveless affair with an obscure actress, Susan Boyce, and resumed the offensive attitude to Annabella. When Murray heard that he had been reduced to selling his library he tried to help, but false pride forced Byron to refuse his offer of £1,500. The bailiffs were sent in on 9 November. They stayed in the house day and night. Although Byron tried to keep their presence a secret from Annabella, she knew and wrote despairingly to Augusta, 'I am afraid *this* bailiff is a sad brute and will proceed to very great inconvenience.'

'Called on Byron,' Hobhouse noted on 25 November. 'In that quarter things do not go well. Strong advice against marriage. Talking of going abroad.' He regularly threatened suicide and drunkenly menaced Annabella until there was fear for her life. Even his loyal servant Fletcher was alarmed and made sure Byron was not carrying pistols when he went into her bedroom. Byron's changed behaviour frightened Annabella so much that she invited the newly pregnant Augusta to stay and began to note down his wild, drunken and unconnected confessions and incomprehensible stories of the nameless hideous crimes he claimed to have committed. He made her so confused that she assumed he must have, at least, committed a murder while touring with Hobhouse in 1809. Augusta regularly waited up until Byron returned in the early hours and sat with him until the maudlin and fighting phases of drunkenness had passed. In a fit of impotent rage against the fates which had dragged him to this dismal situation, he threw his favourite watch into the fireplace and ground it to pieces with the poker.

Augusta Ada Byron was born at one o'clock on the afternoon of 10 December and the baptismal registration was conducted in Annabella's bedroom on 20 December. The actual christening took place the following November but Augusta was not invited or informed.[53] On 22 December, Hobhouse called to congratulate the parents on his way to Holland House, where 'Caroline Lamb came in and cooed a good deal.'

At Christmas, Brocket was full of visitors – Lord Palmerston, a great admirer of Emily Lamb; Henry Brougham, whose name was linked to Caro-George; and William Huskisson, who was married to Lady Melbourne's cousin, Elizabeth Emily. Huskisson was accident-prone. He broke an arm when a child, fell from his horse a few days before his wedding, sprained his ankle jumping a moat at Blair Athol, was knocked down by a carriage as he crossed Horse Guards and later entered history as the first person to be killed by a train when he attended the official opening of the Liverpool & Manchester railway. Caroline did not trust him. 'Just believe what I say, *be cautious,*' she told Murray, 'Huskisson repeats to Lady M *all* that you tell him. Rogers is treacherous, Lord B a mere sieve – be prudent.'[54]

She ended the year soothing Lady Melbourne. 'You are the most amiable of human beings & I the most grateful,' she told her, 'believe me incredibly yours never having been in a passion since I saw you last – I believe I shall soon grow marvellously good tempered.'[55]

7

'Lord Byron, with all his poems is a rogue'

On 5 February 1816 Lady Melbourne told Byron, 'There is a report about you, so much believed in Town, that I think you should be informed of it. They say you and Annabella are parted, and even state the authority upon which it is founded. In general, when reports are as false as I know this to be, I think the best way is to despise them and to take no measures to contradict them. But really, this is so much talked about and believed, notwithstanding my contradictions, that I think you ought to desire her to come to Town or go to her yourself.'[1]

'It is said to be true that Lord and Lady Byron are going to be parted,' Hary-o wrote to Lady Morpeth. 'She has written to him to say that unless he consents to a legal separation she intends bringing it to a Court of Justice.' She added with a little frisson of delight, 'They say his profligacy and ill usage of her have been dreadful.'

Caroline scribbled a note to Murray, 'Can you call on me this evening or tomorrow morning – Do for God's sake tell me – have you breathed what I told you to anyone – and if not have you heard the reports – Is it really true & do you know why – They say it is certain everything rumoured is cause of it – even the worst possible – I have literally been ill on account of it – Pray write.'[2]

Annabella had been so distressed at Byron's erratic and uncouth behaviour in the weeks before Augusta Ada's birth that she had consulted Samuel Heywood, Serjeant-at-law, an old friend of her parents. He advised her not to do anything rash and wait until after her child was born. Both Annabella and Augusta thought that Byron was suffering from mental derangement. Augusta wrote to Hobhouse, 'I am grateful from my heart for your friendship and friendly forbearance towards his infirmities, of whatever kind they may be. His *mind* makes him the most unhappy of human beings.'[3]

Lady Noel, knowing that the lease on 13 Piccadilly ran out in March, suggested that Annabella join her at Kirkby Mallory, the house in Leicestershire she had inherited from Lord Wentworth, and sent a note to Byron asking him to follow when it was convenient.

Byron liked to see Annabella and the baby for a short time each day but on 3 January they had a row which was so loud and vicious that the servants overheard them. Byron ended his tirade by telling Annabella that she had nothing to complain of as he had neither locked her up nor beaten her. They did not speak for three days. During that time Annabella considered her future carefully and came to the conclusion that she could forgive him only if his brutish, drunken fits were manifestations of mental illness.[4]

Byron had hoped to save money by closing down the house, dismissing the servants and persuading Annabella to take Augusta Ada to Kirkby Mallory, but if that failed, he planned to take his family abroad. The bailiffs were still camped in the house and it was only his position as 'a peer of parliament' which prevented them from seizing his possessions. These difficulties did not draw the couple together. They sulked. On 6 January Byron wrote a terse letter which was delivered by Augusta. 'When you are disposed to leave London, it would be convenient that a day should be fixed – & (if possible) not a very remote one for that purpose. Of my opinion upon that subject you are sufficiently in possession – & of the circumstances which have led to it – as also to my plans – or rather intentions – for the future. When in the country I will write to you more fully. As Lady Noel has asked you to Kirkby, there you can be for the present – unless you prefer Seaham – As the dismissal of the present establishment is of importance to me – the sooner you can fix on the day the better – though of course your convenience & inclination shall be first consulted. The child will of course accompany you – there is a more easy and safer carriage than the chariot – (unless you prefer it) which I mentioned before – on that you can do as you please.'[5] She replied stiffly that she would obey his wishes and make arrangements to leave.

During the remaining twelve days in London she made enquires about Byron's mental health. She quizzed Matthew Baillie, who had treated him, as a schoolboy, for his lameness. He assured her that Byron was sane but deeply distressed and should not be left alone with any young woman. Augusta protested, saying that he might commit suicide without anyone to look after him, so the two women invited his cousin and heir, George Byron, to move in to protect them. Baillie, realising that Annabella's presence was a constant reminder to Byron of his inability to look after his family, suggested that she leave him temporarily 'as an experiment' but, until then, she should stop raising subjects she knew annoyed him. Hanson robustly explained away each of Annabella's examples of madness and suggested that she take Byron's own advice, 'Not to mind my words and then we may get along very well.' She searched his desk and rummaged through his trunks looking for damning evidence but all she found were a couple of books he thought too risqué to put in the library and a bottle of laudanum, a common cure-all. Determined to prove she was right, she buried herself in the *Medical Journal* and soon diagnosed that the cause of his agitation, bad temper and violence was hydrocephalus, or water on the brain.

Totally unaware of what Annabella was doing, Byron was convinced that they were reconciled. He thought she wanted to return to her parents and was in a relaxed and playful mood when they went to bed on 14 January, the last night Annabella spent at 13 Piccadilly and the last they spent together 'fully as man and wife'.[6] Annabella did not want to leave Byron and she hoped he would change his mind. Before she left she stroked his favourite spaniel which was lying in the doorway of his room. She said she envied the animal because it was allowed to remain 'to watch over him' but that she must go. She later told Mrs Harriet Beecher Stowe (her American friend, champion and author of *Lady Byron Vindicated*) that she went into the room where he and 'the partner of his sins' were sitting together, and said, 'Byron, I come to say goodbye.' Instead of asking her to stay he tucked his hands behind his back, edged closer to the fireplace, looked at the two women and quoted, 'When shall we three meet again?' Annabella answered in her pedantic way, 'In heaven I trust'. She told Mrs Beecher Stowe that those were her 'last words to him on earth'.[7] However she also claimed, in notes she gave to her lawyer, that the last time she spoke to him was the evening before when she left him 'in a violent agony of tears'.

Two days later, safe in familiar surroundings at Kirkby Mallory, Annabella's sorrows poured out; but she did not tell her parents the full story at once, letting them believe that Byron was ill. The Noels offered to nurse him back to health but he told Hobhouse, 'They want me to go into the country. I shall go soon, but I won't go yet. I should not care if Lady Byron was alone, but I can't stand Lady Noel.'[8]

Augusta's bulletins to Annabella were disappointing. Byron continued to drink and showed no signs of wanting to reform. Over the next few days Annabella gradually revealed details of her tormented marriage to her horrified parents. She painted a dreadful picture that became more shocking as the days went on.[9] There is no doubt that Byron was grossly offensive and on occasions behaved like a drunken oaf, but there is reason to question the more highly coloured versions of events she gave to her parents and later described to her lawyers. Sir Thomas Lawrence, the portrait painter, commented to the diarist Joseph Farington: 'Lord Byron's habits have never been of a domestic kind & since his marriage he has gone on as before; his hours uncertain – breakfasting – dining – etc, irregularly & as his inclination led him. In addition his circumstances are in a very distressed state.'[10]

Francis Le Mann, a physician and Annabella's accoucheur, confirmed on 18 January that although Byron was short-tempered he was not insane, but he was suffering from an unspecified liver disease brought on by drinking but which could be easily treated.[11] Now that it had been shown he was not mad, Annabella decided that he was 'wicked so entirely and irrevocably so as to make it impossible that she could live with him any longer.' Lady Noel, who had never forgiven him for his off-hand treatment of Annabella, was determined that he would never be allowed to keep Augusta Ada. She hurried up to London to see Dr Stephen Lushington, an advocate in the ecclesiastical court, which governed the laws of Domestic Relations and on 2 February the separation procedure began.

Byron was unprepared for such an attack. Annabella's letters had been loving and intimate, she had signed herself, 'ever thy Pippin,' his affectionate nickname. Her responsiveness in the bedroom, not just on the last night but the night before, had not given him any reason to suspect that she was other than in love with him. He had been so engrossed in his own misery that he had not noticed how severely he had hurt her but he could not believe she agreed with her mother's action and blamed Mrs Clermont, her former nurse, and Lady Noel for poisoning her mind. The strain on him was enormous. He ate only once in three days, spending many hours in his room brooding and weeping. Those around him began to fear he was becoming suicidal again. Annabella was indifferent and Lady Noel remarked, 'So much the better. It is not fit such men should live.'[12] Byron appeared to be stunned when Hobhouse saw him on 5 February. At first he would not talk about what had happened, then, 'with tears in his eyes, and in an agitation, which scarcely allowed him to speak, mentioned the proposition he had received from Sir Ralph Noel.' On 9 February Douglas Kinnaird heard that 'the Melbournes are in arms against Lady B. G[eorge] L[amb] called her a d—d fool, but added that C[aroline L[amb] accused B of — poor fellow, the plot thickens against him. He is depressed most dreadfully, yet still laughs as usual & says he shall "go to Court to be presented on his separation".'

Byron told Thomas Moore, 'Her nearest relatives are a **** – my circumstances have been and are in a state of great confusion – my health has been a good deal disordered, and my mind ill at ease for a considerable period. Such are the causes (I do not name them as excuses) which have frequently driven me to excess, and disqualified my temper for comfort.'[13] Hodgson and Hobhouse wrote to Annabella to ask her to reconsider. She refused. 'He married me with the deepest determination of Revenge, avowed on the day of my marriage, and executed ever since with systematic and increasing cruelty, which no affection could change.'[14] Byron was hurt and puzzled, 'Were you then *never* happy with me? Had I not, had we not the days before and on the day we parted, every reason to believe that we loved each other, that we were to meet again?' These words touched her heart and she wept and wondered if she could find a way to return to him with her pride intact but Lady Noel and Mrs Clermont dismissed her tears as weakness and Stephen Lushington urged her forward, anxious for his fee.[15] It was on his advice that Annabella refused to write or see Byron, in case this gave him grounds to apply for the restitution of conjugal rights. Lushington hinted that Annabella's health might be in danger bearing in mind Byron's recent affair with Susan Boyce and he alerted her to Byron's rights as a father. Many years later both Byron's grandchildren agreed that without Lushington's influence, reconciliation might have been possible.[16]

The news of their separation had reached London first in a letter from Miss Selina Doyle, a friend of Annabella's who was staying at Kirkby Mallory. Her brother, Colonel Francis Hastings Doyle, became the chief advisor to the family as the separation progressed and he instructed Annabella to keep copies of all her letters and not to destroy any she received, especially from Augusta.

The unexpected turn of events left Caroline tortured by ambivalent feelings of love, hate and hope. She told Hobhouse, 'Byron has behaved most barbarously to me & I can never feel anything towards him again but resentment – In this quarrel too I differ from you and take her part not his.' However she still hoped he might come back to her when he heard that she had offered to sell her jewellery, worth £300, to pay off some of his debts. She had, of course, sworn Hobhouse to secrecy but knew that the custom of private letters being passed from hand to hand like newspapers was common and the chances of Byron hearing of her sacrifice was high. She asked Hobhouse to tell her why Byron would not agree to the separation and she objected to his blaming her for having a hand in spreading rumours against him. She wrote, 'I need not ask you to tell him this was a most unmerited & ungenerous accusation – I fear no investigation of my conduct from the beginning to end of this affair. I have kept out of it entirely for both their sakes & it is not fit for me to excuse myself for what I never did.'[17]

When Hobhouse did not reply she directed her advice to Byron. 'Go to her – whatever the cause, little or great – it must be made up, nothing can do it but an interview. Lord Byron you will no doubt be angry at my interfering where I have no sort of right or interest. – But I have witnessed some scenes that I cannot forget & the agony I suffer at this moment from suspense and alarm is not affected – If you knew what odious reports people circulate when men part from their wives – you would act in this instance prudently – you would not try to irritate Lady Noel or to speak with harshness to Lady Biron, who loves you, would you but conciliate. I know you & fear you – and fear that you will be too offended & too proud to listen to those [who] would advise you. I have disbelieved all the reports till now – but still I trust they are of far less consequence than some pretend… Could you know what some say – you would really be on your guard.' She continued, 'Those of my family who have seen Lady Byron have assured me that whatever her sorrow – she is the last in the world to reproach or speak ill of you. She is most miserable. What regret will be yours if fake friends or resentment impel you to act harshly on this occasion. Whatever my feeling may be towards you or her I have with the most scrupulous care for both your sakes avoided either calling or sending or interfering'.[18] She signed herself as his 'cousin Caroline'. Byron did not reply. He knew she was in Annabella's camp and that she had spoken against him at Melbourne House.

'If you wish to *see*, or think I can be of use, I will go to you at any time,'[19] Lady Melbourne assured Byron. She did not dare meet him at Melbourne House in case the Milbankes or Caroline got wind of it. The estrangement renewed all Lady Bessborough's fears of an elopement but Caroline dismissed this, saying the mere idea of it would kill her mother.

Byron could not have guessed what trouble he was laying up in store when he had tried to shock Caroline out of love with him at Albany. His horror stories, full of unspeakable crimes and hints, which at the very least implied knowledge of incest and of homosexual experiences at school and abroad, had all been too exciting for Caroline to keep to herself. She confided in Caro-George with the usual rider not to breathe a word but, naturally, she could not resist whispering them to her lover, Henry Brougham, nicknamed Chronique Scandaleuse, who had no scruples in spreading them further afield. He had resented Byron ever since he heard him call Caro-George 'a damned fool'. With his twitching, trumpet-shaped nose and dingy complexion, Hary-o thought he looked like 'something that had been dug up,' but as one of Annabella's legal advisers he was in a position to spread stories which 'were too horrid to mention.'

On 29 February Hobhouse recorded in his journal, 'Mrs Leigh has been forbid all intercourse with her [Annabella] at her lawyers's request. A story has now gone abroad against *HER (MRS L) AND B!!!*' The Devonshire House sisterhood had known the story since 8 February. 'Lady Ossulston told me a horrid report of its [the separation] being in consequence of an improper correspondence having been discovered between him and Mrs Leigh,' Hary-o wrote. She added incredulously, 'It must be impossible.' News of the scandal reached The Duchess of Devonshire in Rome and she immediately wrote to Augustus Foster, now English Minister in Copenhagen. 'Poor Lady Byron's fate is enough to alarm all parents. She is wretched, ill and persecuted by him, who now refuses to sign the deeds of separation.'[20] A few days later, 'Lady Byron's fate is the most melancholy I ever heard, and he must be mad or a Caligula. Caroline [George] will have told you some of the stories. It is too shocking, and her life seems to have been endangered whilst with him from his cruelty.'[21]

From Annabella's point of view everything was going very well. She told Mrs Clermont, 'I was sure Lady C[aroline] L[amb] would take my part. I am rather flattered by the favour of the wicked... William Lamb maintains a becoming silence, & George Lamb declaims against me.' London buzzed with speculation fed by juicy hints and innuendoes. Annabella suggested to her mother that they should prolong the separation proceedings as much as possible in the hope of exasperating and tiring Byron into doing something foolish. Meanwhile she continued preparing notes, statements and comments justifying her actions and laying the groundwork to prevent Byron or Augusta ever obtaining custody of Ada. (The name Augusta was dropped forever.)

At first Annabella had been content to allow the two Carolines, Miss Selina Doyle and a friend of her mother, Mrs Elizabeth Hervey (the writer William Beckford's half-sister), to disseminate vague but damaging rumours. Now she began to fear she herself might be implicated. 'I cannot help repeating my wish,' she told Caroline-George, 'that nothing of any sort should be mentioned to anyone *as coming from me.*' Caro-George bridled, 'Indeed, I cannot agree with you in the propriety of being silent as to your wrongs. I cannot bear that vice should triumph or that conduct so perfect as yours has been, should be in the slightest degree blamed or misunderstood.'

On 8 March the Duchess of Devonshire wrote to her new daughter-in-law, Albina Foster, in Copenhagen, 'We were all astonished here at the separation of Lord and Lady Byron. You will have heard of it from England. Nobody knew the cause when my last letters were written, but everybody seemed to pity her. So do I too; but yet I think that, had I married a profligate man, knowing that he was so, and that I had a child, and was not ill used by him, I would not part from him.'[22] Augustus replied, 'Caroline [George] seems quite shocked at Lord Byron's conduct to poor Annabel but don't give me the particulars. They were certainly two very opposite people to come together, but she *would* marry a poet and *reform* a rake.'[22]

The ground had been prepared so well that before the end of March all London was convinced that Byron had committed a crime too dreadful to be named. He wretchedly told his friends, Scrope Beardmore Davis and Hobhouse, that he might have been '*bereav'd of reason* during his paroxysms with his wife,' but that he had never lifted a finger against her and the harshest thing he had ever said was that she was in his way. 'It appears to me he has made some confession,' Hobhouse wrote, 'I am still, however in the dark utterly.' Augusta wrote, 'what this mysterious charge can be is beyond the utmost stretch of my imagination to guess. He *VOWS HE* knows not.'

Byron's rejection of Caroline's offers of help and money stiffened her resolve to carry out her frequent threat to 'ruin' him. Her obsessive love had been transmuted to hate and revenge. She was enraged at the thought that Byron suspected her as the source of the gossip, though her history of broken promises and her ability to manipulate the truth made her the chief suspect. However she could hardly be held responsible for the tales coming from Piccadilly. They had begun to circulate soon after Ada was born and at first they were trifling – Annabella had not had a square meal since her marriage and Byron had 'no fixed hour for breakfast, and was always late for dinner.' Now the accusations were more serious, that Annabella was afraid for her life and Byron slept with loaded pistols at the bedside and a dagger under his pillow. Hobhouse took Byron to task, listing his alleged crimes: great tyranny towards Annabella, menaces, furies, neglect, real injuries, locking doors, waving of pistols, frowning at her in bed, turning her out of the house and throwing of soda bottles at the ceiling during her labour. (Hobhouse examined the ceiling the following day but he could find no dents or marks.) When Byron was questioned on the story which said that he had asked Annabella during her labour 'whether the child was dead,' – he was horrified and said, 'She would not say that, though, God knows poor thing! It seems now she would say anything; but she would not say that, no she would not say that.' The servants blamed Mrs Clermont; Mrs Milward, the wife of the Noels' butler, was astonished and stayed with Byron until the house was closed down.[23]

Augusta was physically and emotionally drained. She had lived at Piccadilly for almost three months and longed to go home to prepare for her new baby. Annabella had invited her to stay in December to be a buffer between her and Byron and when she returned to her parents in January, Augusta remained, at her request, to look after Byron. Augusta was distressed and repelled at the stories circulating about her. Hobhouse had heard that 'Lady B had said that B had boasted to her of going to bed with his sister. I implied that if he had she was more villainous in mentioning it than he in doing it.' He remarked, 'Lady B will not stick at a trick. I know from her having told B that she was in love with another man in order to hook him – she confessed this to B himself.' He tartly told Caroline that he trusted that 'Lord Byron's enemies would condescend at last to perch upon a fact'.[24]

When Hobhouse called in at Piccadilly on 13 March he found Augusta tearful. She told him that George Leigh had never doubted her innocence but when the Dowager Duchess of Leeds had urged her, for her own sake, to return home, Lady Noel had remarked, 'So she ought, but she is a fool, and perhaps her brother's having left her all he has to dispose of may make her shy of offending him.' On 17 March Augusta left Piccadilly and moved to a grace-and-favour apartment at St James's Place, to which, as one of Queen Charlotte's Bedchamber Women, she was entitled.[25] On the same day the legal preliminaries for the separation were agreed. Byron was penitent and downcast. He had sincerely wanted to be reunited with Annabella and the baby. On a sheet of paper stained with his tears he wrote the haunting poem:

Fare thee well! And if for ever,
Still forever, fare thee well:

Even though unforgiving, never
'Gainst thee shall my heart rebel.

Would that breast were bared before thee
Where thy head so oft hath lain.
While that placid sleep came o'er thee
Which thou ne'er cans't know again:

Would that breast, by thee glanced over,
Every inmost thought could show!
Then thou wouldst at last discover
'Twas not well to spurn it so.

Though the world for this commend thee –
Though it smile upon the blow,
Even its praises must offend thee,
Founded on another's woe:

Though my many faults defaced me,
Could no other arm be found,
Than the one which once embraced me,
To inflict a cureless wound?

Yet, oh yet, thyself deceive not;
Love may sink by slow decay,
But by sudden wrench, believe not
Hearts can thus be torn away:

Still then own its life retaineth,
Still must mine, though bleeding, beat;
And the undying thought which paineth
Is – that we no more may meet:

These are words of deeper sorrow
Than the wail above the dead;
Both shall live, but every morrow
Wake us from a widow'd bed.

And when thou wouldst solace gather,
When our child's first accent flow,
Wilt thou teach her to say 'Father!'
Though his cares she must forego?

When her little hands shall press thee,
When her lip to thine is press'd,
Think of him whose prayer shall bless thee,
Think of him thy love had bless'd!

Should her lineaments resemble
Those thou never more may'st see,
Then thy heart will softly tremble
With a pulse yet true to me.

All my faults perchance thou knowest,
All my madness none can know;
All my hopes, where e're thou goest,
Wither, yet with thee they go.

Every feeling hath been shaken;
Pride, which not a world could bow,
Bows to thee – by thee forsaken,
Even my soul forsakes me now:

But 'tis done – all words are idle –
Words from me are vainer still:
But the thoughts we cannot bridle
Force their way without the will.

Fare thee well! Thus disunited,
Torn from every nearer tie,
Sear'd in heart, and lone, and blighted,
More than this I scarce can die.

'Dearest Bell, I send you the first verses that ever I attempted to write upon you, and perhaps the last that I may ever write at all. This at such a moment may look like affectation, but it is not so.'[27] Annabella did not reply. She claimed it was an act of Machiavellianism on his part to put in her the wrong because it was he not she who had wanted the separation.

Byron showed Murray a copy of *Fare Thee Well* as well as his manuscript, *A Sketch from Private Life* – a vicious attack on Mrs Mary Anne Clermont.

Born in a garret, in the kitchen bred,
Promoted thence to deck her mistress' head;

Next – for some gracious service unexpress'd,
And from its wages only to be guess'd –
Raised from the toilette to the table, – where
Her wondering betters wait behind her chair.
With eye unmoved, and forehead unabashed,
She dines from off the plate she lately wash'd.

Quick with the tale, and ready with the lie,
The genial confidante, and general spy...

Murray published fifty copies of the works for private circulation but it was not long before they found their way into the newspapers. Byron was publicly condemned by many and Caroline was furious, perhaps fearing the touching lines might change Annabella's mind, and hurt that his tenderness was not for her. She wrote furiously to Murray, 'Do you remember some time ago when you were justly indignant with Lord B[yron] and said he was "done for" that I said by no means but what he feels he can describe extravagantly well – & therefore I never did doubt that he would one day or another write again as at first – but for God's sake do not let this circumstance make you forget what a rogue he is.' Caroline knew Byron was a source of Murray's prosperity and that he respected him for his talent and agreed that he should stand by him, 'but for my sake, for Lady Byron's for the sake of honour, justice – every good feeling – never forget what he really is – The sun may shine upon a bit of broken glass till it appears like a diamond but if you take it up you will only cut your fingers – and though the world even, were to be take in by Lord Byron neither you nor I can be. Do not forget the wrong of such as are opprest – Remember that mother & that child – & however *he* may thrive & they be forgot... I swear to you that so far from ever living with him again – however his friends may countenance the report, Lady Byron would far sooner die than do so.'[28]

Annabella had been to see Murray, probably as part of her campaign to alienate Byron's friends. She had spoken to him 'when her heart was breaking' because, according to Caroline, she wanted him to 'believe the truth of her ill usage. She spoke to you as a friend – and then she saw you publish the most infamous verses that ever yet were written'. Caroline warmed to her subject. 'No libel was written no transaction accounted base can equal the mean cowardice of those verses & his whole conduct. – I speak of her wrongs not mine. I was so wrong myself that I never dared resent what I knew however was not the conduct of a man who had one honest feeling in him. But though the belief of his being at length detected & miserable & deserted might soften me, by him who created me I swear that if he ever rises more, though I may die, or ruin myself in the attempt, I will prove his contemptible enemy. Truth & faithfulness can stand even against Genius unsupported by those qualities & Lord Byron with all his poems is a rogue & what is equally bad – a coward – believe me is a most paltry coward. [Big ink blot] I feel I write too warmly – pray forgive me.'[29]

'Are not Lord Byron's leave taking verses beautiful?' Mary Russell Mitford asked her friend Sir William Elford; 'I believe I indulged myself with abusing him to you but ever since those verses I felt certain relentings towards the luckless Author. Partly I believe this effect may be owing to some particles of contrariness in my disposition which have been a good deal excited by the delicate morality of his admirers in this neighbourhood, who excuse themselves for their *ci-devant* admiration by a double portion of rancour towards his Lordship and pity towards his wife – "Poor Lady Byron!" "Unfortunate victim!" "Hapless sufferer;" and so forth are her style & titles at present. Now without at all attempting to vindicate him or accuse her, I cannot help thinking this immense quantity of sympathy rather more than the case requires. Why did she marry him? For, to do the man justice, he was not a hypocrite; his vices were public enough. Why did she marry him but to partake his celebrity and bask in the sunshine of his fame? And by what device of conjugal flattery could that object be attained so fully as at present? She has now the comfort of being "interesting" in the eyes of men, and "exemplary" in the mouths of all woman; she has moreover – and even I, spinster as I am, can feel that *this* must be solid consolation – She has, moreover, the delight of hating her husband, to the admiration and edification of the whole world.'[30]

Annabella's evidence against Byron was flimsy. Charges of cruelty, drunkenness and male moral turpitude were not sufficient to secure a separation. Indeed Byron believed he would win his case. The law was weighted in favour of men, however brutal, who strongly opposed separation and claimed the restitution of their conjugal rights. Lushington knew Annabella suspected Augusta of a crime and advised her to find positive proof, but all she had were her own vague feelings, which Byron had drunkenly fostered during the miserable two weeks they spent at Six Mile Bottom.

Caroline was determined to hurt Byron and if possible wound Augusta too. In the middle of March she wrote to Annabella, playing on her fears that she might lose the custody of Ada. She began with flattering, pious comments about Lady Noel and promises of secrecy. She explained how she had urged Byron to be reconciled, promised never to speak to him again but she could not resist mentioning how she had 'suffered many *deserved* griefs through his Barbarity' and her 'inexcusable & criminal conduct.' She hoped the use of the word 'criminal' would lead Annabella to believe that her affair had been a sexual one. However Lady Melbourne had already told her that Byron had 'resisted the wiles & fascination of her daughter-in-law Ly Caroline, whose attempts to captivate him had become too public to make any reserve necessary'.[31]

Caroline heavily hinted that she knew dreadful secrets about Byron's past which she could only honourably reveal to Annabella should he try to take Ada from her. She advised Annabella to be on her guard and never to forget she was surrounded by 'serpents', to remember that Byron's friends were not hers and to mistrust those who told her he was '*ill* and unhappy' because he was 'crafty'. She repeated a conversation she had had with Lady Melbourne during which Byron had spoken about her kindly, asking 'repeatedly if you were not happy.' He said he knew she loved him and showed the loving letter she had written to him from Kirkby as proof. Caroline continued, 'Mrs Lee too espouses yr part. *It is not natural – how much* she talks it. Oh, mistrust even her – keep all at a distance – say not to one of them what you fear *his* knowing & above all intimate to *him* that you have the knowledge & proof of some secret which nothing but despair shall force you to utter.'

Caroline realised her defection must puzzle Annabella and tried to explain it away by saying that she wanted to spare her the agony of seeing Ada taken away. She conspiratorially told her that Byron had a dreadful secret which he dared not face and that she would rather die than reveal, but if he thought Annabella knew it too he would be in her power and would not dare take the case to an open court. Caroline ended by asking Annabella not to reply to her letter because she wanted to tell Lady Melbourne truthfully, should she ask, that she had not heard from Annabella. In a postscript she warned Annabella that if anyone found out that she knew Byron's secrets, they would know the information had come from her and, Caroline wrote, 'It would seem I had acted the part of a King's evidence.'

A few hours later, Caroline returned to her desk. She had spent the intervening hours planning the best way of undermining Lady Melbourne's support for Byron. Both she and William agreed that an affectionate and pleasant letter from Annabella would make a good beginning and she had drawn up a suitable draft. 'My dear Aunt, you will no doubt be surprised & hurt that at a moment of great affliction like the present I have not written openly or seen you – but I too have been deeply wounded – & have thought by all I have heard that you have rather taken part against me than with me. There are things which I will never communicate to any – which are wholly my own but in all else I wish to shew you confidence.'

Caroline then passed on to Annabella the gist of another conversation she had had with Lady Melbourne, during which Lady Melbourne had said that Byron had agreed that there had been 'disputes' with Annabella but that he did not hold her responsible. He then appealed to Augusta and Hobhouse, 'I know I have been rough at times – but Augusta, have you not seen me go to her? – Kiss her & soothe her? – Have we not been more fond than most married people are before others?' Caroline warned Annabella to be on her guard and to be able to explain away the letter Ann Fletcher had written to her husband from Kirkby, now doing the rounds at Melbourne House, in which she described Annabella's distress after she had agreed to the separation and how she had flung herself on the floor screaming, 'Oh, they have forced me to this, I am lost forever – I am imprisoned.' Caroline repeatedly told Annabella that her case would be ruined if it were known they had colluded. It would be said that 'the cast-off Mistress and the Wife make common cause.' She offered to meet Annabella to discuss tactics any day at eight in the morning or between seven and eight in the evening when she went out riding.[32]

When Lord Holland offered to mediate between Byron and Annabella, Caroline sprang forward with more advice. 'Appear frank & kind,' she told Annabella, 'for he has a good heart but do not trust him as he tells all to Lady H, though he may promise not. Do not strive however to hide that you feel deeply – as they have it now all over Town that you are cold – & do not feel – particularly for *yr child* – When I say this I speak of the narrow circle I live in.' She urged Annabella to sack her maid, Ann Fletcher and reminded her that Ann was married to a loyal servant, William Fletcher, a former farm labourer from Newstead who Byron had trained to be his valet. She suggested that Annabella hint to Lord Holland that she knew something about Byron which was so bad that only despair and the fear of losing Ada would tempt her to reveal it. Caroline continued, 'Say however, that if driven to the last extremity, if yr generous forbearance is not understood – if the family instead of supporting you joins with & supports him – if the causes you can & will name are insufficient – Oh, say that you will come forward yourself & bring such accusations against him that he dares not stand. For God sake speak thus to Lord Holland. – You have no conception of the good it will do.'[33]

'Lord Byron's real character is known but to few,' she told Annabella, 'perhaps 40 or 50 victims may rue the hour they saw him & loved him but he wears a mask to all others – and Hobhouse himself though a good-hearted man in reality is utterly blind. Murray, of all his friends, is the one who has the most warmly espoused yr cause – but even he is imprudent & his situation inclines him to talk. – Fletcher loves Lord Byron. He is not absolutely bad. He blames his Master but

I fear he is not to be trusted.' (It had been suggested that Fletcher be asked to give evidence against Byron.)

Annabella managed to irritate Lady Melbourne by accusing her of secretly meeting Byron. She had been told this by a friend, whose name she could not divulge, but who had been turned away from Whitehall. Lady Melbourne replied that those people that wanted to keep their names a secret 'must be very silly or mischievous people, & in either case the less I know of them the better, one thing I cannot help saying that whoever the person was that told you he was refused at the door because I was with Ld B must have told a positive untruth.'

Once again Caroline urged Annabella to write to Lady Melbourne. 'Be secure that at bottom she has a kind & generous disposition – & it appears to me that were she to think that you had the means – if driven to necessity, of ruining him & abstained from generosity – she would admire & love you. As it is, she is told quite the contrary. That you have only puerile charges, & that he is *Certain* of success.' She finished on a schizophrenic note, 'If you could know how anxious I am for his sake that this might be amicably settled you would not think I took part against him or wished to harm him.'

On 24 March Lord Holland called on Annabella and by the time he left he was confused and bewildered. He shared his impressions with Lady Holland and after weighing up what he had been told and reading between the lines they came to the conclusion that Byron had tried to force Annabella to commit a deviant sexual act. Hobhouse wrote in the margin of his copy of Moore's biography of Byron, 'Lord Holland told me, he tried to — her.'

Annabella knew full well that if anyone guessed that the innocent and wronged Lady Byron had conspired with such a worthless wanton as Caroline, her case might be destroyed. However, curiosity and the opportunity to obtain damaging information against Byron overcame her scruples. A meeting was arranged for Wednesday morning, 27 March, at Caro-George's modest home near Lincoln's Inn Fields.

Caroline opened the conversation with a request for secrecy and the return of her letters. Annabella agreed to keep their meeting secret but she refused to return the letters until after her death. She then turned to the real business and asked Caroline to describe the contents of the papers Byron had shown her at Albany. Caroline tried to avoid answering, saying that she had promised never to reveal the secrets, but she felt guilty for not sharing the knowledge with Annabella before her marriage as this might have saved her from a 'dreadful fate'. Byron had persuaded her to remain silent because he was a reformed character and promised not to sin again. Although Caroline wanted to tell Annabella everything, she needed an excuse to break her promise. Annabella solved the quandary by suggesting that her promise had been invalidated by Byron's subsequent confessions. This soothed the pliant consciences of both ladies, giving Caroline an excuse to speak and Annabella to listen.

She falteringly said that Byron had told her that Augusta had been in his rooms in Bennet Street during her visit to London in 1813 and he hinted that 'criminal intercourse' had taken place. She did not believe him at first but when he said 'Oh I never knew what it was to love before – there is a woman I love so passionately – she is with child by me, and if a daughter it shall be called *Medora*'. Caroline replied, 'I could believe it of *you* but not of *her*'. 'Would she *not?*' he said and began to boast that it had been an easy seduction and that Lady Holderness had separated them when they were small children because of precocious 'improprieties'. Caroline remained unconvinced until Fletcher produced a portfolio from which Byron took some letters and threw them at her. Among the papers were letters from Augusta, which contained what she deduced were references to the act. 'Oh B – if we loved one another as we did in childhood – *then* it was innocent'. Caroline said she was so shocked that she never again 'suffered any intimacy with Ld B'. This was not the end. There were 'other & worse crimes', she said. Byron confessed that he had committed homosexual acts and corrupted Rushton and three school friends. He 'practised it unrestrictedly in Turkey – His own horror of it still appeared to be so great that he several times turned quite faint & sick in alluding to the subject'. He then turned on Caroline threatening at one moment to 'persecute' her and the next asking if she still loved him. Before she left he forced her three times to make a 'most solemn vow never to reveal' what he had told her.[34]

Caroline volunteered the information that she had heard that Rushton used to sleep outside Byron's bedroom in a smaller room when he was at Newstead. Annabella told Caro-George that she 'almost disavowed the belief of Incest' but she did believe Byron had seduced Rushton. All this information was much more incriminating and useful than Annabella had expected and she spent the afternoon preparing her notes for Lushington, who congratulated her. They knew that if evidence could be produced that proved or even convincingly alleged that Byron had committed homosexual acts, he would certainly never gain custody of Ada.

Caroline's story was a mixture of half-truths and deliberate lies but she may not have realised the extent of the damage she had done. She wanted Byron to suffer but her prime aim was to harm Augusta and she used Annabella's cause as her tool. She had never forgiven Augusta for ignoring her, but more than that she was jealous. Byron openly enjoyed Augusta's company. He never found anyone who compared favourably with her. She was loyal, sympathetic, playful and could match his talent for talking nonsense. These qualities endeared her to him, perhaps more than was healthy for either of them. His open admiration had not passed unnoticed. It was foolish and reckless of him to rattle on at Holland House about incest but it was not yet a crime and it was the subject of the moment. Even the highest in the land were not above suspicion. Princess Sophia's illegitimate son, Tom Garth, was supposed to have been fathered on her by the charmless Duke of Cumberland, her brother, or by George III, her father. However it was not a felony – merely an offence under ecclesiastical law. Homosexual acts, in contrast, were considered to be so abhorrent that capital punishment was often seen to be the only suitable sentence for those convicted of the crimes. Their gallows were set apart so they could not, even in death, taint others.

Far from debauching Robert Rushton, Byron protected him by sending him home from Gibraltar in 1809, telling Mrs Byron, 'I would have taken him on (but you *know boys* are not *safe* amongst the Turks.)' There was nothing particularly unusual in personal servants sleeping within call of their masters, as both Annabella and Caroline well knew. Byron had always been susceptible to girls. He fell in love with his cousin Mary Duff when he was eight and with another cousin, Margaret Parker, at twelve, with Mary Chaworth at fifteen and in his late teens he cut a swathe through the maidens of Southwell, where he lived with his mother at Burgage Manor. At nineteen he had a child by Ellen, a young girl he met in London, and a second child by Lucy, a maid at Newstead, when he was twenty.

Caroline returned home after the momentous interview and wrote another of her long, rambling letters to Annabella; 'You have in all things acted so nobly & in so very Superior manner – that God must love & bless & everyone who knows you venerate & admire you.' The flattery was thick but then, Annabella had a high tolerance. 'Make use of what I have told you,' she wrote, 'think of your own & your child's interest – and even if the generous desire of sparing him should seal your lips let it not prevent respectable & numerous friends from being acquainted with part of his atrocious conduct.' She warned, 'His verses are sure to affect many – & is it not a mean & paltry act to give them to a Bookseller to show – I inclose you a copy of a letter I have just sent to Murray'.

Caroline rebuked Murray for publishing *Fare Thee Well*. Then she added, 'You say in your letter to Lady M something as if I were Lady Byron's advocate and confidant. I believe you will find yourself utterly mistaken. I do not fancy she would even extend her compassion to a reprobate like me, and though from my soul I pity her, as I knew that which ought to have made me fly to her and prevent her marriage, yet some day you will find out that Lord Byron's own imprudence alone betrayed to her a thousand circumstances which to this hour I believe Lady Noel and Mrs Clermont have not the remotest idea of. When you suspect me, ask yourself if there are no others who had more interest than I had in causing this disunion.'[35]

Caroline was unwittingly skating on very thin ice. Although she knew that Lady Melbourne suspected her of spying, she did not know that Annabella had taken 'minutes' of their meeting which she had passed on to Lushington. 'I request you take most particular care what you say to Lady M,' she warned Murray. 'You may ruin me if you chuse by shewing any one on earth this letter but you will ruin yourself if you are not extremely guarded. Take a high tone. Seem sure of everything but tell her nothing – & for god sake to not name me. – I think it perfectly useless to trust her – *his* influence over her is such that I feel secure *now* nothing can shake it – pray take care – above all let her not imagine what you know – for were you ever to confide it she would only try & disprove it. I fear nothing can change her – but pray be kind should she call.'[36]

When she discovered that there were written accusations against Byron, she made an astonishing and desperate attempt to play the ends against the middle. Her hand shook as she wrote to him. The words were large, sprawling and blotchy with black ink. 'Hear me – for God sake pause before you rashly believe any report others may make. If letter or reports or ought else has been malignantly placed in the hands of yr Wife to ruin you I am ready to swear that I did it for the purpose of deceiving her. There is nothing, however base it may appear that I would not do to save you or yours from this. Do not, oh, do not, believe those who would lead you for one moment to think that she knows anything for certain. Be guarded, resolve upon seeing her. There is nothing – nothing, a wife cannot and ought not to forgive. I can never believe that she will betray you. The Curse of God will fall on her & her alone if she does. I know not whether it may appear wrong or right to do so, but this I know that if my death could at this moment serve you – little prepared as I am I would seek it.'

Caroline was terrified that Byron would discover her treachery: 'Let it please you to know that amongst those who have most warmly, most zealously supported you against every attack, William Lamb has been the foremost. Oh, Byron believe it. Both himself and me and all our family would gladly bear any calamity, any reproach to save or serve you. Lady Melbourne is unwell and low, we have neither of us been out since this report (not on account of it, but because she is ill). She disbelieves every word against you, and if I tremble more than her – think not at least that I judge you. Do not rashly credit any lie or invention that old Devil Lady Milbanke may invent – Don't even think that Lady Biron may know because she suspects, or if it be a letter deny it at once. There are moments when to deny is a virtue, and this is one. Be firm and do not let mistaken friends gain your confidence.' According to Caroline both her brother William and her husband came to Byron's defence when they heard his name being abused. 'I have said stoutly and without enquiry,' Caroline told him, 'that all such reports were false. Believe me Lord Byron, we all honour you and regard you with attachment and interest that is not altered, and though my misconduct and unhappy circumstances have estranged us you will never find more affectionate relations and friends than in this house.' She condemned Annabella's behaviour as 'blameable' and Lady Noel's 'shameful'. She continued, 'One promise I ask of you. Suppose people tell you anything is known that you think of consequence – swear to me that you will be firm: deny it calmly and to all. Do not – do not fancy because every appearance is against you that it is known. See your wife and she cannot have the heart to betray you – If she has she is a devil – and in mercy be calm.'[37]

Annabella was implacable. The law moved on inexorably and the deed of separation was brought to Byron to sign at three in the afternoon of Sunday 21 April. He left England four days later. Hobhouse and Sir Francis Burdett, one of Lady Oxford's former lovers and a Radical politician, both believed he had over-reacted. 'I have no patience with your saying *poor Byron*,' Sir Francis wrote to Douglas Kinnaird, Byron's banker and friend since their days at Cambridge: 'If any man in the world has shower'd upon him all that God and nature can bestow, it is Byron, *Poor Byron*! What! Even if he were in the wrong, what an *amende* honourable his "Farewell!" In my opinion those lines are worth all he ever wrote, and do him, in every way infinite credit.'[38]

Annabella's hatred of Augusta and her supposed 'crime' did not end with Augusta's death thirty-five years later, nor even with her own in 1860 but was continued into the first quarter of the last century by Ralph Lovelace, Byron's grandson, in his book *Astarte*. Byron's departure did not stop the speculation on the reasons for the separation. A few months before he died he told a friend, 'The causes, my dear sir, were too simple to be easily found out.'[39] His granddaughter, Lady Anne Isabella Noel King, wrote, 'B would have been happy with a woman of a lower but more amiable character who would have bent herself to his will and who had a *sensual* love for him.'

8

'I am on the brink of another ruin'

Caroline was busy during the spring of 1816. She found time to secretly write her novel *Glenarvon*, conspire with Annabella to ruin Byron and to fight for her marriage. Emily, Frederick and George Lamb had wanted William to agree to a legal separation for some time. Lady Melbourne preferred to endure Caroline's vagaries for fear of something worse – damage to the family reputation or William's future – but the opportunity her children had waited for occurred in early April.

Lord Melbourne had forbidden the use of firecrackers in the house and during a game with Caroline a page threw one into the fireplace. The loud explosion disturbed Lord Melbourne and temporarily frightened Caroline, who panicked and threw the hard ball she had in her hand at the boy. The impact cut his head and he began to bleed profusely. He shouted, 'Oh, my lady, you have killed me.' Terrified, she raced down the stairs screaming, 'Oh God, I have murdered the page!' Her shrieks and the general pandemonium echoed out into Whitehall. Lord Brougham, a lawyer and an admirer of Caro-George, was summoned to reprimand her. When he told her that if she were not careful she would end up in the dock at the Old Bailey, Caroline grabbed a poker from the grate and Brougham ran off claiming he was frightened for his life. The incident was too good for a gossip like Brougham, nicknamed Chronique Scandaleuse, to keep to himself and before long garbled rumours were whispered across drawing rooms. Joseph Farington claimed to have heard the boy's skull had been fractured deliberately, that he had recovered but that Caroline 'was in danger of being brought to trial.'[1]

Using the general brouhaha as an excuse, Emily and her brothers persuaded William to have a preliminary meeting with Lord Spencer and other members of her family to discuss Caroline's future. There was talk of a discreet separation but some wanted her committed to a lunatic asylum. Lord Spencer was reluctant to adopt such a Draconian solution but his wife, Lavinia, was equally as enthusiastic as Emily and her brothers. A doctor specialising in diseases of the mind, Mr Moore, was called in to examine Caroline.

She was justifiably terrified at the thought of being confined to an asylum, where it was the common practice to chain women to the wall by an arm or a leg, their only clothing being 'a blanket-gown, with nothing to fasten it with in front.' The report of the Parliamentary Committee, constituted to examine conditions in Bethlehem Hospital (Bedlam), stated in their report of August 1815, published in *The Times*, that the inmates 'were locked up in their cells, naked and chained, on straw.' They lived in conditions that were so squalid that members of the committee 'could hardly imagine a human being in a more degraded and brutalising situation.'[2]

While discussions on her future continued she was banished to Brocket with Augustus. She hid her fears and wrote defiantly to Lady Melbourne, 'I heard with surprise the measures which you propose – In the first place observe that nothing but absolute force shall induce me to consent.' She continued, 'Thank God I have friends to support me – and whatever measures are taken they shall be taken publickly. Wm Lamb has promised to agree to no private attempts to prove the mother of his child insane & the boy's parents & himself and every servant I have will stand by me. I cannot but feel utterly disgusted at Mr Moore's conduct – however you may proceed if it is your pleasure only remember that I utterly & at once deny any authority you may chuse to claim. Whilst I live, be assured I shall ever consider Lady Spencer as my enemy and Lord Spencer as the weak instrument of her intrigues. For fear you should misrepresent this letter as you have others I attest to you I have taken copies of it and send a copy of each to those friends who mean to support me. Yours no longer a Dutiful or Affectionate Caroline Lamb.'[3]

Despite her bravado Caroline was very scared. 'My dearest Lady Melbourne, I am not ungrateful – And whatever happens I shall not easily forget it… What would have been my fate had it been otherwise – God forbid I should say anything harsh of my own relations. The only censure I wish to cast upon anyone – at present is this – Let me remain under your protection till William returns. I wish to see no one. I do not care about going out, but to tell you the plain truth I had much rather be put in prison for any fault I have committed or abide by the law of the country than trust myself in the power of either Lord or Lady Spencer. As to Duncannon, he has a very good heart as well…but he was extremely severe at first and only when he found he could not prevail with Wm to do all he wished he relinquished his point.' Lord and Lady Bessborough had made little effort to save Caroline and she put this down to their fear of Duncannon. She vowed never to speak to Lady Spencer again, even were she 'to kneel here for pardon, which she ought to do.' Caroline refused to honour any promises forced from her when 'a straight waistcoat & a mad Doctor was held forth to view,' including disbanding her little army of pages. She pleaded with Lady Melbourne to be allowed to stay at Whitehall. 'This is the only place I feel safe in – and really when with my own eyes I read a letter not hinting but absolutely declaring me *Mad* – I may be a little afraid of those who had the inhumanity to write it. It is too bad to hear all this is for my *good*.'[4]

Augustus Foster wrote to his mother from Copenhagen, 'It is impossible not to feel some regard for her from old times, and it is really painful to see so delightful a person as she once was in absolute danger of committing so horrid a crime, and so entirely unmanageable. I must say I think her husband is a great deal to blame, for, had he studied a little more of Shakespeare's taming of the shrew, he might have checked her, at least so as to prevent such dreadful and shameful excesses in a disposition not naturally wicked.'[5]

Caroline was grateful for Lord and Lady Holland's support: 'At such a moment any kindness is deeply felt – but to see people attempt to alienate me from my husband – and fail is disgusting.' When Lady Holland advised her that 'the less you talk or write about it the more you will show yourself sensible of the pain you must have inflicted upon those whom you ought to consider beyond all others,'[6] Caroline took offence. She vowed never to forgive Lady Holland for such impertinence. She was even more infuriated when she heard that Hobhouse was passing her letters to Byron round Holland House. He told Lady Melbourne he intended to publish the letters and Caroline responded by upping the ante. 'I vow to God,' she wrote, 'I will on the instant publish not only his, but the whole exact journal I have kept of my acquaintance with him, and his conduct during the last four years. I speak it not in menace, but to apprise you of it.'[7]

Caroline was summoned from Brocket to Whitehall to sign the separation papers. She waited in her huge reception room listening to the movements of the lawyers and members of the family below in Lady Melbourne's apartment. Before the transaction was completed, William went to her to explain that Augustus would continue to live with her, as before, at Brocket. When he failed to return, Duncannon was sent to fetch him. On opening the door he was astonished to see William sitting close to Caroline while she fed him with 'tiny scraps of transparent bread and butter.' The lawyers were dismissed and Caroline wrote, 'We became united just as the world thought we were parted forever.'

On 9 May, when the page incident was dying down, a gothic novel in three volumes, *Glenarvon*, was published anonymously. Hobhouse had read it by the following day and at once recognised the author as Caroline. He went to Whitehall intending to take her to task, only to find Henry Webster already there 'attacking her for her abuse of his mother,' Lady Holland.[8]

Glenarvon was published by Henry Colburn, the rising star in the literary world and a shrewd businessman. He controlled *The New Monthly Magazine* and the weekly *Literary Gazette*, in which he published glowing reviews of his own books. Critics did not stint their praise either, which was not surprising as those he did not bribe he had on his payroll. He employed professional 'diners out' to talk up his books at fashionable dinner tables and catered to the emerging middle class who, he believed, liked to read books written by members of the aristocracy. Walter Scott's *Waverley* had given the public a taste for romantic, historical novels and, riding on his coat tails, Colburn published a best seller, Lady Morgan's *O'Donnel.*

Lady Morgan was an Irish patriot and one of the first novelists to use the political situation in Ireland as a backdrop to her stories. The memory of the 1798 Rebellion was still fresh in people's memory and through her novels and songs she encouraged her readers to sympathise with the rebels and the nationalist cause. These were popular drawing-room topics and Lady Morgan and her compatriot, Thomas Moore, were welcome guests at the great Whig houses where they sang sentimental, poignant songs about dead heroes, harps, shamrocks, minstrel boys and kings with collars of gold. When Caroline offered Colburn a novel set in Ireland he snapped up the opportunity.

Caroline took an active part in editing *Glenarvon,* even teaching herself printers' marks. According to Lady Morgan she said that, 'in *one month* – I wrote and *sent Glenarvon to the press.* I wrote it, unknown to all (save a Governess, Miss Welsh) in the middle of the night. It was necessary to have it copied out. I had heard of a famous copier, an old Mr Woodhead. I sent to beg he would come to see Lady Caroline Lamb at Melbourne House. I placed Miss Welsh, elegantly dressed, at my harp, and myself at a writing-table, dressed in page's clothes, looking a boy of fourteen. He addressed Miss Welsh as Lady Caroline. She showed him the author. He would not believe that this schoolboy could write such a thing. He came to me in a few days, and he found me in my own clothes. I told him William Ormond, the young author, was dead.'⁹ (Lady Morgan misheard Caroline. The governess was Miss Webster.)

Caroline was under a great strain. She believed she had lost everything and was about to be forcibly separated from William. As the lawyers drew up the papers and as the date of the publication of *Glenarvon* got closer she developed severe headaches and could not sleep from excitement. Much of her time had been taken up writing lyrics for six songs which were to be sung to Irish folk tunes by characters in *Glenarvon.* She was exhausted and in her extravagant way she told Colburn she was dying and asked him to 'do justice to my little narrative' and to pay Miss Webster £200. However, should she survive she wanted him 'to publish another MS which is very nearly finished.' She suspected the Lambs would be furious when the book was published, and made a suggestion to Colburn; 'I have thought of an expedient, which, without vexing my family, may excite some attention. When you put "This day is published *Glenarvon* a Novel in 3 Vols??? Add such mark as thus!!! Will not that attract? Or will you like to put "in which a popular Irish air is introduced – with words." This would perhaps obviate the objection. Also taking it without leave.'[10] She was suggesting to Colburn that it would appear that he had published the book without her permission.

The first copy, still smelling of printers' ink and binding leather, made her exclaim, 'It looks beautiful but makes my heart beat!'[11] She took the surprising step, for someone wanting to remain anonymous, of showering half of London with copies, each one inscribed 'From the Author'. The list lengthened hour by hour. Colburn shipped copies to Lady Bessborough, Sidney Smith, Mr Coombe, Mr Dulcean from the French bookshop, the Duchess of Devonshire – Rome, Miss Townsend – Devonshire House, Captain Clifford, Sir Charles Stewart – in the diplomatic bag to Vienna, Madame de Staël staying in Surrey, La Marquise de Coigny – rue de Vaugirad, 'the Miss Berrys in South or North Audley Street', Miss Webster, the Duke of Wellington, The Duke of Devonshire, Mr Hookham and John Murray.[12]

The plot of *Glenarvon* is simple but a tribe of minor characters, rebels, abbesses, evil counts, changelings, bards and a wronged maiden make it seem more complicated. The story begins at Delaval Castle in Ireland, where the widowed Duke of Altamonte lives with his sister, Lady Margaret Buchanan, his sister-in-law, Mrs Seymour, his infant son Sydney and his adolescent daughter, Calantha. Lady Margaret had promised to become the mistress of an Italian admirer, Viviani, on condition that he kills Sydney, leaving her son, George Buchanan, to inherit the dukedom. A murder is carried out and an infant dies, but Lady Margaret refuses to fulfil her promise and Viviani disappears.

Lady Margaret's plans are upset when Calantha falls in love with Lord Avondale instead of Buchanan. They marry and are deliriously happy. Avondale spends many happy hours converting Calantha to his freethinking and liberal ideas, which undermine her religious principles, leaving her vulnerable to the superficial morals of high society in London, which is ruled by the Princess of Madagascar.

A mysterious, handsome foreigner, Glenarvon, arrives intent on inciting a rebellion. Calantha is immediately attracted to him and introduces him to her friends. At the same time she takes under her protection an Italian page, Zerbellini. Lady Margaret immediately sees in him a likeness to the Duke's dead son, Sydney. He is accused of stealing a necklace and disappears.

Calantha and Glenarvon plan to elope but Mrs Seymour is suddenly taken ill and Calantha refuses to go. She says a tender farewell to Glenarvon who leaves for Wales where he meets Miss Monmouth, a demure heiress. He decides to marry her but dallies with an older woman, Lady Mandeville. Tortured by rumours of his infidelity, Calantha bombards Glenarvon with letters until his patience breaks and he spurns her. Avondale discovers her infidelity, rejects her and desperate with remorse, Calantha dies in his arms.

Lady Margaret once more rejects Viviani as her lover and he stabs her. The Duke of Altamonte realises that Zerbellini is his son and that the murdered baby was a changeling. He rushes off to rescue the boy from Viviani who is holding him prisoner. He finds him standing on the edge of the cliff with Sydney in his arms. Before Viviani can leap to his death, the Duke's servants seize him and rip back his cloak, revealing the face of Glenarvon.

The family rejoices at the return of the heir. Glenarvon survives and escapes to take command of a ship and fight honourably at the battle of Camperdown. Overcome by remorse he throws himself to his death from the helm of his ship into the stormy sea. When Avondale realises how badly he has treated Calantha, he dies of a broken heart.

Lady Holland described the book to Mrs Creevey as a 'singular libel' and 'a *plaidoyer*' against William, 'addressed to the religious and methodistical part of the community, accusing him of having overset her religious and moral (!) principles by teaching her doctrines of impiety, &c. The outlines of few of her characters are portraits, but the *amplissage* and traits are exact. *Lady Margaret* is a two fold being – Ds of Devonshire and her mother; *Lady Augusta,* Lady Jersey and Lady Caher; *Sophia,* Lady Granville, who had 6 years ago a passion for working fine embroidery, and she marks most *atrociously* her marriage with Lord Granville. *Lady Mandeville* is Ly Oxford; *Buchanan* is Sir Godfrey Webster; *Glenarvon* and *Viviani* are of course Lord Byron. Lady Frances Webster is sketched and some others slightly. Lady Melbourne is represented as bigoted and vulgar... The *bonne-bouche* I have reserved for the last – myself. Where every ridicule folly and infirmity (my not being able from malady to move about much) is portrayed... The work is a strange farrago, and only curious from containing some of Lord Byron's genuine letters – the last, in which he rejects her love and implores an end to their connexion, directed and sealed by Lady Oxford, is a most astonishing performance to publish... I am sorry to see the Melbourne family so miserable about it. Lady Cowper is really frightened and depressed far beyond what is necessary… The work has had a prodigious sale, as all libellous matters have.'[13]

'Shyness and embarrassment,' William told Lord Holland, prevented him from talking to or seeing anyone 'more particularly those who have been the objects of so wanton and unjustifiable attack. I did not write, because what could I say? I could only exculpate myself from any previous knowledge, the effect of which must be to throw a heavier load upon the offending party.'[14] William knew nothing until the book was published. He told Caroline, 'I have stood your friend till now – I even think you ill used; but if it is true this novel is published – and, as they say, against us all. – I will never see you more.' Then letters full of 'malignant violence' and 'libel' began to arrive from his family and friends but they were so extreme that, as Caroline remarked, 'they over-did it,' and William took her side. She told Lord Granville, 'He saw and feels, deeply feels the unpleasant situation it is for him but he loves me enough to stand firm as a rock, and to despise such as came forward to ruin one who had never hurt them.'[15]

Emily was embarrassed; 'I could not have believed & had I been told beforehand that you would have done such a thing I should have thought myself justified in vindicating you from what I should have conceived a wicked & unwarrantable aspersion,' she told Caroline. 'Human nature is liable to err, and anyone may give way to a fit of passion for everything you ever did I could, and did try, to find some excuse, but for this there is none. It is no accident, no weakness but a deliberate voluntary act and there are none but bad feelings that could dictate such a course, to sit down calmly & write for public inspection all that is malicious and with not an object but to offend and to hold up to ridicule those who have been your friends, to disclose to the world (all the chamber maids and footmen) a story for which most people would have given their fortunes to buy up if any scribbler had threatened to write of them and what is to me still more distressing, to see Wm's character in the world utterly and entirely blasted by it. His name held up to ridicule and contempt and himself the sport of every club where the book is laid upon the table… It makes my heart bleed to see him walking up and down the streets when I know what people are saying of him & if he has no feeling for himself at least his family are bound to have some for him and I must own that I feel his disgrace very deeply.'[16]

Emily exaggerated. William had been furious with Caroline but when he realised, through reading *Glenarvon*, how she had suffered at the hands of his family, he sympathised with her and, in any case, he was rather pleased with her description of his character [Lord Avondale]. He felt touched and even a little proud of her achievement.

Caroline knew that any praise for the book enraged the Lambs so she was alarmed by any publicity. She wrote to Colburn. 'I have just heard with excessive astonishment & anger that at a shop in Duke St, I believe Portman Place, they advertise to be sold or let out *Glenarvon* by Lady Caroline Lamb – I do entreat you go instantly & have it stopped as I shall certainly take every means of doing so – They have no right!'[17]

Hary-o was disgusted, Lady Holland was enraged, Lady Jersey cut Caroline and even Lady Bessborough said that she would have rather seen her dead than to live and publish *Glenarvon*. 'I am on the brink of another ruin,' Caroline told Lady Melbourne. 'Half my friends cut me, all my acquaintances are offended – your protection may save – but I shall never ask for it unless freely offered. At this moment I am doing all I can to stop further mischief. They have written to me to say that the further 1,500 copies are sold & a new edition is wanted. I will either refuse it or make every alteration I suggested – at all events I will leave out anything obnoxious. – You say I have written another novel – I will not deny it – but I have burnt it – Are you satisfied, or do you still accuse me of acting the part of a Grubb St author? – When I said everyone was in my power – I merely meant that in the novel I wrote I had certainly not said one thing malignant of my acquaintance – & except Lady Holland who is there that I have attacked?'[18] She was prepared for unflattering reviews and promised that if they were malicious or made any unpleasant remarks about her, 'Lady Holland and her minions shall have reason to rue the hour they got it done.'

Lady Melbourne told Annabella that she had not been able to read more than the first twenty pages and Caroline accused her of changing her tune. She had obviously forgotten their conversation in which she had said that she did not mind the book being published, 'laughed about the Princess of Madagascar' [Lady Holland] and appeared altogether good-humoured.'

Under pressure from his family, William wrote to Colburn on 17 May. 'The novel of Glenarvon having been published by the Author without any consultation with her friends upon the subject, many parts of it having been applied as they never were intended, objections having been made to some passages of the novel, and others being certainly liable to some objections it is my determination that for the present at least that there shall be published no second edition.'[19] Caroline had not lost her touch and a few days later she wrote, 'I am happy to say that I have obtained leave to publish a second edition, which will be greatly improved without delaying the printer. I have also written you a most beautiful preface – and now wish to have done with the whole thing. It is useless to deny it. Everyone knows who wrote the book. Make therefore what use you chuse of it.' She offered Colburn first refusal on the copyright to include all the pictures, poems and songs, for five hundred pounds, the same amount he had paid Lady Morgan for *O'Donnel*. She told him, 'I should not have asked so much only it has just been offered me.'[20]

Caroline told Lady Melbourne, 'I owe it to all to publish as far as I can, without involving those I love, a full explanation of my conduct and a full repetition of the calumnies that have been spread against me and my infamous book – and an exact recount of Lord Byron's conduct for the last four years.' She told the readers that *Glenarvon* was written and committed to the press 'without permission, communication, advice, or assistance' and its characters were fictitious. She explained, 'This work is not the offspring of calm tranquillity, and cool deliberation, it does not bear the marks of such a temper, or of such a situation. It was written under the pressure of affliction, with the feelings of resentment which are excited by misrepresentation, and in the bitterness of a wounded spirit, which is naturally accompanied by a corresponding bitterness both of thought and expression.'

Caroline was afraid that Lord Granville might forbid Hary-o to see her so she put her position before them and asked them to think. 'Before you judge me you should see and question the Boy to whom I was said to be so barbarous. You should also see my husband, who knows everything and is not blinded by my acts or even by love, and who says that he could not in honour give me up.' She listed her grievances, 'I was ordered out of the house in no gentle language,' (by Lord Melbourne). 'My mother was spoke to with the most barbarous roughness in my presence. My husband received letters telling him he would be a public ridicule and jest if he supported me. I was proved mad. Mr Moore assured me it was so, and entreated me to persuade my husband of it.' She said that she made up her mind to publish *Glenarvon* on the night a 'dreadful scene passed between me and Lord M and Mama.' She said the original book had been much more violent and she was justified in parodying Emily, Lady Melbourne and Lady Holland because they supported Byron for four years even though they knew it annoyed William. She resented being tried at the family council, her character pulled apart and her mistakes, 'wrongs, crimes, follies,' stretching back to 'the days of infancy and all brought forth to view without mercy. To write this novel was then my sole comfort, but before I published it I thought myself ruined past recall, and even then I took out all the passages I thought might reflect upon Lady Melbourne and many others.'[21]

By supporting Caroline, William had antagonised his family. Lord Melbourne declared that he did not want Caroline under his roof and George begged William to leave her. The discontent and unpleasantness had made him ill and depressed. 'He says he wishes he was dead & the like,' Caroline told Lady Melbourne. 'It was on this account I urged you to delay talking of changes – for unless Lord Melbourne wishes us to take a house now – there can be, it seems to me, no use to enter upon the subject just at present – but as I well know he ever imputes the basest motives to me & never since I was in this house believed that

I did one thing from kindness or right feeling. Tell him that he need be under no sort of alarm, he has the power to turn us out tomorrow if he chuses and as George, Emily, the prince, Lord Egremont & all his friends advise it I hope he will be happier when he has given William the greatest pain he can inflict. As to me, whom he thinks to wound and to punish, he knows me but little. He says that my own family have gone against me. That no one receives me. That I am scorned by all – & he acts in a manner to bring this to pass.' The only reason she stayed was to prevent 'William's health and spirits decline'. If, she predicted, Lord Melbourne threw William out 'to gratify the malevolence of those who *hate me*' he would shorten and embitter William's last hours…and when you have made him miserable you will be so yourself. Lord Cowper may then sit in Brooks' unmolested. The stigma of disgrace fixed upon me – indelibly, will gratify the mean jealousy of the triumphant malevolence – but your own hearts will grieve & Lord Melbourne in his later years lament too late his severity – however just… I am accused of taking Lady Byron's part! Lady Jersey could not read *Glenarvon* she was so shocked & disgusted – yet she could receive & approve of Lord Byron. – In all things you have all been able to uphold soothe and assist him [Byron] & me you cannot pardon though insulted & injured past bearing. – All I trust is that those who have been insulting to me – may soon suffer the agony I have felt & when their hearts are bleeding let some cold friend appear to soothe them with a taunting recapitulation of their previous offences… Emily above all has acted most ill – for she has seemed kind – she has abetted her friend Lady Jersey in all that she has done – & let me say – that all this will soon or late cause her regret – for her heart is good I believe & though she hates me & seeks only to mortify me – she will be sorry when she finds the irreparable mischief she has done. I do not like underhand measures – have written openly. Trust me however, I neither seek to deter you from your purpose nor to alarm you. I merely state a fact – as you all do – & God so deal with you all as you have dealt with me. I wish no worse. Can I?'[22]

Because she knew she could not afford to fall out completely with the Melbournes, Caroline approached Emily. 'All I ask you is to write to Lord & Lady M, pray to them, I dare not ask them to forgive me – but bid them burn those horrid letters… I will grow calm & pray to God to make me so. Your brother is violent. I will think upon what he has borne for me.' On the reverse she wrote, 'Let them know my heart is not yet hardened. I am miserable at having been so wicked. Pray obtain their pardon – & God bless.'[23]

Emily refused to believe that Caroline was sorry or unhappy. 'How can this be possible,' she asked, 'when I hear of you going on just as usual with all the train, pages, horses, carriages etc, and to all appearance of having the world instead of being as one should expect from a person of any feeling, abashed & ashamed…

You have chosen to sacrifice Wm's honour & character to your imaginary revenge and this I must resent. He may be so far decided as not to see the case in its true light but I must and cannot help feeling it. What you say as an excuse for yourself I cannot accept. A book is not published in a moment. There is plenty of time for reflection and I cannot but think the provocations you have had about the page's business were very slight and such as you ought to have borne with patience. People's feelings were naturally shocked at hearing of such violence but they were willing to ascribe it to a momentary fit of passion or almost to excuse it as the effect of insanity – & had you retired and appeared sorry for it the whole would have been instantly forgotten.' The last part was a marvellous piece of hypocrisy as it makes no mention of the part she and her brothers had played in trying to ruin Caroline's marriage.[24]

Augustus Foster told his mother that he had found the book hard-going but 'If Lord Avondale reads it, he must be a little conscience struck at his character of a free thinker, for I am convinced that, with all his good and noble qualities, he was used to scout at all fixed principles, and taught her, or helped her, to do the same… She don't give me the idea of being at all cured, notwithstanding her confessions. I sadly fear some bad end for her; she certainly is past all advice.'[25]

'Shall we never hear the last of Lady Caroline Lamb and her vagaries!' Lady Shelley wrote in her diary of 21 June. 'What a strange being this is! First to run all over London after Lord Byron, and then spread all kinds of stories about him, good, bad and indifferent. Holding up her folly for all men to see and smile at, and then to crown it all by the publication of a book like *Glenarvon*!'[26]

The second edition was in the bookshops on 22 June and continued to be a best-seller. Caroline nervously told Colburn, 'I think it as well to say as little about *Glenarvon* as possible. To praise it is only to enrage those who are offended. Those who attack me hitherto have done it in a vulgar and ill-bred manner. They have only lowered themselves by it & done me good. I prefer it much to any attempt at excuse or puff & for God sake, if you cannot stop the mouths of my enemies "deliver me from my friends!" '[27] The songs were popular, especially the 'Waters of Elle' sung by Count Gondimar, alias Thomas Moore, in volume two, chapter XVII. It was sung to the tune of '*Ils ne sont plus*' and performed in theatres by the *demi-monde* and in respectable homes by young girls accompanying themselves on the family piano.

Waters of Elle! Thy limpid streams are flowing,
Smooth and untroubled, through the flow'ry vale;
O'er thy green banks once more, the wild rose blowing,
Greets the young spring, and scents the passing gale.
Here 'twas at eve, near yonder tree reposing,

One still too dear, first breath'd his vows to thee;
Wear this, he cried, his guileful love disclosing,
Near to thy heart, in memory of me.
Love's cherished gift, the rose he gave, is faded;
Love's blighted flow, can never bloom again,
Weep for thy fault – in heart – in mind degraded:
Weep if thy tears can wash away the stain.

Call back the vows, that once to heaven were plighted,
Vows full of love, of innocence and truth.
Call back the scenes in which thy soul delighted:
Call back the dream that blest thy early youth.

Flow silver stream, tho' threatening tempest lower,
Bright, mild and clear, thy gentle waters flow;
Round thy green banks, the spring's young blossoms flower;
O'er thy soft waves the balmy zephyrs blow.

Yet, all in vain; for never spring arraying
Nature in charms, to thee can make it fair.
Ill fated love, clouds all thy path, portraying
Years past of bliss, and future of despair.

In July Byron dined with Madame de Staël, his champion and friend, at Coppet, her home on Lake Geneva. When she leant across the table and asked him if he was the original of the anti-hero, Glenarvon, he coolly replied, '*C'est possible, Madame, mais je n'ai jamais posé.*'[28] With almost motherly solicitude she persuaded him to allow her to broker a reconciliation with Annabella. 'The separation may have been my fault,' Byron conceded, 'but it was her own choice. I tried all means to prevent and would so as much and more to end it – a word would do so, but it does not rest with me to pronounce it. You asked me if I thought that Lady B was attached to me? To this I can only answer that I love her.'[29] Henry Brougham got wind of the plan and immediately informed Annabella that Lady Romilly (Sir Samuel's wife) was bringing a conciliatory letter from Byron. He advised her to ignore it. In a maladroit effort to help, Madame de Staël had let slip that Annabella had met Caroline. Byron was outraged at his wife's complicity 'with that self-avowed libeller & strumpet' and the reconciliation failed.

Armed with Caroline's confession, Annabella began her campaign to force Augusta to admit to incest. Travellers returning from Switzerland brought more gossip as Brougham efficiently spread the story throughout the large English colony. Augusta was upset and her letters to Byron were full of misgivings. He replied, 'I think all these apprehensions – very groundless. Who can care for such a wretch as Caroline, or believe such a seventy times convicted liar? And in the next place, whatever she may suppose or assert? – I never "committed" any one to her but *myself*... And as to her fancies – she fancies anything – and every body – Lady M &c. Really this is starting at shadows'.[30] He replied to the next panic-stricken letter, 'If I understand you rightly, you seem to have been apprehensive – or menaced (like every one else) by that infamous Bedlamite. – If she stirs against you, neither her folly nor her falsehood should or shall protect her. Such a monster as that *has no sex* and should live no more.'[31] Percy Bysshe Shelley reassured him, saying that the 'calumnies' bore no weight, partly because they were so extravagant and partly because they were silly. He compared them to the sparks of a straw fire that vanish when their fuel fails. 'You are destined, believe me, to assume a rank in the estimation of mankind where such puerile hostilities cannot reach.'[32]

Glenarvon continued to sell well. In March 1817 it was reviewed in a Venetian paper and in August it was translated into Italian and Shelley was offered 'a considerable sum to work up the materials of Lady Caroline Lamb's novel' by Thomas Hookham. He declined.

William told Caroline, 'I will stand or fall with you.' His determination to support her grew stronger when he saw how she was attacked and rudely treated and for his sake she made great efforts to redeem her name and regain the respect of society. It was a painful process. Lady Salisbury, a near neighbour of Caroline's and a family friend, went out of her way to be kind and Lord Granville ostentatiously stopped to speak to her. Others made her welcome but in such an enthusiastic way that she was suspicious. Above all else she wanted to be accepted and forgiven by her cousins, Hary-o and Lady Morpeth.

The seal on her rehabilitation would be her acceptance at Almack's, the most fashionable and exclusive club in London. The Ladies Committee governed the club. Emily had been a member since 1813. She was the most popular of the 'Patronesses', Lady Jersey the most ill mannered, Lady Sefton the most kind and amiable, Lady Castlereagh and Mrs Drummond Burrell (later Lady Willoughby d'Eresby) the most self-important, and Princess Lieven the most haughty and exclusive. Their number also included Lady Downshire, Lady Bathurst and the *bon enfant*, Princess Esterhazy. The main business of these ladies was to further their husbands' careers, pay off old scores and maintain Almack's exclusiveness. Membership was controlled by a system of vouchers. To possess one carried almost the same cachet as being presented at court. The rules were strict. No one was allowed in after midnight and even the Duke of Wellington was turned away when he arrived a few minutes after twelve. This enabled Lady Jersey to say, 'No one can ever accuse us now of showing favouritism.'[33]

The Duke maintained his friendship with Caroline to the intense irritation of other ladies. He even tried to advise her how to handle William. 'Whenever you are inclined to do anything to make him very angry, & you forget your great vow remember the promise you made me the last night I saw you at Lady Kinnaird's.' He hoped he had helped and told Lady Shelley, 'the more particularly as my family, which is tolerably numerous, took up her cause very warmly.'[34] He thought her charming and amusing 'especially *her accidents*,' Hary-o told Lady Morpeth, 'which is the charitable term he gives to all her sorties.'

In another attempt to reinstate Caroline, the Duke asked Lady Downshire to give her a precious Almack's ticket. She demurred, saying she must ask her sister Patronesses. With the exception of Lady Bathhurst, who was not present, they declined. The Duke persuaded Lady Bathhurst to leave a slip at the door for Caroline to exchange for a ticket but another Patroness told the door-keepers to refuse to admit her. 'What do you think of that?' he asked Lady Shelley. 'Luckily Calantha did not go, and the shot missed. But, in the meantime all London is in arms, including even the Patronesses who were not parties to giving the directions last mentioned. Caroline was "Fit to be tied", as the Irishman says, on discovering that it was 'Queen Willis [Lady Jersey] alone who gave the order that she should not have a ticket at Almack's, notwithstanding that Lady Bathurst had given her an order for it.'[35]

Caroline was 'cut' at a reception at Anglesey House. Annabella smugly reported to her mother, 'Nobody spoke to her. I cannot help pitying her – for she must see around and *near* her so many whose hypocrisy only has secured them from similar scorn.' The last remark referred to Caro-George, who was crossing Europe to join her mother in Rome and whose name was constantly linked with Brougham's.

At Lady Melbourne's request and as part of her rehabilitation programme, Caroline agreed to write a letter to Annabella. She regretted that they had seen so little of each, other saying she was hesitant to call on her until she could be sure of her welcome and offered her the use of Lady Bessborough's box at Drury Lane. Annabella did not reply. Caro-George wrote approvingly from Valence saying she did not trust either Lady Melbourne or Caroline and their offers of friendship were nothing more than a ploy to protect Caroline's reputation. However, she advised Annabella to cultivate William's goodwill.

It is surprising that Caro-George was not more sympathetic as George Lamb was as passive and indifferent to her as William was to Caroline. In addition to the characteristic Lamb boorishness and violence, he was impotent. Lady Melbourne was annoyed that Caro-George's name was being linked to Henry

Brougham and told her so. Caro-George replied from Geneva in much the same vein that Caroline used. 'I could be happier living out of the world even with loss of reputation with those who loved me, than in it, struggling to appear happy with those who did not care for me. I have struggled seven years, and my courage at last failed me. I was told George appeared unhappy at my absence and wrote to ask if he was so, and this was his answer – "Who the deuce says I am unhappy? If I am it is only at some theatrical worry. I do not like your absence certainly – it fidgets me and unsettles me, and I get through less business in consequence." This was not the language of a person who loved or regretted me, but I suppose he was perfectly unconscious of what was passing in my mind.'[36]

Lady Melbourne probably was not surprised. The emotional hold she had over her sons was enormous. Frederick did not marry until twenty years after her death, Peniston died a bachelor at thirty-five and William and George were unsatisfactory husbands. Their wives were regarded as interlopers. Frederick commiserated with his mother, commenting on his two sisters-in-law, 'How extremely and continually you are plagued by the little beast and with how much reason. I am sure it wears you, and it can not do otherwise. The other Lady I think less about because she is out of the house and you do not see her so continually, but two such curses were never inflicted upon a family which was so perfectly happy and united before they came into it.'[37] Her attitude was in stark contrast to that of Lady Bessborough, who went out of her way to welcome her daughters-in-law.

The proposed separation and the publication of *Glenarvon* had overshadowed William's return to Parliament in April as the Member for Peterborough, a seat his grandfather, Matthew Lamb, had occupied from 1747 until he died in 1768. The cost of taking up the position had, as he predicted four years before, put his budget under great pressure.

Lady Melbourne accused Caroline of extravagance and Lord Melbourne referred to her as 'your Lavishness' but it cannot have been easy for her to run Brocket Hall knowing that all the while the servants were running to Lady Melbourne with tales.[38] 'I wish just to ask you why you take upon trust such very unkind things?' she asked her mother-in-law. 'You owe it to William and me to investigate before you accuse – as very frequently I am accused without the least cause.' The Melbournes accused her of hiring and feeding extra servants which she denied, adding, 'I beg you will just remember that at this time William wants a person entirely for himself to wait on him – at the House of Commons. When we first married that was our establishment… If I have no boy, a footman for me is the least we can do with. If you think this is too much only arrange it as you like… At a time like the present William requires a servant for himself. If you like it we can pay him his board wages – but though he does not say so I know Wm is distressed & this makes me try and make any shift – to prevent adding to the yearly bills... I am very sorry if I have given you the least offence but you do not guess how it wears upon the spirit to try daily & never, never to give satisfaction.'[39]

In September Emily and Lord Cowper took their older children abroad, leaving the two youngest, William and Spencer, with Lady Melbourne. Augustus compared badly with these healthy, jolly little boys. His fits, which had declined in the spring, had returned. 'I never know what to do,' Caroline told Lady Melbourne, 'he has had 4 attacks today, 2 very, very severe ones.' Mr Lucas, the family physician, a strong believer in the efficacy of fresh air, was consulted and it was decided to send Augustus with Miss Webster to Brighton. The boy was blistered and then purged four times with 'Mr Evans powder' before he left.[40]

The Melbournes continued to complain that Caroline wasted money. 'I know you and Lord Melbourne will say how it is impossible that William, having no expenses, should be distressed but just remember going abroad, the child at the sea, the quantity of doctoring for that child & coming into Parliament all makes money very short,' she explained. 'If Busby [a long-time family servant] returns – I can manage very well but now we really scarce know what to do.'[41]

Caroline relied on Busby or Hazzard to control the servants but when Brierly, a servant she regarded as 'thick', complained of bullying she encouraged him to stand up for himself.[42] She gave a trouble-maker, James, a month's notice but he refused to leave. Not even William could budge him until he agreed that he could keep the clothes they had supplied and, to Caroline's annoyance, a pair of new boots. He was allowed to remain at Brocket overnight because it was 'after five and all the coaches had left but instead of being pleasant and grateful James menaced Busby'.[43] Emily described the staff at Brocket to Frederick as appearing and disappearing like shadows on a Chinese lantern. 'They come on and go off.' Thérèse, Caroline's former maid, wrote, 'She sometimes hires a servant, and sends him off the next day for the most absurd reasons; such as "Thomas! You look as if you required a dose of salts; and, altogether, you do not suit me. etc." She is the meanest woman on earth, and the greatest tyrant generally speaking, *quoi qu'elle a ses moments de bonté*; but as to her husband, he is at all times proud, severe, and altogether disagreeable.'[44]

While staying at Tixal with Lady Bessborough, Mrs Peterson (Lady Bessborough's maid) told Hary-o that 'the Brocket ménage is going on terribly now that they are alone there. Caroline more irritable and peevish than ever and going into such furies with her servants that the history of the page was very near being acted over again with a footman one day last week; that Wm is become very nearly as violent and that the scenes going on there are really dreadful.' Mrs Peterson thought that 'Caroline's mind has now decidedly much to do with it;

that she wanders about the house tormenting the servants, swallowing all the physic she can get at and will not cross the walk before the house or take exercise of any kind.'[45] Thérèse corroborated this view. Since leaving Caroline's service she had been hired by the courtesan, Harriette Wilson, who, in the course of her professional duties had entertained all the Lamb brothers and their father.

Caroline had palpitations and told Lady Melbourne, 'My breathing is much affected by the heart fluttering & beating that I literally feel like a person with asthma and I do not find laudanum or ether or valerian of the least use. Whilst the blister was drawing I did not feel it & last night it was easier... Lucas says I am so low he does not like to bleed me but the pulse stops so and the heart beats so that he should like to take blood from the left arm. What do you advise? I believe bleeding is very pernicious.'[46] She lost her appetite and ate only a chicken wing with a glass of sherry for dinner, in contrast to Augustus who ate enormous amounts of food.[47] The trip to Brighton had not cured his fits and he returned suffering from a 'breaking out in the middle of his head at the back'.

Caroline's medicinal glass of sherry gradually turned into a bottle. When she was told to limit her drinking she hid bottles of cognac in her bedroom, slipping back for a glass or two during the day.[48] She had difficulty in sleeping. A frequent guest at Brocket, Bulwer Lytton, remembered how she would send a page to wake the guests at three in the morning and invite them to sit on the stairs as she played the organ that stood on the landing. She would stop after a few minutes and the guests would all join in the conversation. Caroline was so amusing and brilliant that no one noticed how late it was until dawn broke.

Lord Melbourne complained about the cost of the organ and in a fuddled reply Caroline told Lady Melbourne, 'We want a bottle of brandy, & a bottle of spirits of wine... Tell Lord M – he need not think of the organ it is for me – not his and it only costs a guinea – which he may refund in the said bottle of brandy & spirits of wine – as there is none in the house.'[49]

To break the tedium and to curry favour with Lord Melbourne, William and Caroline spent days copying out his 'very dull' papers and, in an attempt to please Lady Melbourne, Caroline grappled with the theory of household management. She ordered cookery books, the *Domestic Cook or Compleat Housewife*, and asked Lady Melbourne for the recipes for 'cold cream & almond paste'. In return she sent her an 'Irish recipe for boiling potatoes' just as it was given to her at Bessborough. 'Take the tatoes & clean the earth off of 'em & put them in cold not in hot water & let 'em simmer till ye've nothing in life to do, that is from early morning until noon then put 'em on a strainer to sweat – till they're dry & mind they burst their own skins before you peel 'em.'[50] Her zeal for domestic perfection led her to write a book on domestic economy but she did not have it published. 'I mention this,' she told Lady Morgan, 'to show you I, too, have been a good housewife, and saved William much; but he says what is the use of saving in one place if you squander all away in another? Alas! What is the use of anything? We may go on saying what is the use, till we really puzzle ourselves, as I did, as to why we exist at all.'[51]

Caroline knew Murray was preparing to publish the third canto of *Childe Harold* and she begged to be allowed to see a copy, promising not to tell anyone. 'Believe me therefore sincerely thankful for what I am going to receive – as the young lady said to the duchess when she was desired by her parent to say "Grace".'[52] Murray did not reply immediately and Caroline asked, 'Are you offended with me or my letter? If so, I am sorry, but depend upon it if after seven years' acquaintance you choose to cut off what you ever termed your left hand; I have too much gratitude towards you to allow of it. Accept therefore every apology for what I have written…let me entreat you to remember a maxim I have found very useful to me, that there is nothing in this life worth quarrelling about, and that half the people we are offended with never intended to give us cause… I think you will relent and send me *Childe Harold* before any one has it. This is the first time you have not done so – and the *Quarterly Review*, pray also any other book that is curious, or at all events tell me of it, as we have much time and I like your judgement… Have mercy and send them or I shall gallop to town to see you.'[53]

By November the scandal over *Glenarvon* had died down and Caroline returned to the social rounds, receptions, Drury Lane and the opera. She gaily described to Murray how she had gone to the opera house dressed in white satin with feathers and diamonds in her hair and while she was standing on the steps someone had recognised her and shouted, 'Lady Caroline Lamb'. A facetious footman replied 'Lady Caroline *Wolf*' and several footmen came to her defence. During the argument she was kidnapped by two sedan chairmen, despite trying to tell them that she wanted to get in to the opera house and not out. Once safely inside, one of her spaniels dashed in behind her covered with mud. A comedian shouted 'a fox!' and began hissing. 'Judge of my situation,' Caroline told Murray, ' I was either obliged to give up this dear shabby cur, or own a friend in such a disguise.' She decided to take the dog home but when she went outside she found her carriage had been 'almost carried away by Irish boys and drunken chair men one of whom to the indignation of the rest, constantly vociferated, "This is my lady" – "Your lady d—n you?" "Yes, my lady" – and sure enough he, like the dog, proved a mendicant pensioner when a blaze of light showed him to me like a ghost. Now, fare thee well; excuse all this nonsense.'[54]

A visit to Albemarle Street on 12 December left her in a nostalgic mood. 'It is strange but my visit to your house today has made me miserable – after all what a life mine has been & how singular our acquaintance.' She told Murray, 'I had a thousand things to say to you but they were all forgotten the moment they said you were at home – is not life strange? Whatever he is, however I have abused him, if I believed him at any hour unhappy would I not go through the fire to save him & that child of his – Will it be like him? But what is all this to me? Your room speaks of him in every part of it, and I never see you without pain, yet is it not strange? It seems to me most unpleasant if I can pass any length of time without seeing you, and what I can safely say I add – that you have been a sincere, upright and manly friend to both him & me through many trying scenes. If ever you are grieved send for me – for I am yours in my heart & soul – & perhaps I reproach myself for the violence with which I have presumed to judge & condemn another. Of all people on earth I am the last to do so – who ever knew so little as myself how to command my own actions yet be afraid? Whatever my faults I feel your kindness with the utmost gratitude & never, never shall forget to name you among my real friends.'[55]

Two days later Hary-o followed a page through 'the dark and winding passages and staircases' of Whitehall to Caroline. She told Lady Morpeth, 'I was received with rapturous joy, embraces and tremendous spirits. I expected she would have put on appearance of something, but to do her justice she only displayed a total want of shame and consummate impudence, which, whatever they may be in themselves, are at least better or rather less disgusting than pretending or acting a more interesting part. I was dragged to the unresisting William, and dismissed with a repetition of embassades and professions. I looked, as I felt, stupefied. And this is the guilty, broken-hearted Calantha who could only expiate her crimes with her death. I mean my visit to be annual.'[56]

In January 1817 Caro-George was still on the continent and Caroline commiserated with Lady Melbourne, 'I am so very sorry by George's letter to see things are not going on well', adding pointedly, 'but pray do not mention it in the least to him as nothing is so unpleasant as to have things repeated.'[57] The story was very popular and when Lady Sefton came to Brocket for a few days Caroline sturdily tried to divert the conversation away from Caro-George. 'There is nothing you can imagine that she did not ask & in so many different ways. It was like being cross-questioned', she told Lady Melbourne. 'I just let her talk and said nothing but general things. She seemed to be quite surprised when I said Mr Brougham had returned. It is wonderful how she hears and questions.'[58]

Augustus was ten in August. He had grown from a fine, fat baby into a strapping handsome, healthy boy but sadly his mental development had not matched his physical growth. William, anxious that he should be as well educated as possible, asked the eminent physician Sir Gilbert Blane (famous for introducing lime juice into the navy to prevent scurvy) for advice. On Blane's recommendation he hired a fellow Scot, the newly qualified doctor, Robert Lee. William explained to Sir Gilbert what he expected of his new employee. 'With regard to the management of the health of his pupil, Dr Lee will, of course, have the entire control. With respect to his education, I beg leave to distinctly state that the principal object of it at present must be to teach him Latin and Greek languages according to the modes practised in our English schools, which I shall be able to point out to him.' As far as other subjects were concerned, Dr Lee had *carte blanche* 'and may teach him as much logic, moral philosophy and metaphysics as he can get in.'[59]

In October William and Caroline took a short holiday in Brighton and in November Byron paid the Duchess of Devonshire the outstanding rent on 13 Piccadilly. The nation was plunged into mourning on 6 November when Princess Charlotte, the Prince Regent's only child, died five and a halfhours after giving birth to a stillborn boy. Richard Rush, the American Ambassador, commented on the numbers of people that he saw wearing black as he walked through London. Caroline thought it was all excessive and remarked, 'I see no end to the mourning, and really believe we shall end by wearing it of an *evening* as long as the Prince Regent. I hear everybody goes still in black gloves to the Pavilion.'

Caroline met Michael Bruce in Paris in 1815. He was famous for being the lover of Lady Hester Stanhope (traveller in the orient and William Pitt's niece) and for conniving at the escape of Count Lavalette, an act for which he was sentenced to death. The Count had served Napoleon and on the return of the Bourbons was imprisoned and tried for high treason by Louis XVIII. He escaped mainly through the bravery of his wife, Emilie Louise, the Empress Josephine's niece, and the emotional appeal Lady Hester made to the King. Bruce had met Byron in 1810 in Greece and his memories of that time fascinated Caroline so much that she asked him to call on her, '& bring any who like to come – as I think such pleasant conversation does William good. If you thought me unamiable pray pardon it. I am not very feminine and gentle something like Catherine the Shrew before she was tamed – and you must bear with these infirmities.'[60] She sent him a card on which she had painted a delicate watercolour of two angels, one stabbing the other. On the reverse she had written:

Love Seiz'd for her his sweet dart
And plunged it in her guilty heart
Even while contained within his arms
She gazed upon his matchless charms.

Even as she pressed his lips of rose
And heard the music of his Vows

The subtle poison through her frame
Burnt like the wild insatiate flame.
Remorse – despair and agony
Mingled with every ecstasy
One kiss – one last fond kiss he cried –
She gave him what he wished and died.[61]

Reminiscing about Byron brought back all Caroline's sorrows. 'If I could believe what you say respecting Lord Byron, it would indeed make me miserable, as it is I cried for an hour upon reading your letter, but I believe it was chiefly because my mind & body are both weakened.' She told Bruce that her heart 'was in torture & my whole soul the same – It is as if there was a sword run through me – or a fire burning in my brain. No ship that ever was lost on a strange sea without daring to anchor anywhere – or in immediate fear of being lost – ever yet was so distressed as I am. I know not how to live & I dare not die. There is but one thing could soothe & calm me & that were Religion – but I know neither how to believe or how to doubt. My heart inclines me to kneel down & pray – & my mind refuses to let me – & my pride also rejects it. You said you could calm me & advise me – but you have only made me much worse. There are such thoughts in me at times that if they continue I must go mad. Human weakness cannot bear up against it and in the night it's dreadful. If this is what is called remorse how can people say there is no Hell... When those who are unhappy say they will kill themselves – they are not to be pitied but when those that cannot live dare not die – believe me their agony should not be mocked at.'[62]

Emily was with Lady Jersey at Middleton on 21 December and preparing to leave for Brocket, 'where there is to be a party, but which will all be soured by the Devil, 'Cherubina'. The only chance we have of getting rid of her, is by committing murder and getting hanged, of which I think there is some chance, for the page has been hardly any lesson and she stabs as she used to do.'[63] Caroline continued her efforts to be accepted. 'She has been quieter lately, as her only object is to push herself on in the world, which is, I assure you, very uphill work, tho' William gives her all the help he can, and now, as he *will* stick to her, I think it is better to give her any lift I can – for her disgrace only falls more or less on him,' Emily told Frederick. 'I have therefore fought a battle for her and put her name down to Almack's Balls in spite of L Jersey's Teeth. Let people do as they like in their own *private* Society but I think it hard to exclude a person from a ball where six hundred people go if they really are received anywhere.'[64]

The year 1818 began with a 'most disagreeable report', saying that the Duchess of Devonshire had become a Catholic and in a fit of remorse confessed to exchanging her new born baby for that of the Duke's first wife, the 'Beautiful Duchess' Georgiana. If this were true it would have made Hartington an impostor and changeling. Emily reminded Frederick that 'in *Glenarvon* there is some allusion to L[ady] M[argaret] having exchanged a child and people trace the story to that; others say it is only a corroboration of its truth, and there was some paragraph about it in the papers which has annoyed Calantha a great deal. But one cannot pity her for any annoyance that comes to her thro' that infernal book, as it is so richly deserved.'[65]

Emily assumed that Caroline had used the circumstances of Hart's birth in Paris as the basis for her plot but she could just as easily have been inspired by a contemporary crime. Slipped into one of her commonplace books are two newspaper cuttings. One describes the kidnapping of a small boy, the heir to a considerable estate, by his cousin, Charles Rennett, who disputed his claim. Rennett was tried in his absence and the judge ordered that 'the most active & intelligent officers were sent in pursuit to Dover, Margate and other ports.' To identify the kidnapper and the boy Mr Horseley, the child's father, and a few of his friends accompanied them. The second cutting vividly describes a ship foundering in a gale near Kinsale, County Cork, which brings to mind Glenarvon's death at the battle of Camperdown.

After Christmas Lady Melbourne complained of pains in her stomach and legs. Dr Lucas and Dr Warren were consulted and they treated her for biliousness and cupped the painful knee. By the middle of January she was in constant acute pain. She disliked the prescribed opium-based medicine, which only gave her temporary relief and made her feel heavy and drowsy. On 18 February Warren recommended she add Rygrathee Oil to her other medicines. In March she bathed twice daily in warm water but nothing could ease the pain, which had spread from her thigh to her foot. She described the pain as feeling a little like gout with the greatest discomfort being felt in her thigh and knee, which prevented her sitting comfortably to write. Hobhouse called to give her his best wishes and Caroline thanked him for his kindness.[66] Lady Melbourne died at Whitehall on the morning of 6 April.

Lady Shelley noted in her diary, 'The death of Lady Melbourne offers food for reflection to the most frivolous. This lady, beautiful, clever, and well read, married in the flower of her beauty a man who did not care for her in the least. As a natural consequence she was surrounded by admirers belonging to the highest walks in life. Unfortunately she was addicted to opium, which broke down her health and dimmed her mental faculties. She suffered latterly the most excruciating pain, and during the last three days of her life she was in convulsions

– without, however, losing her reason. Lady Bessborough, who was with her when she died, told me that Lady Melbourne's appearance at the last was pitiable, and that her sufferings were horrible.'[67] The coffin, accompanied by Lord Cowper, William and George Lamb was taken to Hatfield Church on 14 April and placed in the family vault.

'I think it will please you to know that in almost the last conversation I had with her she spoke kindly of you,' Caroline told Hobhouse. 'You had seen her lately enough to prepare your[self] for this event but it is her loss and not the suddenness of it that all who knew her must regret for I think a kinder heart and a finer mind were never to be found anywhere than there – God bless you – If you like to come to this mournful house, remember that whilst William and I are in it you will be welcome.'[68] On 7 April Hobhouse asked Emily to return Byron's letters. Caro-George was disgusted. She had never liked Hobhouse and she suggested that that the only reason he wanted them was that he feared the contents might be scandalous and might be revealed.

Because of the nature and slowness of her illness, Lady Melbourne had been able to prepare her children for her death. She urged William to exert himself and claim the great political position she had prepared him for. She encouraged Emily to be true, not to her boring husband, Lord Cowper, but to her long-standing admirer Lord Palmerston, for whom she foresaw a dazzling future.

Without Lady Melbourne's protection, Caroline was vulnerable to the machinations of Emily, Frederick and George. Lady Melbourne had opposed any form of separation, fearful that the scandal would harm William's political chances. She knew that her handsome, fascinating son was susceptible to flattery and would be safe from predatory women only if he remained married. His financial situation was too precarious to allow him to agree to an expensive separation settlement without running the risk of bankruptcy. Lady Melbourne exerted her failing strength and all her powerful influence to ensure that Caroline was once again accepted by society and reconciled with her husband. 'Ah', William said later, 'my mother was a most remarkable woman, not merely clever and engaging, but the most sagacious woman I ever knew. She kept me right as long as she lived.'[69]

Once back at Brocket, Caroline began to drink heavily. 'My new French maid has just been telling me a great deal about her late Mistress, Lady Caroline Lamb,' Harriette Wilson wrote to her sister, Fanny. 'Her Ladyship's only son, is I understand, in a very bad state of health. Lady Caroline has therefore hired a stout young doctor to attend on him and the servants at Melbourne House have the impudence to call him Bergami!' [He was the reputed lover of the Princess of Wales]. 'He does not dine or breakfast with Lady Caroline or her husband, who, you know, is Fred Lamb's brother, the Honourable William Lamb; but he is served in his own room, and Her Ladyship pays great attention to the nature and quality of his repasts. The poor child being subject to violent attacks in the night, Lady Caroline is often to be found after midnight, in the doctor's bedchamber, consulting him about her son. I do not mean you to understand this ironically, as the young Frenchwoman says herself, there, very likely, is nothing in it, although the servants tell a story about a little silk stocking very like her Ladyship's having been found one morning, quite at the bottom of the doctor's bed. The doctor, as Thérèse tells me, is a coarse, stupid-looking, ugly fellow.' Emily's spies at Brocket had kept her informed. She told Frederick that 'Cherubina bores very much and looks hideous, and makes up to a Scotch Doctor they have got as Tutor. He is young, and she says like Lord Byron... He is astonished and bored with her absurdities, but she makes herself ridiculous in the eyes of others – and her familiarity with him shocks the maids.'[70]

Thérèse had a bedroom next to William's and she claimed to have overheard William and Caroline talking.

'Lady C: "I must and will come into your bed. I am your lawful wife. Why am I to sleep alone?"

'William: "I'll be hanged if you come into my bed, Caroline, so you may as well go quietly to your own."

'Lady Caroline persevered.

' "Get along, you little drunken —" said William Lamb.

'The gentle Caroline wept at this outrage.

' "*Mais où est, donc, ce petit coquin de docteur?*" said William in a conciliatory tone

' "*Ah! il a du fond, ce docteur-là*" answered Caroline with a sigh!

'Mind, I don't give you all this nonsense for truth; I merely repeat the stories of my young Frenchwoman.'[71]

Despite Harriette's disclaimer, Caroline was furious at these revelations and dashed off a poem condemning her, ending,

In the meantime – we Lambs are seldom civil –
I wish thy book – though not thee – at the Devil!

William shrank from his drunken wife but his rejection and occasional violence aggravated Caroline's eccentric behaviour. He had told Lady Melbourne four years earlier that he wanted more children but it would appear that he did nothing about it. He may, of course, have become impotent like George, and probably his father, but Caroline came from an affectionate, demonstrative family and she craved warmth.

The Caroline Lady Morgan knew bore no resemblance to the one the Lambs described. Her Caroline had a 'good and kind heart, which, in serving and giving pleasure to others, obeys the instinctive impulse of a sanguine and genial disposition – waiting for no rule or maxim – not opening an account for value expected – doing unto others what you wish them to do unto you. This in one word, is Lady Caroline Lamb; for if she does not always act wisely for herself, she generally acts only too well towards others.'[72]

Lady Morgan's literary successes, *O'Donnel*, a new novel, *Florence Macarthy*, and a guidebook on France sold so well that Colburn offered her the unheard of sum of two thousand pounds for a book on Italy. When she arrived in London unexpectedly, Caroline sent her flowers, a basket of fruit and an invitation to visit her at Brocket. When she refused, saying that she could not leave London, Caroline hurried back to Whitehall where, Lady Morgan explained, she 'overlooked all inconvenience of her London house at the season [August] – carpets up and curtains down – She had her couchette put up in one of the sitting rooms at Melbourne House, and there she is stopping whilst we remain, with no other notice than to be of use to us.' Caroline was anxious to please her friend so when Lady Morgan mentioned that she would like to see 'Faust', Caroline arranged it. 'We might have had a fairy godmother', Lady Morgan said as she opened Caroline's note offering the use of the Duke of Devonshire's box.[73]

It intrigued Lady Morgan to see Caroline sitting next to her husband's aunt, 'the lady of supreme London ton and the wealthy old lady *de province*,' to listen to 'the contrast between the lisping, soft voice of Lady Caroline, and the prim, distinct tones of the old lady was curious and amusing.'

Lady Cork sponsored Lady Morgan. As Mary Monckton, she had turned her mother's London house into a literary centre where Dr Johnson, Sheridan, Edmund Burke and Sir Joshua Reynolds were sure to spend an entertaining evening. After her marriage to Edmund, seventh Earl of Cork, her salon was patronised by Canning, Castlereagh, Lord John Russell, Sir Walter Scott and Byron. Her parties were famous. She explained to Lady Morgan, 'I have pink [parties] for the exclusives, blue for the literary, grey for the religious.' While she was groping for a suitable colour for her remaining friends, Lady Morgan exclaimed, 'Oh, call it "dun-ducketty mud colour".' Lady Cork laughed and adopted it.[74]

Lady Cork's failing eyesight made it necessary for her to dictate letters. 'Now my dear,' she said to Lady Morgan, 'begin another to your friend Lady Caroline Lamb, who, tis said, broke her page's head with a teapot the other day.' Lady Morgan rushed to defend Caroline. 'A Tory calumny,' she declared, 'Lady Caroline was at Brocket the very day the adventure was said to have happened at Whitehall.' 'I don't care whether it's true or not,' said Lady Cork, 'all pages are the better for having their heads sometimes broken; now write please; "Dear Lady Caroline, will you come to me to-morrow evening, to my *Blue* party? I send this by that pretty little page whom you admired so, but who, though full of talent and grace, is a little imp, who, perhaps, *you* may reform but I cannot. He is very like that boy you used to take into your opera box with you, and was so famous for dressing salad. I would not advise you to take him, if I did not think he would suit you. Ask any one you like to my Blue *soirée* particularly Mr Moore.'[75] Lady Cork is thought to be the original of Lady Bellair in Disraeli's novel *Henrietta Temple* and Mrs Leo Hunter in Dickens' *Pickwick Papers*.

Sir Samuel Romilly cut his throat on 29 October, three days after his wife died and Caroline used this as an excuse to write to Byron. In fact Byron thought Romilly's death poetic judgement. He had never forgiven him for changing sides during the separation on a technicality. Romilly's death brought back to Caroline the memory of the day in May 1812 when Spencer Perceval was shot, and Byron came to Melbourne House. 'Then', she wrote he was the 'dearest friend I possessed on earth, when I had willingly died to serve you and felt for you what I believe no one ever did before or will, you promised me – Do you remember? – That whatever might happen, whatever my conduct might be, you would never cease to be my friend? If this ever recurs to your mind – if one remembrance of the past ever comes back to plead for me, forgive me before I die. I have sinned against everyone on earth and against you – but from my soul I suffer for all I have done, and accuse no one but myself for all I have and shall suffer.' She told him she had seen Annabella, Lady Noel and Ada who was 'clever & beautiful' and looked a little like him. 'I am grieved for the past. William Lamb though it be strange, likes you, and almost cries when he reads anything you have written.'[76] She mentioned that she had invited Scrope Davies and Lady Frances Webster to see her at Melbourne House. Hobhouse commented, 'SBD is got into the hands of Lady CL and is deep with Lady FW. As they are in some measure *de tiennes*, I suppose he makes love to one and hate to the other with your poetry.'[77]

Romilly's death released one of the parliamentary seats for Westminster and Hobhouse and George Lamb put themselves forward as candidates – Hobhouse for the Radicals and George Lamb the Whigs. William was appointed as George's agent and he put the entire family on election alert.

Caroline boasted to Murray, 'Four years of constant riding in the most intricate streets at a *petit* gallop have given me an ease on horseback that very few possess,' but this did not save her from falling off the back of her favourite chestnut horse, Cameron/Glenarvon, on 15 December. 'Three days after,' she told Lady Morgan, 'I was seized with a most violent nervous fever, accompanied by inflammation in the throat and stomach, so that what with the general lowness and partial fullness no one knew what to do. For one week I never swallowed anything. The moment of danger passed, and now I believe, in truth, I died; for assuredly a new Lady Caroline has arisen from this death. I seem to have buried my sins, griefs, melancholy, now, and to have come out like a new-born babe, unable to walk, think, and speak but perfectly happy. So finding myself – after I had wished for death and died – alive again, I made them carry me out into the air in a blanket, and then to the astonishment of everyone ordered my horse next day, and sat upon it and would ride, and now I am well, only weak. I have positively refused to take any draughts, pills, laudanum, wine, brandy, other stimulants. I live upon meal-porridge, soda water, milk, arrowroot, and all the farinaceous grains. My mind is calm – I am pleased to be alive – grateful for the kindness shown me; and never mean to answer questions further back than the 15th of this month, that being the day of this new Lady Caroline's birth, and I hate the old one. She had her good qualities, but she had grown into a sort of female Timon – not of Athens – bitter, and always going over old, past scenes. She also imagined that people hated her. Now the present Lady Caroline is as gay as a lark, sees all as it should be, not perhaps as it is, and having received your very clever letter, full of good sense, means to profit by it but, at present, like her predecessors, and like one of your countrymen, is going about wanting work. I have nothing necessarily to do. I know I might and ought to do a great many things, but then I am not compelled to do them. As to writing, assuredly enough has been written, besides, it is different writing when one's thoughts flow out before one's pen, and writing with one's pen waiting for thoughts. Would I could be useful!'[78]

Fully recovered, Caroline threw herself into the election and together with Lady Morpeth they spearheaded the campaign in much the same way that their mothers had done for Fox in 1784. It was a typically dirty campaign. The Radicals described George Lamb in their posters as 'A RED HAIRED LAMB, cross bred, got by Regent out of Melbourne, God-son to the great Prince.' To qualify to vote the citizens of Westminster had to have paid their rates, so George's supporters arranged for the City rate collectors to turn a blind eye to defaulting Whigs. They also employed gangs of roughnecks to roam the constituency armed with bludgeons and cleavers, to threaten their opposition, and for good measure several houses were wrecked.

Lady Shelley was repelled by a 'most scurrilous hand bill' which raked up 'all the old stories of Melbourne House! Lady Caroline Lamb is in all the happiness, and in all the anxieties of canvassing, and takes all the greasy voters in her carriage to the hustings, apparently forgetting that she fancied herself dying a week ago! She is now reanimated, and, as the probability of success gains strength every day, I conclude we shall hear no more of her palpitations till the whole bustle is over.'[79]

Caroline was furious when she found out that Hobhouse's supporters had been using her name. 'The election, one way or another will be over, but unkindness remains for life,' she told him. 'I am extremely unwell and scarce know what I have written. Being in the country anxious about William I had it not in my power to call upon a single person in Town. I was only disgusted to find that many of them had however been insulted by a letter beginning – "Lady Lamb hopes for your vote," and suggestions I would pay their taxes. I know it is not of your doing but I entrust that you take care, and remember I feel a very sincere & grateful regard for you & friends are not in this life so extremely common that they need be thus trifled with and unfairly used. I am so very ill I can hardly see to write.'[80]

In her enthusiasm Caroline canvassed the ageing Unitarian philosopher, William Godwin, for his vote. He replied, 'You have mistaken me. Mr G Lamb has my sincere good wishes. My creed is a short one; I am in principle a Republican, but in practice a Whig. But I am a philosopher, that is a person desirous to become wise, and I aim at that object by reading, by writing and by a little conversation. But I do not mix in the business of the world, and am now too old to alter my course, even at the flattering invitation of Lady Caroline Lamb.'[81] She did not gain a vote for George but she did gain a friend.

George Lamb was elected on 4 March 1819. It was not a popular victory. The mob drove him from his committee room, set fire to the house and he escaped by climbing out of a window. He made his way across the roofs of the neighbouring houses and took shelter in a house in Henrietta Street until a detachment of the Life Guards could be found to escort him home. The Guard was doubled at Horse Guards to protect Melbourne House.[82] On the way back from Almack's, Emily's carriage was stoned, a panel broken by a brickbat and her coachman was pelted with mud for wearing George's favour in his hat. Caroline's carriage was also attacked and one of her little pages hit on the forehead by a stone. Caroline got down and addressed the crowd, saying, 'You are all Englishmen, therefore you will not attack a woman. I am not in the least afraid of you.' The mob was mollified but the leaders insisted that her servants remove their election favours before she could complete her journey to Whitehall.

Emily had taken time off from the election in January to hold a children's ball for her daughter Minny. It was such a success that Caroline decided to hold one for Augustus. 'Cherubina has been outdoing herself in absurdity. She will really make Wm the laughing stock of his County,' Emily told Frederick. 'She chose this very bad weather and *no moon* and asked everybody (from fear of offending any Constituents) as if it was only *a little practice for Augustus*. Of course everybody sent excuses, then she got in despair – having prepared a supper for a hundred people.' The ball was postponed until the following day but as Caroline had given away most of the food she had to buy more. Emily sent her children with the French governess. 'The whole House was lighted up. There were several supper tables, a band of twenty-four musicians,' and eleven guests if you counted Dr Lee, Augustus, Miss Webster, William and Caroline. Caroline sent a servant to Luton Hoo to invite Sir Thomas Brand to send 'a party' but ' they excused themselves on the score of their horses being out, upon which she sent her carriage to fetch them in the evening and they sent it back empty. – Did you ever hear of such proceedings?' Emily asked Frederick, adding that Caroline 'is so mad at the failure of her Ball that she will listen to no prudence and only goes on making herself more and more ridiculous and floundering deeper. – Starving her servants to make a dash of this sort, for the expense of these failures is as great as if she succeeded and in a concern of this sort she don't mind what she throws away – but means to make up for it the next week, by the most miserable stinginess. There never was such a Woman!!!'[83]

The death of Lord Dacre and the succession of his son Thomas Brand to the peerage left a vacancy for the Hertfordshire seat in the House of Commons. William was the anointed successor and wrote an open letter on 14 October 1819 'To the Gentlemen, Clergy and Freeholders of the County of Hertford' asking to be nominated for the seat. 'Should I be so fortunate as to succeed in the present object of my ambitions I shall be ever actuated by a regard to truth, liberty & justice and by a strong attachment to the principles of the constitution and a warm zeal for the interests of my country.'[84] William was successful in spite of what George called 'his irresolution and want of decision' and Emily told Frederick that 'Cherubina's husband is a miserable fellow always thinking of the money it may cost.'[85]

Soon after William's election a row broke out between George and Caroline. He had offended her by the way he continually poked fun at William. Caro-George made matters worse by making disparaging remarks about Lady Bessborough. After they left, Caroline reflected on the evening and accepted her share of the blame. She apologised to Emily but said that she still thought that George had deliberately set out to be unpleasant.

Caroline was delighted by Emily's conciliatory reply and responded, 'I will be as gentle, as forbearing, as anxious to please you all as possible in the future. Thank you for your extreme kindness and forbearance. Thank God every day that you have so sweet, so delightful a character. You know not the misery of the contrary, one thing further – make my peace with George... I had friends I would have died for – You were one of my earliest. – You know not how very much I loved you – once – It is this, it is feeling too keenly, it is suspecting evil even perhaps never intended that makes me so harsh, so violent, so odious. Forgive me, dearest Emily, in your hands I put myself. This once plead for me with George. Bring him to dine here tomorrow & by heaven I will cut my throat before I will ever suffer my tongue to say one ill word again. Provoke me as you please. If I am angry permit me to leave the room, make me a sign – and if you do but feel something for me – you may depend on my gratitude – but with deep feelings it seems hard to live with enemies, to wear the mask of friendship – and find oneself the butt and jest and scorn of one's nearest & dearest relations. I remember Lord Byron first told me I had a deadly enemy in Frederick. He said he hated me in secret and to that degree the influence I held with D House and for my imprudence & wrong conduct and that he was forever saying all that was malicious & cruel against me. Think Emily how hard it is to bear this. To feel when your heart burns for friends that all the nearest inmates of your family instead of pardoning and pitying your faults are your greatest backbiters & slanderers… I will from this hour study only what is right. I will try to render you and your dear, kind father happy and comfortable and if in anything I fail – I ask you in your kindness to excuse it, assist me, say also all you think proper and right to George. Say something from me – and whether he forgives me or not, at all events for his father's and brother's sake let not him be the person to stay away.'[86]

William and Caroline joined the rest of the family at Panshanger in December for the annual Hertford Ball. 'By the way,' Emily wrote to Frederick, 'did I tell you that in London, after her fly out with George, that I had had an explanation about her with Wm which I was glad of, as being upon terms of communication with him even in ever so small a degree, destroys the effect of her misrepresentations.'[87]

George continued to be vindictive and urged his father to evict Caroline from Whitehall. The injustice of the situation drove Caroline to write to Emily, 'I forgave him [George] once, he might generously forgive me a hasty word – if not – do as you have all long wished, drive me from this house and add open hostility to secret malice. You hurt no one in it but William – and I do not think you care for him. You have exposed my faults to everyone, spoken of them at all times. Have I ever done the same by you?… I owe you much apparent kindness, the last kindness drew me back to you & to yours but I think you could not endure to see me happy… If in anger with George at Brocket I said things that were cutting – read the letter he wrote to William and remember his excuse that he was angry when he wrote it. I can, I do forgive, then let him – if he will, if you will act only tolerantly, kindly, if you will allow me to be here while it suits your father & William in peace – I pledge myself I will do all I can to guard my temper &

mouth but if when I am absent you do all you can to make yr Father comfortable & happy, as you ought, and upon my return all say to him you now will not come near him or else treat me in a manner ill calculated to conciliate, let me say plainly, it is acting a base & shameful part and even if you succeed as no doubt you all will in making him decide to live away for the sake of quiet & yr company, you can never hope to enjoy peace yourself, for you do not deserve it. I feel much hurt but shall say no more. If George retracts and comes as usual I shall feel indebted & I think he ought, for he is very rude, very ill bred – But if he does not I shall tomorrow return to Brocket or Brighton and you may enjoy the peace again you did before. But will you find it?'[88]

Battle lines had been drawn and Caroline's relationship with the Lambs from now on would be a series of skirmishes and ambushes. William weakly stood on the sidelines, frightened of his sister and half-heartedly protecting Caroline. How times had changed since she wrote in 1807:

If e'er in thought or word I rove,
From thee my first and only love,
If e'er my inmost heart would frame,
A wish thy presence could not name,
May I unworthy of thy care
No more thy faith unaltered prove
Or rest securely on thy love.
But now beyond description blest
My mind employed, my heart at rest,
I tranquil seek thy guardian breast;

And there removed from vain alarms
Find shelter in a husband's arms.
Such love I feel is pure and chaste,
By no unhallowed thought disgraced,
But like a clear stream its course runs even
Admired by man – approved by Heaven.
May blessings crown thy youthful head,
May earth its choicest gifts afford,
May Heaven its fairest bounties shed
To bless my Husband and my Lord.

12. Lady Lavinia Spencer, Caroline's aunt, remarked after being introduced to Byron, 'If I ever read countenances correctly I read either madness or wickedness in Ld. Byron. He is not ill-looking but such eyes!' After seeing him for the first time Caroline wrote in her diary the famed comment – 'Mad, bad, and dangerous to know'.

13. This portrait of Caroline by Thomas Phillips, commissioned by her cousin Hartington, was exhibited next to his portrait of Byron. When Caroline heard that it was being said that the position was deliberate and she was offering the grapes to him, she demanded that her picture be removed.

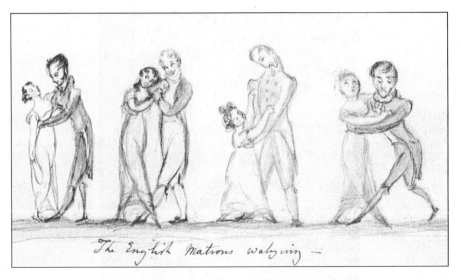

The English Matrons waltzing –

14. Caroline enjoyed the waltz – the fashionable dance that was considered by some to be lewd. In the past the only contact between a young man and his partner was a light touch of the hand but now he could, with perfect propriety, place his arms around his partner who was completely unprotected by petticoats and stays, wearing only a scanty, loosely fitting dress.

15. Annabella Milbanke had an impressive list of suitors but none who measured up to her high standards. Byron said of her, 'She is too good for a fallen spirit to know or wish to know, and I should like her more if she were less perfect'. Annabella refused Byron's first proposal but when he half-heartedly proposed again she seized the opportunity and they were married on 2nd January 1815.

16. **The Duke of Wellington:** On her way to Paris from Brussels in 1815, after nursing her brother Frederick, who had been wounded at Waterloo, Caroline was taken ill. She sent for a doctor but by a strange accident the note was delivered to her new idol, the Duke of Wellington. Hary-o, her cousin, was sceptical, remarking that Caroline had been flirting with the Duke for weeks.

17. Caroline drew this sketch of her family in 1807 soon after the birth of her only surviving child, George Augustus Frederick. He was named after his godfather, the Prince of Wales, and known in the family as Augustus. He suffered from fits when a baby and never reached full intellectual development. He died in 1836.

18. **George IV:** Emily, Lady Cowper, was William Lamb's sister and she rejoiced when Augustus was overlooked and her eldest son, Lord Fordwich, was chosen to be a page at George IV's coronation. She basked in the King's smiles, gloating, 'He will hardly speak to William and Caroline.'

Devonshire

19. 'Hart', Caroline's cousin Lord Hartington, later 6th Duke of Devonshire, was devastated when he was told Caroline intended to marry William Lamb but remained her confidant and friend. He disliked the Lambs and did all he could to comfort and support Caroline when they turned against her. Four years before she died he remarked, 'She might have been saved had she not got into the hands of these blackguards.'

20. Jane, Countess of Oxford liked to think of herself as an intellectual and referred to herself as Aspasia (the Greek adventurer) advocating revolution and free love. Knowing that William disapproved of her, Caroline went out of her way to form a friendship and to adopt some of her views. When she was reprimanded Caroline promised to end the relationship. Lady Oxford later became Byron's mistress; she was forty and he twenty-five.

21. Elizabeth, Lady Holland was satirised as the Princess of Madagascar by Caroline in her novel *Glenarvon*. Ostracised by some sections of society because she had borne an illegitimate child, she was famous for her dinners at Holland House which were attended by writers, Whig politicians and others who did not have to worry unduly about their reputations.

22. Elizabeth, Lady Melbourne, William Lamb's mother, enjoyed Byron's company, later becoming his confidante during his public affair with Caroline. She took Byron's side during the separation negotiations between Byron and Annabella. Byron said of her, 'If she had been a few years younger, what a fool she would have made of me, had she thought it worth her while, and I should have lost a valuable and most agreeable friend'.

23. Caroline St Jules (Caro-George) was universally admired as a child for her sweet disposition and exemplary behaviour. Although thoroughly disapproving of her sister-in-law's conduct, she was at Caroline's bedside when she died.

24. Brocket Hall, in Hertfordshire. This was the Melbourne's country house and where Caroline and William spent their honeymoon. It was Caroline's favourite home and she liked to return there every year to celebrate her wedding anniversary on 3rd June. Her ghost is said to play practical jokes in the bedrooms.

25. This sketch by Caroline shows her taking her dogs for a walk in Cavendish Square – her home before she married William Lamb.

9

'They say she is only wicked from temper and brandy'

When George III died on 29 January 1820, after a reign of sixty years, Parliament was dissolved and the following month a general election was called. George Lamb stood again for Westminster as a moderate Whig. Hobhouse, who had recently been released from Newgate after serving a sentence for writing a seditious pamphlet, and Sir Francis Burdett represented the Radicals. Lamb approached a friend of the Duke of Wellington, the Joint Secretary of the Treasury, Charles Arbuthnot, and proposed that the Tory Government should support him to keep out the Radicals. His request was 'positively refused' and Lady Bessborough took Mrs Arbuthnot to task. She countered this argument by reminding her 'that the conduct of the Whigs had been most infamous as they uniformly join the radicals rather than assist a Tory candidate.'[1] William rounded up a few friends to fight the election but his heart was not in it and he complained that he did not feel well. On the fifth day of the campaign Hobhouse was 700 votes ahead of George Lamb.[2] Emily was preoccupied with a new baby and it was left to Caroline to canvass the voters. She shelved her grudge against George and single-handedly persuaded forty of Hobhouse's supporters in Shepherd Market to change their allegiance, calling Lamb the 'real liberty candidate'. 'As for the mad skeleton,' wrote Hobhouse, 'she rode her a—e bone off, kissed, canvassed and cuckolded, but all in vain, and the bit of fig leaf which half hid her nakedness was torn off and flung in her face. It was a common cry on the hustings, "Where's Caroline?" '[3] He need not have been so vicious as he beat George Lamb by 446 votes and claimed his seat in the House of Commons on 23 April.

At two months Emily's baby still had no name. 'We hesitated,' Emily told Frederick, 'Caroline Seymour Cowper we think pretty and this would be naming her after Ld Cowper's aunt and his present cousin but then we fear it would appear as if she was named after the Beast as the second name seldom appears & this would be disgusting so I am rather inclined to call her Louisa.'[4]

On 18 August the *Morning Chronicle* published an article announcing that Byron had returned to England. London buzzed. Believing Murray had met Byron at Dover, Caroline demanded to know Byron's plans, 'how he looks, what he says, if he is grown fat, if he is no uglier than he used to be, if he is good-humoured or cross-grained, putting his brows down, if his hair curls or is straight as somebody said, if he has seen Hobhouse. Is he going to stay long and a great deal more.' It was all a mistake; Byron was still in Italy.[5]

Using Byron's epic poem *Don Juan* as her theme, Caroline appeared as the Don at a masquerade at Almack's surrounded by a troop of children dressed as devils. She had hired them for the evening from Covent Garden to scamper and run about her. They became uncontrollable nuisances but they fulfilled her purpose, which was to attract attention to a parody she had written of *Don Juan*, called *A New Canto*, which poked fun at Byron's extravagant romanticism:

What joke? – my verses – mine, and all beside,
Wild, foolish tales of Italy and Spain,
The gushing shrieks, the bubbling squeaks, the bride
Of nature, blue-eyed, black-eyed, and her swain.
Kissing in grottoes, near the moon-lit tide,
Though to all men of common sense 'tis plain
Except for rampart and the amphibious brute,
Such damp and drizzly places would not suit.

Byron wrote to Murray on 31 August from Ravenna, 'I only wonder that she went so far as "the *theatre*" for "the *Devils*" having them so much more natural at home – or if they were busy – she might have borrowed the bitch her mother's – Lady Bessborough to wit – The hack whore of the last half century.'[6]

Augustus was growing into a handsome and charming boy but his health had not improved and his fits had become more frequent, unpredictably long, and alarmingly violent. At a ball Caroline held in his honour he had cut a fine figure in his 'light blue velvet jacket with point lace collar falling over his white silk waistcoat and trowsers – white silk stockings, black kid shoes & diamond buckles'. 'You were much admired in the Ballroom, you led off the Ball and danced remarkably well', Miss Webster told him.

Emily saw very little of Augustus after he went to live with Miss Webster and her sister at Rose Cottage, Brompton, but she constantly probed and tormented Caroline with questions. Caroline countered this with glowing reports, claiming that Augustus was quite well and his fits less frequent. Emily commented to Frederick, 'I suppose she is tired of lamenting about it so she wants to hear no more on the subject. I thought she looked foolish when I said I would go and see him & she said don't be surprised if you find him with leeches on his head for it is merely done as a measure of precaution.' Emily and Lord Melbourne saw Augustus at Rose Cottage and he was indeed a little better. Dr Lee attributed the improvement to the starvation diet he had recommended and the application of leeches every ten days.[7] Caroline sketched Augustus, showing his shaven head marked by leeches. She wrote in a shaky hand,

My little yew lamb come you here unto me,
Stretch your little limbs at my feet, Lay yr head on my knee,
And say why your brown eyes so dingy have grown
& your little weak limbs are all sheer skin & bone
& say why they've shaved you so bald & so bare
& why you look full of such sorrow & care?

*   ... My little yew lamb you are come from a school*
Where they've spanked you & made you a regular fool
I tried what I could but I cannot improve you
So all I can do is laugh at and love you –
Then come with your ails and your cares to my heart
I will leave you no more and we'll never live apart
But yr pains & your faults & your aches I'll remove
By a few soothing words & some kisses of love.[8]

Augustus could read and his writing was neat and legible but his hand hurt if he held a pen for too long. In 1821 Frederick Ponsonby wrote, 'Augustus' letters are excellent. They tell us all the news. They are extremely pedantic which makes them more amusing, he speaks of the fund like an old stock jobber, and the state of the world like a worn out politician.'[9]

To Miss Webster he was 'a sweet little darling' and even when he was sixteen she told him he was 'her own *little pet lamb* such he will always be to me, to whatever age or size it grows'. She encouraged him to read and recommended *The Hundred Wonders of the World*, 'It will suit a rational young man like yourself who prefers reality to fiction'. She mothered him and her interest continued long after he had left her care. She sent him presents, a ribbon for his watch, transparent slates for drawing, seeds, a puzzle, a bible, a prayer book, biscuits, coins, books and jokes for his collection. 'A Frenchman,' she wrote, 'having violent pains in the breast and stomach went to a physician for relief. The doctor enquiring where his troubles lay – the Frenchman with dolorous accent – laying his hand on his breast said "Vy sare, I have one big pain in my Portmanteau," (meaning his chest).'[10] William appreciated her efforts and rewarded them with an annuity of fifty pounds, which he was still paying in 1841.[11]

Caroline tried to prepare Augustus for the future by stressing how important it was to be able to write in a 'decent small hand or running hand as, if it pleases God you live, you will have business of this sort to transact, and I should like you to know enough of affairs in general to prevent you being in the power of Ragamuffins of all sorts.'[12]

While Dr Lee remained at Brompton, a substitute, Dr Walker, was hired to take his place at Brocket. He was a friend of Lee's, a Scot and an intelligent and pleasant man who fitted into the household well. When Emily saw him laughing and joking with William and Caroline at a musical evening at Hatfield House, she jumped to the conclusion that he was Caroline's lover and told Frederick that William looked 'like a fool, arriving with them & looking as pleased as Punch & she looked so disgusting with her white cross and dirty gown as if she had been rolled in the Kennel!!'[13] The following year Dr Walker left for Switzerland and he was replaced by an Irishman, Doctor George Hamilton Roe.

'Lord Melbourne was lonely without his energetic wife and concentrated most of his energy on Emily. 'Only think he is just gone (at 11 o'clock),' Emily wrote to Frederick, 'he has been with me *sans cesser* ever since this morning at one. He came for Minnie's dinner [Minnie was Emily's daughter, later Countess of Shaftesbury], went out with me, dined with me and would not even go home to dress for dinner but preferred being *en bottes*.'[14] Like most men of his age and generation, Lord Melbourne had always been a hard drinker but now he spent 'all day and night in a state of complete drunkenness.' He took a 'drink at dinner, which put him to sleep till 12, and then drink again till 2 or 3 o'clock in the morning and then all the next day continual and repeated glasses of sherry.'[15]

Caroline sometimes managed to avoid Emily by pretending to be ill and on 25 September 1820 she remained at Brocket nursing a cold, while William joined a family gathering at Panshanger to discuss Lord Melbourne's future. They agreed that he should spend much of December at Brocket. This was partly because it would break up the winter, partly because he would be near Caroline and he liked 'to abuse her and quarrel with her', but most of all because he wanted to check up on how William and Caroline were managing Brocket and rescue it 'from the aspersions of stingyness under which it labours.'[16] Emily was always willing to listen to the servants gossip about Brocket. She had been told that William was not paying the bills or that they were paid very late. Given the slipshod way Caroline was supposed to be running Brocket, she was at a loss to explain why the butler, Joseph Hazzard, and the housekeeper, Mrs Dawson remained loyal to her. She told Frederick, 'Hazzard's philosophy talking of

Caroline is so good. He says she can't be any worse so one hopes she will get better.'[17] To praise Caroline would have endangered his job.

Surprisingly the ménage at Brocket got on surprisingly well and Lord Melbourne grew quite found of Caroline. The winter brought its share of coughs and colds, which were all lovingly described in letters. More serious were William's painful attacks of sciatica. Emily told Frederick, 'He has had a Lumbago a good while and that foolish wife makes him be cupped continually, which does not cure the lumbago but makes him look fat and white. I am sure it cannot be good. How can he be such a fool as even to be doctored by her – I would manage my own health if I let her have her way in everything else.'[18]

Caroline wrote to Lady Holland, with whom she was enjoying an armistice:

I am at home with William Lamb
And he, I think is rather better.
He says he does not care a D—n
Whether I prate or write a letter.[19]

Although Caroline was not interested in politics beyond the effect they had on her private life, she wanted to help and support William, especially when he spoke in the House of Commons. 'At 4 precisely Wm Lamb will move the writ,' she told Murray, 'I dare say he will speak – could you take me to the Gallery with you? – Oh, do for heaven's sake – at all events go there!' After failing to divorce his long estranged wife, George IV had been sorting through the Book of Common Prayer for some time trying to find a precedent to avoid her being prayed for in church by name and title. Queen Caroline was equally determined to claim the titles and privileges of a Queen Consort but the government sided with the king and she was omitted from the prayer book. Many people believed that she had been badly treated by her deplorable husband and a motion was put proposing that her name be restored to the liturgy. William spoke in her defence. Emily dismissed his arguments as 'twaddling and foolish, speaking on one side and voting on the other, splitting hairs… When you differ with your party about trifles, it is better to hold your tongue.'[20]

Despite being half-starved and drained of blood by leeches, Augustus' fits grew worse and Caroline was willing to consider almost any treatment which promised a cure. She asked Murray to approach his friend, Dr Blake, and told William Godwin, 'I am very anxious about my dear boy, I must speak to you of him. Every one, as usual, is kind to me; I want for nothing this earth can offer but self-control'.[21] Emily told Frederick, 'The fool has a man to magnetise Augustus every evening. This man, who is the greatest charlatan I ever saw, has persuaded her he shall conjure his fits away and draw off the obnoxious fluid which produces them with Metallic tractors'.[22] On 16 March she wrote, 'Brother Wm seems quite well again. Lady C Lamb goes on breaking crockery, fighting Dr Lee & dragooning her people, but to outwards appearance she is much quieter. I should not know of these little home exhibitions if Lee had not made a confidant of Young Jack.'[23] Emily's cousin, Jack Milbanke, had been sent to Brocket to keep an eye on Lord Melbourne and try to reduce his 'boozing' to 'one glass of Negus at supper.' Although his Lordship was watched he still mysteriously managed 'to be drunkish' all the time. George was alarmed and depressed when he realized how happy his father was with Caroline and how well he spoke about 'that old fool William's goings on'.

Emily was ecstatic when Augustus was overlooked and her eldest son, Lord Fordwich, was chosen to be a page at George IV's coronation. She basked in the king's smiles, saying happily, 'He will hardly speak to Wm & Caroline. I don't know why this is, but I suppose, as it is particularly to her, that he has heard of her riding about in the Queen's mobs, or of her saying something about her, for you know she always talks… But she is such a low minded person.'[24]

In the summer Lord and Lady Bessborough left on a continental tour with William and Barbara Ponsonby and their sons, Charles and Henry. Caroline happily agreed to look after her mother's two wards, Frederick Sysonby and Susan Churchill, while her mother was away. Susan was the daughter of Harriet Caroline Spencer, the sprightly fun-loving girl daughter of William Robert Spencer, the wit and poet. Harriet had been seduced in September 1817 – without a great deal of effort – by the Marquis of Blandford; Lady Bessborough offered to take the resulting baby. Frederick Sysonby was one of Lord Bessborough's by-blows. Caroline took the children to Brocket and promised to find a suitable school for Frederick. 'They are both expected to bellow a day, so I shall shut them up together', she told her mother.[25]

Caroline's letters were full of gossip and news. 'Dearest of own heart's blood,' she wrote to her mother, 'I believe I told you how Harriet Stewart [her half sister] danced, how very pretty she looked on the night of the Fête for the King.' She continued, 'Dearest, I would you were in England. There is a strange wild story called *Ada Reis*, written they say, by an American, and if I can get Murray to let me send you a rough printed proof of it I will, as it will amuse you, but I understand that he minds particularly its being seen or getting about, so if it goes to you do take care.' The book was one of several she had offered to Murray without William's knowledge. Presumably she wanted to have her mother's reaction to it before she allowed it to be printed.[26] Although there is no record of Lady Bessborough's thoughts, Caroline's brother, Frederick, made some constructive comments.

Augustus missed Lord Bessborough and tears came into his eyes if any one mentioned him. He was consoled by regular letters, which his grandfather invariably began with comments on the weather followed by a discussion on cricket and card games and ending with health notes. Caroline expected to meet the family in Paris and to see Caro-George and the Duchess of Devonshire, who were already there. Meanwhile, she missed her parents and told them, 'It is a mournful thing to see the gap you have left.'

William and Barbara Ponsonby returned to London to attend the Coronation on 19 July but left England immediately afterwards for Geneva. A few days after they were reunited with their family, their son Henry became ill. They moved from the stifling heat of the town into the coolness of the Alps but he remained weak. It was decided to go on to Parma to find an English physician but the closest, Dr Downe, lived in Florence. They sent for him and as soon as the former Empress Marie Louise, now Duchess of Parma, heard of their distress she sent two of her own physicians.

Henry's symptoms ranged from raging fever to 'deathlike paleness & feebleness, then convulsions'. He revived for short periods and just as his parents began to hope he was plunged into 'a dreadful stupor again'. Doctor Downe and the Italian doctors diagnosed 'water on the head' and twelve days after the onset of the illness, at eleven o'clock at night, Henry gave three deep sighs and died. Lady Bessborough's heart ached 'almost to breaking' as she watched William and Barbara trying to rub warmth and life back into his little cold hands.[27] Within hours, she fell ill, wracked by shivers and a dreadful coldness. It was decided to take her to Florence to consult Dr Downe and a makeshift bed was quickly prepared in a carriage. Lady Bessborough and Mrs Peterson, acting as her nurse, set off on the rough roads to Florence. Despite sending for Dr Downes as soon as they arrived, Lady Bessborough was beyond help. She died on 14 November 1821. Her last thoughts had been of Caroline. She wanted her to know that Dr Downes had 'suffered most terribly till 14 or 15 from epileptic fits, & since that period has had no return,'[28] so perhaps there was hope for Augustus. Lord Bessborough was crushed by the calamity; 'Comfort there can be none, but compose yourself for my sake and your family,' he told Caroline. 'She sent her blessing to you. Kiss Augustus for me.'[29]

Mrs Peterson comforted Caroline, 'I feel more deeply for you than I can express; your angel mother's death was calm, resigned and beautiful. Her illness tho' short was severely painful, but she bore it all with a fortitude beyond my power to express. Her last blessing was for her dearly beloved Caro... It will be late in December before we arrive. Your brother will meet us at Calais. I begged to accompany her sad remains. I will never quit her till I have seen her safely deposited in her grave... It will be a melancholy meeting but pray, dearest Lady

Caroline, be calm, consider *me* a little, if you do not think of *yourself.* I have gone through so much, do not add to my grief by letting me see you miserable. Try to be calm, to fortify yourself to meet your brother and hear all our sad story.'[30]

Everyone dreaded Caroline's reaction to the news but all she would admit to the Duke of Devonshire was that she felt very nervous. Her composure pleased Miss Trimmer, who told her, 'I do not wonder at the way in which it afflicts you. It is a stunning stupefying blow and you can hardly tell as yet how great the loss is.' Mrs Arbuthnot wrote in her Journal, party politics forgotten: 'I do not know when I have been so grieved as at her death. She was much the cleverest & most agreeable woman I have ever known... She was dotingly fond of her children, who were passionately attached to her... She was the kindest hearted person that ever lived, her purse and her good offices were always at the disposal of any one in distress, & she used to laugh & say that no one ever got into a scrape without applying to her to help them out.'[31] Duncannon and the Duke wondered if Caroline would be strong enough to attend the funeral. They questioned William, who replied, 'I cannot resist Caroline's wishes upon such an occasion but it is impossible not to be alarmed for her nerves under such trying circumstances'.[32] He instructed Henry Fox, the agent at Melbourne Hall, the family's seat in Derbyshire, to open up the house in case she was taken ill and asked him to ensure 'that there is not a ring of bells or anything of that nature.'[33]

Caroline returned to Cavendish Square on 22 December to wait for the arrival of the coffins. On Christmas Eve, Hary-o and Harriet Stewart bustled in to express their condolences. 'I went with every feeling of interest and kindness awakened,' Hary-o told Lady Morpeth, but 'Caroline contrived somehow or other to deaden both.'[34] In fact, Caroline told the Duke, their noisy grief was more than she could bear and Hary-o was 'so agitated I did not like to see her.'[35]

On Christmas Day the cortege left Cavendish Square for the Church of All Saints, Derby, where Lady Bessborough was to be placed in the vault next to her sister. Caroline was numb but calm, reassured by the presence of Mrs Peterson and Miss Trimmer, who promised to stay with her until it was all over. On 28 December she wavered; 'I trust I shall be able to do all I ought, but human nature is weak.' She asked the Duke, 'Suppose I really cannot, will you promise to forgive me?' She told Amelia Opie that she did not 'feel equal to bearing any more than the loss and the painful journey'. Too weak to attend the service, she stayed in bed and listened to Miss Trimmer read the burial service. Through the walls they could clearly hear the organ playing in the church.

On 30 December the Duke wrote to his stepmother in Rome; 'The funeral of my poor Aunt took place at Derby yesterday. Duncannon & William, Wm and Caroline, Miss Trimmer, who kindly offered to come with Caroline and Lord Spencer's youngest son arrived at Derby the night before and were lodged at my home there which is in a very quiet and retired situation. Caroline was then remarkably calm and determined to attend the ceremony, but in the night she became agitated and so ill in the morning that she gave up being present. It took place at ten o'clock. I felt it must be too much for William when the coffins of his child & mother were brought in, both he and Duncannon were much agitated but they supported themselves with great fortitude. When it was over they went into the vault and William afterwards took Mrs Peterson down. William Lamb and I went separately and alone – and after that I had it closed. Caroline was persuaded by Mrs Peterson and Miss Trimmer to give up that also.'[37]

Before she left Derby Caroline wrote to her cousin: 'My dearest & kindest Duke of Devonshire, I will not leave this place without once more thanking you and assuring you that the affection & feeling you have shewn on this occasion is felt very much by all and by Mrs Peterson who desired me to tell you this… God Bless you, we are just going. I am better today and slept almost for the first time since.'

William's cynical lessons had stripped away Caroline's simple trusting faith, leaving her with no hope and nothing to cling to during the dreadful days that followed. She replied to Amelia Opie's letter of condolence by saying, 'I was convinced that nothing was really sure and that I might only be dreaming all this time. I was one of those unfortunately prosperous beings who having nothing else to grieve them or try them, to make matter fair was given a violent temper & stubborn disposition to fight with instead of other trials… Next to William I loved her better than anything in life – but if it should please God to spare him & I can grow good enough to dare to die I shall not consider myself as unhappy.'[39]

Lord Bessborough was too distressed to return for the funeral and remained in Florence with his son Frederick.[40] Caroline, always spontaneous, kind and quick to react in a crisis, sent Dr Lee to look after him and a list of practical suggestions. She proposed that Mr and Mrs Peterson and John Daniel, his footman, should be given annuities and sent her father designs for her mother's memorial. Lord Bessborough asked her to deal with her mother's papers and books.[41] In due course the intimate letters from her former lover, Lord Granville, dating back from the first days they met in Naples, twenty-seven years earlier, were taken from the sweet smelling cedar box in Lady Bessborough's bedroom and burnt.

Dr Lee returned to England in August 1822 with Lord Bessborough and they were met by Caroline and Augustus on the quay at Rochester. Lee wrote, 'At first there was a good deal of feeling on all sides, but it was soon over, and in a few instants she seemed to feel as little as if nothing had occurred since their separation. Her conduct is as strange as ever. The boy has grown much, but his

217

head is small and there is a lamentable appearance of vacancy in his look. His attacks are the same.'[42]

With Lady Morgan's encouragement Caroline sought out other women authors. She already knew Amelia Opie and Lydia White, a wealthy Irishwoman noted for her lavish dinners (whom Byron nicknamed 'Miss Diddle' in his poem 'The Blues'), and Miss Elizabeth Ogilvy Benger, a thin and rather plain woman whose sparkling eyes and dazzling conversation more than compensated for her lack of beauty. She was often to be found in the Reading Room of the British Museum, rustling through piles of dusty paper in search of material for her books, now long forgotten – *Elizabeth of Bohemia,* and a life of Mary Stewart. At Miss Benger's small salon in Doughty Street, Caroline met the beautiful Rosina Doyle Wheeler and Latitia Elizabeth Landon, who soon afterwards married the governor of Cape Coast, Africa, George Maclean, and died in mysterious circumstances. Caroline's perfect dress, good taste, gentle, courteous manners, title, carriage and two smart footmen added great tone to the meetings. The ladies admired her advanced and startling views, her fantastic witty conversation and fertile imagination. Women writers were in vogue. Mary Mitford's sketches of country life appeared in the *Lady's Magazine*; Jane Austen's novels were published by John Murray; Fanny Burney was an established author and Maria Edgeworth's Irish tales were so popular that they were imitated by Sir Walter Scott. Lending libraries were doing a roaring trade and had difficulty in keeping Mrs Ann Radcliffe's gothic novels in stock.

Caroline occasionally visited Miss Benger's friend, Miss Spence, who became devoted to her and followed her about like a shadow. Miss Spence was famous for her book *Dame Rebecca Berry* and for the size and exuberance of her blue turbans. In her little room, three flights above Little Quebec Street, she entertained an assortment of reviewers, dilettante authors, old ladies and inferior professional musicians. Caroline impressed them all with her politeness, always behaving as though she was taking tea and muffins at Holland House. To the little coterie at Doughty Street she was 'a gentle, lady-like, little woman with slight remains of comeliness, yet pleasing from the delicacy of her appearance'. A journalist from Bentley's *Miscellany* even thought she was 'somewhat uninteresting – perhaps a little sad,' and was disappointed that 'there was nothing in her appearance of that passion which breathes in every line of *Glenarvon*'.[43]

Among the few men who attended the meetings was Ugo Foscolo, the Italian patriot, writer and protégé of Lady Holland, who was down on his luck. He existed by giving lectures for five guineas apiece. Other guests were Dr Kitchener, a neighbour of Miss Benger and the author of cookery books and the young and charming Edward Bulwer Lytton.

Bulwer, born in 1803, was the youngest son of William, Earl Bulwer and Elizabeth Barbara Lytton of Knebworth House, Hertfordshire, only a few miles from Brocket. He fell in love with Caroline when he was seventeen after he heard that she had helped a man who had been crushed at the races at Hoo. He sent her a 'poetical Bagatelle which tho' far too weak to express your ladyship's merits yet the subject itself like the rays of the sun cast upon it a lustre it little deserves':

Daughter of Feeling, Queen of Love
Tis to thee these lines are due
Beauteous as the Cyprian Dove
Hast thou then her nature too.
… Thy Guardian angel hov'ring near
Soar'd upwards with that deed of thine
And as he dropp'd th' applauding tear
Wrote down the name of Caroline.[44]

At thirty-seven years old, Caroline still looked young. Bulwer thought this was because of her 'slight, rounded figure and a child-like mode of wearing her hair (which was of a pale golden colour) in close curls. She had large hazel eyes, capable of much varied expression, exceedingly good teeth, a pleasant laugh, and a musical intonation of voice, despite a certain artificial drawl, habitual to what was called the Devonshire House Set... Apart from these gifts, she might be considered plain, but she had, to a surpassing degree, the attribute of charm, and never failed to please if she chose to do so. Her powers of conversation were remarkable. In one of Lord Byron's letters to her, which she showed me, he said, "You are the only woman I know who never bored me." ' Bulwer described her conversation as being full of 'a wild originality' which combined 'sudden contrasts from deep pathos to infantine drollery; now sentimental now shrewd. It sparkled with anecdotes of the great world, and of the eminent persons with whom she had been brought up, or been familiarly intimate; and, ten minutes after, it became gravely eloquent with religious enthusiasm, or shot off into metaphysical speculations – sometimes absurd, sometimes profound – generally suggestive and interesting. A creature of caprice, and impulse, and whim, her manner, her talk, and her character shifted their colours as rapidly as those of a chameleon'.[45]

Bulwer frequently visited Brocket to show his work to William while Caroline assumed the role of tutor and gave him sound advice on poetry. As a special favour she arranged for him to meet William Godwin .[46]

Ugo Foscolo encouraged Caroline to write another book 'which will offend nobody; women cannot afford to shock.' She took his advice and by March 1822 she was in daily contact with Colburn preparing her new novel, *Graham Hamilton*. Its heroine, Lady Orville, with her beautiful blue eyes, good nature, tenderness of feeling and love of cards, bore a strong resemblance to her aunt, Georgiana. William was alarmed when he discovered what Caroline planned. He dreaded the repercussions from the family and asked to see the proofs. Caroline returned them to Colburn a few days later with a note: 'It is approved by him who I wished to see it and it would be a pity, he says to let it come out full of common errors for the want of a little time.' Colburn wanted to advertise the book using her name and rank but Caroline was uneasy. She told him, 'It was my wish to put my name – I had rather stand by what I write however bad but as I must consider others & they may not like it I shall abide by my first determination'.[47] She promised that if he kept his 'promise and by no suggestion allow *Graham Hamilton* to be thought mine,' she would 'immediately prepare *Sir Eustace de Grey*' for him. She added, 'but, as Rosalind says "By all the pretty oaths that are not dangerous" I do assure you one puff, one hint will seal my mouth & stop my hand entirely in future.'[48] This still left the difficulty of explaining to William how the book had been written bearing in mind the promise Lady Melbourne had extracted from her, never to write again. One way round the problem, Caroline suggested, would be for Colburn to print a disclaimer. 'This MSS having been placed in my hands two years ago with earnest expectations neither to name the Author now or to publish the work at that time Mr Colburn hopes he has obeyed the wishes of the author in both respects having neither named him nor published the MSS until the present moment.'[49]

On 14 March Caroline gave Colburn the first few pages of her new novel *Rose and Mary,* receiving an advance of one hundred pounds. She asked him to secure the money 'with what interest it can for an orphan child I have adopted & called Ellinor Mowbray. It is none of my own I swear but of a friend. It has nothing to hope for but me. I shall for the next two years write for it. Should I die therefore & *Rose & Mary* be given to you remember my wishes.' She returned proofs for another edition of *Glenarvon* together with a new preface that, she stipulated, must not be published until after her death.[50]

Caroline grew nervous as the date of publication of *Graham Hamilton* drew closer, saying, 'I suppose it will be reckoned stupid'. To her surprise and pleasure William remarked, after reading the specially bound copy she had given him, 'It contains some beautiful verses, the best the authoress ever wrote.'

If thou could'st know what 'tis to weep,
To weep unpittied and alone,

The livelong night, whilst others sleep.
Silent and mournful watch to keep,
Thou would'st not do what I have done.

If thou could'st know what 'tis to smile,
To smile, whilst scorn'd by every one,
To hide, by many an artful wile,
A heart that knows more grief than guile,
Thou would'st not do what I have done.

And, oh, if thou could'st think how drear,
When friends are changed and health is gone.
The world would to thine eyes appear,
If thou, like me, to none wert dear,
Thou would'st not do what I have done.

Frederick Lamb had been in England since September 1821, waiting for a suitable diplomatic post, but in April 1822 he moved to Paris and by July he was Minister Plenipotentiary to the German Confederation and living in Frankfurt. A few days after he left, Emily reported that 'Caroline had been so long restrained by your presence that she burst forth like a volcano as soon as you were gone, and has kept burning on ever since. There have been nothing but storms with her servants and one day with Papa, but nothing to signify; it only made him nervous and she was ashamed of herself… I had no idea that your presence had been such a restraint to her. Jack [Milbanke] and she had one quarrel, and he said that he thought she would have beat him. The *charming* Dr Roe has left the house, never to return; she kicked his door open, threw a looking glass at him, and a bottle and poured a jug of water over him. Her servants say she has been quite drunk for a week. I fancy it's all because people do not come to visit her and do not praise or think about her novel. One mad freak I thought rather comical. She heard on Friday that Mrs Fox Lane was brought to bed, so she came home and strewed her ante-room with hay, at least desired the servants to do so. When William came home he began damning and swearing, upon which she came out and said: "Mrs F Lane is brought to bed, and why should not I?" '51 Caroline would have liked another child. This pathetic gesture of bravado was probably the result of William's constant coldness and sexual neglect. Caroline once said that she believed husbands and wives should live in different house and only call on each other. William had replied that 'those who are not rich ought not to marry at all.

221

People who are forced to live much together, are confined to the same room, the same bed etc are like two pigeons under a basket who must fight.'[52]

William continued in good spirits and often dined at Panshanger but Caroline, according to Emily, was 'odious and ill, always raging or fainting, and Aug[ustus] is in a state worse than ever'. Caroline, frightened he might die, called in six more doctors to see if a new French treatment, burning the skull, would improve his condition. 'To please her they agreed to try it, but with Caustic, upon which she turned them all out, flew into a rage, abused them all, and threw everything in the room at Dr Roe'. The Brocket spies reported that she was 'more mad and drunk than ever'.[53]

Emily never questioned the truth in the gossip from disaffected or toadying servants from Brocket. Although there is evidence that Caroline was a volatile and at times difficult employer, she was always a kind one and invariably helped her servants find new positions if they decided to leave or were dismissed. It is impossible to know what incident sparked the spat with Dr Roe but she did her utmost to help him obtain a new post when he left. She wrote to eminent members of the medical establishment as well as to Lady Morgan who she hoped might have some influence through her doctor husband. 'I am anxious to serve a physician who is with me, whose name is Dr Roe, who was and is highly recommended... He has done everything he could for my dear and only child; I therefore have done and will do everything for him.'

Another story, which reached the eager ears at Panshanger, described the preparations for a large dinner. Caroline thought the table decorations were dull and told Hazzard that they were too flat and needed 'something picturesque or elevated; a group of figures, or at least of flowers, high above the rest.' When he ignored her she 'peremptorily ordered the centre piece to be taken away, and then without disturbing the surrounding garniture stepped lightly into the vacant place and stood in a graceful attitude to illustrate her idea.' Hazzard ran to find William. 'The moment he saw her, he said only in the gentlest tone of expostulation, "Caroline, Caroline!" then took her in his arms and carried her out of doors into the sunshine, talking of some ordinary subject to divert her attention to what had happened.'[54] It is difficult to think of anything more calculated to make one furious than to be treated like a foolish doll.

Things went from bad to worse and in October William confided in Emily. 'He says he is quite miserable,' she told Frederick, 'and does not know what to do about her, that he never has a day's peace, and that her violence increased so much that he is always afraid of her doing some serious mischief to some of her servants, and that he has written to W Ponsonby to say something must be done. He says she is the greatest bore in the world, and that there never was such a temper, because her fits of passion instead of being succeeded by a calm are only

222

changed for the most eternal crossness and ill humour. He is a *great ass*, for having borne her as he has done, but one cannot help feeling for him just particularly when it appears that he is not blinded about her, and he really sees her as she is.'[55]

John Murray was only seven years older than Caroline but he had a steadying influence on her and no doubt would have helped her fulfil her writing ambitions if he had not felt constrained by the Lambs' disapproval. He had read two of her novels, *Rosamund* and *Ada Reis*, and chose to publish the second. William was dismayed to see *Ada Reis* advertised in the list of forthcoming books. He did not forbid Caroline to publish but he wrote Murray a letter damning the book with faint praise and asked him to show it to his literary advisor, William Gifford. It was obvious that he hoped Gifford would advise Murray to cancel the publication.[56] A month later he wrote again, 'If Gifford thinks there is in the first two volumes anything of excellence sufficient to overbalance their manifest faults I still hope that he will press upon Lady Caroline the absolute necessity of carefully reconsidering and revising the third volume and particularly the conclusion of the novel.'[57] Murray ignored the heavy hint and continued to work with Caroline.

Caroline based the exotic setting of *Ada Reis* on stories William Bankes and Michael Bruce had told her. Bankes had recently returned to England, having spent eight years travelling in Greece, Asia Minor and Egypt. Both men had been briefly acquaintances of Byron and dined out on it. Caroline had researched the novel carefully and of all her books it was her favourite. She filled it with notes taken from Baron Alexander von Humboldt's *Tableau de la Nature* and Antonio Herrera y Tordesillas's history of the Americas and *Descripción de las Indias Occidentales*.

In the autumn of 1822 Caroline gave Murray another novel, *Pennruddock*. When she heard nothing she wrote on 8 December, 'I am in great anxiety about your not informing me what Gifford says. I think it might be a civil way of giving my death warrant – if *Penruddock* does not.' In another letter, written the same day, she began, 'My dear and most obstinately silent Sir', and continued to invite Murray to dinner, playfully suggesting that he might like to apologise for his 'inexorable and inhuman conduct'.[58] Whether Gifford did not give the book his blessing or Murray was intimidated, the book disappeared. When Murray published Ada Reis, Caroline novels was not paid a fee nor did she share in the profit, receiving just four free copies in exchange for the copyright. As Murray was accustomed to paying his authors fairly, it was undoubtedly William who forced the meanness of this transaction on him.

The story takes place in Peru and involves a handsome pirate, Ada Reis; his daughter, Fiormonda; a page, Zevahir; and Kabarra, who represents the forces of darkness. Fiormonda becomes a hermit and writes her story on a scroll, preserved by friendly Indians. Lady Holland had read the book by 21 March and was scathing in her comments. 'The dedication to Lydia White is well imagined & literally executed; but as there is some feeling expressed probably Wm Lamb worded it. There is Greek in the Motto I believe. The book is called *Ida Rees* or *Reis*, but to tell the truth, I could not wade through, & guessed the author very soon, & found was right upon enquiry. Some one said of Ly Caroline, that her head was *red*, her heart was *black*, her liver *white*.'[59] Emily sent a copy to Frederick with the comment, 'It is a strange farrago, but you may think it worth fifteen shillings to satisfy your curiosity.'[60]

Emily and her family went to Brighton in March. She had hoped to be able to get close enough to the King to encourage him to recommend promotion in the diplomatic service for Frederick, but George VI was beginning to show serious signs of wear and tear. He had an infection in one of his legs running from his toes to his thigh. He was delirious and queasy as, according to Creevy, his stomach was being 'literally soused with Opium and Bark, Brandy and Wine,' which he 'sucked in like mother's milk.' In the following delirium he imagined he had taken part in martial exploits. He gave the Duke of Wellington a graphic description of how he had charged with the Household Brigade at Waterloo and on another occasion he claimed he had visited Lady Melbourne almost daily in the fortnight before she died in his arms. Emily was nonplussed. She had never left her mother's side during that time and, far from dying in his arms, the King had not even enquired about her health. Mrs Arbuthnot remarked, 'This is lying with a vengeance!'[61]

William and Caroline were also in Brighton, with Lord Bessborough, William Ponsonby and Lady Barbara. 'I hope to see very little of her', Emily told Frederick. 'She is here with all her train, - Roe, Susan, Augustus &c.'[62] 'I saw Calantha at Brighton,' the Duke of Wellington told Mrs Arbuthnot, 'as mad as a March Hare. She jumped out of her Carriage to come to me on the East Cliff, and did not wait to have the steps let down! She has written another book, called I don't know what; but she is to send it to me and you shall have it.'[63]

'All I have asked of Murray is a dull sale or a still birth,' Caroline told Lady Morgan. 'This may seem strange, and I assure you it is contrary to my own feelings of ambition; but what can I do? I am ordered peremptorily by my own family not to write... I ask you my dear Lady Morgan, if one descended in a right line from Spencer, not to speak of the Duke of Marlborough, with all the Cavendish and Ponsonby blood to boot, who you know were always rebellious, should feel a little strongly upon any occasion, and burst forth, and yet to be told to hold their tongues and not write, by all their relations united – what is to happen? You cannot do me a greater favour than to recommend and set abroad

Ada Reis. I will send you three copies.'[64] She asked Colburn, 'I hope you received & liked *Ada Reis, Rose & Mary* shall be ready – or, if you prefer it, *Sir Eustace de Grey,* or if you like better anything else. Let me know as I hate to feel confined.'[65]

Caroline was delighted to receive praise from Amelia Opie and she told Lady Morgan, 'Your kindness about *Ada Reis* I feel the more, as everybody wishes to run down and suppress the vital spark of genius I have, and, in truth, it is but small (about what one sees a maid gets by excessive beating on a tinder-box). I am not vain, believe me, nor selfish, nor in love with my authorship; but I am independent, as far as a mite and a bit of dust can be.'[66] In a letter to her cousin, the Duke, she told him that she was working on a new novel called *The Witch of Edmonton* and sent him a scrap of paper dated 12 July, 'I have just found these which I wrote at Chiswick once to you:

Oh that my feeble verse had power
To wake thy thoughts to times of yore
To mind thee of each former hour
Departed to return no more.

When we were friends in joy and sorrow,
With hand in hand and heart to heart.
Regardless of the coming morrow
Which two such firm bound friends might part.

Had we been born of Indian Race
Our kindred blood had linked us fast
And strangers ne'er had gained the place
My right hand given me with my cast.

Thy father loved me as his own
Thy mother ever cherished me
And I though older far was thrown
In thy young years to tend o'er thee.

Thy first thy earliest love was mine
And now though chill'd and cold I seem
I cannot look on thee or thine
Nor dream again my former dream.[67]

She gave Colburn permission in September to put her name on the title page if he ever reissued *Glenarvon* or *Graham Hamilton,* telling him that 'I never again mean to publish anything without.' In her usual kind way the letter was accompanied by a brace of partridges.

Lady Morgan began her research on a new book, the life of the Neapolitan poet and landscape painter, Salvador Rosa, by asking Caroline for help. Caroline rose to the occasion by writing to everyone she knew who had a Rosa in their collection and she had replies from the Duke of Devonshire, Lord Palmerston and Lord Cowper. The Duchess of Devonshire provided a list of all the Rosa paintings she could find in Rome and William Ponsonby sent a long letter full of helpful notes. When Lady Morgan mentioned that she had been asked by Lady Cloncurry if she knew of a suitable governess, Caroline recommended a Miss Bryan: 'She is about twenty-two, very clever, good and with a good manner, writes a beautiful hand, knows music thoroughly, both harp and pianoforte. She is attached to an old mathematician in Russia – a Platonic attachment; his name is Wronsky, so that as they are not to marry or meet for ten years, she is very anxious to go into any respectable and comfortable family where she will be well treated.' Before any arrangments could be made, Miss Bryan was laid low by a cold. 'I would not, for the world,' Caroline told Lady Morgan, 'have Lady Cloncurry wait for her; but if she chances to be without a proper person, when well, Miss Bryan would assuredly go. However, it is no loss to the girl, as I feel sure she wishes to die or marry Wronsky... She has a cold and cough, and is in love. I cannot help it. Can you?'[68] Miss Bryan was hired and was last heard of on holiday in Torquay with Lady Cloncurry in October 1824.[69]

In March Caroline developed what Miss Webster called a 'bilious complaint' and ran a high temperature.[70] At the height of her delirium she found it difficult to sleep but when she did suffered from nightmares. She dreamed that she saw Byron looking at her and grinding his teeth. 'He did not speak; his hair was straight; he was fatter than when I knew him, & not near so handsome. I felt convinced I was to die.' She leapt out of bed, screaming. She said, 'This dream took possession of my mind. I had not dreamed of him since we had parted'. Her description of Byron matches a sketch Murray bought in 1819 made by John Harlow in Venice, which showed him with greasy hair hanging round his face like curved rats' tails.

On Easter Day, 18 April 1824, Byron died at Missolonghi, killed by fever, bleeding and starvation, surrounded by arguing doctors, his plans for the liberation of Greece still unfulfilled. The news reached England on 14 May. Caroline told Medwin, 'Judge what my sorrow was, as well as grief, when long after the news came of his death it was conveyed to me in two or three words – "Caroline, behave properly, I know it will shock you – Lord Byron is dead" – This letter I received when laughing at Brocket... It is impossible for me to express all I feel. Poor Byron, I would to God he had lived to return to her to be happy.'[71] She wrote to Hobhouse, 'Perhaps it may please you & his family to know that Ld Melbourne, Lady Cowper & *William* all put on mourning for him and it is my earnest wish if you have carriages to follow his funeral to have theirs attend.'[72]

Byron had given his memoirs to Thomas Moore in October 1819 with the words, 'It is not a thing that can be published during my lifetime.' It proved not to be a thing that could be published after his death either. Hobhouse insisted they be burnt and had no trouble in persuading timid Augusta Leigh who, just two days after receiving the news of her brother's death wrote, 'It is my very decided opinion that the memoirs ought to be burnt, and I think the sooner the better.' On 17 May, page by page the journal was torn up and fed to the flames in the elegant marble fireplace in John Murray's office. Lady Holland thought it was rather pointless as there was very little of interest in them and they had been read by many people. Caroline described them to Dr Lee and William as being 'of no value – a mere copy book, and that they contained an account of the profligate amours; that they were worse than Rousseau's Confessions, and that there were passages that could not be published.'

On 12 July Caroline felt well enough to go out in an open carriage. She told Medwin, 'As I was slowly driving up the hill here, – Lord Byron's hearse was at that moment passing under these very walls, and rested at Welwyn. William Lamb, who was riding on before me, met the procession at the turn-pike, and asked whose funeral it was. He was very much affected and shocked. I, of course was not told, but, as I kept continually asking where & when he was to be buried, & had read in the papers it was to be at Westminster Abbey, I heard it too soon, and it made me very ill again.' Caroline dictated a letter to Murray the next day, 'Lord Byron's hearse came by our gates yesterday – you may judge what I felt. Pray write to me. Lord Byron's death has made an impression on me, which I cannot express. I am so very sorry I ever said one unkind word against him.'[73] She later told Bulwer Lytton that 'all the hideous calumnies concerning himself and Mrs Leigh (indeed, of all calumnies involving the charge of crime)' were untrue.[74] She continued, 'He had pleasure in shocking people and making himself out worse than he was,' and he did this 'from an affectation of '*rouerie*', a common fault among the Whigs.

Caroline asked Murray to negotiate with Hobhouse for the return of her correspondence with Byron. 'Our quarrel,' she told Hobhouse, 'was about Mrs Lee, yet I do pity her so much that I am most anxious to shew her every respect and kindness... I should very much wish you to get into your own hands, if you are able, all letters relating to Mrs Lee. Ld Byron was excessively imprudent... All I ask you, for his sake is – get everything in your own hands and burn whatever you think proper... I shall not live long – to you I leave even the rose – the carnation he first gave me at my mother's.' On 22 May Caroline saw Hobhouse and told him that she was not worried about her own letters but there were two or three of Lord Byron's that she wanted to keep. On reflection she refused to hand over any of the letters, instead she offering to seal them with instructions that Hobhouse should have them when she died. He refused, saying that they were 'the only guarantee against her making a novel out of Byron's letters. I shall give the same answer,' he told Murray, 'about Lady Melbourne's letters and all to whom I have spoken agree with me in the propriety of this measure.'[75]

Caroline wrote to Lydia White; 'I do not like to trouble you yet, as you are always kind to me and know Moore, Hobhouse & Mr Murray – be so good as to say that I wish for Lady Melbourne's letters to William Lamb sealed, and they shall be burned if they like in their presence. My own letters and two pictures of me and my drawings I particularly request.'[76] The row rumbled on and William Ponsonby tried to mediate. He met Hobhouse and they agreed that he would try to persuade Caroline to destroy the entire correspondence.[77] She refused.

On 30 March the Duchess of Devonshire died at the Palazzo Spade in Rome. The young Duke had forgiven her long ago for marrying his father and dutifully escorted her to Derby to be reunited with Georgiana and Harriet. The Duchess remembered Caroline in her will, leaving her a diamond watch, a present from Lord Bessborough, and a trinket box. 'My dearest kindest Cousin,' Caroline wrote to the Duke on 19 May, 'I have put on mourning for the poor Duchess. My heart too is in mourning at hearing of Ld Byron's death. He has abused me I know. He has long been absent from me, yet I hope I shall be forgiven if I say how deeply I feel his death. To me it is an awful lesson.'[78]

Depressed by Byron's death, William's indifference and not being allowed to write, Caroline consoled herself with large glasses of brandy and sherry, which made her belligerent. She complained of a multitude of minor illnesses and alternated between gorging and starving herself. William's unrealistic hopes for Augustus alarmed her. 'Write often,' he told him, 'and tell me what you do, and what passes in the most minute particular. As you are so much improved in your health take pains to improve also in your manners & your understanding... Take pains with your writing; work hard at it & at Arithmetic. It will do you no harm to write three letters every week, one to your Mama, one to your friend & one to me & pray seal and disc it for yourself – you have the use of your fingers, I believe, and any man who has that, can if he pleases, do whatever another man can do with an implement.' He reminded him to clean his teeth night and morning and to remember his hair, 'If you do not make yourself agreeable,' he warned, 'nobody much will care for your society.'[79] The Ponsonbys tacitly accepted that Augustus would never be capable of fending for himself. They accepted his limitations and loved him for the cheerful, affectionate boy he was; unlike Emily, who regarded him as an idiot, or his father, who once referred to him as a 'hideous fellow'. Augustus used to play cards with Lord Bessborough: 'He did not revoke, and was even shrewd in his play, but it was too like the cleverness of the automaton. When those about him talked he listened, and when they laughed he smiled.' He rarely got the point of a joke and seldom joined in conversations. When Caroline tried to stimulate him and got little response she became upset and he would sit next to her and gently stroke her hand, saying, 'God Bless you, dearest Mama.' He generally lived at Brocket and played with younger children, Susan Churchill, Ellinor Mowbray, Dr Roe's son James and 'little Mary' at the stables.

Caroline knew that the Lambs loathed her. Their ringleader, Emily, was supported by Frederick. Hary-o described him as being 'uncommonly clever and agreeable but he sees life in the most degrading light and he simplifies the whole thing by thinking all men rogues and all women —'. She thought he had 'a sort of rude polish which his brothers want. He is less like an animal, does not roll about and snore as they do. At meals the real Lamb breaks out, but at other times he is civil, gentlemanlike… I think him very like Lady Cowper, they are both remarkable for good temper and ill nature and the question is whether one should not prefer a blow or a little praise. It is one sweeping condemnation of man, woman and child and if there is one exception to the word "fools" it is qualified by "d—d disagreeable".' On another occasion Hary-o wrote, 'There is about him a degree of kindness and coarseness that goes against my taste and his manners are occasionally too *laisser aller*-ish.'[80] William shared the family tendency to curse and Caroline wrote:

Yes I adore thee, William Lamb,
But hate to hear thee say God D—
Frenchmen say English cry D—, d—,
But why swear'st thou – thou art a Lamb.

All Caroline's eccentricities and light-hearted pranks in the past were now being carefully collated for future use. Nothing escaped. The incident of her leaping onto the dining-room table at Brocket was embroidered into a story that she had herself served naked in a tureen. Her desperate attempts to help Augustus and her pathetic endeavours to win back William's affection were mocked; her illnesses dismissed.

After a stormy dinner, William quietly ordered horses and set off for Brocket. He had only been in bed for a few moments when he heard an unusual noise in the corridor. After a few minutes when it did not stop, he opened the door to find Caroline crouched on the floor in tears. Instead of feeling sorry for her, 'the absurdity and scandal of such incidents wounded his sensibility to the quick.'[81]

On her way back to Melbourne House late one night, Caroline staggered into Horse Guards and tried to fight her way through to Whitehall. The sergeant on duty refused to let her pass and her screams of rage attracted a crowd, which stood, watching and mocking her. A few minutes later William arrived with servants but Caroline would not go quietly. Lady Holland told her son, Henry Fox, that 'the violence continued; & she is now attended by two women from a mad doctor. William Lamb is going abroad, the son is put to Mrs Trimmer & she is to remain confined at Brocket. All this is brought on by immoderate drinking and a violent ungovernable temper. It will be a relief to William, as the physician declared he could not answer for the lives of those about her. She is kept low, which means being limited to one bottle of sherry daily. There is something horrid in such a termination to a person one has known so intimately from infancy; but she never had a particle of good in her whole composition.'[82] Caroline was released a few days later and returned to Brocket because, Lady Holland wrote, 'The physicians will not sign to her being mad enough to be confined. They say she is only wicked from temper & brandy'.[83]

During a visit to Panshanger the Duke of Devonshire wrote, 'It's dull here with these indifferent damn your eyes people. F[rederick] Lamb is odious'. He told Hobhouse, 'I rode late to Brocket, found poor Caro there in a state of sad degradation. She might have been saved had she not got into the hands of these blackguards'.[84]

Life smiled on Hary-o and she was prepared to be less censorious about her unfortunate cousin, whose marriage was now over. She told Lady Morpeth that 'Caroline Lamb is in a much calmer state at Brocket and under the surveillance of two women, that William is with her *de temps en temps* but lives chiefly with Lord Melbourne at Whitehall.'[85] In October Caroline was banished to Melbourne Hall, to stay with the George Lambs. The Duke told Hary-o, 'I went to Melbourne for 2 nights, poor Caro tries her best to be cheerful there, but it is the most dismal place in the world, the soil so spongy it is never dry, and the two Lambs damn & whistle in the room with their hats on, very cross too... Don't tell Caro that I mentioned their being so but it is really terrible for her and when I come to settle here in November I shall try to rescue her from that gloomy den. In the meantime there is no good, no charity you can do, equal to the kindness [of] your writing her a few lines and love. – She lives upon her letters & they cheer her up.'[86] Rather missing the point, Hary-o replied four days later, 'What distress for poor dear Wm Lamb! I will write to her soon but for the moment I feel so nervous & bewildered that it would not be a kindness.'[87]

At the end of October, Thomas Medwin, a cousin of Percy Shelley and a Pisan acquaintance of Byron's, published *Journal of Conversations with Lord Byron*. He claimed that Byron described Caroline as having 'scarcely any personal attractions to recommend her,' and that her marriage was a 'match of *convenance*, and no couple could be more fashionably indifferent to, or independent of, one another, than she and her husband'. He also claimed that 'she had never been in love, at least where the affections were concerned, and was perhaps made without a heart, as many of her sex are, but her head more than supplied the deficiency.' Even worse he boasted that, 'I was soon congratulated by my friends on the conquest I had made, and did my utmost to show that I was not insensible to the partiality.' Caroline read his scathing poem, 'Remember Thee, Remember Thee,' for the first time and was cut to the quick. She told the Duke, 'Those bitter lines are a legacy which grieves me; allow me therefore to send you the copy of the last letter written to me by Ld Byron, "when we two parted in silence & tears." '[88] In a long letter to Medwin, outlining her affair, Caroline told him that 'Byron did not affect, but he loved me as never woman was loved. I have had one of his letters copied in a stone press for you; one just before we parted... I grew to love him better than virtue, Religion – all prospects here. He broke my heart, & still I love him – witness the agony I experienced at his death & the tears your book has cost me.'[89] Hobhouse talked to Caroline for two hours on 1 November. Afterwards he wrote in his journal, 'She is in the utmost rage at Medwin's *Conversations* representing her as not having been the object of Byron's attachment, and she showed me a very tender letter of his which she wishes to publish. She gave me a ridiculous account of the attempt lately made to confine her as a mad woman, and mentioned that she had sent 16 quarto volumes of her journals kept by her since 1806 to Godwin, the author, to do what he would with.'[90] Caroline had already sent Colburn Byron's letters and her journals with instructions not to publish them until she was dead, an event she expected daily.[91] She told the Lambs that she had been in touch with the newspapers. They were so unnerved that they were polite to her for a few weeks.

On 14 December she reconsidered, telling Colburn. 'I have been so very ill that it was supposed I could not recover. I therefore sent the journal and letters to you. It has pleased God, after a struggle, to send me back again upon all your hands and as this is the case, and I have met with such excessive kindness from Mr Lamb & all others around me, let me request you to return the MS & the letter by Dr Roe – only delivering it into his hands. I will then, if I live, set about something, which I shall put my mind to. It will amuse me – may it instruct others. It is Lady Morgan's advice that I should write. You may depend upon having it, whatever it is, if you will accept it. If on the contrary I have any relapse and die – you will receive again the *Journal MSS* but with some passages crossed out.'[92]

'Have you read Captain Medwin?' the Duke of Wellington asked Lady Shelley. 'Calantha is in a nice way. They tell me that that which displeased her most is that Medwin should have said that Lord Byron was not in love with her! She says that she can prove he was so, and will publish his letters!! Hobhouse has informed her that if she publishes a line, he will publish *all her's which he has got*!! What delightful society these people of genius make!!'[93]

Hobhouse threatened William Ponsonby that he would keep Caroline's letters until she agreed to burn or return Byron's. William replied, 'I fear Lady Caroline's disinclination to the terms proposed by you throw some difficulty in the way and yet if she shd persist in refusing to comply (which she does at the present moment) I still hope that Ld Byron's friends if they fairly consider the case may think themselves authorised either to give up or destroy the letters in their possession. Lord Byron's honour was solemnly pledged to Lady Bessborough, Lady Cowper & others that these letters were actually destroyed & it was not till Lady Byron told Lady Caroline that she had seen them that there was the least suspicion of their being in existence... In the very improbable event of Ld Byron's letters in Lady Caroline's possession becoming public she & he wd suffer abuse... If Lady Caroline's letters to him shd by any accident get into print it wd do her harm but it wd also be considered as a most unjustifiable breach of confidence on his part, & as a most ungenerous act of retribution on the part of his friends.'[94]

Caroline's friendship with young Edward Bulwer had developed into a cloud of 'sentiment and romance which looked like love, but it never came to that'. He commented that 'we had every opportunity of acting ill; though I was young and almost in love, though everything conspired to tempt her, I believe she resisted what few women would have done.' No doubt, after her recent buffeting Caroline enjoyed the admiration of the good-looking young man who would listen fascinated by her memories of Byron. She allowed him to wear a ring that belonged to Byron and to read his letters. Bulwer concluded that 'despite the evident passion that dictated and coloured them, there was no trace of the selfish and heartless libertine; rather a desire to save her, as it were, from herself, and a consideration for her happiness, chastening and predominating over the thought of his own. What ever the connection between them and however blameable, regarded from the mildest point of view I cannot think him the seducing party; and certainly, from her own confession, he was not the betraying one.' In a retrospective mood Caroline told Bulwer that she believed that Byron's popularity depended on the truth of his writing, describing what he had seen and felt, but when he broke this rule his work became affected or obscure. Bulwer respected Caroline's opinions. 'She was no mean judge of human character, and viewing Byron then from a point of view no longer obscured by passions, I think her estimate of him was sound'.

Early in January 1825, Bulwer joined Caroline and her friends at a ball at Panshanger. Included in the group was Mr Russell, a natural son of the Duke of Bedford, a good-looking young man about the same age as Bulwer and, like him, a protégé of William and Caroline. At first Bulwer thought Caroline was merely trying to make him jealous as she paraded round the ballroom on Russell's arm, but when she ignored him as well he became angry. When they arrived back at Brocket he told her curtly, 'I go tomorrow, before you are up. Good-bye.' In the morning he found a note in his room asking him not to leave before he spoke to her. He went to her room and she threw her arms round him, begging him to stay and asking him to go riding with her. She did not tell him that Russell had also been invited and during the ride she fawned over him. Bulwer rode back to Brocket alone. Caroline found him in his room, weeping. She gave an evasive answer to his question – whether he had a reason to be jealous of Russell. However, he dried his tears and joined the other guests. When he saw Russell was wearing Byron's ring he was full of resentment. He flung himself on a couch after dinner, closed his eyes and pretended to be lost in the music until he sensed Caroline standing over him. 'Are you mad?' she asked and called out to the musicians, 'Don't play this melancholy air. It affects Mr Bulwer so, that he is actually weeping.' This cruel betrayal brought him to his senses. He leapt up, laughed, talked and was the life of the company. At the end of the evening he went over to Caroline and said, 'Farewell forever. It is over. Now I see you in your true light. Vain and heartless you have only trifled with my feelings in order to betray me. I despise as well as leave you. Instead of jealousy, I only feel contempt. Farewell. Go and be happy.'[95]

William and Caroline were at Melbourne Hall at the end of the month where, according to Caro-George, 'We go in better than I expected and they are as amiable as *they can be*. Ever since the journey she has annoyed him and when we arrived she flung herself out of the carriage saying "Let me out, for God's sake, let me out," and, "Oh will nobody stop that clamour," at some children who were running to welcome us... I am all day trying to pacify her. She walks out in our dingy lanes in sattins, and feathers & thin shoes which all get spoilt.'[96]

By the spring of 1825 it seemed as though the worst was over and William, as Caroline had once told Lady Morgan, became to her 'a guardian angel. I love him most dearly; and my boy, though afflicted, is clever, amiable and cheerful.' Her own health had improved and Emily showed signs of being genuinely friendly by taking her to the theatre.

On Maundy Thursday William wrote to Caroline from Brighton, 'Dear Car, It is dull & cold here – Have a good fire in my room – Let us go to Brocket. I shall be sure to be with you Sunday.' The next day she received a another letter in which, she told the Duke of Devonshire, he said 'he had been urged to part with me, that I had often proposed it & that it was well to settle the matter now. Upon the Monday he sent me word that as my answer was far from conciliating he would follow the advice of his friends & not return until something was settled. Upon Tuesday he wrote to Frederick & said he had done it but was miserable *and desolate...* Save me if you yet can – and above all do not mention it as, thank God at present it is not known.'[97]

William wrestled with the love he still had for Caroline but after a good nudge from Emily, he told her that his life was unendurable and that they must part. Typically he left for Paris, leaving the necessary legal duties to his brothers. Caroline asked the Duke to write to Hary-o and 'beg her if she see William at Paris to ask for a delay at least – do, I implore you.' She offered him copies of her letters saying, 'It is destruction to me, no arrangement, no future kindness can make up for it; 20 years I have not only been tolerated but loved with such devotion that when I have offered & begged to go away I have been detained. I see too by William's letter to Frederick Lamb that he is wretched at the step he is taking, that he has been urg'd to do it. Can you retard it at least until I have gone out a little, & in some measure restored myself to the good will of a few friends & relations?... Were it done from jealousy or for any particular reason just now I could bear it with more composure as feeling it to be just, but the whole transaction has been brought about by mean arts... Farewell, pity me & love me, even me also, whatever my sins or errors, for I love you dearly.'[98] In another letter she described herself as being 'No more mad than a March Hare only now and then combustible when misunderstood – Be kind to me.'[99]

Hary-o tried to sway William but he was determined to obtain a separation. His attitude led her to believe that if Caroline continued to resist, the family would resort to harsher measures. Hary-o told her brother, 'I think you might hold out to her the different impression that her resigning herself to a separation and behaving well about it will make upon us all however she may have disgusted, offended, and estranged us. She had a great deal still in her power to regain but if she now defies, resists and exasperates, she is lost.'[100]

On 15 April, George Lamb wrote to the Duke; 'We found her on our arrival quite changed from the unhappy reasonable creature which you had represented her, for she had resumed her natural character of violence and threats of all sorts, and now says she is determined to agree to nothing unless William come back. Of course the only safe method is to believe not one word she says, otherwise Frederick would certainly have some reason to complain of the speeches she had put into your mouth. You seemed to think it cold that William had gone away and left nobody to settle it. Certainly it would have been so, if he had, but the fact is he left Frederick fully authorised to arrange the whole, and we now, I think, have much reason to complain that William Ponsonby puts off the whole himself and will not facilitate any settlement. If we are at last forced to take forcible steps the blame will all be on the heads of her own family. The suddenness of William's determination arose from a proposition which had been made her by him and which she was requested to think of at leisure being answered by a letter full of the grossest abuse.'[101]

The Duke replied that he was sorry that Caroline had been in an 'intractable state' but that she had said nothing at which Frederick could take offence; 'She represented him as having been extremely kind to her, at which I expressed my satisfaction as I had not thought him likely to be so disposed. It seems to me however, unnecessary to explain this, as he and all who knew her unfortunate temper & way of talking without reflection must know also what allowances are to be made for her assertions.' He declined to act for Caroline in the separation negotiations, leaving that to William Ponsonby. 'All that I wish to venture in the way of interference is to intreat you & your brother to act with as much indulgence as possible which I am sure you are inclined to do. Unlimited indulgence has, I know been the cause of her ruin & misfortunes but I am quite sure that with all her impetuosity & spirit of provocation it is only by kindness & temperance that this difficult affair can be arranged'.[102]

Sitting in the cold grandeur of Melbourne House, Caroline wrote to Lady Morgan. 'You know not what misery and illness I have suffered since last I wrote to you. My brother, William, my kind guardian-angel – informed me today that you were in town, and as I am too ill to go out, and wish to consult you about publishing my journal and many other things, would you do me the favour to call here.' She added a postscript, 'They have broken my heart – *not my spirit* and if I will but sign a paper, all my rich relations will protect me, and I shall, no doubt go with an Almack's ticket to heaven.'[103]

Caroline fought back and within a short time her tactics became clear. Frederick exclaimed to Charles Cookney, the family lawyer, 'This infernal woman has advertised her memoirs for publication. Pray ascertain whether the Chancellor would grant an injunction to stop it on the application of her Husband.'[104] Cookney advised him that an injunction would be possible only if the work could be considered the 'property of the Husband,' adding 'but I know of no precedent.' Frederick snapped, 'This affair is serious and you must take the best Chancery opinion upon it… There is every reason to believe that it will be of the most libellous nature upon a great number of persons. She has said that it will contain my brother's letters to her before she was married… Pray take the best opinions upon the case… The expense is no consideration.'[105] Mr Pepes of Lincoln's Inn advised the Lambs that there had to be evidence that Caroline had a publisher for the material.[106] She backed down. Whether this was because of the legal argument, because she took her brother's advice or because she was browbeaten by Frederick is not known, but Frederick told Cookney on 6 May that 'what I wrote to you about has been done through another channel therefore proceed no further in this business.'[107]

William returned from Paris and was surprised at how calm Caroline seemed when they met. 'She was not violent – she was cross – at first but at length grew quite good-humoured and rattled away in such a manner that I could not help laughing immediately. She said that she would do everything that I desired her, that she wished to go to Brocket for a few days to fetch her things then to Brighton & then abroad.'[108]

In reply to William's question, 'What do you want?' she wrote:

You ask my wish – the boon I crave
O grant it – leave me what I have.
Leave me to rest upon my bed
With broken heart, with weary head.

No stormy passions now arise,
No tears relieve these suffering eyes,
No age, no love, disturb me now,
To God's avenging power I bow.

You've yielded to a wicked crew,
Who ruin me, who laugh at you;
Sweep out the gore, and while you can
Think for yourself, and be a man.

Before Frederick left to take up his new post as Minister to Spain he hired two nurses to look after Caroline. Her emotional outbursts, brought on by rage and frustration, had frightened Lord Melbourne and the nurses had orders to keep her out of his way. Emily thought she was frightened of them but Caroline told Lord Egremont that she was glad to have them as they protected her from George Lamb's violence. Caroline wandered about the house at night and made friends with 'the women' offering them a guinea if they would show her the 'straight waistcoat', which they refused.[109]

William moved out of Melbourne House into the University Club but he often called to see Caroline. This worried Emily, as she feared that she would take advantage of him. On 12 May she reported angrily 'He wants energy so much and somebody at his back to push him on… Caroline has now turned again to the sickly mood, and says she shall not live and has not ate for four days. However it is very easy to rouse all her energy's by merely disagreeing with her.' (Caroline claimed that during this time she was not able to eat or walk because she was suffering from typhus.)

The push to evict her from Melbourne House began. George instructed Charles Cookney 'to proceed immediately against the tenant in question'. He consulted a colleague, Samuel Marryatt of the Temple. 'Favour me with a consultation this evening – sending you the outline. – Upon the marriage of A with B, A's father gave up part of his house (being a suite of rooms on the first floor, quite unconnected with the ground floor where the father resided) to be occupied by A, his wife and family as a separate establishment. Great differences having arisen between A & his wife – and a separation wished for – the father is desirous to possess the whole of his house again – and A is desirous he should, but A's wife being in possession the difficulty is how *legally* to remove her.'[110]

The Duke of Devonshire, Lord Brougham and William Ponsonby supported Caroline while Emily, Frederick, the George Lambs and Lord Cowper were against her. Lord Spencer did not oppose the separation and Frederick Ponsonby, now a Major General, commanding troops in the Ionian Islands, was unavailable. Duncannon, who had never really liked Caroline, was convinced she was mad. Caroline relied on her younger brother William to defend her and his written advice was to settle for nothing less than three thousand pounds a year, the payment of her debts up to the date of the agreement and a carriage and horses. William Lamb saw the letter and told Ponsonby that he 'considered the terms proposed entirely inconsistent with the fortunes which she brought, or with the fortune which I possessed; that I should immediately consult with my solicitor upon the subject, & that I begged he would upon his part name a person in order to negotiate the arrangement.' Ponsonby's reply, according to William, was 'nearly as offensive & insulting as it is possible to conceive – He began by saying that tho' he could not defend his sister, he would not suffer her to be trampled upon either by my family or by me. That the arrangement he had proposed was not his own, but had been suggested by another person who was anything but favourable to Caroline (this person I understand to be Lady Holland) that it rested upon the grounds that tho' his sister had brought a small fortune I had, by the marriage, obtained a brilliant connection which my family wanted. That I had indulged her in unlimited expense & that [she] could not be expected to submit to any sacrifices to facilitate an arrangement which was entered into solely for my convenience & to her utter ruin – that he had written his letter to Caroline in a hurry & under the impression produced by a person's coming from Melbourne House & representing to him the harshness & violence

of my conduct in my last interview with her as well as her dreadful situation…
That he would have no further communication with me upon the subject & that
he could not but repeat the misfortunes which my alternate violence &
indulgence had brought upon his unfortunate sister.'[111]

The reference to William's socially brilliant marriage struck a sensitive nerve.
Emily called William Ponsonby 'an ass & a Jackanapes,' but his letter had played
into her hand. 'It steadied our brother and put the other in the wrong.' She told
Frederick that 'William was foolish and used to go and see her and listen to her
stories, and laugh – but then came the quarrels, and she misrepresented him and
told William Ponsonby of his beating her, which was not true and he and our
William quarrell'd upon which the latter took the wise determination of seeing
her no more and wrote her word so… I think the thing now settled or as good
as settled, for she is anxious for an arrangement, finds all idea of putting it off
impossible, & is desirous of avoiding publication. This is a favourable change and
I take all the merit of it to myself, for in a way I have bullied the bully. She
threatened and ranged for the first half hour I was with her about the book & the
letters, & when she had done I said in the quietest way, "Well, I see all
accommodation is impossible," for this is exactly what Wm said to me last night
– He said it was only trifling to try a private arrangement & that he now had
quite made up his mind to go into Court, that many things might be said
disagreeable on both sides, but that this in his opinion was quite a trifle
compared with the advantage of having everything finally and completely settled
– & so I went on saying I was not quite of that opinion but as she and Wm had
both made up their minds there was no help for it. This produced a violent
abusive letter to him next Morn which he did not understand till I explained it,
& next Morn came a letter from her to Lord C[owper] begging him to speak to
the Duke of D and saying how anxious she was for *any* settlement which would
keep them out of court – as there was not use in their appearing in Court like Mr
and Mrs Bang reviling each other & so Lord C[owper] is to meet the Duke and
I hope it will all be settled. I think the arrangement will be 2,500 now and 3,000
on Papa's death, a great deal more than she deserves – but I think it well worth
while to get rid of her, and to have the whole thing settled quietly, for of course
on this arrangement she will be bound to publish nothing. The fact is that the
books are still completely in her own possession so that there is not fear of them
coming out except in a moment of fury.'[112]

An agreement was reached by the beginning of June in which Caroline would
receive an annual income of £2,500 (about £120,000 today) and a flat payment

of £2,000 (£96,000) to allow her to set up her own establishment. 'I always think it better to be handsome about money and it puts everybody on your side – and then it may settle the thing (and quietly too) which is a great advantage and Papa can afford it,' Emily told Frederick. The Duke of Devonshire was anxious that the arrangement should be concluded swiftly and Caroline go abroad or make some plan for herself. She seemed reluctant to take any action and retreated to Brocket, continually asking William to join her.[113] She wrote to Lady Morgan on 2 June, 'I am too miserable. You have not yet advised me what to do. I know not, care not, Oh, God, it is punishment severe enough; I never can recover from it; it is fair by William Lamb to mention that since I saw you he has written a kinder letter, but if I am sent to live by myself, let them dread the violence of my despair... Pity me for I am too unhappy. I cannot bear it. I would give all I possessed on earth to be again what I once was, and I would now be obedient and gentle but I shall die of grief... My life has not been the best possible. The slave of impulse I have rushed forward to my own destruction.'[114]

In reply to an invitation to a party by a friend (the name is obliterated on the original letter) Caroline wrote, 'Do me a favour, ask of those you think great scholars the meaning of the word *amicable* separation after 20 years of mutual attachment, resentment, forbearance, eagerness to part and making it up again – but no, I will explain it; It is to idolise, to flatter to be entirely governed by a Woman who every day errs and is never restrained nor reproved whilst she is young, in health and accounted clever. It is to retain her by protestations of kindness and love when others wished to take her away – It is to laugh at her termagant humour, independent ideas – & encourage her in these and when, perhaps by her own fault, she becomes miserable, ill & lonely – to find out all her errors, blaze them to the world & have straight waistcoats, physicians, with all the aristocracy of the country to say she had better go – go where? Will you find that out & do not say as John Bull, Frederick Lamb, Lady Cowper and others would say, answer to the D—, let them go there if they like – I will not if I can help it. Excuse me for troubling you and pray mark that in the truly *amicable* arrangement I am accused alone of being *passionate* (when ill-used) did they never find that out before? *I however, "still love the hand upraised to shed my blood"*.'[115]

Caroline loved Brocket best in the early summer, when it blossomed as it had on her wedding day. She marked the twentieth anniversary, the first without William, by an entry in her commonplace book: '200 May girls & the Tenants all came to wish me goodbye on my Wedding day.

Little Birds in our Grove,
Making nests and making love,
Come, sing upon my favourite tree
Your sweetest song once more to me.
An exile from these scenes I go,
Whither I neither care nor know,
Perhaps to some far distant shore,
Never again to hear you more.
The river Lee glides smoothly by,
Unconscious of my agony.
This Bursting sigh, this last sad tear
On quitting all I hold so dear,
Are felt, are seen, are heard by none
Left as I am by every one –
Farewell to Brocket's gladsome Hall
Farewell to Dawson's fruitful wall
Farewell to Hazzard's charming smile,
His hearty laugh which could beguile
Each gloomy thought – until a tear
Dimmed his bright eye for me this year.
Farewell the faithful Welwyn Band
The poor, the kind – my own dear land.
Where e'er I go God bless you all
And thus I leave you – Brocket Hall.
Time was a thoughtless happy child
Fearless, untutored, frank and wild;
I left my home and parents dear
To find a home and Husband here.
Those days of joyous youth are fled
My friends are mostly changed or dead.
My faults, my follies these alone
Live in the minds of every one.
Yes, those survive when all is gone,
Hark how the tenants shout and say
Rejoice on this – thy Wedding day
This is my twentieth Marriage year
They celebrate with Hazzard's beer.
They dance, they sing they bless the day
I weep the while – and well I may –
Husband nor child to greet me come

Without one friend – without a Home –
I sit beneath my favourite tree
Sing then my little birds to me,
In music, love and liberty.[116]

On 30 June Caroline received a terse note from Cookney: 'Lord Melbourne desires me to inform your Ladyship that he is tired of the delay which has taken place in the matter of the separation between Mr Lamb and yourself and urges a speedy completion of the business as he is truly anxious to possess to himself the whole of the House, both in London and at Brocket Hall, and therefore trusts your Ladyship will consider his situation and age and settle and arrange matters without loss of time.'[117] Caroline replied, 'I was surprised at receiving your letter – Will you be kind enough to *call* upon me – then & then only will I answer you.'[118]

'William's affair is not yet settled,' Emily wrote to Frederick on 7 July, 'but I think it will be soon now, for the Duke of D is returned to town and says he will keep her to her agreement, but he may fail and in this case Wm has no alternative but to take a house in some street and order her into it. This is much better than Shilly-Shally, trying to get her to keep to any one plan for two days together. She is irresolute, and changeable, and drunken, but I think there is method in all these variations. She hopes to try everybody's patience to get hold of Wm and to remain where she is. But this there is no chance of; he is completely stout and completely disgusted, and aware of her tricks, and he had made Papa through Cookney give her notice to go, which produced a violent turmoil for two days, but nothing more (thanks to the Women)... She has written to Papa to ask for Melbourne but all I believe to gain time to avoid doing anything.'[119]

'The only question I want you to solve is, shall I go abroad?' Caroline asked Lady Morgan. 'Shall I throw myself upon those who no longer want me, or shall I live a good sort of a half kind of life in some cheap street a little way off, viz The City Road, Shoreditch, Camberwell, or upon the top of a shop. – Or shall I give lectures to little children, and keep a seminary and thus earn my bread? Or shall I write a kind of quiet every-day sort of novel, full of wholesome truths or shall I attempt to be poetical, and failing, beg my friends for a guinea a-piece, and their name to sell my work, upon the best foolscap paper; or shall I fret, fret, fret and die?... I never can love anything better than what I thus tell you; William Lamb, first; my mother, second; Byron third; my boy fourth; my brother Fred, (myself), my cousins next, and last my *petit* friend, young Russell, because he is my aunt's godson; because when he was but three I nursed him; because he had a hard-to-

241

win, free and kind heart; but chiefly because he stood by me when no one else did.'[120]

Caroline agreed to leave Melbourne House by 1 August but she refused to be put in a house and asked to take a room at Thomas' Hotel in Berkeley Square, uncomfortably close to Emily's house in George Street. 'This is what she said yesterday, but her plans vary every hour, and she trusts to time bringing back Wm into her power, and she thinks the best chance of this is to avoid all regular separation, and to rely upon him to arrange everything for her, so as never to leave him in peace'. Emily wanted William to leave London, 'for he has not the strength and decision to resist this sort of warfare'.[121] His inertia exasperated Emily; 'He wants energy so much & somebody at his back to push him on. In his own determination of parting I see no wavering but he does not know what to do & instead of taking a House for her *coûte qui coûte* & ordering her into it, he hesitates and thinks of the price & fancies she will go abroad or to Melbourne'.[122] William continued to visit Caroline. Emily thought he was foolish. 'She is sure to take advantage of everything... Never did I in my life see so irresolute a person; every trifle turns his purpose and makes him waver. This, however, is only on the means and the different arrangements for I have not seen him waver the least upon the main point – that of getting rid of her.'[123]

On 23 July everything was in place for the deed to be signed. George was uneasy, fearing his father might have fallen under Caroline's spell and relented. The abrupt tone of Cookney's note announcing that he was sending the deed for her signature offended Caroline. She replied, 'I have waited three months for this infernal Deed – just as long I mean to take before I either sign or consent to it. On Monday I am engaged. My father and brother William will no doubt see you – I cannot.' The deed was returned unsigned.[124] 'It differed materially from yr agreement with Ld Cowper,' Caroline told the Duke; 'There was no mention of 3 thousand if I outlived Ld Melbourne, no mention of 2 thousand down, and I think there was only 2 thousand a year. My father told me this, & I of course did not sign it.'

Augustus was invited to dine with the family when he arrived in London on 26 July, and Caroline sent him to Lord Melbourne to tell him that he could not join them if she was not welcome too. Lord Melbourne sent the boy back with the message that he was sorry but in that case he would not see Augustus either. When William told Emily that he intended to take Augustus to Melbourne, she was pleased: 'He ought to make acquaintance with him & see what can be done with him, but it is a sad case. The boy is very strong and healthy but with the mind of a child always in mischief & rolling the maids about.' Augustus had been known to chase his nanny while half dressed. 'He sits on her *n'est-ce pas incroiable?*' Emily asked Frederick, '& this at 18 years old... I went last night to the play to see *Frankenstein* & the huge creature without sense put us all in mind of Augustus. I am glad he is now with William, that he may really see by his own eyes what ought to be done with him, for having only seen him occasionally, I really think he has never been aware of his strange state & I never liked to speak to him about him for fear he should think it unkind, if he was not quite aware himself of what a creature he is… He should have some tutor of a very decided Character who should insist upon his behaving with propriety & keeping himself decently clean & well dressed & not acting like a baby – & at least try to make him behave like a gentleman'.[125]

On 1 August the family were still waiting for Caroline to leave. 'Till then,' Emily told Frederick, 'I am obliged to mount guard, but all preparations are making, and I really think now that she will be off in a day or two to Paris.' She thought Caroline's settlement was large 'but it was worthwhile to get rid of her, and she would not have gone without and in this case force would have been difficult if she had been determined to fight every point; now the separation is regularly drawn up, so that I hope it is now done, and forever. William has been to Kent for three days with Lord Cowper, gay as a lark; what an easy man he is to live with, and what a foolish Caroline she is to have thrown away such cards.'[126]

When Caroline heard that it would take six weeks to draw up the separation papers, she decided to leave and told the Duke of Devonshire that she had said goodbye to her friends and Augustus and left for Calais, intending to return in time to sign the papers.

'Conceive what luck!' Emily wrote triumphantly to Frederick on 14 August. 'She marched out without beat of drum last Friday morning at 8 o'clock by the steam boat to Calais, so that I think there is little fear of her wheeling back now. She will, I trust, have been so sick as to feel little anxiety to cross the water again directly… The rooms are now locked up safely, so I think there is no fear of her making lodgement there again (even if she wished it). She went off in a better temper & in a better frame of mind than I have seen her for a great while. She behaved remarkably well when I took her down the last night before she went to wish Papa goodbye. She was very quiet & said nothing to worry him.'[127]

Emily was still gloating on 19 August; 'She is safely off, a change of plans at Calais frightened us but now she has again sent to have her carriage sent out so I hope she is safe. The house in Whitehall was all put into a state of preparation to maintain a siege… She went off in peace and Christian charity with us all.'[128]

10

'I feel returned to my God and my duty'

The deed of separation arrived in Calais on 8 September 1825. Caroline refused to sign and wrote bitterly to William, 'I remain here that I may not exceed my allowance as from want of knowing how to manage… Thank you for keeping the boy with you. I always told you it would be better for him than sending him to stupid places where he remains with women and children, learns nothing and grows silly… The more I think of the mean barbarous manner in which I have been sacrificed the less I can understand you. *You* could bring yourself to sanction it. I still maintain that the proceedings have been as illegal as they were cruel – that taking advantage of my sorry and severe illness with the assistance of the basest & most hypocritical of men – by intimidation & every sort of unkindness I was forced from your father's house. Lady Cowper on the bed of death & Frederick Lamb & that abhorred scoundrel Jack Milbanke *shall* remember me – and when my memoirs appear with all my faults then in this world some will pity me… As to Lord Melbourne who seemed so fond of me & kind to little Susan – he is the mere tool of those arts which have been my ruin… You are cruel – cowardly – & selfish – The abhorred deed is here. I have not looked at it. No message came with it. The De'il take the deed that took my Willy from me.' She turned to practical things, asked for her horse and returned her little spaniel bitch, Bijou, 'for I fear she is with pup'. She wrote sadly, 'Remember me to my son, sweet kind boy. No one wrote to me on his birthday.'¹ She enclosed with the letter:

Though all at once unheard, reprove me,
Left alike by friend and foe,
I will not shrink, if thou but love me
No hand but thine can strike the blow.
And say'st thou that I dare not face
The storm that burst above my head?

245

The proud must keenly feel disgrace,
And 'tis disgrace, alone, I dread.
I fear not censure's bitter sneer,
I heed not envy's venomed tongue
Nor hadst thou seen one woman's tear
If my own heart had known no wrong.
And even though wrong, if thou canst love me,
Or friend, or foe, may frown on me;
Their barbarous rage shall never move me,
If blest by one kind word from thee.[2]

Hary-o offered her refuge in Paris, telling Lady Morpeth, 'I think this may be a terrible corvée but on the other hand I feel just now a little quixotic about it.' A few days later she wrote, 'Today Caro Wm has desired the messenger to look for an apartment. I hear she has been all this time lodged at an apothecary's running up large bills and sitting up to a late hour at night drinking champagne.' Hary-o was disappointed when she heard that Caroline intended to return to England, telling her sister, 'She would not be beyond a mark troublesome to me, but to Lady Cowper, Mrs Lamb etc, she is a calamity. I had a few lines from her yesterday, ending, "Sometimes I think, like Mr Brummell, I shall stay here for ever." Why not?'[3]

Caroline took rooms at the Ship Tavern in Water Lane, Dover, with Dr Goddard, Dr Roe's successor, to whom she had taken a great dislike. 'I have no servants, page, carriage, horse, nor fine rooms – the melancholy of my situation in this little dreary apartment is roused by the very loud, jovial laughter of my neighbours, who are smoking in the next room,' she told Lady Morgan. 'I seem to be left to my fate most completely, and to take my chance, or rough or smooth, without the smallest interest being expressed for me. It is for good purposes, no doubt; besides I must submit to my fate – it being without remedy.'[4] She sent a note to Colburn offering him her memoirs, saying that the sale of *Graham Hamilton* was brisk and that she had seen a French edition of *Glenarvon* in Calais. 'Many strange things have happened to me since I saw you. I am now seriously going to write and shall request you to be my publisher – if you like it.'[5]

Emily despondently told Frederick that Caroline 'is now in the White Cross Inn, Smithfield, where the packet arrives. Last Monday morning I received a letter from her from Calais in very good humour saying she should stay there for a month and then go on to Paris and giving an amusing account of the society they had there. – Two hours afterwards I heard of her in London having come on the steam boat with young Arbuthnot, very riotous all the way abusing the captain and the sailors and her Doctor Goddard, telling him he was a rascal. I suppose she must have been quite drunk. She proposed to young Arbuthnot to come with her to *Whitehall* or to Panshanger. He tried to quiet her and at last lodged her in this little inn where the packet stops. What a bore it is to have all this bother again. She wrote to William to intreat he would come and see her and take a house for her, as she would leave England no more. He sent her word he could not come and could not take a house for her in their circumstance of separation. But all this worries him and will continue to do so and therefore he intends to keep his departure secret.'[6] William intended to stay with Frederick in Spain and Emily hoped this would force Caroline to find a house alone. She warned, 'Jack [Milbanke] must take care she does not get into Whitehall and then everything will settle itself.'[7]

William, on the advice of Sir George Tuthill, a physician at Westminster Hospital, employed two nurses who specialised in disorders of the mind to look after Caroline. She was very frightened and secretly sent Mrs Peterson to Devonshire House with a letter to the Duke. She wrote that before she left London she had looked at over fifty houses but none satisfied William and that Dr Goddard had laughed in her face when she threatened to dismiss him. He had stolen the separation deed and returned it to William and told him, 'every thing he could against me & at last said I was mad.' This, she believed, probably pleased William because it gave him an excuse to avoid paying her allowance. Caroline thought they were looking for a quiet house in the country to put her away.[8]

Emily had been careful to keep Caroline from Lord Melbourne in case he weakened. Now she prevailed on him to have Caroline re-examined for signs of madness. On 19 October Goddard submitted his report: 'Lady Caroline has a predisposition to the high form of insanity, which shows itself at certain times, and particularly so, when exposed to any excitement, whether mental or physical. – Such is my answer to your letter of enquiry which I had the honour to receive this morning. I have hesitated in forming my decision but her conduct lately has been very inconsistent, and certainly proclaims that many of her actions proceed from other causes than the more impetuosity of passion. – Positive coercion is seldom justifiable in any, with respect to Lady Caroline it is by no means requisite. – I consider that her Ladyship, with kind treatment and occasional restraint, ought to recover, or at any rate become calm and rational – But there are friends who *could* be removed from her; measures *must* be chosen where she can be governed with every appearance of favouring herself. Lady Caroline is very suspicious & therefore I have only had time to write these few lines.'[9]

No longer allowed to live at Whitehall, Caroline was forced into lodge with Mr and Mrs Thomas Crosby in Conduit Street until she could find a house of her own. Knowing how much Caroline resented Dr Goddard's interference, William appointed Thomas Crosby to look after her financial affairs. Kept short of money and depressed by her dreary surroundings, Caroline tried to dull her emotions in alcohol. After a particularly bad bout on 24 October, she addressed a scrap of paper to Mr Crosby, 'After having drunk (shame on me) exactly one quart and fi of wine – 10 drops of laudanum, half a bottle of sherry and a tablespoon of brandy.' She crossed this through and began again; 'Sir, being unhappy today I have drunk 1 whole bottle of wine, which I bought for myself all at once without [illegible] and I did it upon learning Mr Lamb wished to speak to me. – I still was able to do everything he wished.'[10] She scribbled a note to a neighbour apologising for disturbing him. 'All I wish you to know is this – that the same house which witnessed a quarrel between myself and my husband also witnessed a reconciliation (observed by Mr & Mrs Crosby).' She added, 'I have enough enemies, pray pardon my inadequacy – on my part I have had a very difficult time. I love Mr Lamb dearly.'[11]

'William Lamb saw me last night,' Caroline told the Duke of Devonshire, '& once more agrees that if you & my brother will be my trustees he will allow me my liberty & sign the deed. For God's sake do so, & be assured that whatever my faults or imprudences William himself will own I am perfectly exact about money. Let me go to Paris or Switzerland, let some lady who is accomplished & kind be my companion.' She implored, 'Save me from the most horrible of fates, confined away from friends in the power of a weak mercenary doctor & a common keeper. I am not mad, & never was, but am inexpressibly wretched, unless you get me off this once more. Do my dearest cousin & God reward you for it. I will in such case go & live at Brighton with Mrs Peterson, who shall answer for me, or go abroad & trouble no one any more, although ultimately I do hope to have a house in town'. She added ruefully, 'I am to be pitied for I always mean well & only get into most scrapes by detestation of shabbiness & hypocrisy… Oh, my dearest cousin, for pities sake do not join with them against me this once. It will drive me to utter despair. I trust to your generosity, and above all see me before you judge me.'[12]

Emily crowed, 'William is at Whitehall in great glee having I really believe done (at last) the right thing about Caroline. He has placed her with Mrs Peterson, Doctor Goddard and the Woman who inhabited the long room at Whitehall… Goddard says he thinks her reason might be restored if wine was kept away, and everything she has been accustomed to, that even getting on her Mare drives her wild from different associations, and she is therefore sent to Brocket, and he says she ought not to be allowed to see any of the people she has been accustomed to. In this state of things of course Wm must remain on the spot… He is in great spirits and seems very comfortable, cottons very much to us, and seems to like being at Panshanger, and I should think would very likely come to us at Brighton.'[13]

On 2 November Charles Cookney received a letter from Ferrars & Company, Lord Bessborough's lawyers, informing him that Caroline had 'executed the Separation Deed & that they were ready to exchange it for the part to be executed by Lord Melbourne & yourself.' He warned William, 'It is a matter of serious consideration – now you have absolute control over her Ladyship as her husband but when the separation deed is executed this power will be gone, as you covenant thereby not to molest or disturb her Ladyship. It is true that her Ladyship agrees to do the same but this is of little use unless someone will lend himself as a bond with a penalty that she shall not molest or disturb you. – Indeed I think Lord Bessborough and Mr Ponsonby (her Ladyship's brother) should do this and take upon themselves the care and management of her Ladyship's person & that she will not become troublesome to you hereafter.'[14]

On 17 November Caroline signed a contract with a tailor, Mr Henry Moore of 39 Conduit Street, to rent an apartment for £450, the lease to take effect on 31 December 1825. From her new living room windows Caroline had an unrestricted view, past Emily's house and the elegant white pillars of St George's Church, to the green of Hanover Square.[15]

George Agar Ellis, Lady Morpeth's son-in-law, told Lady Holland, without indicating his source, that Caroline was living in Phoenix Yard, a mews off Oxford Street, and had been seen driving an open carriage, with the nurses in the back, 'evidently with the design of breaking their necks'. As Agar Ellis had the wrong address and since it was well known that Caroline revelled in driving fast, the whole story may have been a fiction. This did not worry Emily, who complained to Frederick that Caroline was always rioting, showing off and driving 'a pony chaise with four bay ponies in hand and her horses following her and a mob at her heels.'[16]

Caroline developed a peripatetic life and spent a great deal of time travelling between London, Roehampton, Brocket and Kingston, where Augustus lived with Mrs Harding. He had flourished and grown so fast that, after a visit to see him on 7 December, she wrote to William telling him to be prepared to buy the boy new winter clothes. Augustus had recently learnt of his parent's separation and the shock 'caused him such violent grief that it gave him 3 fits.' Caroline suggested they meet at Brocket to discuss his future but her ruse to see William again was unsuccessful. With nowhere to go apart from her lodgings, she put on a cheerful face and told him her plans for the rest of the year; 'I shall either go to Brighton, the Isle of White, or France till Xmas. I hope you are glad all things are concluded & you will often see me without a cloud on your brow... God bless you Dearest Wm.'[17]

The weeks passed, punctuated by Caroline's persistent requests to Crosby to lend her money and the arrival of duns. She owed £21.11s.6d. to Pulford and

Nichol, tailors in St James' Street and was menaced by their debt collector. In desperation she sent a scrawled message on an undated slip of paper to Crosby, 'I *command* you to come to me in my bed and that your wife come with you. Mind I *command*'. On 13 December she asked Mrs Crosby for her accounts and '£40 as we have not got a penny and I must shew my accounts to my father.'[18]

Caroline had forgiven Dr Goddard and made friends with his sons Alfred and William, taking them on outings to Roehampton and introducing then to Susan. Despite these diversions, Caroline was unhappy for most of the time. Dr Goddard wrote to her: 'You say you continually cry, pray do not do so. If you do not govern your passions your passions will govern you… I know when every barrier of decorum has been broken down & when public censure had been braved to the utmost that women, in particular, lose every excitement except that which results from the whispering of conscience. The house in Conduit St will soon be yours, make it your home, live in it, be careful whom you select for your friends and confidants, all will be well – Lady Caroline will again be beloved, will again be happy.'[19]

In an attempt to occupy her mind Caroline turned to poetry and renewed her friendship with the musician, Isaac Nathan; 'I am and have been very ill; it would perhaps cure me if you could come and sing to me "Oh Marianne" – now will you? I entreat you the moment you have this letter, come and see me and I promise you that if I get well I will come to your Theatre – but I use no bribe. I merely ask – come and soothe one who ought to be happy, but is not.'[20] In 1814 Nathan had been working on a selection of traditional Hebrew music and had asked Byron to write the lyrics. The result of this co-operation was Hebrew Melodies, published in October. Caroline also collaborated with Nathan on a duet, which was publicly performed in London:

The man sings:

The kiss that's on thy lips impress'd
Was cold as parting kiss should be;
And he who clasp'd thee to his breast
Again can never feel for thee;
The chain he gave – a true love token
Thou sees't in every link is broken.

The woman replies:

Take back the ring, take back the chain
These gifts thy love I here resign;
Take back thy heart, since pledged in vain
But Oh! Restore what once was mine.[21]

Caroline did little to help her reputation. She over-dramatised her problems and provided ammunition for gossips that, however fanciful, was always believed. There are more letters from her enemies preserved in archives and libraries than from her friends. Emily's letters are spectacular for their vindictiveness but those from Isaac Nathan, Lady Morgan and John Murray are for the most part kind and understanding. Nathan thought she was 'generous and kind hearted in the extreme' and a person who 'would forget all personal danger to forward the views of any distressed person and in her own words, the knowledge that a human being was unhappy, at once erased from her mind the recollection of enmity or of error.' When Caroline asked him to produce a benefit concert for a friend who had fallen on hard times, he suggested she invite a popular singer called Miss Love, and she exclaimed, 'Oh, do ask her to come – Will my writing to her assist you?' Instead of sending a standard letter, she sketched on a small card a little cupid praying to a bank of cloud with the caption, 'Love implores Love to come to' and next to the chubby baby stood a little woolly lamb.

At Christmas Caroline wrote, 'Thank you, dearest William for your kind letter. Bell (her dog) sends you the "compliments of the season". Once, when more refined, she would not have made use of a vulgar phrase; but now we mix with common fellows in common society we shall speak the vulgar tongue.' Enclosed with the letter was a poem: 'In my opinion these verses are very full of feeling, although they have faults.'

Loved one! No tear is in mine eye
Though pangs my bosom thrill,
For I have learn'd when others sigh
To suffer, and be still.
Passion, and pride, and flatt'ry strove,
They made a wreck of me;
But Oh! I never ceased to love,
I never loved but thee.
My heart is with our early dreams
And still thy influence knows,

Still seeks thy shadow on the stream
Of memory as it flows;
Still hangs o'er all the records bright
Of moments brighter still,
Ere love withdrew his starry light
Ere thou hadst suffered ill.
'Tis vain! 'tis vain! No human will
Can bid that time return;
There's not a light on earth can fill
Again love's darkened urn.
'Tis vain – upon my heart, my brow,
Broods grief no words can tell;
But grief itself were idle now –
Loved one, Fare thee well.

Despite skirmishes with the Lambs and the protracted separation discussions, Caroline, with typical energy and fluency, had transferred her journals, twelve quarto volumes, into manuscript form ready for Colburn to publish. In May 1825 she received a pathetic letter from J Wilmington Fleming, an amateur poet, writer and full-time confidence trickster who specialised in begging letters. She felt sorry for him, giving him small sums of money and promising to approach John Murray on his behalf. She rashly lent him three short stories and some of her journals. He promised to give her his professional opinion on the works and return them. Instead he used the journals to attempt to blackmail her and passed off her stories as his own. Caroline described to Colburn how she had first met Fleming. She was 'all but dead', weak from typhus and from shock following William's decision to separate and had gone to Brocket Hall. Fleming had appeared on her twentieth wedding anniversary, when her emotions were in turmoil and she was still so ill that she had to be carried from her bedroom to watch the local young girls and boys dancing in Lady Melbourne's elegant white and gold ballroom. He 'had walked to Brocket & remained there,' she wrote, 'prowling about & writing verses to me of the most flattering kind. It was natural that at such a moment when so entirely deserted I should be pleased with these effusions. In return I kept giving him pound after pound until the little money I had was gone.' Fleming received ten pounds from Caroline and five pounds from William Ponsonby's solicitor to encourage him to return the journals.[22]

Fleming wrote to Caroline again before she left for Calais. She replied, 'I have often wondered that a person who seems to feel violently as you do and can write so well should not have a little patience with a woman under the unfortunate circumstances I am at the moment… My heart is tortured my mind gone. I leave everything I love on earth and am perfectly indifferent as to where I go.' In her state of misery and preoccupation with the separation she did not care what he did. She told him that she was wrestling with the 'same desperate feelings and passions which I had when I was 3 years old – I have them still but not half so violent. I know I deserve punishment – but the severity, the barbarity and the meanness with which I have been dashed to destruction, a common felon going to be hang'd would not, by the laws of this country, be permitted to suffer.'[23] Fleming returned with more menaces in January 1826. Caroline explained that although she still did not have any money, she had given her journals in manuscript form to Colburn and was waiting to see if he would buy them.

In February Fleming turned his attention to Hobhouse, sending him a begging letter; as a prominent Member of Parliament known for his humanitarian views, Hobhouse ignored it. On 22 February Fleming wrote again. This time he enclosed a sample of his own verses based on *Childe Harold*, a copy of his last published poem *The Destroying Angel* and passages he had copied from Caroline's journals. He assumed that Hobhouse 'would not wish them to become the property of a mercenary publisher.'[24] Hobhouse remained silent.

On 8 March Fleming tried his luck with Augusta, asking for money and telling her that he had Caroline's private journals and details of her relationship with Byron and Annabella. He explained that he was driven to take this action because he was the sole support of his mother who expected daily to be evicted from her home, and that if his demands were not met he would be forced to take the information to a publisher. Augusta showed the papers to Hanson, the family lawyer, and wrote to Annabella enclosing the letter, saying, 'I cannot believe her *mad* – but *excessively bad* & as anybody might become by giving loose to ungoverned passions.' She then described how, while she was waiting for a carriage with the Dowager Duchess of Leeds at Lady Salisbury's, Caroline had 'suddenly jumped before us like Beelzebub *mad* or drunk!' She accosted them and held out her hand. 'I believe I *just* touched it & made her the most profound curtsey! Then she made off somewhere – thro' a trap door I believe – for the whole apparition was to me like something from the lower Regions.'[25] Annabella took copies of the papers and informed William.

Fleming had already received an advance of five pounds from Colburn for two of Caroline's three stories and arrangements had been made for the journals to be published and sold through E Lloyd's in Harley Street, a bookseller well known to Caroline and who probably warned her. (He published advertisements for governesses and Caroline had used his services in the past.) She approached Edward Blaquiere, of 24 Great Marlborough Street, another bookseller, and asked him to act as a go-between. 'Lady Caroline is extremely anxious to obtain the restitution of the MS, which was in the hands of Fleming and originally printed for Mr Lloyd. It is of the utmost importance to her future peace that the work should be withdrawn and if this be granted she is very willing to indemnify Mr Colburn for any expenses he may have incurred and he may be assured of her friendship with Mr Colburn & should like very much to see him for a few minutes if he knew of any evening when she could meet him at Mr Blaquiere's. In the meanwhile she is ardent and persevering.'[26] Edward Blaquiere had been a member of the Greek Committee in London, which urged Byron to take up the Greek Cause, but he had left Greece before Byron arrived, leading Byron to make sarcastic remarks about his 'mania for book-making.'

Caroline lapsed into an illness brought on by nervous strain. She refused Dr Goddard's offer to act as her secretary and insisted on writing to Colburn herself. In a shaky hand she wrote, 'I will send you back the £5 and request you to send me my drafts. This you will observe is an actual right and I am grieved to see that you, who have ever conducted yourself so well towards me, should now treat me with so much want of delicacy and that too at a time when I am unfortunate. Fleming's conduct is so infamous that I wonder you can think for a moment of giving him more money. He has no right to any.' She described Fleming as 'an impostor and a dangerous person. It is no use to bribe him into silence. He knows all about me, of course since he read my journal. If he likes to abuse me money cannot prevent him & he has no papers or letters of mine I care about.'[27] What really enraged Caroline was not the threat of the unauthorised publication of her journal but that Fleming, 'the greatest scoundrel', had sold two of her novels to Colburn and now Colburn, 'another scoundrel', refused to return them even though William had been to see him.

'Now with regard to the 3 tales,' Caroline wrote to Colburn, 'I must read them myself or they must not be published… Will you let me see the stories one after the other as fast as they are being printed. I will leave it as it was – secure that Mr Lamb will never do anything unhandsome about it. His only care, I am sure being that they should be good. I will not have any of them published if a single word of Wilmington Fleming is in them (observe this)… My brother's solicitor called the other day upon a man called Ball who wrote to me – I suspect & so does this gentleman – that it was another trick of Fleming in order to frighten me – I am in no sort of way in his power assure yourself this is true. I have been too good to him – & his ingratitude proves him worthless. As to my imprudence in lending him my journal, I have endeavoured to explain it. I was miserable and could not care what became of me.'[28]

Despite Augusta's urging, neither Murray nor Lamb would give Fleming any money. Murray explained to her that once begun the payments would never end, as Fleming would use other parts of the journal to blackmail the family. Augusta was not appeased and exclaimed to Annabella, 'I wish that Woman could be sent to the Tread Mill as well as that shameless man her husband!' Fleming lapsed into silence. The affair was over and the blackmailer vanished back to 39 Great Andrew Street, in the rookery of Seven Dials. The incident was forgotten until 1831 when William received a letter from J H Burn, a former printer, who said he had 'produced for publication Lady Caroline Lamb's statement, in her own hand of her connexion with Lord Byron, the proceedings which led to them and various anecdotes of the family.' Mr Burn had 'lost a large sum in business' and was now unemployed but, he suggested, if William would find him a job 'in the state paper office or in some way connected with the preservation of the records, so that I may fairly earn my subsistence', he would refrain from publishing.[29] William did not reply.

In January Caroline moved into 39 Conduit Street. Her French bedstead was moved into the bedroom and a new Brussels carpet was laid. The nightstand and wardrobe were badly damaged and chipped but the cheap bamboo wash-stand, small looking-glass, writing table, ink stand and the round table with its four chairs were sound. A linen airer stood on the hearthrug in front of the fireplace with the steel fender and fire irons. The window curtains hid two broken panes of glass. Only one room in the entire apartment, the front attic, did not have either broken or cracked windows. These were disguised by broken spring blinds and blue moreen curtains. Water was brought up in a 'suitable apparatus' and the landlord was responsible for providing 'a bell to communicate from the said back bedroom with the room occupied by the servant.' Caroline was forced to share 'the use of the Kitchen and the Offices jointly'. She provided her own 'plate, linen and china' but kitchen utensils were included in the rent. Almost all the items on the inventory were cracked, broken or chipped, from cups to wash basins. The condition of the kitchen was matched by the other rooms, which housed shabby furniture including a sofa with four dirty cushions, a sofa table (broken) and two satinwood board tables (green cloth soiled). The miscellaneous collection of broken bric-a-brac included glass shades and figures (beading broken) marble slab (broken) plaster ornament and stand (broken). The list of damaged, cracked and broken furniture and ornaments marched from the front and back attics, the front drawing-room, side drawing-room, end drawing-room, second floor front best bedroom, small front bedroom to Caroline's bedroom. A copper coalscuttle stood on the landing at the top of the stairs.[30] It was a far cry from Cavendish Square, Brocket Hall, Chatsworth or Melbourne House.

Caroline returned to Brocket in the middle of February and on 24 April she sub-let her ramshackle apartment to Mrs Anne Gibbes. Once free of her lodgings her natural ebullience returned and she cheerfully quizzed Murray: 'have you quite forsaken me? I entreat you to write to me – and to send me the *Quarterly Review* and Mrs Ellis' book – *The Man in the Iron Mask* to lend. How are you, what is going on?'[31] She lent the three stories Colburn had returned to Lady Morgan with instructions that 'If Mr Lamb, Mr Peterson or Dr Goddard, in short if any one calls about my affairs, be out & take as much pains in correcting my tales as if they were yr own.'

Caroline spent her time writing poetry and outlines for novels in children's exercise books. The hero of one of her short stories is George Morrison. He falls in love with a beautiful gypsy, Betsy Grey, and to gratify her desire for pretty things he becomes a highwayman. He eventually tires of her and falls in love with a virtuous virgin, Fanny. Betsy turns king's evidence and Morrison is hanged.[32]

A general election was called for June and William half-heartedly offered to stand for the Hertford seat. It promised to be a hard fight and the candidate needed to be full of energy and enthusiasm, neither of which William possessed. Even his opponent, the Radical Thomas Duncombe, told Lord Jersey that William would lose the seat 'by want of activity.' He was lacklustre and a bad canvasser. Emily thought it was a great pity he had put his name forward. He eventually withdrew in favour of twenty-three-year-old Bulwer Lytton, who lost to Duncombe. The rest of the family showed more resolution; William Ponsonby was returned for Poole, Lord Duncannon for Kilkenny and George Lamb for Dungarvan.[33]

The children were growing up. Caroline asked Colburn to help her look for a governess for Ellinor Mowbray. Susan and Frederick Sysonby were both at boarding schools and Augustus was with his tutor, the Reverend Stewart, at Sawbridgeworth. Caroline asked Miss Richardson, her new companion, to write to Augustus. After discussing the weather and the fruit crop at Brocket, Miss Richardson admitted that she never walked in the shrubbery without thinking of him and added that 'Your dear father has been at Tunbridge Wells but found it so dull he is gone to Hastings. – Your little wife, Susan, improves very much in every way. She would have written to you herself but is doing her sums as she means to be your housekeeper by and by. She is very anxious to become a good arithmetician.'[34] Despite an age gap of almost eleven years, Susan and Augustus got on very well and she wrote to him regularly from school; 'Now you are learning to write, you can write me a nice letter. I am ashamed of this but it is the fault of my ink. Pray give my love to Bell and to all other enquiring friends.'[35] Miss J A Monk ran Susan's boarding school and her fees were paid out of Caroline's allowance. The cost for 'half a quarter' amounted to £1.18s.0d. This covered the extra tuition for writing, drawing and the purchase of copying and spelling books, J Ouiseau's *Practical Geography* and silk thread and material to make a sampler.[36]

On 26 July, Caroline wrote to Augustus, 'I am glad to hear you are well and have given up snuff which in such quantities as you take must injure your health. I hope you will abstain from taking that vast tower of bread with that immense sea of tea as I am convinced the mammoth and the ostrich alone could digest anything like the quantity.' After passing on good wishes from other guests at Brocket to the Reverend Stewart, Caroline got to the purpose of her letter: 'I do sincerely hope that you will not be ungrateful enough to lay your bad tricks & attacks & bad words to our doors – as I think I may with truth say that you were reminded in rather severe terms once or twice by me that pinching people & dogs and such other idle habits were neither agreeable to us at Brocket nor to your father, nor to Mrs Stewart. Do try and seriously break yourself off from doing these things. They can give you no pleasure and they give all living things upon whom you inflict them real pain. I shall send you some balls which will save many heads – and windows – your father kindly sent me some. Miss Wheeler actually spat blood and is not yet well from the blow she received in her chest from your cricket ball'.[37]

Bulwer Lytton renewed his friendship with Caroline and they were frequently seen together at parties and literary gatherings. It was during a visit to Miss Benger's that Lytton met Rosina Wheeler who, despite suffering from all the unpleasant effects of a heavy cold, charmed him completely. They were attracted to each other at once and throughout the spring were inseparable. In July Caroline invited them to Brocket, where they declared their love for each other in the shrubbery. The pair were married in August the following year against Mrs Bulwer Lytton's wishes. She considered Bulwer too young and Rosina 'a penniless girl, vain and flighty, with a mocking humour and conspicuous lack of principle,' who lied about her age, wore rouge and was the 'spoilt pet of Lady Caroline Lamb'. She was not a fit life-companion for her favourite son.

Caroline lived quietly at Brocket. She described her days to Bulwer, 'Happy, healthy, *quiet*, contented; I get up at fi past 4, ride about with Hazzard & see harvest men at work in the pretty confined green county – read a few old books, see no one hear from no one and occasionally play at chess with Dr Goddard or listen to the faint high warblings of Miss Richardson. This contrast to my *sometime* hurried life delights me – besides I am well – and that is a real blessing to oneself and companions. When you saw me and were so kind to me, how miserable I was. If there be a place of punishment hereafter, assuredly the lost souls must feel as I did then. Pray write to me as you then did even although your opinion of me and affections, boyish affection, be utterly changed – your letters were beautiful and soothing. I detest wit and humour and satire. I fear you are now given to all this, and have lost the freshness of youthful feeling, the noble sentiments, and the warm vivid hopes and aspirations of an uncorrupted and unworldly heart. I drew my Good Spirit, in *Ada Reis*, from you, as I imagined you. Pray do not turn into a Bad Spirit… William Lamb says he will come. He has been at Hastings with which he was delighted as far as scenery goes and climate but he found himself dull there, knowing no one and having nothing to do – without wife or Parliament or trouble he ought now to have found the true enjoyment. He pined quite, yet if I mistake not, he is less happy than when plagued by those two apendages – If there are two p's in that word imagine one and pray excuse my spelling.'[38]

No one dared to tell Lord Melbourne that Caroline was living at Brocket. Emily thought William was too weak to tell her to go which was 'monstrous stupid of him', so she was relieved when William told her that Caroline had taken a house in Hastings, but that still left the problem of Augustus. His fits were more frequent, his memory was bad and the only thing he liked to do was to play games. Emily dreaded the trouble he could cause if he was not kept under strict control. She told Frederick that 'he evidently will never get any better' and that there was the danger that 'he might make bad associations & marry the chambermaid or any person who found out he had expectations. Evidently the only thing to be done is to get him a person to have care of him and to live with him always and look after him and control him – a physician something like a Tutor & establish him at Brocket when he leaves – or send him with this person to travel abroad or in England to amuse him, for his ever being his own master seems to me quite out of the question. She should have directly a good servant to look after him and keep him clean.'[39]

Caroline felt cut off at Hastings and asked Augustus to speak to Caro-George and ask her to send her the London gossip: 'If she will do so I will write her a letter of thanks but there is nothing here which could interest her except the recalling to her mind, as the place does to mine, the happy days we once spent here and the long walks we took when both our mothers were alive'. She sent Augustus a 'box of bonbons' and reminded him not to eat too much and to take exercise.[40]

In December William Ponsonby invited Caroline to join him and Lady Barbara for Christmas at their new home, Canford Manor in Dorset. He encouraged her to 'fight against melancholy thoughts & always try to make the best of any situation in which you may be placed, instead of giving way to & exaggerating to yourself the evils of it.' He suggested that she could make life easier for William and Augustus if she ran 'a respectable household & a small society, not of exquisites but of family.' He believed that faced with the prospect of comfort, William's natural indolence would ensure he did not roam. 'If you have no object to interest you, you might create one. Attend to some of the poor people, to some of the schools, & be assured that even worry is better than no object at all. All this however is not the object of my note, which is to say that we should both be delighted if you like to come here & eat your Christmas dinner.'[41]

In January the Reverend Stewart became so ill that he was forced to ask Caroline to take Augustus home. Augustus was confused – he liked the Stewarts, got on very well with their children and did not understand why he had to leave.[42] Caroline sent him a note saying, 'Dearest boy, Your papa sends you a pheasant & as you wish it so much and have so little amusement in this life, I cannot refuse you staying on if they will be troubled with you till next Tuesday. But should they wish to be rid of you pray let them call for a hacking coach and send you here immediately where a fine fire and your mama wait you. If you want anything say so. Your books are all here. The coachman can do anything you require. – God bless you.'[43]

In February William was at Panshanger, Caroline at Hastings and Augustus alone at Brocket under the supervision of a servant. Although William knew he should find his son another tutor, he did nothing, telling Emily that the boy was comfortable and well and, to her relief, he refused her offer to bring him to Panhanger.[44] Eventually Augustus was placed in the hands of the redoubtable sixty-one year old Miss Trimmer, who took him to Melbourne House.

Dr Goddard developed symptoms that looked suspiciously like those of tuberculosis and Caroline took him to Hastings in the hope that the sea air would improve his health. Emily told Frederick on 20 March, 'Wm, like a fool is going down to Hastings to see Caroline; when will that child have cut his wise teeth?'[45]

Safely settled in her comfortable lodgings at 6 Castle Hill, Caroline wrote to Augustus, 'My own boy, write me a few lines and tell me if you often go and see Ld Bessborough & how you like London. Do you care for shells? There are plenty here. I hope your father will bring you here for a week soon... The weather is beautiful these last 2 days & I have found some acquaintance here. I think I will never quite leave Hastings except for a visit now and then to dear Brocket just in May & 3rd June [her wedding anniversary].'[46] Susan chimed in, 'Today at Hastings has been beautiful, the sands and beach crowded with people. I wish you were here to enjoy it. Ask your Papa to let you come for a day or two. We have a house perched on a hill overlooking the sea, and an old castle behind us. Are you not tired of London? Do write and tell me all about yourself &c &c.'[47]

Preoccupied with politics, William was grateful when Lord Bessborough offered to accompany Augustus to Hastings, and with an astonishing lack of memory he remarked to Caroline, 'You say that Mr Stewart is very ill. I forget who he is & all about him.' The instinct to instruct, which had been the hallmark of the early years of his marriage, returned: 'I shall remit you by your brother,' he told her, 'Brougham's preliminary essay. You know they are going to try to make all science, knowledge &c more easy & accessible than it is at present, & this is the opening treatise, which is to be followed by others upon every subject. Pray read it carefully. Do not be terrified by the Arithmetic at the beginning but go through it. Understand of it as much as you can & write me word what you think of it. I know you have a notion, hastily taken up, that instruction & education dispose people to be turbulent, & render them difficult to be governed. I am quite of a contrary opinion... However, read the treatise.'[48]

William won the parliamentary seat of the Borough of Newport in Hampshire on 24 April 1827 and before the end of the month the Prime Minister, George Canning, made him Chief Secretary to the Lord Lieutenant of Ireland. This appointment required William to stand for re-election. He resigned his Newport seat and stood for Bletchingley, where he was elected on 7 May. He was uniquely qualified for the post in Ireland and won the support of many members of both parties, Whig and Tory. He had no direct financial interests in the country and his agnostic religious views were a comfort to the Catholic and Protestant lobbies. Emily rejoiced: 'Now he has everything open to him and is in his proper station, whether he goes to Ireland or stays at home, and will feel much happier than he has done for a great while. What a happy thing it is that he parted with that Woman, she would have been a millstone round his neck.'[49] William decided to take Augustus to Dublin but when Emily heard of the plan she told Frederick, 'Somebody was here so I could say nothing, but I intend to speak to him seriously about it – but you have no idea of the difficulty of getting Wm's ear. All the afternoon he is at the House and all morning at his office.'[50] Despite Emily's misgivings Augustus went to Ireland with his father.

Within days of his arrival at Phoenix Park, William met Lady Brandon, the former Elizabeth La Touche and daughter of Colonel David La Touche. She had married the Reverend William Crosbie in 1815, the same year that he became 4th Baron Brandon. They were immediately attracted to each other and it was not long before Dublin society was whispering about his habit of paying her calls at the unsociable hour of eleven o'clock at night. Their presence at the theatre and balls attracted the attention of those looking for advancement and they made sure of including Lady Brandon in any event to which William had been invited. Like Caroline, she was breathtakingly indiscreet and before long it was assumed that they were lovers. This is unlikely because William was too lethargic to enter the turmoil of deception. He later expressed his regret to Lady Brandon for 'lost opportunities,' but this may have been just politeness. However, in 1829 Lord Brandon accused him of having 'criminal intercourse' with Lady Brandon after he read his wife's correspondence with William. He had, at first, offered to overlook its compromising nature if she would persuade William to award him a bishopric. When she refused he began the court action. It was soon abandoned when crucial witnesses failed to appear. Mrs Arbuthnot, a true Tory, wrote in her journal in 1829, 'There is not one among that party who have one grain of honour or principle. Ld Melbourne talked the other day to a person, who repeated it to me, of having given the best living that fell vacant while he was Secy for Ireland to Mr Latouche [Lady Brandon's brother] that he might help to support his mistress, Lady Brandon. I think a man who could do that wholly unfit to be trusted with anything.'[51]

William's relationship with Lady Brandon bore noticeable similarities to his marriage; indeed Emily remarked that Elizabeth Brandon 'was very like in her ways to poor Caroline!'[52] In an early letter to William, Lady Brandon told him, 'I will not do anything to annoy you such as biting hitting and so forth – but you must do something more to quiet me than looking stern and cunning. This is all a most unsatisfactory way of spending an evening designed for better purposes.' On another occasion she wrote, 'I had no idea that I could have felt so strong an aversion and almost thirst for revenge as I did after you left me the night you nearly broke my arm.' William carried the Lamb family's tradition of boisterousness to the edge of brutality. He took a keen interest in the disciplining of Lady Brandon's daughter, Lily, and recommended that she should be beaten regularly. 'A dozen smart stripes would, I have no doubt be amply sufficient[53]... I remember a governess who used to say when her pupils were begging not to be whipped, "If I hated you or were indifferent to your future welfare I should forgive you, but as I love you dearly and am anxious for your doing well hereafter, I shall whip you severely." Was this not admirable?'[54] He warmed to his theme, 'It should be seldom only *pour les grandes fautes* & those of a particular description. It is most in keeping for enforcing obedience and for that purpose one whipping is generally quite sufficient.' He enthusiastically promised to write a treatise on the principle of whipping.[55]

He sent Lady Brandon an illustration he had cut from Les Dames Gallantes, a publication of French erotica, which showed a child being beaten. 'They are designed by Devaria, a very clever artist at Paris & are done with great truth, nature & spirit.'[56] He pointed out the finer points of the technique used by the persecutor: 'She is employing her right hand, which is much more usual & natural than her left. She seems quite intent & determined upon what she is doing in spite of the other child [cringing beside her] & she lifts her arm with great neatness & grace. The figure of the child is also good. It is trying to turn itself round which children always very naturally do in such circumstances & which the left arm of the woman prevents.'[57] He described an article in the Monthly Magazine: 'The eldest daughter of a gentleman in Russell Square, aged six, received a card whence ran this "Miss B – at home at 7, punch at 8, quadrilles." It elicited the following reply, the father being some what of our way of thinking in these matters: – Miss R – presents her compliment to Miss B – and regrets to say that she is to be well whipped at 7, and in bed by 8".' A cutting from the Morning Chronicle described how a 'girl of fourteen was publicly flogged in the school-room *au derrière* with a birch rod,' and how 'on the second day after this flogging, when the child was seen by its mother, no inflammation had, it seems, appeared, and, except for a few scratches, no marks of the birch remained.'[58] William continued to send Lady Brandon tit-bits on the subject for several years, sometimes expounding on his pet theories, for example, the futility of beating dogs, which were protected by their coats, as against the efficacy of 'a few twigs of birch applied to the naked skin of a young lady,' which, 'produces with very little effort a very considerable sensation.'

After Lady Bessborough's death, her ward, little Susan Churchill, was disciplined by William at Brocket. In 1842, five years after her marriage to a Swiss banker, Aimé Cuénod, she consulted William on the best way to control her own children: 'I have not forgotten your *practical* lessons on whipping and follow up the system with great success upon Caroline [she was three years old] at least, for William is too young don't you think so? He is only 10 months. I remember as though it was yesterday the *execution* then being thrown in the corner of a large couch... I remember you coming back one day and saying, "*Well, cocky does it smart still?*" at which of course I could not help laughing instead of crying but I do not know at what age this began.'[59] Susan compared various methods with William, 'the *rod* produces a very good effect but I think it *marks* her more than the hand. I whipped her the other day for hurting a dog although she is very fond of him. I am sure you will say I did right.'[60]

As well as beating children, William sometimes had a desire to beat women. He told Lady Brandon in 1830, 'A letter from you excites me more than the full possession of others... I wish I were with you. I would administer promptly what is necessary on such occasions... If I did not think that you were too angry to be jested with I should say that I would certainly get a rod for you and apply it smartly the first time that I see you.' In the same year he told a friend that he never thought of a certain woman without wishing he had the power to 'order her a brisk application of the birch upon that large and extensive field of *derrière*, which is so well calculated to receive it.'[61] Emily had vehemently denied William Ponsonby's accusation that Caroline had been beaten. It is unlikely that she was unaware of the violent attitude that both George and William adopted towards their wives when they were crossed. The only surprise is that Caroline said nothing for so long.

Augustus celebrated his twentieth birthday in Dublin but Caroline did not let the milestone pass without a celebration. She invited 125 tenants and their families to a magnificent picnic at Brocket, where they devoured 'fat sheep and a round of beef and pudding,' accompanied by the 'proper quantity of beer.' At the end of the day they all shouted 'Huzza three times three for Augustus.' She told him that 'all the neighbourhood sent their respects to you & you have been loudly proclaimed by Mr Cross who said, "Lord love him, I feel as though he were my own boy" – how very good your father has been about writing – Susan wishes much for a letter. She sent you the only sovereign she has got to buy you a birthday present and I 4 for the same purpose.' She offered to send him books and suggested he might enjoy reading Baldwin's History of England.[62] He replied that his father kept him well stocked with books and sent his 'best love to Susan'. He reassured Caroline that he was in 'very good health' and that 'the attacks' were 'not near so frequent'.[63] She was pleased with his reply, especially as he had taken the time and trouble to write it himself and replied with a long letter full of local news and gossip. Susan asked him how he spent his time and if Phoenix Park was as 'pretty as Brocket'. She described how beautiful the lake looked now it had been cleaned out and how Caroline liked to go out on it in a boat. A passion for archery seized the county and Caroline made sure Susan had all the equipment. She took the sport seriously and practised with Dr Goddard. 'I stand at 30 yards, Dr Goddard at 60 or 70. Yesterday I got 93 in one hour', she told Augustus proudly. The three of them went to a party given by Mrs Faithful, the local vicar's wife, where Susan challenged the 'Miss Faithfuls and their friend Miss Chester who were all very good marksmen.'

For the first time for many years Caroline was enjoying a quiet and well-ordered life. She had no exciting political news to report to William but she did mention seeing the Duke of Wellington when she dined with the Salisburys at Hatfield. He had 'looked uncommonly well'. She derived a great deal of pleasure from hearing that Augustus was 'behaving very dutifully and very well'. As usual she tried to stimulate his mind and suggested he play chess by letter with Dr Goddard. 'The first move to save time shall be yours (and allowing it to be the King's pawn two moves as he supposes it will be) his next will be the same. Place your board in some room that is not used and you will find it a good plan. It will give you plenty of time to think.'[64]

As the summer turned to autumn it became clear to Dr Goddard that Caroline was not well. He called in Dr Lucas, who had treated Augustus when a baby, and another colleague, Dr Thomas, to examine her. They were not satisfied and examined her four times in September. Dr Goddard wrote to William on 2 October, 'Lady Caroline has just desired me to let you know how she is. Some time ago I wished to do so, but her Ladyship prevented me as she by no means would unnecessarily frighten or distress you. It has been with the feelings of deepest regret that I have lately observed symptoms of water collection about her. At present the case is too clearly manifest and from the quantity of fluid contain'd and evidence felt in the abdomen, and from the visceral obstruction and disease I have apprehensions of the greatest danger, – of course Dr Lucas has occasionally seen her but the idea of any further advice, and the remedies that may be the result, seem to trouble her much. Her conduct has been very amiable; indeed, her behaviour of late has altered very much in every respect for the better. She appears convinced she cannot ultimately recover – but with feelings of perfect resignation she says she does not mind to die.' Caroline dictated the rest of the letter: 'I really feel better – The medicines agree with me and I have everything I possibly want. I am sure you will be glad to know that Frederick Lamb came over with Emily to see me and sat with me nearly an hour. He was very entertaining and with his usual satire seemed to abuse every place but particularly Spain. You know of course that he is appointed to Lisbon... He does not look at all well and wears very long bushy hair, which I think, makes him look older, but it is not as ours is turning grey... I hope you will go and see Duncannon & pray remember me to them all.'[65]

Caroline was examined eleven times in October and almost every day and sometimes twice a day in November. The bills show that she was dosed with Epsom salts, sassafras, tincture of rhubarb, tincture of ginger, boluses (enormous pills), lineaments, draughts (usually six a day), lotions, spirits of wine, tincture of cardamom, tincture of Hyoscymus, unspecified powders (up to ten times a day) and occasionally eight to ten leeches were applied. All this care and medicine amounted to £57.6s.5d. It was to no avail. As the insidious symptoms of dropsy became more apparent so the medicines increased to include blue pills, squill (sea onion), and sweet spirit of nitre with an infusion of cascarella bark.[66]

On 16 October Caroline made a special trip to London to meet Lady Morgan at Thomas's Hotel, to ask her to 'see William and my son, and write and tell me all you think about them, and Ireland, and when you next will be out. I write this solely to fulfil my engagement – saying, I leave you when I die Lord Byron's picture, now under the care of Goddard – the original by Saunders [George Sanders].'[67]

It was obvious that Caroline was failing and Dr Goddard and Dr Lucas decided that it would be better for her if she were in London, closer to professional help and her family. She did not want to leave Brocket and sulked when she left, telling the servants that she would be back in a week or so.[68] William Ponsonby had taken rooms for her at 107 Pall Mall, very close to his own home in St James's Square and had hired furniture to make her comfortable. Her French bed was installed together with a sofa bed and bedding for the daytime.

She was bloated with water and Dr Goddard persuaded her to submit to an operation to ease the pressure. She told William, 'I have suffered much, and I hope patiently, since I wrote last. Tapping is by no means an agreeable sensation. It does not give pain like a tooth drawn, but it turns you deadly cold and sick. The operation was more troublesome than usual.' She was pleased to receive visitors; 'All the county have been to see me. My dear brother has read to me and soothed me, and is coming back. I never met with such affection and kindness, as for persons of both our families, and dear Emily and Caroline, but what pleased me most was your dear letter saying you loved and forgave me. God bless you dearest.'[69]

Mrs Georgina Hawtre told Lady Morgan on 22 November, 'since the operation, her symptoms have assumed such varied appearances that at this moment we have no confidence of an ultimate recovery. The natural strength of her constitution is very great, and we have all ardent hopes much good may result from that favourable circumstance. The situation is most distressing to the many kind friends that are interested for her recovery. We must derive consolation from witnessing her perfect calm resignation.'[70] Lady Morgan noticed at a dinner party in Dublin on 27 November, that 'Mr Lamb was in the lowest spirits from the bad accounts that had come of poor Lady Caroline'. Knowing how fond Lady Morgan was of Caroline, he allowed her to read all the reports before he forwarded them to Duncannon.

On 29 November the Duke of Devonshire called at 107 Pall Mall and sat with Caroline and Barbara Ponsonby for a while. Caroline refused to be trapped like an invalid and the following day she and Dr Goddard made their way to the hairdressers at 5 Haymarket, where they had their hair cut and Caroline bought an ivory comb, rose water and vegetable extract.[71] She continued to run her home and made lists of things she had to do or buy. On a scrap of paper she wrote, 'Robinson's patent barley & Groats for the children – to enquire for my letters in St James's Square – 6 lemons – 20£ to pay my bills if Mrs Crosby will be kind enough to send for them – a box of wax lights – and – the Morning Post newspaper every day – a barrel of oysters.'[72] Susan was not forgotten – on 8 December Caroline ordered for her 6 plain cotton hose and a pair of green gloves from Ralf Lonsdale, Hosier & Glover, 193 Regent Street.

Caroline did not want to die without being reconciled to Duncannon. She told his wife, Maria, 'I never hear Duncannon's name without crying. My own dear brother – but I owe it to myself to say that except for Wm Lamb, Lady Cowper, my kind brother William – all the other people & Dr Roe told me he was the person [who] spoke most severely against me and wanted me locked up in a madhouse, so that I feared his very name. I consider my painful illness as a great blessing. I feel return'd to my God & my duty & my dearest husband, & my heart which was so proud & insensible is quite over come with the greatest kindness I receive. I brought myself to be quite another person & broke that horrid spell which prevented my saying my prayers, so that if I were better, I would go with you & your dear children to church. I say all this, dearest Maria, lest you should think I flew to religion because I was in danger. It is no such thing, my heart is softened. I see how good & kind others are & I am quite resigned to die. I do not think myself, there is a chance for me.'[73]

On 13 December Dr Goddard wrote to William, 'I regret very much that I have but a melancholy account to give you today of Lady Caroline's health. Saturday she seemed in good spirits, but on that night she began to complain of pain in her side, accompanied with a cough and shortness of breath. These symptoms are, I think, partly accidental, and may not continue, but should they, they will certainly give us great cause of alarm. There is another change, also, she is inattentive to what is going on. She speaks with difficulty, and seems unwilling to see many people. You may gather from these symptoms the unwelcome news that her ladyship is getting worse, her sufferings she still bears with fortitude and complains but little.'[74]

Caroline rallied. On 6 January, William wrote, 'I received your little line yesterday, & I also received with great pleasure Dr Goddard's account that you were better. My heart is almost broken, that I cannot come over directly but your brother, to whom I have written, will explain to you the difficult situation in which I am placed. How unfortunate & melancholy that you should be so ill now & that it should be at a time when I, who have had so many years of idleness, am fixed & chained down by circumstances. Augustus is very well. I gave him today Dr Goddard's letter with which he was much pleased.'[75]

It was a false hope. Caroline was sinking and the coldness of approaching death made it almost impossible to keep her warm despite the use of a new warming pan. To support her swollen body Dr Goddard ordered '2 feather bolsters covered in green leather, 2 down pillows covered in chamois leather, 2 thick hair cushions covered in green leather, one with a square aperture in the centre.' There were special loose covers to make them more comfortable.[76] On 15 January Dr Goddard sent for William, who arrived with Augustus at Holyhead on 18 January after a 'dreadful passage. Heavy gale of wind right against us.' He told Lady Brandon, 'Did not get here till one o'clock – more than fifteen hours – suffered horribly.'[77] On 22 January the Duke of Devonshire visited Caroline. On 23 January William told Lady Brandon, that 'she is dying, dying rapidly and that with a perfect understanding, namely deep regret and repentance of the course which she has run and the conduct which she has pursued.'[78]

For much of the time Caroline remained insensible but when she roused herself she appeared clear-minded with a perfect memory. She talked over her life and its mistakes and pleasures with William, her brother and Mr Faithful who gave her Holy Communion twice. William Ponsonby told Duncannon, 'She was anxious to be released from the state of suffering in which she was; at the same time not a word of impatience has escaped her from the first moment of her illness, & she has shown nothing but the greatest gentleness, & kindest feeling towards all about her. Wm was much affected, but it was a great satisfaction to her to see him once again.'[79]

In the afternoon of 25 January Lady Morpeth saw her cousin and although she thought her face was excessively shrunken, she did not think she looked near death. At about nine o'clock that evening Caroline died from complete exhaustion. Emily told Frederick, 'Mrs Lamb had hold of her hand at the time. She only fetched one sigh and she was gone. Mrs Lamb could hardly believe she was really dead and only felt she was so by the placid look her features assumed.'[80] When Lady Morpeth called on Caro-George the next day she was surprised that Caroline was dead. She was particularly distressed as the mention of it made William violently emotional. 'However', she told her daughter, Lady Caroline Lascelles, 'he got over it, after crying a good deal, and talking with very great interest on political subjects; he cannot be expected to feel it really as a loss, tho' very much affected whenever he mentioned her.'[81] Emily briskly told Frederick, 'Wm was not there at the time but he had been with her a few hours before. He was hurt at the time and rather low next day, but he is now just as usual, and his mind filled with politics. Augustus looked a little grave when he saw her, and when he heard of her death, but nothing makes any impression upon him. He is good-natured, but in intellect I think rather worse than he was, in short he ranks in intellect with a child of six or seven.'[82]

'You will not be surprised,' William wrote to Lady Brandon, 'when I tell you that poor Caroline died on Friday evening. Nothing could exceed her composure, patience and resignation. Her great errors seem now to have been in the nature of a mercy. Had she been always as she was during her illness we never could have borne her loss. The blow is most severe[83]... I felt a sort of impossibility of believing that I should never see her countenance or hear her voice again, and a sort of sense of desolation, solitude and carelessness about everything when I forced myself to remember that she was really gone.'[84]

'A kinder or better heart has never ceased to beat,' William Ponsonby told Lady Morgan. 'It was to her a great consolation, and is now to us, that her mind was fully prepared and reconciled to this awful change. She viewed the near approach of death with the greatest calmness and during the whole of her severe sufferings, the patience with which she endured them, or her kind and affectionate feelings for those about her never failed for one moment. Mr Lamb has felt and acted, as I knew he would, upon this sad occasion.'[85]

Mrs Peterson had little time to mourn. She was in charge of making arrangements for the servants to attend the funeral, the breakfast on the day, removing Caroline's personal possessions from Pall Mall, paying the servant's wages and providing mourning clothes for Susan, Betsy, Caroline's maid and the other servants.

Shortly before she died, Caroline gave her brother all her letters from Byron and all his to her and asked him to destroy them. William Ponsonby lost no time in carrying out her wishes and on the day of her funeral he wrote to Hobhouse to invite him to set a date to burn all the correspondence between his sister and Byron. Caroline's journals almost certainly suffered the same fate. On 10 February Dr Goddard completed arrangements with Lady Morgan to deliver 'the portrait of Lord Byron in the morocco case.' It became a prime exhibit in the small ebony cabinet in the little red boudoir of her town house in Kildare Street, Dublin. When she died in 1859 it was sold at Christie's to a 'gentleman residing near Carlshalton.'[86]

On 4 February Caroline's hearse left Pall Mall for the journey to the Lamb family vault at Hatfield church. Two mourning coaches and six empty carriages belonging to the Duke of Devonshire, Earl Spencer, Earl Carlisle, Earl Bessborough, Lord Melbourne and Viscount Duncannon followed it. The procession followed the hearse to northern edge of London where the carriages turned back leaving the two mourning coaches and the chief mourners, William Lamb and William Ponsonby, to follow the coffin to the church. William wrote to Lady Brandon from Panshanger, 'I am just returned from the funeral and melancholy as the scene has been, I feel relieved by it. It seems as if everything had been done that could be and every duty paid.'[87]

Many years later, when the Duke of Devonshire was preparing his Handbook for Chatsworth and Hardwick, he described the happy days he spent with Caroline in the schoolroom at Chatsworth and the pain he felt when she broke their childhood promise to marry. He had adored her and loved her for her 'great feeling and tenderness,' and her 'extraordinary mixture of cleverness and inconsistency'. He had stood by her during the dark days of her separation and blamed the Lambs for blighting her life. He wrote, 'Her end was melancholy, and what can be more so than these lines?'

My lyre is like to me – neglected;
A useless burden now it stands,
By all who once admired, rejected –
The sport and scorn of vulgar hands.

Time was when decked with ribbons rare
Across thy bosom it was hung;
And only touched with tenderest care,
It answered to the voice that sung.

But now – for all its charm is o'er
Of former talent but a token –
Too rudely struck, 'twill sound no more;
Its chords are as my heart is – broken.[88]

Caroline had described herself to William Godwin as 'the wreck of a little boat, for I never come up to the sublime and beautiful – merely a little gay merry boat, which perhaps stranded itself at Vauxhall or London Bridge; or wounded without killing itself as a butterfly does in a tallow candle. There is nothing marked sentimental or interesting in my career, all I know is that I was happy, well, rich, surrounded by friends. I have now one faithful friend in William Lamb, two more in my father, brother, but health, spirits and all else gone – gone how? O assuredly not by the visitation of God but slowly, gradually by my own fault.'

The Memoir in the Literary Gazette, widely believed to have been written by William Lamb, read: 'For her friends she had a ready and active love; for her enemies no hatred; never perhaps was there a human being who had less malevolence; in all her errors hurt only herself, so against herself only were levelled her accusation and reproach... Lady Caroline was indeed one of those persons who can be much wiser for others than for themselves; and she disdained all worldly advice of the most judicious of worldly advisers.'[89]

Many years later William remarked, 'In spite of all, she was more to me than anyone ever was or ever will be.' His eyes would fill with tears at the mention of her name and he was heard to mutter, 'Shall we meet? Shall we meet in another world?'[90]

EPILOGUE

Old Lord Melbourne died quietly, with Emily by his side, at Melbourne House on 22 July 1828.

Augustus never recovered and his fits became more frequent as he grew older. William, now Lord Melbourne, often sat with him and on the evening of 26 November 1836 Augustus, who was lying on a sofa apparently asleep, suddenly said in a quiet and reflective tone, 'I wish you would give some franks, that I may write and thank people who have been kind in their inquiries. Astonished, William wrote, 'The words and the manner were as clear and thoughtful as if no cloud had ever hung heavily over him. I cannot give any notion of what I felt; for I believed it to be as it proved, the summons they call the lightening before death. In a few hours he was gone.' Twelve days later he wrote, 'That fullness of sorrow is great, but how much greater is its emptiness.' Frederick, with typical Lamb compassion, remarked that 'one cannot but feel it is a good thing'. Sir Henry Halford, Dr Hamilton Roe and Dr Thomas Copeland held a post-mortem. They found that Augustus had 'a most unusual thickening of the bones of the skull, particularly of the bones of the forehead and temples. There were marks of former attacks of inflammation on the membranes and the substance of the brain was unusually dense, so much so as to resist the knife in an uncommon manner. There was a larger portion of fluid at the back of the brain than is common, probably of recent origin, the ventricles also contained more water than usual. With this evidence of great disease within the Brain we did not open the chest or abdomen.'

William was made Home Secretary in 1830 and appointed his favourite brother, George, to the position of Under-Secretary, a post he held until he suddenly died on 2 January 1834. His wife, quiet Caroline St Jules, lived on until 1861. She remained on the fringes of the Lambs' political ambitions, always supportive and eager to help.

In April 1839 Frederick was elevated to the peerage, taking the title Baron Beauvale. William appointed him Ambassador to Austria in 1831 and it was while he was in Vienna that he met and married the daughter of the Prussian Ambassador, Alexandrina Julia (Adine) in February 1841. Although his wife was forty years his junior it proved to be a very happy marriage, which lasted eleven years before Frederick died of gout. His young widow was inconsolable and Emily wrote, 'Frederick is gone, I have lost almost the best friend I ever had.'

When Lord Cowper died on 21 June 1837 Emily's close friend, Henry John Temple, third Viscount Lord Palmerston, the probable father of four of her children, urged her to move to London where he could see her more often. They were married on 16 December 1839 at St George's Church, Hanover Square. Lord Palmerston had fulfilled all Lady Melbourne's expectations, rising from being the most effective Foreign Secretary this country has ever known to Prime Minister. Emily achieved her mother's ambition by becoming a successful political hostess and a power to be reckoned with. The pair lived happy and fulfilled lives until in October 1865 Lord Palmerston caught a chill, which he treated with mutton chops washed down with port. Two days later he died in his bed with Emily and her children at his side. This is a less colourful end to his life than the popular story that he died in the act of seducing a maid on the billiard table at Brocket, but it is a compliment to his vitality, strength and virility that people believed it could be true.

Emily lived for almost four years after his death. She never lost her interest in politics but in August 1869, a few months after her eighty-second birthday, she began to fade. She died on 11 September and her son-in-law, Lord Shaftsbury, wrote, 'Poor, dear beloved Mum it is a very terrible thing to have lost her.' It is difficult to believe he is talking about the Emily Lamb who harried Caroline out of Melbourne House. She was buried with Lord Palmerston in Westminster Abbey.

William was Prime Minister when young Queen Victoria came to the throne in 1837 and, until Prince Albert shouldered him out of her affections, he was her teacher and her guide. It was a familiar position and one he had enjoyed with Caroline. The eighteen-year-old, enthusiastic Queen enjoyed questioning him on the customs and habits of her 'wicked' uncles, George IV, William IV and an even more fascinating topic, Lord Byron. In May 1841 Melbourne's government's budget proposals were dismissed and he resigned. Out of office and out of the Queen's affections, William suffered a stroke in 1842. A fall, jaundice and epileptic fits further weakened him. He became progressively deaf and his list of ailments increased but they were eased a little by his habit of drinking three bottles of wine a day. On 21 November 1848 while at Brocket, he had four fits, lost the power of speech and died three days later. Emily wrote, 'His mind was quite composed and peaceful and I believe he felt no anxiety or painful thoughts now, tho' he had no doubt long contemplated his own death, and his mind was quite prepared to the awful change. At last, thank God his end was peaceful and he only breathed one sigh.'

On 1 December, after a modest funeral attended by his family, servants and Mr Cookney, William joined his parents, Augustus and Caroline in the family vault at Hatfield Church. Visitors looking for his grave are directed to a section of paving covering the vault. The only memorial for William is a modern brass plaque. The resting places of Lord and Lady Melbourne, Augustus and Caroline are not marked.

NOTES

CHAPTER 1

1 Foster, *The Two Duchesses,* p.223
2 Chatsworth, 5th Duke's Group, Duchess of Devonshire to the Dowager Countess Spencer, 4 June 1805
3 Leveson Gower, *The Face Without a Frown,* p.18
4 Ibid, p.9-11
5 Ibid, p.27
6 British Literary Journal, 1986, Dr Frances Harris, *A Gothic House at St Albans*
7 Hobhouse C. *Fox,* p.76
8 Leveson Gower, *The Face Without a Frown,* pp.103-113
9 Chatsworth, 5th Duke's Group, Dowager Countess Spencer's Journal 12 November 1785
10 West Sussex RO, Bessborough Papers, F.268
11 Leveson Gower, *The Face Without a Frown,* pp.134-137
12 Bessborough, *Extracts from the Correspondence of Georgiana, Duchess of Devonshire,* pp.120-121
13 West Sussex RO, Bessborough Papers, F.163(1)
14 Chatsworth, 5th Duke's Group, Journal kept by Ann Scafe, Paris 1790
15 Castle Howard, Carlisle Papers, J18/37-6
16 Chatsworth, 5th Duke's Papers, Dowager Countess Spencer to Miss Selina Trimmer, 15 February 1792
17 Leveson Gower, *The Face Without a Frown,* p.185
18 Bessborough, *Lady Bessborough & her Family Circle,* p.104
19 Ibid, p.103
20 Ibid, p.106
21 Chatsworth, 5th Duke's Papers, 1338
22 Ibid, 1346
23 Ibid, Miss Trimmer to Dowager Countess Spencer, 6 September 1796
24 Leveson Gower, *The Face Without a Frown,* p.211
25 Castle Howard, Carlisle Papers, J18/35-98
26 West Sussex RO, Bessborough Papers, F.271
27 Leveson Gower and Palmer, *The Letters of Lady Harriet Cavendish 1796-1809,* p.49
28 West Sussex RO, Bessborough Papers, F.163, (Typescript)
29 Chatsworth, 5th Duke's Papers, 1560
30 West Sussex RO, Bessborough Papers, F.272

31   Ibid, F.163 (1)
32   Ibid.
33   Leveson Gower and Palmer, *The Letters of Lady Harriet Cavendish 1796-1809*, p.29
34   Granville, *Private Correspondence of Lord Granville*, Vol 1, p.346
35   Leveson Gower and Palmer, *The Letters of Lady Harriet Cavendish*, p.23
36   Granville, *Private Correspondence of Lord Granville*, Vol 1, p.317
37   Hertford RO, Panshanger Papers, D/Elb F.64
38   Granville, *Private Correspondence of Lord Granville*, Vol 1, pp.413-414
39   West Sussex RO, Bessborough Papers, F.273
40   Esher, *The Girlhood of Queen Victoria, 1832-1840*. Vol 2, p.64
41   Morgan, *Memoirs*, Vol 2, pp.210-213
42   Granville, *Private Correspondence of Lord Granville*, Vol 2, p.67
43   Ibid, 15 September 1803
44   Ibid, p.67
45   Ibid, Vol 2, pp.68-69
46   Bessborough, *Lady Bessborough & her Family Circle*, pp.130-131
47   British Library, Althorp Papers, Box F.92
48   Bessborough, *Lady Bessborough & her Family Circle*, pp.129
49   Granville, *Private Correspondence of Lord Granville*, Vol 2, pp. 72-74

CHAPTER 2

1   Chatsworth, 5th Duke's Group, 1813
2   West Sussex RO, Bessborough Papers, F.163
3   Granville, *Private Correspondence of Lord Granville*, Vol 2, p.79
4   Chatsworth, 5th Duke's Group, 1814.1
5   Castle Howard, Carlisle Papers, J18/35
6   British Library, Althorp Papers, Box F.92
7   Granville, *Private Correspondence of Lord Granville*, Vol 2, p.81
8   Ibid, Vol 2, p.88
9   Foster, *The Two Duchesses*, p.232
10   Granville, *Private Correspondence of Lord Granville*, Vol 2, p.85
11   Castle Howard, Carlisle Papers, J18/35 1
12   Foster, *The Two Duchesses*, p.242
13   Leveson Gower and Palmer, *The Letters of Lady Harriet Cavendish*, p.118
14   Ibid, p.122
15   Ibid, p.125
16   Castle Howard, Carlisle Papers, J18/35 67
17   Forster, *The Two Duchesses*, p.257
18   Granville, *Private Correspondence of Lord Granville*, Vol 2, p.128
19   West Sussex RO, Bessborough Papers, F.161
20   Leveson Gower and Palmer, *The Letters of Lady Harriet Cavendish*, p.137
21   Ibid, p.139
22   Ibid, p.150
23   Chatsworth, 5th Duke's Group, 1849
24   Bessborough, *Lady Bessborough & her Family Circle*, p.144
25   Leveson Gower, *The Face Without a Frown*, p.227

26   Wharton, *The Queens of Society*, p.157
27   Bessborough, *Lady Bessborough & her Family Circle*, p.145
28   Ibid, p.145
29   West Sussex RO, Bessborough Papers, F.274
30   British Library, Holland House Papers, 57560/124
31   John Murray Papers
32   Leveson Gower and Palmer, *The Letters of Lady Harriet Cavendish*, p.159
33   Ibid, p.138
34   Esher, *The Girlhood of Queen Victoria*, Vol 2, p.291
35   Granville, *Private Correspondence of Lord Granville*, Vol 2, p.229
36   Chatsworth, 5th Duke's Papers, Lady Elizabeth Foster's Journal, 19 December 1806
37   Castle Howard, Carlisle Papers, J18/35-40
38   West Sussex RO, Bessborough Papers, F.274
39   Ponsonby, *The Ponsonby Family*, p.130
40   Foster, *The Two Duchesses*, p.307
41   British Library, Althorp Papers, Box F.92
42   West Sussex RO, Bessborough Papers, F.275
43   Leveson Gower and Palmer, *The Letters of Lady Harriet Cavendish*, p.201
44   Castle Howard, Carlisle Papers, J18/35 28
45   West Sussex RO, Bessborough Papers, F.16292 (Typescript)
46   Castle Howard, Carlisle Papers, J18/35 44
47   Granville, *Private Correspondence of Lord Granville*, Vol 2, pp.292-293
48   Hertfordshire RO, Panshanger Papers, D/Elb F.101
49   Leveson Gower and Palmer, *The Letters of Lady Harriet Cavendish*, pp.228-229
50   Ibid, p.242
51   British Library, Althorp Papers, ADD. MSS F.174
52   British Library, Hodgkin Papers Vol X, ADD MS 388855 F.225
53   Granville, *Private Correspondence of Lord Granville*, Vol 2, p.308
54   Berry, *Extracts from the Journal and Correspondence 1883-1852*, Vol 2, p.346
55   Ibid, Vol 2, p.348
56   Leveson Gower and Palmer, *The Letters of Lady Harriet Cavendish*, pp.263 and p.265
57   Castle Howard, Carlisle Papers, J18/35-49
58   West Sussex RO, Bessborough Papers, F.276
59   West Sussex RO, Bessborough Papers F.163 (3)
60   Hertfordshire RO, Panshanger Papers, D/Elb F.32
61   Leveson Gower and Palmer, *The Letters of Lady Harriet Cavendish*, p.327
62   Hertfordshire RO, Panshanger papers, D/Elb F.32/4
63   Chatsworth, 6th Duke's Group, 1954
64   Ibid, 11 October 1809
65   Hertfordshire RO, Panshanger Papers, F.163 (2)
66   Bessborough, *Lady Bessborough & her Family Circle*, p.195
67   Hertfordshire RO, Panshanger Papers, F.163 (2)
68   Chatsworth, 6th Duke's Group, 1962
69   Leveson Gower and Palmer, *The Letters of Lady Harriet Cavendish*, p.334
70   Chatsworth, 6th Duke's Papers, 1965
71   West Sussex RO, Bessborough Papers, F.163 (3)

72   Chatsworth, 6th Duke's Group, 1966
73   West Sussex RO, Bessborough Papers, F.277
74   British Library, Lamb Papers, ADD MS 45546/13
75   Ibid.

CHAPTER 3
1   British Library, Holland House Papers, 51560 159
2   Airlie, *In Whig Society*, pp.118-120
3   British Library, Lamb Papers, ADD MS 45546/16
4   Ibid, ADD MS 45546/20
5   Ibid.
6   British Library, Holland House Papers, 51560/162
7   Ibid, 51560/166
8   Ibid, 51560/151
9   Ibid, 50560/190
10   Ibid, 57560/133
11   Ibid, 51560/169
12   Castle Howard, Carlisle Papers, J18/35-52
13   Bessborough, *Lady Bessborough & her Family Circle*, pp.215-215
14   British Library, Holland House Papers, 51560/137
15   Ibid, 51560/141
16   Ibid.
17   British Library, Lamb Papers, ADD S 45546/25
18   West Sussex RO, Bessborough Papers, F.163(2) Typescript
19   Castle Howard, Carlisle Papers, J18/35-95
20   Chatsworth, 6th Duke's Group, 1993
21   Ibid.
22   British Library, Holland House Papers, 51560/137
23   Ibid, 51560/137
24   Morgan, *The Book of the Boudoir, Vol 1, p.145*
25   British Library, Holland House Papers, 51560/177
26   West Sussex RO, Bessborough Papers, F.163 (3)
27   Granville, *Private Correspondence of Lord Granville*, Vol 2, p.405
28   Chatsworth, 6th Duke's Group, 36
29   Bessborough, *Lady Bessborough & her Family Circle*, p.218
30   Airlie, *In Whig Society*, p.123
31   Castle Howard, Carlisle Papers, J18/35-53
32   Foster, *The Two Duchesses*, pp.353-354
33   Ibid, p.352
34   Dyce, *Table Talk of Samuel Rogers*, p.231-232
35   Moore, *Letters and Journals*, p.161
36   John Murray Papers
37   Morgan, *Memoirs*, Vol 2, pp.199-213
38   Moore, *Letters and Journals, p.615*
39   British Library, Althorp Papers, G297
40   Morgan, *Memoirs*, pp.119-213

CHAPTER 4

1   Ibid.
2   Esher, *The Girlhood of Queen Victoria*, Vol 1, p.342
3   Kemble, *Record of a Girlhood*, Vol 1, p.74
4   Mayne, *The Life of Lady Byron*, p.37
5   John Murray Papers (see Vol 2, Chapter 15 *Glenarvon.*)
6   John Murray, *Commonplace Book*
7   Foster, *The Two Duchesses*, pp.367-368
8   Marchand, *Byron's Letters & Journals*, Vol 2, p.175
9   Leveson Gower, *The Letters of Harriet, Countess of Granville*, Vol 1, p.34
10 Foster, *The Two Duchesses*, p.376
11 Dyce, *Table Talk of Samuel Rogers*, pp.232-233
12 Foster, *The Two Duchesses*, p.364
13 John Murray Papers
14 Ibid.
15 Foster, *The Two Duchesses*, p.362
16 John Murray Papers
17 Blessington, *Conversations of Lord Byron*, p.80
18 British Library, Lamb Papers, ADD MS 45546/46
19 Moore, *Life of Lord Byron*, p.164
20 Marchand, *Byron's Letters and Journals*, Vol 2, p.176
21 British Library, Lamb Papers, ADD MS 45546/46
22 Dyce, *Table Talk of Samuel Rogers*, pp.234-235
23 Torrens, *Memoirs of Viscount Melbourne*, Vol 1, pp.106-107
24 Eden, *Letters from India*, Vol 1, p.5
25 West Sussex RO, Bessborough Papers, F.272
26 Castle Howard, Carlisle Papers, J18/35-69
27 Foster, *The Two Duchesses*, p.369-370
28 West Sussex RO, Bessborough papers, 272
29 Ibid.
30 Lewis, *Journal and Correspondence of Miss Berry*, Vol 2, p.497
31 Lee, *Diary of Dr Robert Lee*, p.38
32 Pope, *Diary of Benjamin Haydon*, Vol 2, p.490
33 Murray Papers
34 Dorchester, *Recollections of a Long Life*, Vol 1, p. 43
35 West Sussex RO, Bessborough Papers, F.272
36 British Library, Lamb Papers, ADD MS 45546/77
37 Ibid, ADD MS 45546/128
38 Joyce, *My Friend H*, (Journal reference, 29 July 1812)
39 Sussex RO, Bessborough Papers, F.272
40 British Library, Lamb Papers, ADD MS 45546/29
41 Ibid, ADD MS 45911/58, 59
42 British Library, Lamb papers, ADD MS 45548/62
43 Paston and Quennell, *To Lord Byron*, p.44
44 British Library, Lamb Papers, ADD MS 45911/58, 59
45 Marchan, *Byron's Letters and Journals*, Vol 2, p.184-185

46 British Library, Lamb Papers, ADD MS 45546/52
47 Marchand, *Byron's Letters and Journals*, Vol 2, p.184
48 Elwin, *Lord Byron's Wife*, p.146
49 Ibid, p.493
50 British Library, Lamb Papers, ADD MS 45548/75
51 Ibid, ADD MS 45546/53
52 Marchand, *Byron's Letters & Journals*, Vol 2, p.187
53 Granville, *Private Correspondence of Lord Granville*, Vol 2, pp.447-449
54 Ibid.
55 British Library, Lamb Papers, ADD MS 45548/58
56 Airlie, *In Whig Society*, pp.128-130
57 Ibid, pp.129-130
58 Granville, *Private Correspondence of Lord Granville*, Vol 2, pp.453-454
59 Ibid, Vol 2, pp.452-453
60 British Library, Lamb Papers, ADD MS 45546/31
61 Marchand, *Byron's Letters and Journals*, Vol 2, p.188
62 Airlie, *In Whig Society*, pp.130-131
63 British Library, Broughton, ADD MS 39672
64 Morgan, *Memoirs*, Vol 2, p.204-306
65 Marchand, *Byron's Letters and Journals*, Vol 2, pp.192-193
66 Joyce, *My Friend H*, p.40
67 Marchand, *Byron's Letters and Journals*, Vol 2, p.192-193
68 Ibid, Vol 2, p.199-200
69 British Library, Lamb Papers, ADD MS 45547/43-45
70 Ibid, ADD MS 45546/42
71 Marchand, *Byron's Letters and Journals*, Vol 2, p.203
72 British Library, Lamb Papers, ADD MS 45546/40
73 Granville, *Private Correspondence of Lord Granville*, Vol 2, pp.461-462
74 British Library, Lamb Papers, ADD MS 45546/50
75 Ibid, ADD MS 45546/34
76 West Sussex RO, Bessborough Papers, F.272
77 Airlie, *In Whig Society*, p.110
78 British Library, Lamb Papers, ADD MS 45548/67
79 Ibid, ADD MS 45546/37
80 Marchand, *Byron's Letters and Journals*, Vol 2, pp.235-236
81 John Murray, *Lady Caroline Lamb's Commonplace Book*
82 British Library, Lamb Papers, ADD MS 45546/61
83 Ibid, ADD MS 45911/56
84 Marchand, *Byron's Letters and Journals*, Vol 2, p.199
85 Ibid, Vol 2, p.222
86 Ibid, Vol 2, p.243
87 Airlie, *In Whig Society*, p.150-153
88 British Library, Lamb Papers, ADD MS 45546/46
89 Ibid, ADD MS 45548/69-73
90 Dorchester, *Recollections of a Long Life by Lord Broughton*, Vol 1, p.345
91 John Murray Papers

92   Leveson Gower, *Letters of Harriet, Countess of Granville*, Vol 1, p.40-41
93   West Sussex RO, Bessborough Papers, F.272
94   John Murray Papers
95   Marchand, *Byron's Letters and Journals*, Vol 2, p.246

CHAPTER 5

1   Marchand, *Byron's Letters and Journals*, Vol 3, pp.8-9
2   John Murray Papers
3   Marchand, *Byron's Letters and Journals*, Vol 3, pp.10-11
4   Ibid Vol 3, p.17
5   British Library, Holland House Papers, 50560/199
6   West Sussex RO, Bessborough Papers, F.279
7   Hertfordshire RO, Panshanger Papers, D/Elb/F12
8   British Library, Lamb Papers, ADD MS 45 547/46-47
9   Marchand, *Byron's Letters and Journals*, Vol 3, pp.35-36
10   John Murray Papers
11   West Sussex RO, Bessborough Papers, F.161
12   John Murray Papers
13   British Library, Lamb Papers, ADD MS 45546/61
14   Marchand, *Byron's Letters and Journals*, Vol 3, pp.43-44
15   John Murray Papers
16   British Library, Lamb Papers, ADD MS 45547/53-54
17   Marchand, *Byron's Letters and Journals*, Vol 3, p.67
18   Murray, *Lord Byron's Correspondence*, Vol 1, pp.163-164
19   Marchand, *Byron's Letters and Journals*, Vol 3, p.71
20   British Library, Lamb Papers, ADD MS 45547/57-58
21   Airlie, *In Whig Society*, pp.154-155
22   Smith, *Sydney Smith – Selected Letters*, pp.69-70
23   British Library, Holland House Papers, 50560/201
24   John Murray Papers
25   West Sussex RO, Bessborough Papers, F.279
26   Edgecombe, *The Diary of Lady Frances Shelley*, Vol 1, pp.52-53
27   John Murray Papers
28   Ibid.
29   Ibid.
30   West Sussex RO, Bessborough Papers, F.279
31   John Murray Papers
32   British Library, Althorp Papers, F.40
33   Ibid.
34   Marchand, *Byron's Letters & Journals*, Vol 3, p.26
35   John Murray Papers
36   Ibid.
37   British Library, Althorp Papers, F.40
38   Marchand, *Byron's Letters and Journals*, Vol 3, pp.29-30
39   John Murray Papers
40   Marchand, *Byron's Letters and Journals*, Vol 3, pp.34-35

41   John Murray Papers
42   Ibid.
43   Ibid.
44   Dorchester, *Recollections of a Long Life by Lord Broughton,* Vol 1, p.98
45   John Murray Papers
46   Marchand, *Byron's Letters and Journals,* Vol 4, p.19
47   Ibid, Vol 4, p.104
48   John Murray Papers
49   Ibid.
50   Ibid.
51   Ibid.
52   Ibid.
53   Marchand, *Byron's Letters and Journals,* Vol 4, p.133
54   Hertfordshire RO, Panshanger Papers, D/ELb F.67
55   John Murray Papers
56   Ibid.
57   Morgan, *The Book of the Boudoir,* Vol 1, pp.86-87
58   Brightwell, *The Life of Amelia Opie,* pp.161-162
59   Blanche, *Harriette Wilson's Memoirs,* p.340
60   Marchand, *Byron's Letters and Journals,* Vol 4, pp.135-136
61   John Murray Papers
62   Ibid.
63   Ibid.

CHAPTER 6

1   Marchand, *Byron's Letters and Journals,* Vol 4, pp.178-179
2   Smiles, *Memoir and Correspondence of the late John Murray,* p.251
3   Marchand, *Byron's Letters and Journals,* Vol 4, p.185
4   John Murray Papers
5   Marchand, *Byron's Letters and Journals,* Vol 4, p.180
6   Ibid, Vol 4, p.194
7   Langley Moore, *Ada, Countess of Lovelace,* p.24
8   John Murray Papers
9   Marchand, *Byron's Letters and Journals,* Vol 4, p.228
10   Esher, *The Girlhood of Queen Victoria,* Vol 1, p.341
11   John Murray Papers
12   Marchand, *Byron's Letters and Journals,* Vol 4, pp.203-204
13   Ibid, Vol 4, p.231
14   Dorchester, *Recollections of a Long Life by Lord Broughton,* Vol 2, p.198
15   John Murray Papers
16   Ibid.
17   Dorchester, *Recollections of a Long Life by Lord Broughton,* Vol 3, p.49
18   Ibid, Vol 1 p.191-192
19   Ibid, Vol 1 p.193
20   Marchand, *Byron's Letters and Journals,* Vol 4, p.266
21   Murray, *Byron's Correspondence,* Vol 1, p.302

22 Hodgson, *A memoir by his son the Reverend James T Hodgson*, Vol 2, pp.16-17
23 John Murray Papers
24 Edgecombe, *The Diary of Lady Frances Shelley*, Vol 1, pp.81-82
25 Smiles, *Memoirs and Correspondence of the Late John Murray*, p.267
26 John Murray Papers
27 Ibid.
28 West Sussex RO, Bessborough Papers, F161
29 Ibid.
30 Bessborough, *Lady Bessborough & her Family Circle*, pp.246-247
31 West Sussex RO, Bessborough Papers, F161
32 Cole, *Fouché*, p.274
33 Airlie, *In Whig Society*, pp.171-172
34 Jenkins, *Lady Caroline Lamb*, p.90
35 West Sussex RO, Bessborough Papers, F17
36 Ibid.
37 West Sussex RO, Bessborough Papers, F161
38 Villiers, *The Grand Whiggery*, p.295
39 Simpson, *Paris after Waterloo*, pp.191-197
40 Ibid, p.109-128
41 Leveson Gower, *Letters of Harriet, Countess of Granville*, Vol 1, pp.66-67
42 Simpson, *Paris After Waterloo*, pp.191-197
43 Ibid.
44 Marchand, *Byron's Letters and Journals*, Vol 4, p310
45 Ibid, Vol 4, p.312
46 Kemble, *Record of a Girlhood*, Vol 1, pp.74-75
47 Dorchester, *Recollections of a Long Life by Lord Broughton*, Vol 1, p.323
48 Foster, *The Two Duchesses*, pp.408-409
49 Leveson Gower, *Letters of Harriet, Countess of Granville*, Vol 1, p.75
50 British Library, Lamb Papers, ADD MS 45546/87
51 John Murray Papers
52 Ibid.
53 Lovelace, *Astarte*, pp.66-77
54 John Murray Papers
55 British Library, Lamb Papers, ADD MS 45546/82

CHAPTER 7
1   Murray, *Lord Byron's Correspondence*, Vol 1, p.307
2   John Murray Papers
3   Dorchester, *Recollections of a long Life by Lord Broughton*, Vol 2, p. 359
4   Lovelace, *Astarte*, p.39
5   Ibid.
6   Beecher Stowe, *Vindication of Lady Byron*, p.294
7   Dorchester, *Recollections of a Long Life by Lord Broughton*, Vol 2, pp.215-216
8   Ibid, Vol 2, p.202
9   Lovelace, *Astarte*, pp.40-42
10 Care, *Diary of Joseph Farington*, Vol XIV, p.4816

11   Dorchester, *Recollections of a Long Life by Lord Broughton*, Vol 2, pp.244-45
12   Ibid, Vol 2, p.207
13   Moore, *Letters and Journals*, p.293
14   Hodgson, *A Memoir by his son the Reverend James T Hodgson*, 2 Vols, pp.28-33
15   Dorchester, *Recollections of a Long Life by Lord Broughton*, Vol 2, p.266
16   Lovelace, *Astarte*, pp.17-19
17   John Murray Papers
18   Ibid.
19   Murray, *Lord Byron's Correspondence*, Vol 1, p.3
20   Foster, *The Two Duchesses*, pp.413
21   Ibid.
22   Ibid.
23   Dorchester, *Recollections of a Long Life by Lord Broughton*, Vol 2, pp. 277-78
24   Ibid, Vol 2, p. 284
25   Mayne, *Lady Byron*, pp.208-215
26   Moore, *Letters and Journals*, pp.302-303
27   Marchand, *Letters & Journals*, Vol 5, pp.51-52
28   John Murray Papers
29   Ibid.
30   Mitford, *Recollections of a Literary Life*, Vol 1, p.329
31   John Murray (Transcripts) and Langley Moore, *The Late Lord Byron*, pp.231-238
32   Ibid.
33   Lovelace, *Astarte*, pp.34-36
34   John Murray (Typescripts) and Langley Moore, *The Late Lord Byron*, pp.240
35   John Murray Papers
36   Ibid.
37   Ibid.
38   Prothero, *The Works of Lord Byron*, Vol 6, p.19
39   Moore, *Letters and Journals*, p.296

CHAPTER 8
1   Care, *The Diary of Joseph Farington*, Vol XIV, p.484
2   *The Times*, August 25 1815
3   British Library, Lamb Papers, ADD MS 45548/141-142
4   British Library, Lamb Papers, ADD MS 45,546/89
5   Foster, *The Two Duchesses*, pp.416-17
6   British Library, Broughton Correspondence, ADD MS 36457
7   John Murray Papers
8   Dorchester, *Recollections of a Long Life by Lord Broughton*, Vol 1, p.338
9   Morgan, *Memoirs*, Vol 2, pp.199-213
10   National Art Museum, Foster Collection MSS XXVII (F.48 E. 22) Catalogue No. 238, letter no. 6
11   Ibid, letter no. 46
12   Ibid, letter no. 45
13   Gore, *Thomas Creevey's Papers*, p.153
14   British Library, Lamb Papers, ADD MS 51558/19

15   Granville, *Private Correspondence of Lord Granville*, Vol 2, p.541-43
16   British Library, Lamb Papers, ADD MS 45548/143-144
17   National Art Museum, Foster Collection MSS XXVII (F.48 E. 22) Catalogue No. 238, letter no. 17
18   British Library, Lamb Papers, ADD MS 45546/91
19   National Art Museum, Foster Collection, MSS XXVII (F.48 E. 22) Catalogue No. 328 V & A, Foster Collection, letter no. 12
20   Ibid, letter no. 13
21   Granville, *Private Correspondence of Lord Granville*, Vol 2, pp.541-43
22   British Library, Lamb Papers, ADD MS 45546/119-122
23   Ibid, ADD MS 45548/149
24   Ibid, ADD MS 45548/146
25   Foster, *The Two Duchesses*, p.148
26   Edgecombe, *The Diaries of Lady Frances Shelley*, Vol 1, pp.186-88
27   National Art Museum, Foster Collection, MSS XXVII (F.48 E. 22) Catalogue No. 328, letter no.18
28   Morgan, *Book of the Boudoir*, Vol 1, p.249
29   Marchand, *Byron's Letters and Journals*, Vol 5, pp.87-8
30   Lovelace, *Astarte*, pp.264-65
31   Ibid, pp.268-70
32   Murray, *Lord Byron's Correspondence*, 29 September 1816
33   Walford, *Old London, Westminster to St James's*, pp.197-98
34   Edgecombe, *Diaries of Lady Frances Shelley*, Vol 1, pp.295-96
35   Ibid, pp.229-30
36   Airlie, *In Whig Society*, p.187
37   Ibid, p.177
38   Torrens, *Memoirs of Viscount Melbourne*, Vol 1, pp.188-89
39   British Library, Lamb Papers, ADD MS 45546/109-110
40   Ibid, ADD MS 45546/93
41   Ibid, ADD MS 45546/109-110
42   Ibid, ADD MS 45546/95
43   Ibid, ADD MS 45546/111
44   Blanche, *Harriette Wilson's Memoirs*, p.193
45   Leveson Gower, *Letters of Harriet, Countess of Granville*, 27 October 1816
46   British Library, Lamb Papers, ADD MS 45546/116
47   Ibid, ADD MS 45546/104-106
48   Blanche, *Harriette Wilson's Memoirs*, p.192
49   British Library, Lamb Papers, ADD MS 45546/98
50   Ibid, ADD MS 45546/100
51   Torrens, *Memoirs of Viscount Melbourne*, Vol 1, p.189
52   John Murray Papers
53   Ibid.
54   Smiles, *Correspondence of the late John Murray*, Vol 1, pp.380-81
55   John Murray Papers
56   Leveson Gower, *Letters of Harriet, Countess of Granville*, Vol 1, p.90
57   British Library, Lamb Papers, ADD MS 45546/107

58   Ibid, ADD MS 45546/101-102
59   Lee, *Extracts from the Diary of Dr Robert Lee*, p.12
60   Bruce, *Lavalette Bruce*, p.296
61   Ibid, p.298
62   Ibid, pp.299-300
63   Lever, *The Letters of Lady Palmerston*, p.15
64   Airlie, *Lady Palmerston and her Times*, Vol 1, p.43
65   Ibid.
66   John Murray Papers
67   Edgecombe, *The Diaries of Lady Shelley*, Vol 2, p.6
68   John Murray Papers
69   Torrens, *Memoirs of Viscount Melbourne*, Vol 1, p.133
70   Lever, *The Letters of Lady Palmerston*, p.16
71   Blanche, *Harriette Wilson's Memoirs*, pp.193-94
72   Morgan, *Memoirs*, Vol 2, pp.23-5
73   Ibid.
74   Ibid, p.29
75   Ibid, pp.34-5
76   John Murray Papers
77   Burnett, *The Life and Times of a Regency Dandy*, p.38
78   Morgan, *Memoirs*, Vol 2, pp.280-82
79   Edgecombe, *The Diaries of Lady Shelley*, Vol 2, pp.28-9
80   John Murray Papers
81   Torrens, *Memoirs of Viscount Melbourne*, Vol 1, p.137
82   Edgecombe, *The Diaries of Lady Shelley*, Vol 2, pp.29-31
83   Airlie, *Lady Palmerston and her Times*, Vol 1, pp.44-5
84   John Murray Papers
85   Lever, *The Letters of Lady Palmerston*, p.19-20
86   British Library, Lamb Papers, ADD MS 45548/153-156
87   Lever, *The Letters of Lady Palmerston*, p.24
88   British Library, Lamb Papers, ADD MS 45548/157

CHAPTER 9
1   Bamford, *The Journal of Mrs Arbuthnot*, Vol 1, p.10
2   Lever, *The Letters of Lady Palmerston*, p.28
3   Joyce, *My Friend H*, p.136
4   British Library, Lamb Papers, ADD MS 45550/110
5   John Murray Papers
6   Marchand, *Byron's Letters and Journals*, Vol 7, p.168
7   British Library, Lamb Papers, ADD MS 45550/57
8   Hertfordshire RO, Panshanger Papers, D/Elb F.65
9   West Sussex RO, Bessborough Papers, F.16
10   Hertfordshire RO, Pansanger Papers, D/Elb F.77
11   Ibid, D/Elb F.39/28
12   Ibid, D/Elb F.7610
13   British Library, Lamb Papers, ADD MS 45550/52

14 Ibid, ADD MS 45550/57

15 Lever, *The Letters of Lady Palmerston*, pp.62-63

16 Ibid, p.47

17 British Library, Lamb Papers, ADD MS 45550/57

18 Ibid, ADD MS 45550/93

19 Ibid, ADD MS 51558/125

20 Lever, *The Letters of Lady Palmerston*, p.70

21 Torrens, *Memoirs of Viscount Melbourne*, Vol 1, p.178

22 British Library, Lamb Papers, ADD MS 45550/93

23 Airlie, *Lady Palmerston and her Times*, Vol 1, p.88

24 Ibid, Vol 1, p.91

25 West Sussex RO, Bessborough papers, F.161

26 Ibid.

27 Ibid, F.17

28 Bessborough, *Lady Bessborough and her Family Circle*, pp.267-69

29 West Sussex RO, Bessborough Papers, F.16

30 Bessborough, *Lady Bessborough and her Family Circle*, pp.271-72

31 Bamford, *The Journal of Mrs Arbuthnot*, Vol 1, pp.128-29

32 Chatsworth, 6th Duke's Group, 577

33 British Library, Lothian Papers, Box 234/47

34 Leveson Gower, *Letters of Harriet, Countess of Granville*, Vol 1, p.217

35 Chatsworth, 6th Duke's Group, 581

36 Bessborough, *Lady Bessborough and her Family Circle*, p.275

37 Chatsworth, 6th Duke's Group, 586

38 Ibid, 588

39 British Library, Lamb Papers, ADD MS 50142

40 Bessborough, *Lady Bessborough and her Family Circle*, p.270

41 West Sussex RO, Bessborough Papers, F.16

42 Lee, *Extracts from the Diary of Dr Robert Lee*, p.39

43 Wharton, *Queens of Sociey*, pp.435-50

44 Hertford RO, Lady Caroline Lamb's Correspondence with Edward Bulwer Lytton, C1/45, C24/21, Clutterbuck Vol V1 p.362

45 Lytton, *Life of Edward Bulwer first Lord Lytton*, Vol 1, p.118-20

46 Torrens, *Memoirs of Vicount Melbourne*, Vol 1, p.171

47 National Art Museum, Foster Collection, MSS XXVII (F.48 E 22) Catalogue No. 328, letter no. 39

48 Ibid, letter no. 57 (Caroline is quoting Rosalind in Shakespeare's 'As You Like It', Act IV)

49 Ibid, letter no. 22

50 Ibid, letter no. 20

51 Lever, *The Letters of Lady Palmerston*, p.96

52 Lee, *Extracts from the Diary of Dr Robert Lee*, p.23

53 Lever, *The Letters of Lady Palmerston*, p.102

54 Torrens, *Memoirs of Viscount Melbourne*, Vol 1, p.190

55 Lever, *Letters of Lady Palmerston*, p.111

56 John Murray Papers.

57 Ibid.

58 Ibid.

59 Ilchester, *Lady Holland to her Son*, p.17

60 Airlie, *Lady Palmerston and her Times*, Vol 1, p.110

61 Bamford, *The Journal of Mrs Arbuthnot*, Vol 1, p.154

62 Airlie, *Lady Palmerston and her Times*, Vol 1, p.110

63 Wellington, *Wellington and his Friends*, p.37, letter no.37

64 Morgan, *Lady Morgan's Diary*, pp.68-71

65 National Art Museum, Foster Collection, MSS XXVII (F.48 E. 22) Catalogue No. 328, letter no. 23

66 Morgan, *Memoirs*, Vol 2, pp.210-13

67 Chatsworth, 6th Duke's Group, 817a

68 Morgan, *Memoirs*, Vol 2, pp. 176-79

69 Ibid, Vol 2, pp.195-196

70 Hertford RO, Panshanger Papers, D/Elb F.77

71 John Murray Papers

72 Ibid.

73 Ibid.

74 Chapman, *Byron and the Honourable Augusta Leigh*, p.176

75 John Murray Papers

76 Joyce, *My Friend H*, p.172

77 John Murray Papers

78 Ibid.

79 Chatsworth, 6th Duke's Group, 966

80 Hertfordshire RO, Panshanger Papers, D/Elb F.76

81 Leveson Gower, *Letters of Harriet Countess of Granville*, Vol 1, p.144

82 Torrens, *Memoirs of Viscount Melbourne*, Vol 1, pp.190-215

83 Ilchester, *Lady Holland to her Son*, pp.28-29

84 Ibid, p.29, note no. 1

85 Chatsworth, 6th Duke's Group, 767, 448,1824, 33-36

86 Leveson Gower, *Letters of Harriet, Countess of Granville*, Vol 1, p.307

87 Chatsworth, 6th Duke's Group, 1041

88 Ibid, 1045

89 Ibid, 1130

90 National Art Museum, Foster Collection, MSS XXVII (F.48 E. 22) Catalogue No. 328

91 Dorchester, *Recollections of a Long Life by Lord Broughton*, Vol 3, p.83

92 National Art Museum, Foster Collection, MSS XXVII (F.48 E. 22) Catalogue No. 328, letter no. 1

93 Ibid, letter no. 26

94 Edgecombe, *The Diary of Lady Frances Shelley*, Vol 2, p.12

95 John Murray Papers

96 Lytton, *Life of Edward Bulwer, first Lord Lytton*, Vol 1, pp.118-24

97 Chatsworth, 6th Duke's Group, 1105

98 Ibid, 1129

99 Ibid.

100 West Sussex RO, Bessborough Papers, Copied from the Devonshire House Papers, Ref. 806.19

101 Leveson Gower, *Letters of Harriet, Countess of Granville,* from Countess Granville to the Duke of Devonshire and Lady Morpeth, 31 March 1825

102 Chatsworth, 6th Duke's Group, 1131

103 Ibid, 1132

104 Morgan, *Memoirs,* Vol 2, pp.208-9

105 British Library, Lothian Papers, Box 1, bundle 5/1-3b

106 Ibid, Box 1, bundle 5/1-4

107 Ibid, Box 1, bundle 5/1-6

108 Ibid, Box 1, bundle 5/8-8

109 Hertfordshire RO, Panshanger Papers, D/Elb F.85/15

110 University of Southampton, Hartley Library, Broadlands Papers, BR30 Box 1, folder 5,12 May 1825

111 British Library, Lothian Papers, Box 1, bundle 5/8-9

112 British Library, Lamb Papers, ADD MS 45548/159

113 Airlie, *Lady Palmerston and her Times,* Vol 1, p.166

114 Hertfordshire RO, Panshanger Papers, D/Elb F.85/16

115 Morgan, *Memoirs,* Vol 2, pp.203-4

116 British Library, Hodgkin Papers, Vol X DD. MSS 38855/234

117 Hertfordshire RO, Panshanger Papers, D/Elb F.68

118 British Library, Lothian papers, Box 1, bundle 5/17-18

119 Ibid, Box 1 bundle 1/17-20

120 University of Southampton, Hartley Library, Broadlands Papers, BR30 Box 1, folder 5, 7 July 1825

121 Morgan, *Memoirs,* Vol 2, p.206-8

122 University of Southampton, Hartley Library, Broadlands Papers, BR30 Box 1, folder 5, 14 July 1825

123 Airlie, *Lady Palmerston and her Times,* Vol 1, pp.118-19

124 Ibid, Vol 1, pp.121-22

125 British Library, Lothian Papers, Box 1, bundle 5/24-25/26

126 Airlie, *Lady Palmerston and her Times,* Vol 1, pp.122-24

127 University of Southampton, Hartley Library, Broadlands Papers, BR30 Box 1, folder 5, 14 July 1825

128 Ibid, letter dated 1 August 1825

CHAPTER 10

1 Hertfordshire RO, Panshanger Papers, D/Elb F.32/5

2 Torrens, *Memoirs of Viscount Melbourne,* pp.190-215

3 Leveson Gower, *Letters of Harriet, Countess of Granville,* Vol 2, p.352

4 Morgan, *Memoirs,* Vol 2, pp.209-10

5 National Art Museum, Foster Collection, MSS XXVII (F.48 E. 22) Catalogue No. 238 letter no. 25

6 University of Southampton, Hartley Library, Broadlands Papers, BR29 Box 2, folder 4, 26 September 1826

7 Ibid.

8   Chatsworth, 6th Duke's Group, 1217
9   Hertfordshire RO, Panshanger Papers, D/Elb F.33/1
10   Ibid, D/Elb F.62/1
11   Ibid.
12   West Sussex RO, Bessborough Papers, F.161
13   University of Southampton, Hartley Library, Broadlands Papers, BR30 Box 1, folder 7, 27 October 1825
14   British Library, Lothian Papers, Box 1, bundle 6/1
15   Coutts Bank
16   Leconfield, *Three Howard Sisters*, p.49
17   Hertfordshire RO, Panshanger Papers, D/Elb F.26
18   Ibid, D/Elb F.62
19   Ibid, D/Elb F.32
20   Nathan, *Fugitive Pieces and Reminiscences*, p.50
21   Sanders, *Lord Melbourne's Papers*, pp.78-79
22   National Art Museum, Foster Collection, MSS XXVII (F.48 E. 22) letter no. 58
23   Ibid, letter no. 52
24   British Library, Broughton Papers, ADD MS 36461/438
25   Lovelace, *Astarte*, p.31
26   National Art Museum, Foster Collection, MSS XXVII (F.48 E. 22) letter no. 53
27   Ibid, letter no.58
28   Ibid.
29   Hertfordshire RO, Panshanger Papers, D/Elb F.39/1
30   Coutts Bank
31   John Murray Papers
32   Hertford RO, Panshanger Papers, D/Elb F.69
33   Lever, *The Letters of Lady Palmerston*, p.145
34   Hertfordshire RO, Panshanger Papers, D/Elb F.78/1
35   Ibid, D/Elb F.76
36   Ibid, D/Elb F.75/52
37   Ibid, D/Elb F.76/11
38   Ibid, D/EK C14
39   University of Southampton, Hartley Library, Broadlands Papers, BR30 Box 1, Folder 5, 12 September 1826
40   Hertfordshire RO, Panshanger Papers, D/Elb F.76/13
41   Bessborough, *Lady Bessborough and her Family Circle*, pp.285-6
42   University of Southampton, Hartley Library, BR29 Box 2, Folder 5, 1 January 1827
43   Hertfordshire RO, Panshanger Papers, D/Elb F.76/18
44   British Library, Lamb Papers, ADD MS 45551/76
45   University of Southampton, Hartley Library, BR29 Box 2, Folder 5, 20 March 1827
46   Hertfordshire RO, Panshanger Papers, D/Elb F.76/14
47   Ibid, D/Elb F.76
48   Bessborough, *Lady Bessborough & her Family Circle*, p.287-88
49   Lever, *The Letters of Lady Palmerston*, p.166
50   University of Southampton, Hartley Library, Broadlands Papers, BR29 Box 2, Folder 6, 28 May 1827

51 Bamford, *The Journal of Mrs Arbuthnot*, Vol 2, p.311
52 Hertfordshire RO, Panshanger Papers, D/Elb F.82/92
53 Ibid, D/ELb F.40
54 Ibid.
55 Ibid, D/ELlb F.41/58
56 Ibid, D/ELb F.42/2
57 Ibid, D/ELb F.56
58 Ibid, D/ELb F.42/18 and 19
59 Ibid, D/ELb F.35/3
60 Ibid, D/ELb F.35/5
61 Ibid, D/ELb F.42
62 Ibid D/Elb F.76/16
63 West Sussex RO, Bessborough Papers, F.161
64 Hertfordshire RO, Panshanger Papers, D/Elb/9
65 Ibid, D/Elb F.33/2
66 Ibid, D/Elb F.75/98
67 Morgan, *Memoirs*, Vol 2, p.209
68 Hertfordshire RO, Panshanger Papers, D/Elb 40
69 Torrens, *Memoirs of Viscount Melbourne*, Vol 1, p.297
70 Morgan, *Memoirs*, Vol 2, p.247
71 Hertfordshire RO, Panshanger Papers, D/Elb F.75/33 and 58
72 Ibid.
73 Bessborough, *Lady Bessborough and her Family Circle*, p.290
74 Morgan, *Memoirs*, Vol 2, p.248
75 Bessborough, *Lady Bessborough and her Family Circle*, p.290
76 Herfordshire RO, Panshanger Papers, D/Elb F.75
77 Ibid, D/Elb F.40
78 Ibid.
79 Bessborough, *Lady Bessborough and her Family Circle*, p.291
80 British Library, Lamb Papers, ADD. MS 45551/110
81 Leconfield, *Three Howard Sisters*, p.107
82 British Library, Lamb Papers, Add. MS 45551/110
83 Hertford RO, Lamb Papers, D/Elb F.43/24
84 Ibid.
85 Morgan, *Memoirs*, Vol 2, p.253-254
86 Torrens, *Memoirs of Viscount Melbourne*, Vol 1, p.304
87 Hertfordshire RO, Pansanger Papers, D/Elb F.40
88 Devonshire, 6th Duke, *Handbook of Chatsworth and Hardwick*, pp.140-41
89 Annual Biography and Obituary for the year 1829, Vol XIII, p.51-2
90 Torrens, *Memoirs of Viscount Melbourne*, Vol 1, p.303

FAMILY TREE

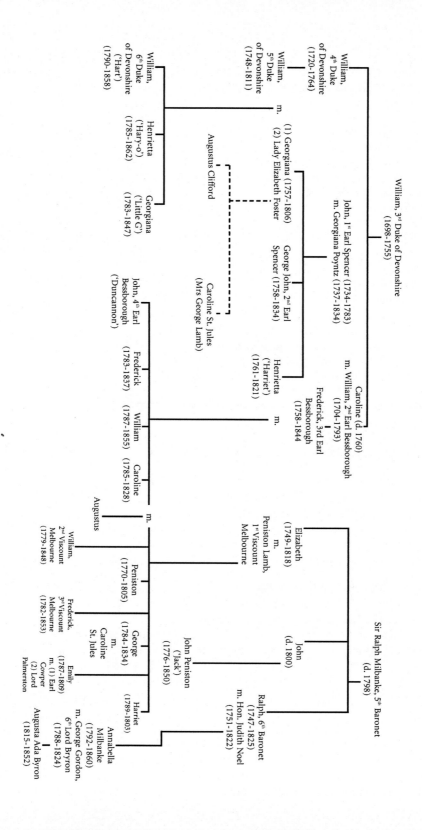

William, 3rd Duke of Devonshire
(1698-1755)

William, 4th Duke of Devonshire
(1720-1764)

William, 5th Duke of Devonshire
(1748-1811)

John, 1st Earl Spencer (1734-1783)
m. Georgiana Poyntz (1737-1834)

m.

William, 6th Duke of Devonshire ('Hart')
(1790-1858)

Henrietta ('Hary-o')
(1785-1862)

Georgiana ('Little G')
(1783-1847)

Augustus Clifford

(1) Georgiana (1757-1806)
(2) Lady Elizabeth Foster

George John, 2nd Earl Spencer (1758-1834)

Henrietta ('Harriet')
(1761-1821)

Caroline St. Jules (Mrs George Lamb)

John, 4th Earl Bessborough ('Duncannon')

Frederick (1783-1837)

William (1787-1855)

Caroline (1785-1828)

Caroline (d. 1760)
m. William, 2nd Earl Bessborough
(1704-1793)

Frederick, 3rd Earl Bessborough
(1758-1844)

m.

Augustus

m.

Elizabeth (1749-1818)
m. Peniston Lamb, 1st Viscount Melbourne

John (d. 1800)

William, 2nd Viscount Melbourne
(1779-1848)

Peniston (1770-1805)

Frederick, 3rd Viscount Melbourne
(1782-1853)

George (1784-1834)
m. Caroline St. Jules

John Peniston ('Jack')
(1776-1850)

Emily (1787-1869)
m. (1) Earl Cowper
(2) Lord Palmerston

Harriet (1789-1803)

Sir Ralph Milbanke, 5th Baronet
(d. 1798)

Ralph, 6th Baronet
(1747-1825)
m. Hon. Judith Noel
(1751-1822)

Annabella Milbanke (1792-1860)
m. George Gordon, 6th Lord Byron
(1788-1824)

Augusta Ada Byron
(1815-1852)

THE MAIN CHARACTERS

Bessborough, Frederick, 3rd Earl of (1758-1844), formerly Viscount Duncannon; Lady Caroline's father.

Bessborough, Henrietta Frances, (Harriet), Countess of (1761-1821), formerly Viscountess Duncannon, daughter of John, 1st Earl Spencer; Lady Caroline's mother.

Byron, George Gordon, 6th Lord (1788-1824), poet. Notorious for his love 'affair' with Lady Caroline.

Byron, Lady Anne Isabella, (1792-1860) wife of Lord Byron and daughter of Sir Ralph Milbanke; Lady Caroline's cousin by marriage.

Cowper, Emily, Countess (1787-1869), sister of William Lamb. Married John Henry Temple, third Viscount Palmerston, in 1839.

Devonshire, Elizabeth, Duchess of (1759-1824), formerly Lady Elizabeth Foster, second wife of William, 5th Duke of Devonshire.

Devonshire, Georgiana, Duchess of (1757-1806), sister of the Countess of Bessborough; Lady Caroline's aunt.

Devonshire, William, 5th Duke of (1748-1811), married Georgiana, daughter of John, 1st Earl Spencer; Lady Caroline's uncle.

Devonshire, William, (Hart) 6th Duke of, (1790-1858), formerly Marquis of Hartington; Lady Caroline's cousin.

Duncannon, John William Ponsonby, Viscount, (1781-1847), later 4th Earl of Bessborough; Lady Caroline's brother.

Duncannon, Maria, Viscountess, (1787-1834), later Countess of Bessborough; Lady Caroline's sister-in-law.

Foster, Augustus, (1780-1848), son of Elizabeth, Duchess of Devonshire, by her first husband, John Thomas Foster.

Granville, Harriet, (Hary-o) Countess (1785-1862), daughter of Georgiana, Duchess of Devonshire; Lady Caroline's cousin.

Holland, Henry Richard Vassal Fox, 3rd Baron (1773-1840), Whig leader and family friend.

Holland, Elizabeth, wife of the 3rd Baron (1770-1845), friend of Lady Bessborough and mother of Sir Godfrey Webster.

Lamb, Augustus, (1807-1836), son of Lady Caroline and William Lamb.

Lamb, Frederick, Baron Beauvale, later 3rd Viscount Melbourne (1782-1853), William Lamb's brother.

Lamb, William, 2nd Viscount Melbourne (1779-1848), Queen Victoria's first Prime Minister.

Lamb, George, (1784-1834), William Lamb's brother.

Leveson Gower, Lord Granville, 1st Earl Granville (1773-1846), Lady Bessborough's lover. Later married Lady Harriet Cavendish (Hary-o).

Melbourne, Peniston, 2nd baronet, 1st Viscount Melbourne (1745-1828), William Lamb's father.

Melbourne, Elizabeth, Viscountess, (1750-1818), mother of William Lamb.

Milbanke, Sir Ralph, 6th baronet (1747-1825), brother of Lady Melbourne and father of Anne Isabella (Annabella), later Lady Byron.

Morgan, Lady Sydney, (1776?-1859), popular Irish author and supportive friend of Lady Caroline.

Morpeth, Georgiana, (Little G) Countess of (1783-1858), daughter of the Duchess of Devonshire; Lady Caroline's cousin.

Ossulston, Corisande, Lady (d. 1865), later Countess of Tankerville; daughter of the Duke of Grammont and brought up at Devonshire House; friend of Lady Caroline.

Oxford, Jane Elizabeth, Countess of (1772-1824), first a friend to Lady Caroline and then her rival for Lord Byron's affections.

Ponsonby, Lady Barbara, (d. 1844), married William Ponsonby, later 1st Lord de Mauley. She was the mother of Charles and Henry Ponsonby.

Ponsonby, William Francis Spencer, 1st Lord de Mauley (1787-1855), Lady Caroline's favourite brother.

St Jules, Caroline, (1786-1862), later Mrs George Lamb; daughter of the 5th Duke of Devonshire and Lady Elizabeth Foster.

Spencer, John, 1st Earl Spencer (1734-1783), Lady Caroline's grandfather.

Spencer, Georgiana, Countess (1738-1814), Lady Caroline's grandmother.

Spencer, George John, 2nd Earl Spencer (1758-1834) son of the 1st Earl Spencer; Lady Caroline's uncle.

Spencer, Lavinia, (1769-1831), wife of the 2nd Earl; Lady Caroline's aunt.

Trimmer, Miss Selina, (1765-1829), governess to the children in the Devonshire nursery, including those of the Duchess, Lady Elizabeth Foster and Lady Bessborough.

Webster, Sir Godrey Vassal, (1789-1836), son of Lady Holland and the subject of Lady Caroline's first extramarital love 'affair'.

CHRONOLOGY

(Some major and some very minor events.)

1779   15th March, birth of William Lamb

1785   29th August, birth of Lady Harriet Cavendish (Hary-o)
13th November, birth of Lady Caroline Lamb

1788   22nd January, birth of George Gordon, 6th Lord Byron

1789   George Washington first President of the USA
14th July, the French Revolution begins

1790   21st May, birth of Hartington (6th Duke of Devonshire)

1792   17th May, birth of Annabella Milbanke

1793   21st January, King Louis XVI of France is executed
16th October, Queen Marie Antoinette is executed

1794   Lady Bessborough falls in love with Lord Granville in Naples
The Bessboroughs spend the winter at 'Stone House', Teignmouth, Devon

1801   21st March, Lady Georgiana Cavendish (Little G) marries Lord Morpeth
In August Lady Caroline flirts with William Lamb while on holiday in
      Ramsgate

1802   Peace of Amiens
The Bessboroughs join Lady Elizabeth Foster in Paris

1804   William Lamb is admitted to the Bar

1805   3rd June, Lady Caroline Ponsonby marries William Lamb
21st October, Nelson dies at the Battle of Trafalgar

1806   3rd January, Prime Minister William Pitt dies
31st January, Lady Caroline's first child, a daughter, is stillborn
30th March, Georgiana, Duchess of Devonshire, dies
13th September, Charles James Fox dies

1807 29th August, Lady Caroline gives birth to a son, Augustus

1808 Peninsular War; 21st August, Wellington defeats the French at the
Battle of Vimeiro

1809 30th January, Lady Caroline gives birth to a daughter who dies within
hours
19th October, the 5th Duke of Devonshire marries Lady Elizabeth Foster
24th December, Harriet Cavendish (Hary-o) marries Lord Granville
Leveson Gower

1810 Lady Caroline begins an affair with Sir Godfrey Webster

1812 In March, Byron publishes *Childe Harold* and is taken up by society
In April and May Lady Caroline conducts a public affair with him
In June and July Byron attempts to bring it to an end
In August she tries to trick him into eloping with her; Lady
Bessborough becomes ill
In September Lady Caroline agrees to go to Ireland with her parents
and William
In October Byron is now living with Lady Oxford and writes his final
letter to Caroline
In November the Bessboroughs return to England
In December Lady Caroline burns Byron in effigy at Brocket Hall

1813 In January Lady Caroline forges Byron's signature to obtain his
miniature from John Murray
In July Lady Caroline stages a scandalous scene at Lady Heathcote's

1814 18th March, Georgiana, Dowager Countess Spencer, dies

1815 2nd January, Byron marries Annabella Milbanke
In June Lady Caroline travels to Brussels to nurse her brother Frederick
who was wounded at Waterloo
In August/September William and Lady Caroline are in Paris, where she
flirts with the Duke of Wellington

1816 15th January, Annabella leaves Byron and asks for a separation
25th April, Byron leaves England forever
Lady Caroline accidentally hurts a page; William's brother and sister
take advantage of the scandal to persuade him either to separate
from Lady Caroline or to commit her to a lunatic asylum
9th May, Lady Caroline's novel, *Glenarvon*, is published anonymously
and is an instant success

1818 6th April, Lady Melbourne dies

1819 In February George Lamb is elected to Parliament as a member for
Westminster

1820 Lady Caroline writes her second novel, *Graham Hamilton*
20th January, George III dies
25th March, General Election – George Lamb loses his seat

1821 10th November, Lady Bessborough dies in Florence
14th December, Henry Colburn publishes *Graham Hamilton*
anonymously

1823 John Murray publishes Lady Caroline's third novel, *Ada Reis*

1824 19th April, Lord Byron dies at Missolonghi

1825 William agrees with his family to separate from Caroline and she is
driven out of Melbourne House

1827 7th May, William is elected as the MP for Bletchingley and is
appointed by George Canning, Prime Minister, to be Chief
Secretary to the Lord Lieutenant of Ireland. He moves to Phoenix
Park, taking his son Augustus with him
Autumn, Lady Caroline develops dropsy

1828 15th January, William is summoned from Ireland as Lady Caroline is
now seriously ill
25th January, Lady Caroline dies
22nd July, Viscount Melbourne dies and William succeeds to the title

1830 William is appointed Home Secretary by the 2nd Earl Grey
26th June, George IV dies and is succeeded by William IV

1831 First Reform Bill introduced by Lord John Russell

1832 The Great Reform Act passed

1834 2nd January, George Lamb dies
14th July, Lord Melbourne becomes Prime Minister; resigns in
October in favour of Sir Robert Peel

1835 18th April, Lord Melbourne again becomes Prime Minister

1836 27th November, Augustus dies

1837 20th June, William IV dies and is succeeded by his niece, Victoria
21st June, Emily Lamb's husband, 5th Earl Cowper, dies
Lady Caroline's brother, the Hon. Sir Frederick Ponsonby, dies

1839 16th December, Emily Lamb marries Henry John Temple, 3rd Viscount Palmerston

1840 10th February, Queen Victoria marries Prince Albert of Saxe-Coburg Gotha

1841 28th August, the Whigs are defeated in Parliament and William resigns as Prime Minister

1844 Lady Caroline's father, Frederick, 3rd Earl of Bessborough, dies

1847 Lady Caroline's eldest brother, John William, 4th Earl of Bessborough, dies

1848 26th November, William Lamb, 2nd Viscount Melbourne, dies

1853 29th January, Frederick Lamb, Baron Beauvale, 3rd Viscount Melbourne, dies

1855 Lady Caroline's youngest brother, William Ponsonby, 1st Lord de Mauley, dies

1858 Georgiana, Countess of Carlisle (Little G), dies

1865 18th October, Lord Palmerston dies at Brocket

1869 11th September, Emily Lamb, formerly Lady Cowper, now Lady Palmerston, dies

BIBLIOGRAPHY

MANUSCRIPT SOURCES

BODLEIAN LIBRARY
Correspondence and papers of Michael Bruce.

Lovelace-Byron archive; correspondence and papers of Anne Isabella, Lady Byron, with Lady Caroline Lamb and others 1812-1824.

Diaries of Joseph Farington.

BRITISH LIBRARY
Althorp (Spencer) Papers: Correspondence and papers of Margaret, Georgiana Countess Spencer including letters to her daughters, Georgiana, Duchess of Devonshire and Henrietta, Viscountess of Bessborough, her grandchildren and family friends.

Hobhouse MSS: The diaries, letters and papers of John Cam Hobhouse.

Holland House Papers: Correspondence of Henry Richard Vassall Fox, 3rd Lord Holland and Elizabeth Lady Holland with the Lamb family and the Earl of Egremont.

Huskisson MSS: Correspondence and papers of Emily Huskisson née Milbanke and her husband William Huskisson.

Lamb MSS: Correspondence and papers of Lady Caroline Lamb, Frederick Lamb and other members of the family.

Lothian Papers: Papers concerning the 1825 Separation of William Lamb and Lady Caroline Lamb.

CASTLE HOWARD
Correspondence of Georgiana, 6th Countess of Carlisle, with Lady Harriet Cavendish, later Countess Granville, Georgiana, Duchess of Devonshire and the Marquis of Hartington.

CHATSWORTH SETTLEMENT
Cavendish family correspondence, papers and archives, in particular the 5th and 6th Dukes' Groups, including letters from Lady Caroline Lamb to her cousin William, Lord Hartington, later 6th Duke of Devonshire and his sisters Lady Georgiana Morpeth and Lady Harriet Granville.

COUTTS & CO.
Inventory and papers regarding the letting and subletting of 39 Conduit Street.

HARTLEY LIBRARY, UNIVERSITY OF SOUTHAMPTON
Broadlands Archive: Letters of Emily, Lady Palmerston, née Lamb, to her brother Frederick Lamb during the years 1825-27.

HERTFORDSHIRE RECORD OFFICE
Panshanger Papers: Lamb family correspondence including letters from Emily, Lady Cowper, Frederick and William Lamb, Lady Caroline Lamb and Augustus Lamb.

Lytton MSS: Correspondence between Lady Caroline Lamb and Edward Bulwer Lytton.

LEICESTER RECORD OFFICE
Correspondence between Lady Caroline Lamb and the Dowager Countess Spencer.

NATIONAL ART MUSEUM, VICTORIA AND ALBERT MUSEUM
Foster Collection: Correspondence between Lady Caroline Lamb and Henry Colburn.

WEST SUSSEX RECORD OFFICE
Bessborough MSS: Family correspondence between Margaret Georgiana Countess Spencer and her daughters, grandchildren, friends and servants.

PRINTED SOURCES

The place of publication is London, unless otherwise stated

AIRLIE, MABELL, *Lady Palmerston and her Times*, 2 vols, Hodder & Stoughton, 1922.

ASPINALL, ARTHUR, *Letters of George IV*, 3 vols, Cambridge, 1938.

BAILY, F E, *The Love Story of Lady Palmerston*, Hutchinson & Co. Ltd.

BAMFORD, FRANCIS AND THE DUKE OF WELLINGTON, *The Journal of Mrs Arbuthnot 1820-1832*, 2 vols, Macmillan, 1950.

BARBER, THOMAS GERRARD, *Byron and Where he is Buried*, Henry Moreley & Sons, Hucknall, 1939.

BESSBOROUGH, THE EARL OF, *Lady Bessborough and her Family Circle*, John Murray, 1940.
Georgiana – Extracts from the Correspondence of the Duchess of Devonshire, John Murray, 1955.

BIRKENHEAD, SHEILA, *Peace in Piccadilly, The Story of Albany*, Hamish Hamilton Ltd, 1958.

BLAKISTON, GEORGIANA, *Lord William Russell and his Wife, 1815-1846*, John Murray, 1972.

BLANCH, LESLIE (ed.), *Harriette Wilson's Memoirs*, Folio Society, 1964.

BLESSINGTON, MARGUERITE, COUNTESS OF, *Journal of the Conversations of Lord Byron with the Countess of Blessington*, Henry Colburn, 1834.

BLYTH, HENRY, *Caro, The Fatal Passion*, Rupert Hart-Davis, 1972.

BRIGHTWELL, CECILIA LUCY, (ed.), *Memorials of the Life of Amelia Opie selected and arranged from her Letters, Diaries and other Manuscripts*, Longman, Brown & Co. 1854.

BROWNLOW, EMMA SOPHIA, COUNTESS, *The Eve of Victorianism*, John Murray, 1940.

BRUCE, IAN, *Lavalette Bruce*, Hamish Hamilton, 1953.

BURFORD, E, *Royal St James's, Being a Story of Kings, Clubmen and Courtesans*, Robert Hale, 1988.

BURNETT, T A J, *The Life and Times of Scrope Berdmore Davis*, Oxford University Press, 1981.

CAMBELL, MARY, *Lady Morgan, The Life and Times of Sydney Owenson*, Pandora Press, 1988.

CARE, KATHRYN, (ed.), *The Diary of Joseph Farington, Vol XIV, January 1816-December 1817*, Yale University Press, 1984.

CALVERT, BRIGADIER MICHAEL, YOUNG, BRIGADIER PETER, *A Dictionary of Battles (1715-1815)*, Mayflower Books, New York, 1979.

CECIL, DAVID, *Melbourne*, Reprint Society, 1955.

CHANCELLOR, E BERESFORD, *The History of the Squares of London*, Kegan Paul, Trench, Trübner, 1907.

CHAPMAN, JOHN S, *Byron and the Honourable Augusta Leigh*, Yale University Press, 1975.

CLAY, EDITH, *Lady Blessington at Naples*, Hamish Hamilton, 1959.

CLUNN, HAROLD P, *The Face of London*, Phoenix House Ltd, 1951.

COLE, HUBERT, *Beau Brummell*, Mason/Charter, New York, 1977.
Fouché, The Unprincipled Patriot, McCall Publishing Company, New York, 1971.

COLERIDGE, ERNEST HARTLEY (ed.), *The Complete Works of Byron*, 1878-1903.

CREEVEY, THOMAS, *Correspondence and Diaries*, (ed.), Sir Herbert Maxwell, 2 vols, John Murray, 1904.

DALLAS, R C, *Recollections of the Life of Lord Byron from the Year 1808 to the end of 1814*, Philadelphia, 1824.

DORCHESTER, LADY (ed.), *Recollections of a Long Life by Lord Broughton (John Cam Hobhouse) with additional extracts from his private diaries*, 6 vols, John Murray, 1911.

DOUBLEDAY, H ARTHUR, (ed.), *The Victoria History of the Counties of England – History of Hertfordshire*, 4 vols, Archibald Constable and Company Ltd, 1902.

DUNKLEY, HENRY, *Lord Melbourne*, Sampson, Low, Marston, Searle & Rivington, 1890.

DYCE, THE REVEREND ALEXANDER, (ed.), *Samuel Rogers, Recollections of the Table*, H A Rogers, 1887.

EDEN, THE HON EMILY, *Letters from India*, 2 Vols, Richard Bentley & Son, 1872.

EDGECOMB, RICHARD, (ed.), *The Diary of Lady Frances Shelley*, 2 vols, John Murray, 1912.

ELLIOTT, MARIANNE, *Partners in Revolution – The United Irishmen and France*, Yale University Press, 1982.

ELWIN, MALCOLM, *Lord Byron's Family.* John Murray, 1975.
Lord Byron's Wife, New York, Harcourt Bruce & Word Inc. 1963.
The Noels and the Byrons, Macdonald, 1967.

ESHER, VISCOUNT, (ed.), *The Girlhood of Queen Victoria, 1832-1840*, 2 vols, John Murray, 1912.

FINDEN, EDWARD AND WILLIAM, *Illustrations of the Life and Works of Lord Byron*, John Murray, 1833.

FOREMAN, AMANDA, *Georgiana, Duchess of Devonshire*, HarperCollins, 1998.

FOSTER, VERE, (ed.), *The Two Duchesses*, Blackie & Son, 1898.

FOX, SIR JOHN C, *The Byron Mystery*, Grant Richards Ltd, 1924.

GIBBS, LEWIS, *Sheridan*, JM Dent & Sons Ltd, 1947.

GILLIS, JOHN R, *For Better for Worse, British Marriages 1600 to the Present*, Oxford University Press, 1985.

GLENBERVIE, LORD, *Journals*, ed. Walter Sichel, Constable & Co., 1910.

GORDON, ARMISTEAD C, *Allegra, the story of Byron and Miss Clairmont*, Methuen & Co. Ltd, 1927.

GORDON, DOROTHY M, *Hogarth to Cruikshank: Social change in Graphic Satire*, Alan Lane, The Penguin Press, 1967.

GORE, JOHN, (ed.), *Thomas Creevey's Papers*, Penguin Books, 1948.

GRANVILLE, CASTALIA, COUNTESS, *Private Correspondence of Lord Granville Leveson Gower, 1781-1821.* 2 vols, John Murray, 1916.

GRAY, AUSTIN K, *Teresa, The Story of Byron's Last Mistress,* George G Harrap & Co. Ltd, 1948.

GROSS, JONATHAN DAVID, *Byron's 'Corbeau Blanc', The Life and Letters of Lady Melbourne,* Rice University Press, 1997.

GROWNOW, CAPTAIN R H, *The Reminiscences and Recollections of Captain Grownow, being anecdotes of the Camp, Court, Clubs and Society 1810-1860,* 2 vols, John C Nimmo, 1892.

GUNN, PETER, *My Dearest Augusta,* Bodley Head, 1968.

HASLIP, JOAN, *Lady Hester Stanhope,* Penguin Books, 1934.

HAYDON, BENJAMIN, *The Diary of Benjamin Robert Haydon,* 5 vols. (ed.) WEB Pope, Harvard University Press, 1969.

HAYWARD, A, *Diaries of a Lady of Quality from 1797 to 1804,* Longman, Roberts & Green, 1864.

HEROLD, J CHRISTOPHER, *Mistress to an Age, A life of Madame de Staël,* Readers Union, 1960.

HIBBERT, CHRISTOPHER, *George IV, Prince of Wales,* Readers Union, 1973.

HOBHOUSE, CHRISTOPHER, *Fox,* Constable & Co. Ltd, and John Murray, 1934.

HODGE, JANE AIKEN, *Passion & Principle – The Loves and Lives of Regency Women,* John Murray, 1966.

HODGSON, REV. JAMES T, *The Reverend Francis Hodgson, BD – A Memoir by his son the Reverend James T Hodgson, MA,* 2 Vols, 1878.

HOLLAND, HENRY RICHARD VASSALL, 3RD LORD HOLLAND, *Further Memoirs of the Whig Party, 1807-1821,* John Murray, 1905.

HOWELL-THOMAS, DOROTHY, *Lord Melbourne's Susan,* Gresham Press, 1978. *Duncannon,* 1992.

ILCHESTER, COUNTESS OF AND LORD STAVORDALE, (ed.) *The Life and Letters of Lady Sarah Lennox 1745-1826,* John Murray, 1904.

ILCHESTER, EARL OF, *The Home of the Hollands 1605-1820,* John Murray, 1937. *Chronicles of Holland House 1820-1900,* John Murray, 1937. *Elizabeth, Lady Holland to her Son, 1821-1845,* John Murray, 1946.

The Journal of Elizabeth Lady Holland 1791-1811, 2 vols, Longmans, Green and Co., 1909.
The Journal of the Hon Henry Edward Fox, 4th Lord Holland 1818-1830, Thornton Butterworth Limited, 1923.

JENKINS, ELIZABETH, *Lady Caroline Lamb*, Sphere Books, 1972.

JERNINGHAM, HON LADY FRANCES, *Correspondence and Diary of Lady Jerningham to her Daughter, Lady Bedingfield, 1780-1843*.

JOYCE, MICHAEL, *My Friend H John Cam Hobhouse, Baron Broughton de Gyfford*, John Murray, 1948.

KEMBLE, FRANCES ANN, *Record of a Girlhood*, 3 vols, Richard Bentley and Son, 1878.

KNIGHT, CHARLES, (ed.), *London*, 6 vols, Charles Knight & Co., 1841.

KNIGHT, G WILSON, *Lord Byron's Marriage, The Evidence of Asterisks*, Routledge and Kegan Paul, 1957.

LAMB, LADY CAROLINE, *Glenarvon*, 3 vols, 1st & 2nd editions, Henry Colburn, 1816.
Graham Hamilton, 2 vols, Henry Colburn, 1822.
Ada Reis, 2 vols, John Murray, 1823.

LANGLEY MOORE, DORIS, *The Late Lord Byron*, John Murray, 1961.
Lord Byron's Accounts Rendered, John Murray, 1974.
Ada, Countess of Lovelace, John Murray, 1977.

LECONFIELD, Lady Maud, *Three Howard Sisters*, John Murray, 1955.

LEE, K L, *Extracts from the Diary of Dr Robert Lee FRS (1821-1822) while resident with the Hon William Lamb (afterwards Viscount Melbourne)*, Hatchard, 1897.

LEES-MILNE, JAMES, *The Bachelor Duke, A Life of William Spencer Cavendish, 6th Duke of Devonshire, 1790-1858*, John Murray, 1991.

LEVER, TRESHAM, (ed.), *The Letters of Lady Palmerston*, John Murray, 1957.

LEVESON GOWER, SIR GEORGE AND PALMER, IRIS (eds.), *Hary-o, The Letters of Lady Harriet Cavendish, 1796-1809*, John Murray, 1940.

LEVESON GOWER, HON F, (ed.), *Letters of Harriet, Countess of Granville 1810-1845*, 2 Vols, Longman, Green & Co. 1894.

LEVESON GOWER, IRIS, *The Face Without a Frown, Georgiana, Duchess of Devonshire*, Frederick Muller Ltd., 1944.

LEWIS, JUDITH SCHNEID, *In the Family Way, Child Bearing in the British Aristocracy 1760-1860*, Rutgers University Press, 1986.

LEWIS, SAMUEL, *Topographical Dictionary of Ireland*, 2 vols, 1837.

LEWIS, LADY TERESA (ed.), *Extracts from the Journal and Correspondence of Miss Berry, 1783-1852*, 3 vols, Longmans, Green, and Co., 1865.

LONGFORD, ELIZABETH, *Byron*, Hutchinson, 1976.

LONGMAN, REES, ORME, BROWN AND GREEN, *Annual Biography and Obituary for the year 1829*, vol XII.

LOVELACE, 2ND EARL OF, *Lady Noel Byron and the Leighs*, Privately printed, 1887.
Astarte, A Fragment of Truth concerning George Gordon, Sixth Lord Byron. New Edition with many additional letters, Christopher, 1921.

LOVELL, ERNEST J R, (ed.), *His Very Self and Voice, Collected Conversations of Lord Byron*, New York, Macmillan, 1954.

LYTTON, EARL OF, *Life of Edward Bulwer, First Lord Lytton*, 2 vols, Macmillan, 1913.

MARCHAND, LESLIE A, (ed.), *Byron's Letters and Journals*, 12 vols, John Murray, 1973-1994.
Byron, a Biography, 3 vols. New York, Alfred A Knopf, 1957.
Byron a Portrait, The Cresset Library, 1971.

MAYNE, ETHEL COLBORN, *The Life and Letters of Anne Isabella Lady Noel Byron*, Constable, 1929.
A Regency Chapter, Lady Bessborough and her Friendships, Macmillan, 1939.
Byron, Methuen, 1912.

MEDWIN, THOMAS, *Journal of the Conversation of Lord Byron noted during a residence with his Lordship at Pisa in the years 1821 and 1822*, Henry Colburn, 1824.

MITCHELL, L G, *Lord Melbourne 1799-1848*, Oxford University Press, 1997.

MITFORD, MARY RUSSELL, *Recollections of a Literary Life*, 3 vols, 1852.

MOORE, THOMAS, *The Life, Letters and Journals of Lord Byron*, John Murray, 1838.

MORGAN, LADY SYDNEY, *Book of the Boudoir*, 2 vols, Henry Colburn, 1829.
Passages from my Autobiography, Richard Bentley, 1859.

Memoirs, Autobiography, Diaries and Correspondence, 2 Vols, William Allen & Co., 1862.

MAUROIS, ANDRÉ, *Byron*, Appleton & Company, New York, 1930.

MURRAY, JOHN, *Lord Byron's Correspondence*, John Murray, 2 vols, 1922.

NATHAN, ISAAC, *Fugitive Pieces and Reminiscences of Lord Byron (new edition of Hebrew Melodies). Also some original poetry, letters and recollections of Lady Caroline Lamb*, Henry Colburn, 1829.

PARK, S J AND NAFZIGER, *The British Military, its System and Organization 1803-1815*, 1983.

PASTON, GEORGE AND QUENNELL, PETER, *To Lord Byron*, John Murray, 1939.

PIERSON, JOAN, *The Real Lady Byron*, Robert Hale, 1992

PONSONBY, MAJOR-GENERAL SIR JOHN, *The Ponsonby Family*, The Medici Society, 1929.

POPE BISSEL, *The Diary of Benjamin Haydon, 1816-1824*, Harvard University Press, 1963.

PRIESTLEY, J B, *The Prince of Pleasure and his Regency 1811-1820*, Heinemann, 1969.
(ed.), *Tom Moore's Diary*, Cambridge University Press, 1933.

PROTHERO, ROWLAND, (ed.), *The Works of Lord Byron, A New Revised and Enlarged Edition*, 6 vols, John Murray, 1901.

RAB, FÉLIX, *Les Maîtresses Authentiques de Lord Byron*, Nouvelle Librairie Parisienne, Paris, 1890.

RUSH, RICHARD, *A Residence at the Court of London from 1817-1825*, Century, 1987.

SADLEIR, MICHAEL, *Blessington D'Orsay, A Masquerade*, Constable, 1933.
Bulwer: A Panorama – Edward and Rosina 1803-1836, Constable, 1931.

SAKES, CHRISTOPHER SIMON, *Private Palaces*, Viking, 1985.

SANDERS, LLOYD C, (ed.), *Lord Melbourne's Papers*, Longmans, Green and Co. 1899.
The Holland House Circle, Methuen, 1908.

SICHEL, WALTER, *Sheridan*, Constable, 1909.

SIMPSON, JAMES, *Paris after Waterloo*, William Blackwood & Sons, 1853.

SMILES, SAMUEL, *A Publisher and his Friends, Memoirs and Correspondence of the late John Murray with an Account of the Origin and Progress of the House, 1768-1843*, 2 vols, John Murray, 1891.

STONE, LAWRENCE, *The Family, Sex and Marriage in England 1500-1800*. Weindenfeld and Nicolson, 1977.
Road to Divorce – England 1530-1997, Oxford University Press.

STOWE, HARRIET BEECHER, *Lady Byron Vindicated*, Sampson Low, Sons, and Marston, 1870.

STRICKLAND, MARGO, *The Byron Women*, Peter Owen, 1974.

STUART, DOROTHY MARGARET, *Dearest Bess*, Methuen, 1955.

SWINTON, THE HON MRS J R, *A Sketch of the life of Georgiana, Lady De Ros*, John Murray, 1893.

TORRENS, W M, *Memoirs of the Right Honourable William Lamb, second Lord Melbourne*, 2 vols, Macmillan, 1878.

TURNEY, CATHERINE, *Byron's Daughter, a Biography of Elizabeth Medora Leigh*, Charles Scribner's Sons, New York, 1972.

TWIGGER, ROBERT, *Inflation: the Value of the Pound 1750-1996*, House of Commons Library, 1997.

USHER, HOWARD, *The Owners of Melbourne Hall*, The Derbyshire Heritage Series, 1993.
William Lamb, Viscount Melbourne, Melbourne Hall Publications, 1998.
Fatal Females.

VILLIERS, MARJORIE, *The Grand Whiggery*, John Murray, 1939.

WALFORD, EDWARD, *Old London, Westminster to St James's*, Alderman Press, 1989.

WALKER, VIOLET W, *The House of Byron. A History of the Family from the Norman Conquest 1066-1988*, revised and completed by Margaret J Howell, Quiller Press, 1988.

WELLINGTON, 7th DUKE, (ed.), *Wellington and his Friends. Letters of the first Duke of Wellington to the Rt Hon Charles and Mrs Arbuthnot, the Earl and Countess of Wilton, Princess Lieven, and Miss Burdett-Coutts*, Macmillan, 1965.

WHARTON, GRACE AND PHILIP, *The Queens of Society*, 2 vols, JW Jarvis & Son, 1890.

WHITE, R J, *Life in Regency England*, Batsford Putnam, 1963.

WILSON KNIGHT, G, *Lord Byron's Marriage*, Routledge & Kegan Paul, 1957.

WYNDHAM, THE HON MRS HUGH, (ed.), *Correspondence of Sarah Spencer 1787-1870*, John Murray, 1912.

ZIEGLER, PHILIP, *Melbourne, A Biography of William Lamb, 2nd Viscount Melbourne*, Collins, 1976.

INDEX

C